Human-Computer Interaction Series

T0137735

Human-Computer Interaction is a multidisciplinary field focused on human aspects of the development of computer technology. As computer-based technology becomes increasingly pervasive - not just in developed countries, but worldwide - the need to take a human-centered approach in the design and development of this technology becomes ever more important. For roughly 30 years now, researchers and practitioners in computational and behavioral sciences have worked to identify theory and practice that influences the direction of these technologies, and this diverse work makes up the field of human–computer interaction. Broadly speaking it includes the study of what technology might be able to do for people and how people might interact with the technology. In this series we present work which advances the science and technology of developing systems which are both effective and satisfying for people in a wide variety of contexts. The human–computer interaction series will focus on theoretical perspectives (such as formal approaches drawn from a variety of behavioral sciences), practical approaches (such as the techniques for effectively integrating user needs in system development), and social issues (such as the determinants of utility, usability and acceptability).

For other titles published in this series, go to
www.springer.com/series/6033

Aaron Marcus · Anxo Cereijo Roibás
Riccardo Sala
Editors

Mobile TV: Customizing Content and Experience

Mobile Storytelling, Creation and Sharing

 Springer

Editors

Aaron Marcus
Aaron Marcus and Associates, Inc. (AM+A)
1196 Euclid Avenue, Suite 1F
Berkeley, CA 94708-1640
USA
aaron.marcus@amanda.com

Anxo Cereijo Roibás
3 Birchfield Street
London
Unit 12
United Kingdom E14 8ED
anxo.cereijo@gmail.com

Riccardo Sala
Riccardo Sala Ltd.
21b Bradbury Mews
N16 8JW London, UK
riccardosala@gmail.com

ISBN 978-1-4471-2531-0   e-ISBN 978-1-84882-701-1
DOI 10.1007/978-1-84882-701-1
Springer London Dordrecht Heidelberg New York

British Library Cataloguing in Publication Data
A catalogue record for this book is available from the British Library

Printed on acid-free paper

Springer is part of Springer Science+Business Media (www.springer.com)

Contents

Part VI   Advanced Interaction Modalities with Mobile Digital Content

Contributors

Lynne Baillie
Telecommunications Research Center Vienna (ftw.), Donau-City Str.1,
1220 Vienna, Austria
baillie@ftw.at

Evangelos Bekiaris
Hellenic Institute of Transport, Centre for Research and Technology Hellas,
P.O. Box 361, 6th Km Charilaou-Thermi Road, GR-57001, Thermi,
Thessaloniki, Greece
abek@certh.gr

Emmanuel Blain
Massachusetts Institute of Technology, Communications Futures Program,
32 Vassar Street, 32-G820, Cambridge, MA 02139, USA
eblain@mit.edu

Bjoern-Michael Braun
Schweizer Strasse 78, 60594 Frankfrut am Main, Germany
bjoernibraun@gmail.com

Renan G. Cattelan
Faculdade de Computação, Universidade Federal de Uberlândia,
1B129, Av. Joao Naves de Avila, 2121, 38400-902, Uberlandia – MG, Brazil
renan@facom.ufu.br

Pablo Cesar
CWI: Centrum Wiskunde & Informatica, Science Park 123,
1098 XG Amsterdam, The Netherlands
P.S.Cesar@cwi.nl

Konstantinos Chorianopoulos
Department of Informatics, Ionian University, 49100 Corfu, Greece
choko@ionio.gr

Lieven De Marez
MICT-IBBT Ghent University, Korte Meer 7-9-11, 9000 GENT, Belgium
lieven.demarez@ugent.be

Sebastian Egger
Telecommunications Research Center Vienna (ftw.), Donau-City Str.1,
1220 Vienna, Austria
egger@ftw.at

Tom Evens
MICT-IBBT Ghent University, Korte Meer 7-9-11, 9000 Gent, Belgium
tom.evens@ugent.be

Giliard B. Freitas
Departamento de Ciências de Computação, Universidade Federal de São Carlos,
13565-905, Sao Carlos - SP, Brazil
giliard_freitas@dc.ufscar.br

Peter Fröhlich
Telecommunications Research Center Vienna (ftw.), Donau-City Str.1,
1220 Vienna, Austria
froehlich@ftw.at

Dr. David Geerts
Centre for User Experience Research (CUO), IBBT/K.U.Leuven,
Parkstraat 45 Bus 3605 – 3000 Leuven, Belgium
david.geerts@soc.kuleuven.be

Dimitris Giakoumis
Informatics and Telematics Institute, Centre for Research and Technology Hellas,
P.O. Box 361, 6th Km Charilaou-Thermi Road, GR-57001, Thermi,
Thessaloniki, Greece
dgiakoum@iti.gr

Thomas Grechenig
Vienna University of Technology – Institute for Industrial Software (INSO),
Wiedner Hauptstrasse 76/2/2, 1040 Vienna, Austria
thomas.grechenig@inso.tuwien.ac.at

Gunnar Harboe
Applied Research and Technology Center, Motorola, 1303 E Algonquin Rd,
Schaumburg, IL 60202, USA
gunnar.harboe@motorola.com

Jussi Impiö
Nokia Research Center, P.O. Box 1000, 33721 Tampere, Finland

An Jacobs
Studies on Media, Information and Telecommunication, Vrije Universiteit Brussel
and Interdisciplinary Institute for BroadBand Technology, Pleinlaan 2 – 1050
Brussel, BE
an.jacobs@vub.ac.be

Dionysios D. Kehagias
Informatics and Telematics Institute, Centre for Research
and Technology Hellas, P.O. Box 361, 6th Km Charilaou-Thermi Road,
GR-57001, Thermi,
Thessaloniki, Greece
diok@iti.gr

Daeeop Kim
#304 N25, Human-Centered Interaction Design Lab, Industrical Design KAIST,
Gwahangno 335, Yuseunggu, Daejeon, South Korea
daeeop.kim@gmail.com

Ji Hye Kim
101-1104 Samsung Raemian APT, Jongam 1 dong, Seonbuk gu,
Seoul, 136-780, South Korea
gimjee@gmail.com

Frederick Lee Kitson
Senior Vice President, Motorola Labs, 1295 E. Algonquin Road,
Schaumburg, IL 60196, USA
fred.kitson@motorola.com

Natalie Klym
Massachusetts Institute of Technology, Communications Futures Program,
32 Vassar Street, 32-G820, Cambridge, MA 02139, USA
nklym@cfp.mit.edu

Hendrik Knoche
Department of Computer Science, University College London,
Gower Street, London WC1E 6BT, UK
h.knoche@cs.ucl.ac.uk

Kun-pyo Lee
Professor & Head, Human-Centered Interaction Design Lab,
Industrial Design, KAIST, Gwahangno 335, Yuseunggu,
Daejeon, South Korea
kplee@kaist.ac.kr

Bram Lievens
Studies on Media, Information and Telecommunication,
Vrije Universiteit Brussel and Interdisciplinary Institute for BroadBand
Technology, Pleinlaan 2 – 1050 Brussel, BE
bram.lievens@vub.ac.be

Jaakko Lehikoiner
Nokia Research Center, P.O. Box 1000, 33721 Tampere, Finland

Aaron Marcus
Aaron Marcus and Associates, Inc. (AM+A), 1196 Euclid Avenue,
Suite 1F, Berkeley, CA 94708-1640, USA
aaron.marcus@amanda.com

Erick L. Melo
Departamento de Ciências de Computação, Universidade Federal de São Carlos,
13565-905, Sao Carlos – SP, Brazil
erick_melo@dc.ufscar.br

Alexander Meschtscherjakov
HCI & Usability Unit, ICT&S Center, University of Salzburg,
Sigmund-Haffner-Gasse 18, 5020 Salzburg, Austria
alexander.meschtscherjakov@sbg.ac.at

April Slayden Mitchell
Hewlett-Packard Labs, 1501 Page Mill Rd., Palo Alto, CA 94304, USA
april.mitchell@hp.com

Koji Miyauchi
Hewlett-Packard Laboratories Japan, Hewlett-Packard Japan, Ltd.,
3-29-21, Takaido-Higashi, Suginami-ku, Tokyo, 168-8585, Japan
koji.miyauchi@hp.com

Marie-José Montpetit, Ph.D.
Massachusetts Institute of Technology, Communications Futures Program,
32 Vassar Street, 32-G820, Cambridge, MA 02139, USA
mariejo@media.mit.edu

Frank Nack
Human-Computer Studies Group (HCS), Institute for Informatics,
University of Amsterdam, 1098 XG Amsterdam, The Netherlands
nack@uva.nl

Kenton O'Hara
CSIRO ICT Centre, Cnr Vimiera and Pembroke Roads, Marsfield,
NSW 2122, Australia
Kenton.O'hara@csiro.au

Marianna Obrist
HCI & Usability Unit, ICT&S Center, University of Salzburg,
Sigmund-Haffner-Gasse 18, 5020 Salzburg, Austria
marianna.obrist@sbg.ac.at

Hiromi Oda
Hewlett-Packard Laboratories Japan, Hewlett-Packard Japan, Ltd.,
3-29-21, Takaido-Higashi, Suginami-ku, Tokyo, 168-8585, Japan
hiromi.oda@hp.com

Jo Pierson
Studies on Media, Information and Telecommunication, Vrije Universiteit Brussel
and Interdisciplinary Institute for BroadBand Technology, Pleinlaan 2 – 1050
Brussel, BE
jo.pierson@vub.ac.be

Maria da Graça C. Pimentel
Departamento de Ciências de Computação, Universidade de São Paulo,
13560-970, Sao Carlos - SP, Brazil
mgp@icmc.usp.br

Erika Reponen
Nokia Research Center, P.O. Box 1000, 33721 Tampere, Finland

Anxo Cereijo Roibás
Vodafone Group Services Limited, 1 Kingdom Street, London W2 6BY
anxo.cereijo@gmail.com

Riccardo Sala
Information Architect, 21b Bradbury Mews, London N16 8JW, UK
riccardosala@gmail.com

Raimund Schatz
Telecommunications Research Center Vienna (ftw.), Donau-City Str.1,
1220 Vienna, Austria
schatz@ftw.at

Dimitri Schuurman
MICT-IBBT Ghent University, Korte Meer 7-9-11, 9000 GENT, Belgium
Dimitri.schuurman@ugent.be

Taro Sugahara
Hewlett-Packard Laboratories Japan, Hewlett-Packard Japan, Ltd.,
3-29-21, Takaido-Higashi, Suginami-ku, Tokyo, 168-8585, Japan
taro.sugahara@hp.com

Cesar A. Teixeira
Departamento de Ciências de Computação, Universidade
Federal de São Carlos, 13565-905,
Sao Carlos – SP, Brazil
cesar@dc.ufscar.br

Richard D. Titus
Controller Future Media, A&M and Mobile, BBC Future
Media & Technology, Henry Wood House, Room 819, 3-6 Langham Place,
London, UK W1B 3DF
richard.titus@bbc.co.uk

Manfred Tscheligi

HCI & Usability Unit, ICT&S Center, University of Salzburg,
Sigmund-Haffner-Gasse 18, 5020 Salzburg, Austria
manfred.tscheligi@sbg.ac.at

Dimitrios Tzovaras
Informatics and Telematics Institute, Centre for Research and Technology
Hellas, P.O. Box 361, 6th Km Charilaou-Thermi Road, GR-57001,
Thermi, Thessaloniki, Greece
dimitrios.tzovaras@iti.gr

Marian F Ursu
Narrative and Interactive Media, Department of Computing, Goldsmiths,
University of London, London, SE14 6NW, UK
m.ursu@gold.ac.uk

Eva Vanhengel
Studies on Media, Information and Telecommunication, Vrije Universiteit Brussel
and Interdisciplinary Institute for BroadBand Technology, Pleinlaan 2 – 1050
Brussel, BE
eva.vanhengel@vub.ac.be

Radu-Daniel Vatavu
Research Center in Computer Science, University "Stefan cel Mare"
of Suceava, 13, University Street, 720229 Suceava, Romania
vatavu@eed.usv.ro

Alex Vorbau
Hewlett-Packard Labs, 1501 Page Mill Rd, Palo Alto, CA 94304, USA
alex.vorbau@hp.com

Marion Wiethoff
Delft University of Technology – Faculty TPM, Transport Policy and logistics'
Organisation (TLO), Jaffalaan 5, 2628 BX Delft, The Netherlands
m.wiethoff@tudelft.nl

Prof. Carola Zwick
Product Design Department, Kunsthochschule Berlin Weissensee,
School of Art, 13086 Berlin, Germany
zwick@kh-berlin.de

Mobile TV: Customizing Content and Experience

Aaron Marcus, Anxo Cereijo-Roibas, and Riccardo Sala

Introduction

This book showcases new mobile TV systems that require customization according to specific users' needs in changing physical environments. These projects and studies, carried out in academia and in industry, promote the awareness of interdisciplinary methods and tools for designing novel solutions. Their objective is to enhance the value of the information they convey while improving the users' enjoyment of it on the move.

Users' adoption of sophisticated handheld devices, together with the increasing interoperability among platforms, has resulted in the expansion of TV consumption beyond a domestic context. Providing a remarkable user experience for mobile TV requires a special attention to pervasive, interactive multimedia systems. These systems enable users' presence and contextual awareness, and they support social use and active participation of users. Some primary challenges for good design are the possibilities for technology to support and encourage communication and interaction among different users and between users and places/events. The vision of mobile TV playing a central role in content broadcasting and narrowcasting involves the emergence of user communities that create and share contextualized digital content on the move.

The design of a high-quality mobile TV experience outside the home implies the understanding of "soft user data," such as multifaceted emotional aspects, strictly related to the context of usage, e.g., to privacy, trust, etc.

The novel methods and design solutions presented here intend to extend the field of action for people on the move, with special attention to the contextual and social usage of mobile TV. The ultimate objective is to encourage the design of systems that are more usable, useful, and appealing, and provide solutions that are relevant

A. Marcus
Berkeley, California, USA

A. Cereijo-Roibas and R. Sala
London, UK

A. Marcus et al. (eds.), *Mobile TV: Customizing Content and Experience*,
Human-Computer Interaction Series, DOI 10.1007/978-1-84882-701-1_1,
© Springer-Verlag London Limited 2010

for the nomadic and peripatetic user. These solutions include user interfaces that support creativity, sociability, content creation and sharing, context awareness, and convergence of platforms in entertainment, work, and government settings.

Some of the issues that need to be addressed in this scenario are the following:

- What are the immediate and long-term advantages for Mobile TV users in the future?
- What are the core issues regarding usability and accessibility for input–output devices in Mobile TV?
- How will other non-technophile users respond to a new interaction model for TV in mobility?
- What are the interoperability issues that need to be addressed?
- How can mobile TV gain from the application of context awareness to mobile services?
- What other paradigms exist beyond having contextualized access to information?
- How will users create and share their own content?
- What does it mean to become a "producer" in a convergent media society?
- How can content be copyrighted by individual media producers?
- Will a mobile TV users' community be created?
- Will this community communicate and share content one-to-one?
- Would content move toward richer media?

The book tries to answer some of the above questions, and leaves some of the others open to further discussion. The book is structured into six topics.

The first topic generates interdisciplinary debate around mobile TV as a medium for digital storytelling and what this medium entails in terms of sociability and the user experience in general.

The second topic shows how conceptual and participatory design can bring innovation to mobile and pervasive multimedia systems.

The third topic looks at understanding the context through experimental research, including novel data gathering and analysis, identification of requirements, and evaluation methods.

The fourth topic addresses the issues related to how mobile and pervasive interactive digital systems can be contextualized to the users' changing physical needs and also to empower their social needs.

The fifth topic explores advanced interaction modalities with mobile digital content through case studies of innovative applications for mobile and pervasive systems. These case studies demonstrate new interaction modalities regarding the use of handhelds with suitable user interfaces to access contents such as programs, diagrams, texts, images, music, and new forms of content.

Finally, the sixth topic has the ambitious conclusive scope to probe the future of mobile TV's technology and its implications for the user experience.

Part I
What It All Means: Six Perspectives on Mobile TV

Mobile TV's Time to Shine Has Arrived

Fred Kitson

MoFilm, the first mobile film festival, achieved some legitimacy when multiple Academy Award-winning actor Kevin Spacey hosted the show in 2009. Spacey commented: "[I]n some countries, this might be the first time they [people] ever see a movie. ... They won't see it on that big screen; they'll see it on a small one."[1] According to a 2007 Gartner report, sales of cell phones skyrocketed for the first time to more than 1 billion.[2] In 2008, the number of worldwide subscribers topped 4 billion, covering 60% of the world population.[3] There are more mobile phones than TVs (there are 1.4 billion TVs worldwide[4]). Spacey concluded: "The quality of work and the simple ability at storytelling, the thing that ignites someone and inspires them to tell a story, can really come from anywhere."[5]

The Nielsen Company reports that three-screen viewing (video on television, the Internet, and mobile devices) continues to grow, reaching a new high water mark. Americans who watch video over the Internet consume 3 hours of online video per month, and those who use mobile devices watch nearly 4 hours per month.[6]

A new study from ABI Research predicts that there will be 500 million Mobile TV viewers by 2013 and the mobile TV market will be worth more than $50 billion. A catalyst for this growth is the conversion, in the U.S. and other regions, to all-digital TV transmissions, which will foster opportunities for over-the-air TV broadcasts directly to mobile devices incorporating TV tuners. At the 2009 International Consumer Electronics Show in Las Vegas, the Open Mobile Video Coalition

F. Kitson
Corporate Vice-President, Motorola Applied Research Center, Motorola, Inc., 1303 E. Algonquin Rd., Schaumburg, IL 60196 USA

[1] *Putting Movies on Mobiles*, Digital Planet broadcast on BBC World Service blog, 27 February 2009

[2] *Cell Phone Sales Hit 1 Billion Mark*, Marguerite Reardon on CNET News blog, 27 February 2008

[3] *Cell Phone Activations Hit 4 Billion Worldwide*, Jamie Lendino on Gearlog blog, 24 December 2008

[4] *Media Statistics: Television (most recent) by Country*, NationMaster.com

[5] *Putting Movies on Mobiles*, Digital Planet broadcast on BBC World Service blog, 27 February 2009

[6] *TV, Internet and Mobile Usage in U.S. Keeps Increasing, Says Nielsen*, Robert Seidman on TV by the Numbers blog, 23 February 2009

A. Marcus et al. (eds.), *Mobile TV: Customizing Content and Experience*,
Human-Computer Interaction Series, DOI 10.1007/978-1-84882-701-1_2,
© Springer-Verlag London Limited 2010

(OMVC) announced that 63 stations in 22 US cities committed to provide over-the-air digital television to mobile devices in 2009.[7]

Mobile TV is real and growing with new applications and content. To quantify the growth of Internet video consumption, consider that the duration of an average video viewed online at Hulu.com during the month of November 2008 was 11.9 minutes on 221 million streams, compared to all online videos at 3.1 minutes and 52.3 videos per viewer on YouTube.com.[8]

What are the major challenges or impediments to growth globally? Technical issues include spectrum bandwidth, coding, distribution, content ownership, digital rights management, power, computation, and the inconsistency of standards. The availability of a $5 TV chipset in the 700 MHz spectrum, which can reach deep inside buildings and travel two to three times further than other higher frequencies, makes Mobile TV broadcast cheaper than cellular alternatives.

The Internet will become essentially video-oriented, comprising 90% of all traffic by 2012.[9] The major transformation in content consumption is the movement from bundled services (the current offering of video, Internet, wireless, and fixed voice) to blended services (social TV or Mobile TV).

The Future Is Personalized Content On Demand

This book focuses on how content will be customized to enhance and optimize the user experiences of consuming and creating content. The future illuminated in this book is "Aaron's TV." In addition to the video explosion, two additional trends in consumer demands are the transition from "prime time" to "my time" and "broadband on the go." The prediction for 2010 estimates that 55% of all Internet video consumed in the USA will be user-generated.[10]

The mobile phone will be sourcing video TV. As an example of the migration to IP video: the 30 November 2008 episode of the US television program *The Office*, was watched more than 5 million times on the Internet and 16 million on traditional broadcast TV.[11]

Designing intuitive Mobile TV user experiences will be a key challenge. User interfaces must account for a combination of:

- Hundreds, growing to thousands, of traditional channels
- All the Internet video that one is trying to access through regional delivery markets such as broadcast and various roaming cellular carriers
- New fixed mobile convergence devices that support WiFi with cellular
- The pressure of content within the limited viewing display and I/O (input/output)

---

[7]*Half a Billion Mobile TV Viewers by 2013*, Chris Albrecht on NewTeeVee blog, 10 February 2009

[8]*Americans View 34 Percent More Online Videos in November 2008 Compared to a Year Ago*, Press Release comScore Video Metrix, 5 January 2009

[9]*Big Growth for the Internet Ahead, Cisco Says*, Om Malik on GIGAom blog, 16 June 2008

[10]*User Generated Online Video: Consumer Usage Exploded in 2006 but Revenues will Prove Slow to Develop*, Press Release, Screendigest, 15 January 2007

[11]NBC Universal's new Total Audience Measure Index (TAMi)

Customization Makes the Mobile TV Experience Compelling

Mobile phones contain location information (e.g., GPS), sensors (e.g., accelerometers), information about contacts (e.g., when and where they are accessed), billing information, etc. The next paradigm shift is to combine this personalized information and predicted analytics (e.g., gender, age, vocation, and commute patterns) with information about consumption patterns and interests from set-tops and personal computer usage. New, open environments such as the Open Cable Application Platform (OCAP) on set-tops and Android-enabled phones make this paradigm possible, with control of one's DVR from a mobile phone.

Web 2.0 development environments enable one to create custom applications quickly with great leverage (e.g., a real estate application that uses Google Maps to plot home addresses). Because the Internet is now *really about video*, the inherent switching and networking components may address basic transcoding that will adapt content from one file format to another (e.g., MPEG2–MPEG4), making it more amenable to a mobile phone. Use of media bundles helps here because, in addition to the video content, one can send metadata about that content plus related content in different formats (e.g., still images, audio, optimized decoders for the specific devices, and viewer preferences). This technology brings a richer, more complex experience to viewing video than previously seen and heard.

As for the mobile device itself, extreme technological advances have revolutionized its form, particularly displays, decoders, computation, and power. Foldable displays and projection displays address the limited visual real estate. The photographs below illustrate an imager from Display Tech in Longmont, Colorado, that uses a

3M micro-projector as a Bluetooth companion to a mobile phone for group display of content or even movie watching. Other novel mobile phone capabilities include 3D user interfaces and accelerators (e.g., from NVidia or Texas Instruments) that help provide psychological focus, using perspective and occlusion to deal with limited screen size and resolution.

Sports fans want mobile content. Companies such as Sportvision, a global provider of digital enhancements for sports television, have devised specific techniques for Mobile TV, such as colored vapor trails on footballs or soccer balls that indicate velocity and direction. Motorola supported a test deployment of the TuVista video-on-demand system for mobile phones at several sporting venues including Azteca Stadium in Mexico City (soccer), Purdue University (football), and Carnegie-Mellon University (professional hockey), as well as the 2009 BT (British Telecom) Para-Olympics.

Application Environments Control the Next Level of Content Customization

The mobile phone will be sourcing video TV, and it is estimated using the Cisco Visual Networking Index that "almost 64% of the world's mobile traffic will be video by 2013."[12] As an example, Motorola developed an internal application environment called Screen3 and deployed it via AT&T/Cingular. Screen3 enabled mobile widgets to appear on the idle screen, such as weather, stocks, or news, which could be user-customized, based on location and/or preferences. The user interface included a ticker-tape-like banner that enabled content to be displayed at its highest level, called a *bite*, which might contain a news story headline, for example. Clicking on the banner brought the user greater detail, which would appear as the first paragraph of a news text, called a *snack*. Both items in the hierarchy were cached on the device by being downloaded when the phone was idle. Clicking one more time directed the user to a live Web site containing full detail (with a higher level of transmission delay or latency), called the *meal*.

The principle used for a Mobile TV guide works as a general paradigm. A user interface can filter program guide content dynamically to match the user's choice of video content, channels, and advertisements. One can have "clickable advertisements" because it is a personal TV experience in which one can opt-in for something that *does* match the user's interest. The screen display is coupled with a voice-input system and search capability, so that one can say "find Sopranos" without needing to know the network or channel. The user interface allows one to set up a buddy list of friends, with whom to jointly watch a movie or sporting event with simultaneous voice connection. This type of user interface continues the trend toward *push*, as

---

[12]*Cisco Visual Networking Index: Global Mobile Data Traffic Forecast Update*, 29 January 2009

Rarely is just one display on in a typical dorm room. Photo courtesy of Don Tapscott.

opposed to *pull* environments, or ambient applications that are aware of the user and the user's preferences, particularly those triggered by location.

Another use of Mobile TV while watching "wired TV" is illustrated in the photograph above. A companion device (similar to laptops) enables customized interactive TV services similar to the startup, *Airplay*, which enables "friendly wagering" and social games on the mobile phone as a companion to sports on TV.

As screen icon Robert Redford stated at the MoFilm mobile film festival, "human creativity is really the one thing that can drive new technology forward [be]cause there's exciting times to come. ... This is the next wave of new opportunities that are driven by new technology."[13] This notion of a customized TV channel is now becoming a reality, as users actively search, aggregate, filter, and present video in an individualized way to other users, anywhere, at any time. Both mobile broadcast TV and *mobilized TV*, that is, cached on the mobile device typically from the set-top, are in our future.

Mobile TV promises new, engaging, and customized experiences. Join us as this book explores in detail these exciting, challenging developments as they unfold.

---

[13]*MOFILM – The world's biggest global mobile short film festival*, about MoFilm video, MoFilm.com

Saddlebags, Paperbacks and Mobile Media

Carola Zwick

Information is shaped by its format. The printing press with its repeatable layout laid ground for footnotes and references from other sources, and thus can be seen as the technology that initially generated the concept of hyperlinks. In the fifteenth century, printed matter quickly developed other formats like the paperback book or the flyer. These formats changed the content in almost every aspect significantly: books that fit in a saddlebag are mobile media and thus not as precious as the gigantic and prestigious folio placed on a lectern stand in a monastery. So books became a widespread, "ordinary" mobile medium and developed a multitude of purposes, aimed at different audiences, and generated a wide range of ideas for adequate content. The flyer in its limited size and public nature generated other forms of organizing and designing content: in order to fit the format and draw attention it uses a condensed form of messaging and an exaggerated typography.

The motion picture as a medium is highly influenced by its form of distribution and context of perception. The presentation in a movie theatre provides not only a large screen and an immersive visual experience, but also demands effort and dedication from the visitors: they need to go out to see the film. In this scenario, the film can also count on the undivided attention of the audience for a period of more than an hour. The TV changed that relationship quite a bit: the movie became a visitor in people's living rooms and was part of, or integrated into, daily routines. The remote control turned the movie into an interactive multiple-choice experience. These use patterns influenced the specific formats that were developed to provide content for what was then called "small screen" content, which became segmented and condensed in order to adapt to the attention span of the TV audience. The TV also standardized "the stage" to a 4:3 ratio for a long time.

When the media became digital, another paradigm shift occurred: the separation between the author and the audience vanished. The desktop revolution that started with desktop publishing took over all areas of media production and distribution.

C. Zwick(✉)
Product Design Department, Kunsthochschule Berlin Weissensee | School of Art, 13086, Berlin, Germany
e-mail: zwick@kh-berlin.de

A. Marcus et al. (eds.), *Mobile TV: Customizing Content and Experience*,
Human-Computer Interaction Series, DOI 10.1007/978-1-84882-701-1_3,
© Springer-Verlag London Limited 2010

The users of today are not only consumers of all kinds of media, but are also writers, film makers, art directors, producers, and publishers themselves.

The video became a convenient and quick format to document, communicate, or comment. Content can be created quickly and by the tools nowadays at hand without a lot of effort. The "multimedia" is characterized by the synchronous use of visual and auditory perception channels. This specific redundancy of multimedia information is much easier to digest than reading longer passages of text on a screen. In today's digital world, the video turns into a serious rival for the written word.

A platform like YouTube particularly exemplifies this development: you find private videos of birthday parties, and at the same time artists start their career on YouTube or established artists release their new song/video on this platform. Video is also increasingly used to document scientific explorations or research results. The classic format of the scientific paper seems to become too rigid or too slow in describing complex matter and thus claiming innovation.

Particularly the fact that video does not need to rely as much on language as the written word helps to turn video imagery itself into a global language. When released on a global platform, the speed of propagation is breathtaking. Hyperlinks that comment or recommend the content and draw connections to similar content unleash the power of this medium: response time and quality of feedback increased significantly from the old footnote.

Not by accident are these films short. Films used to have a linear format; thus, they did not offer techniques like browsing through them, skipping parts, or searching for a particular fragment of the content. These were techniques we were accustomed to from our experience with books. The digital video player tool bar containing features like the slider as well as stop and go buttons give the user a higher level of control. Still the options to annotate, link, grab interesting items, or manipulate parts of the content are missing.

Initially caused by the download size of video, the typical video screen size delivered online became the blueprint for the small mobile screens of today. The variety of output media is still influencing the design of the content. Because the screen proportions in use are varying, a video gutter has been developed similar to the gutter in a book. In the case of small-screen videos, the important content is kept in the middle of the screen to avoid unwanted cropping. The specifics of the format influence both content and aesthetics: Small screens seem to prefer a clear focal point and are in favor of a centerline composition. Because small screens do not take up all of the user's field of vision, they can develop a greater speed: motion and cuts can be much faster than on the big screen. Both the dramaturgy and visual language start to depart from their counterparts on bigger formats. Thus, trying to design specifically for this condensed form of messaging presents new challenges.

The challenge of designing for small mobile screens is adapting the interaction to peripatetic use scenarios. Enabling the user to carry this medium in his or her "saddlebag" means also to offer equally intuitive and enjoyable interactions as with other physical objects that a user can easily operate, like a key, a wrench, or shoelaces. If these interactions call on the manual skills of the user, they are memorized in a way that they can soon be executed blindfolded. This simplicity allows people to operate many functions single-handed without stopping other activities like walking.

Other options to ease and speed up search and browse activities come into play by using metadata of the content as well as keeping track of the user's habits and preferences. This increased ease and speed might help to shortcut navigation paths, thereby reducing the interactions needed to a minimum. Nevertheless, for absorbing visual content, the user needs to give the screen a look or hold eye contact depending on the format.

The inherent properties of screen-based mobile devices will trigger eventually new formats and a specific design of the content: such formats might augment the user's current location or situation with useful additional information or offering narrative and interactive formats for entertainment *en route*.

But the most exiting task ahead is to develop tools for producing or editing multimedia information. Why? We are well trained in "reading" multimedia content and some have already started to "write" in multimedia format as well, but we deserve tools that allow us to do this as nonchalantly as taking notes or making scribbles in our Moleskine!

The Path Tells a Story

Frank Nack

Stories have been shared in every culture because they are a powerful means to entertain, educate, and preserve traditions or instill values. In the history of storytelling technological evolution has changed the tools available to storytellers, from primarily oral representations that have been enriched with gestures and expressions to the sophisticated forms we enjoy today, such as film or complex layered hypermedia environments. Despite these developments the traditional linear presentation of a story is still the most dominant. Yet, the first decade of the twenty-first century established a technology that finally, after many attempts, can challenge the dogma of passive linearity. It is mobile technology that makes people aware that a digital environment opens opportunities to everybody to freely socialize through and with stories relevant for the current spatial, temporal, and social context.

The path to this now open gate to the land of creative communication was long, winded and, like all relevant paths, with a forking origin. One of those was Paul Otlet's Mundaneum, an archive in Brussels with more than 12 million index cards and documents that showed a first glimpse of what information combination could achieve. A more technological inspired vision was presented by Vannevar Bush (1945), who described a futuristic device, the Memex, which is electronically linked to a library, able to display books and films from the library, and automatically follow cross-references from one work to another. The Memex was the first simple and elegant approach toward multimedia information access and it formed the inspirational space for Ted Nelson (1974) to establish what is now known as "Hypertext" and "Hypermedia." The exploration of hypertext as a technology as well as an art form was certainly influenced by the post-structuralism as well as postmodernism movement within literature and philosophy. Hypertext also emphasizes that the linear narrative typical of print is not the only acceptable model of storytelling. The second important vision of Hypertext is that the reader's physical as well as cognitive encounters with the text as much form the basis of the text as

F. Nack
HCS, University of Amsterdam

A. Marcus et al. (eds.), *Mobile TV: Customizing Content and Experience*,
Human-Computer Interaction Series, DOI 10.1007/978-1-84882-701-1_4,
© Springer-Verlag London Limited 2010

the words and links provided by the author (Bernstein 1998; Landow 1994; Murray 1997). Digital fiction in the form of hypertext or hypermedia is interactive, but it is not structureless. Hypermedia narratives follow common patterns that provide coherence through tight organization of material on the basis of composition and aggregation. Famous examples are the interactive novels "Afternoon" by Michael Joyce, or "Victory Garden" by Stuart Moulthorp. Interactive fiction also found resonance in the domain of adventure games, also known as collaborative fiction, of which "Adventure" and "Gateway" are well-known examples. The fascination of hypertext still lies in the use of technology to better exploit the dynamics between author, reader, and material, where the center of attention still lies on the craftsmanship of the writer to create works of imaginative, technical, or scholarly writing (Nack & Hardman 2001).

The notion of the "digital" as the capability to combine atomic information fragments was not reserved to hypertext research only. The cognitive possibilities of the digital combined with the idea of "semantic and semiotic productivity," allowing an endless montage of signs, also inspired a great deal of research in artificial intelligence (AI) that embody mechanisms to interpret, manipulate, or generate stories in different media. The basic vision was that the machine should not only support the author, but also become an active partner in the pleasures of immersion and interaction.

Around the early 1970s AI research on story generation and understanding investigated in particular the dynamic aspects of a plot that refer to mental or conceptual objects such as themes, goals, events, or actions. The inspiration was drawn from theories propagated by the structuralist movement, which understood narration in terms of states and transformational rules. In analogy, AI approaches at that time considered the applicability of story grammars as a solution to the representation of narrative structure, where the main influences came from Propp's work on Russian folktales and Chomsky's transformational grammar (Colby 1973; Rumelhart 1977). For nearly a decade sophisticated grammars had been developed that supported the generation as well as understanding of textual stories. By the end of the 1970s, Black and Wilensky (1979), Graham (1983), and Black and Bower (1980) provided the main arguments that terminated the age of story grammar. They showed that not only were the formal properties of the grammars insufficient, but also that the computational costs of the representation were too high. The number of deletion and reordering transformations in the proposed grammars became extremely large, and yet the grammars were unable to produce a sufficiently varied set of stories. More importantly, through experiments it could be demonstrated that the structures of story-grammars do not reflect the human memory structures that are related to story parts. Black, Bower, Graham, and Wilensky arrived essentially at the same result: a story is a mental process based on different aspects of people's knowledge, of which structure is but one.

Other innovations developed during the late 1970 and the early 1980s made use of methods long employed by linguists, cognitive psychologists, and narrative theorists, resulting in less stringent and dynamic techniques. The main corner stone of this research direction was that memory is structured in the form of meaningful "stories" (not merely inert decontextualized information) and that problem solving progressed by using "cases" or examples stored in memory. This theory takes a schema as the building block of a cognitive framework, where the schema determines what a person knows about the world, the objects it contains, and the tasks to be performed in this world (Schank & Abelson 1977). In combination with automated planning, which concerns the realization of strategies or action sequences typically used in processes that result in creative behavior, it is now possible to establish textual storytelling engines with a far greater degree of freedom and user adaptability. Traces of this technology could be found in interactive fiction where players use text commands to control characters and influence the environment, mainly text adventures, where the entire interface is text only. This type of interaction fiction combined elements of role-playing games, hack and slash, and online chat and later developed further into wholly graphical adventures such as Myst. In that way it guided the way towards digital game playing. The progress in schema and planning eventually stalled mainly because schemata as well as automated planning used in digital storytelling still followed the strains of traditional written communication by supporting the linear representation of an argument resulting in a final document of context-restricted content. Technology, however, changed and with it also the requests of the ordinary user. In the late 1980s it was in particular the development of new digital consumer electronics that allowed computing to leave the realm of research and enter society in large. The development of personal computers in the 1980s as well as the appearance of digital scanner, photo, and video technology changed the world of digital storytelling drastically.

The shiny example of research in digital storytelling in the 1990s was the Interactive Cinema Group at the MIT Media Lab. This group, headed by Glorianna Davenport, internalized the history of storytelling and applied it to all digital media. The essential outcome of research performed by this group did not only inform the theory of digital storytelling with respect to the representation and exploitation of temporal, stylistic, and interaction attributes, but also demonstrated that works on digital storytelling need to be rooted in the real world for making an impact (Interactive Cinema Group). Leaving the realm of research and entering society at large is one of the great achievements of work in this period, of which Terminal Time (Terminal Time) is another good example. Terminal Time is a machine, which combines historical events, ideological rhetoric, familiar forms of TV documentary, consumer polls, and artificial intelligence algorithms to create hybrid cinematic experiences for mass audiences.

In the 1990s also the agent paradigm emerged, which addressed the restricted reaction patterns of planners and thus provided new interaction methods not known until then. Agents perform as an autonomous entity, which observes and acts upon an environment (i.e., a story world) and directs its activity towards achieving goals, supported by learning strategies as well as knowledge it collects over time. The emerging technologies, such as dynamic programming, reinforcement learning, and combinatorial optimization facilitated digital storytelling to be applied in responsive environments in which the user can engage with characters in a story world that was to some extent or in its totality created by the user himself or herself. The most famous examples are the SIMS, a strategic life-simulation computer game of daily activities of one or more virtual persons in a suburban household (The SIMS). The other, more research-oriented example is Façade, an interactive story that puts the player in the role of a close friend of Grace and Trip, a couple who has recently invited the player to their home for cocktails. The story evolves in the form of a dialogue, where the system allows the player to type sentences to either support the couple through their troubles, or driving them farther apart (Façade).

The emergence of the web, new mobile technology, and the rise of media technologies, such as the digital photo and video camera, or midi and MP3 player, stimulated new directions of digital storytelling. In particular, a combination of web and mobile technology provides new challenges for digital storytelling, as the second generation of Web users – most likely their successors, too – are flighty and loyal mainly to the information they create, consume, and distribute. The target for these users is to interact with content and through that content with their peers wherever and whenever. It is now in the field of digital storytelling to provide solutions for authoring, reuse, and presentation in environments mainly built out of media items. Production and consumption must blur into one interaction process, driven by the individual in-group settings and it all needs to be done on a mobile device. The works described in this book are the yellow stones of the path that is the story of digital storytelling.

References

Bernstein, N. (1998). Patterns of hypertext. *Proceedings of the 9th ACM conference on Hypertext and Hypermedia* (pp. 21–29; June 20–24). Pittsburgh, USA.

Black, J. B., & Bower, G. H. (1980). Story understanding as problem solving. *Poetics, 9,* 223–250.

Black, J. B., & Wilensky, R. (1979). An evaluation of story grammars. *Cognitive Science, 3,* 213–230.

Bush, V. (1945). As we may think. *The Atlantic Monthly, 176*(1), 101–108.

Colby, B. N. (1973). A partial grammar of Eskimo folktales. *American Anthropologist, 75,* 645–662.

Graham, A. (1983). What is wrong with story grammars? *Cognition, 15,* 145–154.

Landow, G. P. (1994). The rhetoric of hypermedia: Some rules for authors. In D. Paul & P. George (Eds.), *Landow hypermedia and literary studies* (pp. 81–103). Cambridge, MA: MIT Press.

Murray, J. (1997). *Hamlet on the Holodeck: The future of narrative in cyberspace.* New York: Free Press.

Nack, F., & Hardman, L. (2001). Denotative and connotative semantics in hypermedia: Proposal for a semiotic-aware architecture. *The New Review of Hypermedia and Multimedia 2001, 7,* pp. 39–65.

Nelson, T. H. (1974). *Computer lib/dream machines.* South Bend, IN: Distributors.

Rumelhart, D. E. (1977). Understanding and summarizing brief stories. In D. Laberge & S. J. Samuels (Eds.), *Basic processes in reading: Perception and comprehension* (pp. 265–303). Hillsdale, NJ: Lawrence Erlbaum.

Schank, R. C., & Abelson, R. (1977). *Scripts, plans, goals and understanding.* Hillsdale, NJ: Lawrence Earlbaum.

Interactive Cinema Group – MIT Media Lab, from http://ic.media.mit.edu/
Terminal Time, from http://www.terminaltime.com/
The SIMS, from http://thesims2.co.uk/pages.view_frontpage.asp
Façade, from http://www.interactivestory.net/

Introduction to Social TV

Gunnar Harboe

Mobile TV typically involves accessing television content from handheld devices. The most ubiquitous of these devices, mobile phones, are primarily designed for communication. It is therefore natural to look at how those communication features can be integrated with television viewing. Issues of sociability are also relevant to Mobile TV in other ways, such as in analyzing how watching video in public spaces affects and is affected by the social context, and in the case of communication by video messages and video conferencing.

Researchers have indeed been working on integrating communication as another way to transform how television is experienced. Interest in *Social TV*, social experiences around television content, has increased dramatically in recent years, leading to a flood of research and novel systems. Typical Social TV systems include presence (what channel and program someone is watching), text, voice, and sometimes video conferencing. While the majority of studies and prototypes have utilized stationary setups, much of what has been learned is also relevant to mobile social television.

Neither the term nor the idea of "Social TV" are in fact recent. When first conceived of, Social TV and television were not imagined as separate things. Early visionaries assumed that screens for remote viewing would allow two-way communication, and that audiences would be able to both watch a performance and applaud together from their own homes (Robida 1882, 2004).

Instead, TV developed into the stereotypically one-way, passive medium known today. Still, it was recognized decades ago that a lot of social activity does take place around television (Lull 1990), and the social uses of television have been the subject of significant research ever since. It has been shown that television serves a number of social purposes, both at the time of watching and after the fact, such as providing topics for conversations, easing interaction, and promoting feelings of togetherness. By exploring the social usage of mobile TV, the authors in this book are now extending these findings to settings outside the home.

Social TV proponents, then, see television viewing as a social experience capable of reinforcing bonds in strong-tie relationships, and attempt to extend the effect beyond

G. Harboe
Motorola Applied Research and Technology Center

A. Marcus et al. (eds.), *Mobile TV: Customizing Content and Experience*,   21
Human-Computer Interaction Series, DOI 10.1007/978-1-84882-701-1_5,
© Springer-Verlag London Limited 2010

co-located groups, connecting people across distance and time. Early efforts include the 1995 Prisoner Chat system (O'Sullivan 2005), AOLTV (Hill 2001), and 2BeOn (Abreu et al. 2001). More recently, support for shared viewing has become available for on-line videos and some Blu-ray discs, though not yet for TV broadcasts.

Social TV Research as It Relates to Mobile Social Television

Research around Social TV has mainly clustered around a few big questions. These can be summed up as: validating the effectiveness and appeal of social features around video; exploring and comparing specific features and communication modalities to produce more optimal designs; and studying the behaviors around use of social television systems (Harboe et al. 2009).

Through this work, the ability of the Social TV systems to provide a social experience has been well-established, and the appeal of this experience has been validated in several instances. Observations of users in test sessions show that they take advantage of the social nature of the experience to engage in a rich set of behaviors (Harboe et al. 2008). The two most important features to support the experience appear to be presence awareness and freeform communication.

With Social TV presence awareness, users know when their friends are watching TV. Because television viewing accounts for a great deal of people's leisure time, they often appear as present to each other, and this can make them feel closer and encourage them to strike up conversations. At the same time, when others are immediately aware of you as soon as you turn on the TV or log into the system, this imposes social pressures, not just to communicate, but also around the patterns of viewing (Harboe et al. 2008).

In order to meaningfully share a viewing experience remotely, the ability for users to communicate in their own words turns out to be critical. In systems where users are restricted in the messages they can send, for example to only a set of graphical emotions or recommendations of particular TV programs, they have a lesser feeling of togetherness (Baillie et al. 2007) and feel frustrated and dissatisfied (Metcalf et al. 2008).

While lab studies indicate that both text and voice chat are good ways to offer freeform communication (Weisz & Kiesler 2008), tests in natural environments suggest that in practice, users strongly prefer text (Tullio et al. 2008; Huang et al. 2009). More important than their specific preference, however, is the observation that choice of modality is primarily determined by the dynamic of the communication initiation and by contextual factors of the setting. Since public spaces and changing physical environments are likely to differ significantly from the living room in these regards, this insight calls for a better understanding of these properties for mobile television.

Although the overall impact of social television on social interaction and relationships appears to be positive, based on current findings, some negative effects have been remarked. When freeform communication is available, tension can be seen between the nature of the television screen as "public within the home" and the sometimes personal nature of the communication. This raises a number of privacy concerns (Harboe 2008), and points to mobile television on personal handheld devices as a potentially better platform.

A displacement of sociability is another negative consequence of social television that has occasionally been observed in living room settings. By bringing outsiders into the family space, social television can intrude on important "quality time," and weaken the closest ties even as it builds relationships with more (physically) distant people (Harboe et al. 2009). Because mobile television viewing in many cases takes place in less intimate settings, one could imagine that this would be less of a concern as well. However, attempting to communicate in situations where it is not socially appropriate is very much a relevant issue for mobile social television, in the same way that mobile phone use in public spaces has often been criticized as intrusive and for reducing casual social contact between strangers (Ling 2002). Potentially, if not designed in such a way as to enable and encourage socially appropriate use, mobile social television could lead to increased negative attitudes toward mobile phones.

Work on Mobile Social Television

Prior to this book, very little substantial research specifically on mobile social television has been published. The only systematic exploration of the topic has been by Baillie, Fröhlich, Schatz, and their colleagues at FTW, comprising conceptual models, technology architectures, application prototypes, experiments and user studies (*see Chapter 19*). They conclude that mobile social television is promising although it faces a number of challenges.

That finding is supported by a focus group study described in Massey and Harboe (2009). A specific usage scenario of mobile social television called "place shifting" (here combined with personal content) was presented to participants: "Bill's flight is delayed, so he uses his cell phone to connect to the TV system, and is able to see the home movie. He chats with Susan and the children, and then he joins them as they all watch the rest of the home movie together." This use-case proved particularly controversial, inspiring some strong negative reactions. At the same time, 34% of participants were positive to the idea, which indicates that there is a market for this kind of product.

Beyond Mobile Social Television

Mobile social television is largely driven by, and at the same time a great example of, convergence between media and communication technologies. But this same convergence is also undermining the definitions of "mobile," "social," and "television" as distinct categories, potentially rendering the whole concept obsolete. With ubiquitous access to media content and social networks from a variety of screens and devices, rich and pervasive presence, and a wide range of video experiences (including interactive and user-generated formats as well as video conferencing), mobile social television becomes just one point in a great spectrum of content-enriched communication and communication-enriched content.

References

Abreu, J., Almeida, P., & Branco, V. (2001). 2BeOn: Interactive television supporting interpersonal communication. In J. A. Jorge, N. Correia, H. Jones, & M. B. Kamegai (Eds.), *Proceedings of the Sixth Eurographics Workshop on Multimedia 2001* (pp. 199–208). New York: Springer Verlag.

Baillie, L., Fröhlich, P., & Schatz, R. (2007). Exploring social TV. In *Proceedings of the 29th International Conference on Information Technology Interfaces (ITI 2007)* (pp. 215–220). IEEE.

Harboe, G. (2008). The TV is watching you. In *UXTV 2008 Social TV Workshop Position Papers,* from http://www.uxtv2008.org/program/social-tv-workshop-papers.html

Harboe, G., Huang, E., Massey, N., Metcalf, C., Novak, A., Romano, G., & Tullio, J. (2009). Getting to Know Social Television. In P. Cesar, D. Geerts, and K. Chorianopoulos (Eds.), *Social Interactive Television: Immersive Shared Experiences and Perspectives* (pp. 158–186). Hershey, PA: Information Science Reference.

Harboe, G., Metcalf, C. J., Bentley, F., Tullio, J., Massey, N., & Romano, G. (2008). Ambient social TV: Drawing people into a shared experience. In *Proceeding of the Twenty-Sixth Annual SIGCHI Conference on Human Factors in Computing Systems (CHI 2008), New York, ACM Press,* pp. 1–10.

Hill B (2001) AOLTV for dummies. Wiley, New York

Huang, E. M., Harboe, G., Tullio, J., Novak, A., Massey, N., Metcalf, C. J., & Romano, G. (2009). Social Television Comes Home: A field study of communication choices and practices in TV-based text and voice chat. In *Proceeding of the Twenty-Seventh Annual SIGCHI Conference on Human Factors in Computing Systems (CHI 2009)* New York, ACM Press, pp. 585–594.

Ling, R. (2002). The social juxtaposition of mobile telephone conversations and public spaces. In *Proceedings of the Conference on the social consequences of mobile telephones,* from http://www.richardling.com/papers/2002_juxtaposition_public_spaces.pdf (downloaded 26 Feb 2009)

Lull J (1990) Inside family viewing: Ethnographic research on television's audiences. Routledge, London

Massey, N., & Harboe, G. (2009). Social television through iterative design. In *Proceedings of the 6th IEEE Consumer Communications and Networking Conference, 2009 (CCNC 2009)* (CCNC, Jan. 10–13, 2009).

Metcalf, C., Harboe, G., Massey, N., Tullio, J., Romano, G., Huang, E. M., & Bentley, F. (2008). Examining presence and lightweight messaging in a social television experience. *Translations on Multimedia Computing, Communications and Applications* (TOMCCAP) 4, 4(Oct. 2008), 1–16.

O'Sullivan, D. (2005). *Prisoner Chat,* from http://itp.nyu.edu/~dbo3/proj/prisoner.htm

Robida, A. (2004). *The Twentieth century.* (P. Willems, Trans.; A. B. Evans, Ed.). Middletown, CT: Wesleyan University Press (original work published 1882).

Tullio, J., Harboe, G, & Massey, N. (2008). Investigating the use of voice and text chat in a social television system. In M. Tscheligi, M. Obrist, & A. Lugmayr (Eds.), *Proceedings of the 6th European Conference (EuroITV 2008)* (pp. 163–167). Berlin: Springer.

Weisz, J. D., & Kiesler, S. (2008). How text and audio chat change the online video experience. In *Proceedings of UXTV 2008,* New York, ACM Press, pp. 9–18.

The Sociability of Mobile TV

David Geerts

Both mobile phones and television are known for the social practices they enable. Television has been a social medium since its introduction in households all over the world. Although its main aim is entertaining and informing its viewers, people often watch television together with close relatives or good friends, talk about what is going on while watching television or even structure their social activities around a television show (e.g., eating dinner while watching the news) (Lull 1980). But television programs are also part of social interactions away from the television set, when discussing favorite television programs around the water cooler at work, or recommending shows to watch to good friends. The main function of mobile phones on the other hand has always been social from the start: communicating with other people, when and wherever you want, first using voice communication and later also with text messages and video communication.

So what happens when these two social media are combined? It is clear that mobile TV cannot be successful without taking social practices when watching TV on a mobile device into account. Although one approach could be to let the users appropriate the device in their social environment, as happened with text messaging, the risk that it does not match their current practices is too big. A better approach is to design mobile TV applications that take direct advantage of the social aspects of each medium, which means adding interactive features that will enable and support social interaction between users on different levels. In order to get an idea of the possibilities, it is interesting to look at recent research in the closely related domain of interactive television.

During the last decade, a new brand of interactive television applications is being developed: social interactive television systems that allow remote viewers to interact with each other via their television set. In the beginning of this century, systems such as AOL TV (Time Warner 2000), 2BeON (Abreu et al. 2002), and AmigoTV (Coppens et al. 2004) were designed to allow people at different locations to talk or chat with each other while watching television, also offering other

D. Geerts
Centre for User Experience Research (CUO), IBBT/K. U. Leuven, Parkstraat 45 Bus 3605,
3000 Leuven, Belgium

A. Marcus et al. (eds.), *Mobile TV: Customizing Content and Experience*,
Human-Computer Interaction Series, DOI 10.1007/978-1-84882-701-1_6,
© Springer-Verlag London Limited 2010

social features such as presence information, messaging, or even sending cartoons to other viewers. Since then, more and more interactive TV systems incorporating different forms of social interactions have sprung up: Social TV (Harboe et al. 2008), ConnecTV (Boertjes et al. 2008), CollaboraTV (Nathan et al. 2008), Ambulant Annotator (Cesar et al. 2006), etc. Although at the time of writing none of these systems have been commercialized yet, we can expect commercial social iTV systems to hit the shelves in the near future.

It is useful to discuss some of the most prominent features of these systems, as this gives insight into the possible social features that could be interesting for mobile TV as well. First of all, some systems support mainly synchronous interaction, allowing direct communication between viewers, while others are mainly focused on asynchronous interaction, for example, when they enable leaving messages for other viewers. Both modes of interaction are interesting, and so a social interactive TV system should support these two forms. A similar dichotomy can be found in the communication modalities: some systems support remote talking with other viewers, while other systems choose to implement text chat as communication tool. The choice between voice and text chat is currently actively debated (see, e.g., Geerts 2006), and is still not concluded. However, offering both options allows users to choose the communication modality that best fits the situation and their own experiences, as users who are less proficient in typing might prefer voice chat, or certain circumstances are more beneficial for text chat, for example, when the children are sleeping. Another common feature is the use of presence information in varying forms. Users can see whether other viewers are watching TV or not, what television programs they are watching, or can even get a full viewing history of their friends or relatives. Some systems use this information to include features such as following another viewer automatically when switching channels, or by including a social EPG that shows the favorite television shows of someone's buddies. Less frequent, but nevertheless interesting, social features are the ability to share content (synchronously as well as asynchronously) with other viewers, clipping and annotating video content, or enabling team-based play, for example, by playing along with a game show as a team with remote players.

Based on user tests and field studies with several of these systems and an analysis of the use of these different features, 12 sociability heuristics for social interactive television were created (Geerts & De Grooff 2009):

1. Offer different channels and levels for communicating freely
2. Use awareness tools for communicating availability
3. Allow both synchronous and asynchronous use
4. Support remote as well as co-located interaction
5. Exploit viewing behavior for informing and engaging other viewers
6. Give the user appropriate control over actions and system settings
7. Guarantee both personal privacy and group privacy
8. Minimize distraction from the television program
9. Notify the user of incoming events and situation changes
10. Adapt to appropriate television program genres
11. Let users share content flexibly
12. Encourage shared activities

These heuristics offer designers and evaluators of social interactive television systems guidance when implementing or evaluating tools for supporting and stimulating social interaction.

The systems and their features mentioned in the previous paragraphs are all designed for use on a normal television set using a kind of set-top box and are mainly intended for use in a living room, with a very specific context of use: a big screen, a large distance from the screen, and multiple people watching the same content at the same time. One need to only look at the Internet, and the many social television and video sites that are being introduced recently on the web, to see the impact of using a different device in a different context. The PC is an excellent medium for communication between remote viewers, but is a less sociable medium for co-located viewers as it is intended for solitary use, due to the smaller screen size and a "two-foot experience" (in contrast to the "ten-foot experience" of a television set). As some social features as well as sociability heuristics are useful in this context as well, many others are not. Similarly, merely exporting the same functions to mobile TV is not useful, as some of these will come in conflict with the highly personal and nomadic use of mobile devices. Likewise, the sociability heuristics for interactive television cannot all be used for mobile TV. However, using the aforementioned systems as inspiration, similar social functions can be used as a starting point and can explore how they can manifest itself in a mobile TV system. When combining research into social interactive television with thorough knowledge of the – social as well as general – practices of mobile phones, new functions and features can be thought of that will ensure that mobile TV applications will fit the context of use.

Several chapters in this book deal with these social aspects of mobile TV in different ways: using mobile TV in everyday social interactions, letting social information help in finding and selecting interesting videos to watch, sharing presence information as well as content with other mobile TV users, etc. The possibilities are diverse, and as mobile TV is still in the early stages at the moment, much research is needed on the different approaches to this important but complex phenomenon. In any case, as mobile TV will no doubt be used in rich and varying social contexts, paying attention to well-designed social features will be a prerequisite for successful mobile TV services.

References

Abreu, J., Almeida, P., & Branco, V. (2002). 2BeOn: Interactive television supporting interpersonal communication. In *Proceedings of the sixth Eurographics workshop on Multimedia 2001* (pp. 199–208). Manchester, UK: Springer-Verlag.

Boertjes, E., Schultz, S., & Klok, J. (2008). *Pilot ConnecTV. Gebruikersonderzoek* [Pilot ConnecTV. User research. Public report of the Freeband Project, TNO]. Retrieved 18 December, 2008, from http://www.tno.nl/content.cfm?context=markten&content=publicatie& laag1=182&laag2=1&item_id=267

Cesar, P., Bulterman, D. C. A., & Jansen, A. J. (2006). An architecture for end-user TV content enrichment. *Journal of Virtual Reality and Broadcasting, 3.*

Coppens, T., Trappeniers, L., & Godon, M. (2004). AmigoTV: Towards a social TV experience. In J. Masthoff, R. Griffiths, & L. Pemberton (Eds.), *Proceedings from the second European conference on Interactive television "Enhancing the experience,"* University of Brighton, Brighton.

Geerts, D. (2006). Comparing voice chat and text chat in a communication tool for interactive television. In *Proceedings of the fourth Nordic conference on Human-computer interaction: Changing roles* (pp. 461–464). Oslo, Norway: ACM.

Geerts, D., & De Grooff, D. (2009). Supporting the social uses of television: Sociability heuristics for Social TV. In *Proceedings of the twenty-seventh annual SIGCHI conference on Human factors in computing systems,* Boston, MA, USA (April 04–09). CHI '09, New York: ACM.

Harboe G, Massey N, Metcalf C, Wheatley D, Romano G (2008) The uses of social television. Computer Entertainment 6(1):1–15

Lull, J. (1980). The social uses of television. *Human Communication Research, 6*(3).

Nathan, M., Harrison, C., Yarosh, S., Terveen, L., Stead, L., & Amento, B. (2008). CollaboraTV: Making television viewing social again. In *Proceedings of the first international conference on Designing interactive user experiences for TV and video* (pp. 85–94). Silicon Valley, California, USA: ACM.

Time Warner. (2000). *AOL launches AOLTV – The first interactive television service for the mass market.* Press release June 19, 2000. Retrieved December 14, 2008, from http://www.timewarner.com/corp/newsroom/pr/0,20812,666719,00.html

Interactive TV Narrativity

Marian F. Ursu

Looking back over the past 25 years, the impressive developments in information and communication technologies generated a booming popularity of the new forms of media consumption that allow for interactivity and mobility, such as Web information and entertainment and games. This was and still is particularly evident within the younger generation, who are the most avid adopters of both new technologies and new forms of media consumption (Schadler 2006; KPMG 2007). When asked, in 2006, which device they could not live without, 37% mentioned their PC, 26% their mobile phone, whereas only 17% mentioned their TVs (Schadler 2006); and all these were before the launch of products such as the iPhone, which offer increasing flexibility and mobility of the media experiences.

Television, whose dominance started to be seriously shaken by this, responded by embracing interactivity: interactive television (iTV) made its debut in earnest 20 years ago, in the late 1990s. However, until quite recently, interactivity did not apply to narrativity, to the stories told by the programs themselves, but was provided in parallel with and more or less disconnected from the actual programs. Examples of such interactive services include "enhanced TV" (Jensen 2005), which is an advanced version of teletext, electronic program guides, betting, shopping, e-mail access, Internet browsing, and game-play. Their invocation can happen more or less at any point during the viewing of a program, as they are not aligned or synchronized with the moving image narration.[1] They reflect television's attempts to assimilate services that emerged and grew successfully on other delivery platforms, in more or less their original formats, rather than to develop its own forms of interactivity. In this approach, iTV emphasizes its position as a delivery platform for, more or less, disjoint interactive services, of which the traditional linear television narration is the one always present.

M.F. Ursu
Narrative and Interactive Media, Department of Computing, Goldsmiths,
University of London, London, SE14 6NW, UK

[1]The exception of sending content via teletext that is synchronized with and overlaid on the main visual narration may be regarded as representing a simpler case of multistream delivery (discussed next).

A. Marcus et al. (eds.), *Mobile TV: Customizing Content and Experience*,
Human-Computer Interaction Series, DOI 10.1007/978-1-84882-701-1_7,
© Springer-Verlag London Limited 2010

Shifting the point of view on the narrative role of television, on its excellence at telling stories with moving image, a natural question arises: could this role, itself, be enhanced by interactivity? There is clear evidence that the answer is yes (Ursu et al. 2008b). Interacting with narrations has become possible, has started to happen, is gathering momentum, and is becoming more and more sophisticated. Nevertheless, new forms of narrative interaction require new technological capabilities. Requirements for the former may be identified and specified, but the technology necessary for their implementation may not be available; certain forms of narrative interactions have to wait until such technology is created. This is because truly interactive narrativity, regarded as the ability of each active viewer to influence, at viewing time, the narration that is recounted to them, necessarily requires that a part of the narration is carried out automatically, by software. Only in this way, each active viewer or groups of viewers can receive, during each viewing, their own personalized narrations. And only now, the computing capabilities, including both processing speed and bandwidth, are ripe to support personalized interactive TV narrations – made with moving image and delivered to many.

The most rudimentary form of interacting with a TV narration is the ability to move backward and forward (stop, replay, rewind, fast-forward) through linear programs. Although inherently available for locally stored moving image (e.g., DVD), iTV had to wait until recently to make this interaction mode available for broadcast TV programmes, in the paradigm denoted ShapeShifting TV. They can be denoted "brute force" technologies, as they either allow TV content to be sent directly to the viewer, when the viewer wants it (video on demand), or permit local storage of a significant amount of TV broadcast content. Another brute force technology, in the form of multistream synchronous delivery, supports a seemingly more developed form of interaction, namely the ability to choose a point of view from which to receive a narration, such as, for example, the viewing perspective (camera) or the voice of the narrator. However, behind the scenes there is nothing more than a number of synchronized streams delivered in parallel, their synchronicity allowing viewers to switch between them at any time they wish. In all these, established by now, forms of iTV, storytelling is still carried out, essentially, by linear programs, as it was since the inception of television. The actual narrations are still not interactive.

The newest approach to interactive television exploits cross-platform content delivery in the conveying of different interconnected facets of main narratives, while at the same time providing rich active viewer engagement, through direct interaction, around the topics of the narratives. This was foreseen in 2000 by Steve Billinger of Sky Interactive as "content continuum" in which "television will continue to be used to build the primary compelling brand position, and all platforms (broadcast, radio, broadband) will deliver slices of the content pie" (Forrester 2000). Highly interactive spaces surrounding main narratives are now provided as places in which viewers can enhance their experience of consuming linear narrations by accessing supplementary content, discussing matters of interest related to the topics of the narratives, participating in related activities, and even providing their own generated content. In turn, such spaces are being used by content creators to elicit preferences and interests from the (active) viewers in order to prepare subsequent narrations. The Sweden's SVT participatory drama *The Truth*

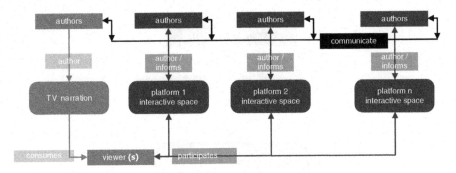

Fig. 1 Separation of narrative and interactive spaces: communication between them happens mainly via human operators

About Marika (Jarnhed 2007), which gained immediate success, is representative of this versatile approach. Nevertheless, even here, the main TV narration is still authored and consumed in a linear fashion, as is illustrated in Fig. 1. The link between the different interactive spaces and the narrative space is done via their authors and not automatically.

In 2008, BBC published compelling words in support of multi-platform interactive narrative delivery. Referring to dramatic productions, it stated: "We are looking to find major multi-platform dramas which allow the user to explore the world of a drama ... by allowing audiences to engage and become involved with the characters and their world. We want to allow our audiences to explore and create the new worlds originally imagined by the linear narratives and be able to share their ideas and experiences with others ... [and] to create their own content in [the world of the drama] but without fundamentally changing it. We want to ... expand linear programme[s]" (BBC-Drama 2008). These words could be interpreted as suggesting more: the convergence of narration with interaction, the organic integration of interaction into narration, the creation of interactive narrative spaces that are able to unravel differently at each viewing by responding to viewers' interaction through automatically compiled high-quality linear narrations (refer to Fig. 2). This view appears to be supported even more by what BBC stated about documentaries: "We want to move beyond the constraints imposed by traditional linear film to tell important stories in new ways, with formats that are more immersive and interactive" (BBC-Documentary 2008).

The development of interactive TV narratives which, on the one hand, maintain the high quality associated with traditional linear narratives and, on the other, provide for appropriate viewer agency poses challenges at all levels: conceptual, pragmatic (especially regarding technological support), and economic. The challenge at the conceptual level is about crafting an explorable interactive narrative space, which provides active viewers with the appropriate means of exploration and communication, and which results in different individual (linear) narrations, for each viewer's interactive experience, of the same or better quality as those told directly by expert creators. Addressing this challenge depends a great deal on the provision of appropriate support for both authoring and delivery, as, interactive TV narratives, by their own nature, have to be automatically compiled at the time of viewing.

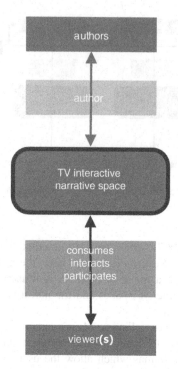

Fig. 2 Organic integration of interaction and narrativity resulting in an interactive narrative space

Expert content creators should be provided with tools that support and nurture their creative thinking, and also allow them to create robust interactive programs. Such tools should allow different formats of audio–visual material to be ingested and annotated, narrative structures to be created and associated with the actual content, and programs to be tested and validated at different stages in their development. They should support highly iterative development methods and should address the creative processes from concept formulation, through design and sketching, to the production of the final program. Not least, they should be production-independent, otherwise the solutions provided would not be cost-effective.

Delivery also imposes substantial requirements on technology: reasoning engines should be able to interpret the participating viewers' input on the basis of the editing know how embedded in the authored narrative structures, and thus produce contiguous playlists in between the viewers' interactions; compositing engines should be able to render such playlists, dealing with multilayered timeline arrangement of different media types and the application of cinematic and digital effects; transmissions from servers to end users or in between end users, in whatever chosen network architecture, has to be done without loss and in good time. Timing is crucial: each playlist has to be calculated sufficiently early, so that there is sufficient time to render and deliver it, such that, given the delays over the transmission medium, each subsequent narrative fragment reaches the engager before the previous fragment was completely played. Scaling of processing is also crucial: personal narrations are to be provided to extensive numbers of active viewers.

The ShapeShifting Media paradigm (2008), which includes a generic technology for authoring and delivery (Ursu et al. 2008a), and a number of associated experimental interactive TV productions that both inspired and validated the technology (Williams et al. 2007; Ursu et al. 2008b), has initiated successful answers to significant conceptual and technological challenges regarding interactive TV narratives. No other such paradigm appears to have been reported so far, neither in the research nor in the commercial arenas. However, ShapeShifting Media is still just a "road opener": indeed, it provides both a technology and a collection of forms of interactive narratives, but these are not more than a valuable framework for further developments.

Questions regarding the economy of interactive TV narrativity production, such as whether participant viewers enjoy interactive TV narratives and whether such productions are cost-effective, cannot soundly be answered until a statistically significant sample of productions has been made, delivered, and evaluated. The recent growth in momentum regarding the development of interactive TV narrativity, the newly developed ShapeShifting Media Technology, and the productions made with it, will probably promote and inspire such further developments. Will interactive TV narratives become successful? The belief expressed here is: yes.

References

BBC-Documentary. (2008). *Documentary on Multiplatform*, commissioning document published by BBC on March 2008, from http://www.bbc.co.uk/commissioning/tv/network/genres/docs detail.shtml# multiplatform

BBC-Drama. (2008). *Drama on Multiplatform*, commissioning document published by BBC on March 2008, from http://www.bbc.co.uk/commissioning/tv/network/genres/drama detail. shtml# multiplatform

Forrester, C. (2000). *Business of digital television*. Oxford: Focal Press.

Jensen, J. F. (2005). Interaction television: New genres, new format, new content. In *Proceedings of the Australasian conference on Interactive environment* (pp. 89–96). Sydney, Australia.

KPMG. (2007). *The impact of digitalization: A generation apart*. KPMG.

Schadler, T. (2006). *Gen X and Gen Y can't live without their PCs*, Forrester, Cambridge, published on September 8, from http://www.forrester.com/Research/Document/Excerpt/0,7211,40283,00.html

ShapeShifting-Media. (2008). *ShapeShifting media portal*, from http://www.shapeshift.tv

Jarnhed, R. (Director). (2007). *The truth about Marika (Sanningen om Marika)* [Television series episode]. Sweden: The Swedish Public Broadcasting Company (SVT) and The Company P.

Ursu, M. F., Kegel, I., Williams, D., Thomas, M., Mayer, H., Zsombori, V., Tuomola, M. L., Larsson, H., & Wyver, J. (2008a). ShapeShifting TV: Interactive screen media narratives. *ACM/Springer Multimedia Systems, 14*(2), 115–132.

Ursu, M. F., Thomas, M., Kegel, I., Williams, D., Tuomola, M., Lindstedt, I., Wright, T., Leurdijk, A., Zsombori, V., Sussner, J., Maystream, U., & Hall, N. (2008b). Interactive TV narratives: Opportunities, progress and challenges, *ACM Transactions on Multimedia Computing, Communications and Applications, 4*(4), Article 25.

Williams, D., Kegel, I., Ursu, M. F., Pals, N., & Leurdijk, A. (2007). Experiments with the production of ShapeShifting media: Summary findings from the project NM2 (New Millennium, New Media). *ICVS-Virtual Storytelling 2007, LNCS, 4871*, 153–166.

Part II
User Experience and Design of Mobile TV in Everyday Life

Culture, Interface Design, and Design Methods for Mobile Devices

Kun-pyo Lee

Abstract Aesthetic differences and similarities among cultures are obviously one of the very important issues in cultural design. However, ever since products became knowledge-supporting tools, the visible elements of products have become more universal so that the invisible parts of products such as interface and interaction are getting more important. Therefore, the cultural design should be extended to the invisible elements of culture like people's conceptual models beyond material and phenomenal culture. This chapter aims to explain how we address the invisible cultural elements in interface design and design methods by exploring the users' cognitive styles and communication patterns in different cultures. Regarding cultural interface design, we examined users' conceptual models while interacting with mobile phone and website interfaces, and observed cultural difference in performing tasks and viewing patterns, which appeared to agree with cultural cognitive styles known as Holistic thoughts vs. Analytic thoughts. Regarding design methods for culture, we explored how to localize design methods such as focus group interview and generative session for specific cultural groups, and the results of comparative experiments revealed cultural difference on participants' behaviors and performance in each design method and led us to suggest how to conduct them in East Asian culture. Mobile Observation Analyzer and Wi-Pro, user research tools we invented to capture user behaviors and needs especially in their mobile context, were also introduced.

Cultural Design Beyond Aesthetic Stereotypes

The late Professor Jay Doblin (1920–1988) stated "Product is frozen information." The phrase tells us that what is more important is not product itself – while it generally is the primary goal of designers – but the information reflected into product. The information in regards to cultural value of society, life, and user manifests into product.

K.-P. Lee
Human-Centered Interaction Design Lab, Department of Industrial Design, Korea Advanced Institute of Science and Technology

A. Marcus et al. (eds.), *Mobile TV: Customizing Content and Experience*,
Human-Computer Interaction Series, DOI 10.1007/978-1-84882-701-1_8,
© Springer-Verlag London Limited 2010

However, designers often merely focus on product itself; form, color, material, or any other physical attribute. Naturally when we – designers – talk about cultural design, we refer to the aesthetic stereotype such as nationwide preferred shape or color. "Rigor" for German, "flair" for Italian, "compact and cute" for Japanese, and "tail fins" for American are good examples for such ideal preferences. Whereas aesthetic differences and similarities among cultures are obviously one of the very important issues in cultural design, the issue of culture in design should be extended to the invisible "frozen information" beyond material and phenomenal culture. As an example, I would like to share a story of my own which goes back to the time I lived in Chicago, USA I bought one piece of frozen pizza and the recipe on the top of its container said "To enjoy the best taste, preheat the oven and put the pizza on the second rack." I took for granted that "the second" meant "from the top" but very interestingly, or rather surprisingly, most of my American colleagues counted it "from the bottom"! This startling difference of conceptual model puts significant influences on the way that users interact with products. Particularly nowadays, the cultural affordance plays critical role as interaction and interface design have become one of the most important factors in digital information appliances, mobile devices, and web sites than ever before. However, the invisibility of user's conceptual model is not easy to deal with since designers are mainly concerned with visible problems.

When addressing the problem of invisibility in culture, two issues are raised about design: the users' cognitive styles in different cultures and design methods for culture. Firstly, the users' cognitive styles are strongly associated with ways of approaching a task. For the same task, user with a different cognitive style may have a different perception on how to interact with the product. Many researchers, including Nisbett, have proved through various experiments that Asians and Westerners have different cognitive styles; Asians tend to think thematically (relationally) whereas Westerners tend to think functionally (individually). Secondly, a very critical topic in culture and design is about design methods for cultural design. Typically, most major design methods for cultural design are limited in the designer's personal intuition or, at best, surveys or interviews. These conventional methods cannot effectively work for identifying cultural characteristics or for applying them to design because of the invisibility of culture. The other issue related with design methods for culture is about "different methods for different culture." For understanding a particular culture, the user is one of the most significant elements. However, design methods developed for a specific culture and in which only the native users have been taken into consideration may not effectively work in a different culture simply because the users are different. This paper introduces and demonstrates several cases of researches regarding these two subjects of cognitive style and design methods for culture carried out in HCIDL (Human Centered Interaction Design Lab), KAIST, Korea.

The Structure of Culture

The myopic definition of culture comes from the wide diversity of definitions of culture. A brief look-up of the word "culture" at Google generates as many as 49,000 results. Images shown are mostly "high arts," "fashion," "pop," or "tradition" implying "a social class" or "classy taste." We frequently hear someone say "He is a pop culture celebrity." However, definitions of culture which are widely used throughout the academic society are related to the "behavioral" and "cognitive" aspects of culture; "Culture consists in patterned ways of thinking, feeling, and reacting, acquired and transmitted mainly by symbols, constituting the distinctive achievements of human groups, including their embodiments in artifacts." This definition leads to the model of culture having the different depths or levels, which many culture-related researchers agreed on. Table 1 shows different models of cultural structure by various researchers (Lee, 2001).

Table 1 can be summarized by the diagram of Fig. 1 having three levels of "Artifact," "Value," and "Basic Assumptions." As shown in Fig. 1, three levels differ from each other in the degree of observability, concreteness, and consciousness. Top layer of culture, "Artifact" consists of the observable, objective, concrete, and tangible elements of culture such as language, food, housing, monuments, clothing, tools, arts and all artifacts human-created. People can consciously and explicitly describe this phenomenal layer of culture. This layer of cultural element – Artifact – is the manifested symbol of deeper layers of cultural element which reminds us of the phrase, "Product is frozen information." Middle layer of cultural element "Value" includes something that people know but cannot exclusively talk about or elaborate. People know clearly what they prefer or not but cannot articulate the reason. Finally, as we come down to the bottom line, the deepest layer of cultural

Table 1 Comparison of models of cultural structures

Authors/layers	Top	Middle	Bottom
F. Bosa	Nature	Human relationship	Neither of both
L. White	Technical	Sociological	Ideological
J. P. Spradley	Artifact	Behavior	Knowledge
E. T. Hall	Technical	Informal	Formal
F. Trompenaars	Explicit artifacts	Norm & value	Basic assumptions
N. Hoft	Surface	Unspoken rules	Unconscious rules
Vask & Grantham	Symbols	Rituals	Myths
F. Kluckhohn	Covert		Overt
Stewart & Bennet	Subjective		Objective

Fig. 1 Cycling and mutually complementary relationship between different levels of cultural elements

element "Basic Assumptions" consists of things in people's minds that are out of conscious awareness, taken for granted, and difficult to know or elaborate.

These three levels of cultural elements are mutually reinforcing through the intertwined cycle. The top level of artifacts is linked to the bottom level of basic assumptions through the middle layer of value and norm. Artifacts are embedded in norm and value which are in turn embedded in basic assumptions. The artifacts impart meaning to behavior through the rules prescribed by norm and value, but the meaning of behavior only makes sense in the context of basic assumptions that surround such behavior. This cyclic model also reveals the process of how the product is evolved. At first, a new product is introduced to the real world as a functional artifact (e.g., car for transporting), and later people get to form their individual values of its image (e.g., "sexy" car). Next, if the value lasts long enough to be shared by a society, it would be gradually absorbed deep into a subconscious level (e.g., car as society's icon). Once the cycle reaches the bottom level, we really need creative people to cross the chasm and start the reverse cycle, i.e., from basic assumption (frozen information) to artifact (product) level. Why **"creative"** people? Because the core of creativity is nothing but breaking fixed mental blocks (basic assumptions) everybody takes for granted. So far, the first half of the cycle has been dealt with by social scientists, typically in the field of marketing. They go out to the market (artifact or street), carry out marketing research on people, and, consequently, results made of very abstract keywords come out, like, "Trend of back to the basic." In other words, "information" melts out of a "product." Then the result of market research (the melted information) is handed over to designers who hardly share the real meaning and background of the information from the former half of the cycle. Naturally, designers handed over with tons of marketing data begin to "freeze the information into product" without understanding the true message of that marketing data. In the future, designers will be increasingly required to be capable of connecting these two half-cycles by crossing over the chasm between them.

Cultural Cognitive Styles and User Interface Design

Cultural Cognitive Styles

Anthropological and psychological studies continue to suggest that cognitive style is culturally different. Particularly, Nisbett reports plausible evidence of such cultural difference, empirically supporting what has been extensively asserted in other disciplines by explaining where this cognitive difference comes from. Nisbett and his colleagues have found cognitive differences between East Asians and Westerners in regard to perception, attention, categorization, and inference.

Masuda and Nisbett (2001) found perceptual differences between East Asians and Westerners through an experiment where they presented animated vignettes of underwater scenes to Japanese and American participants, and asked the participants

to report what they had seen from memory. The result indicated Japanese participants to be more likely to report field information such as the color of the water,
plant formation, and inert animals than Americans. This study revealed that East
Asians are more focused on the context and the relationships among objects,
whereas Westerners are more focused on central objects and tend to detach objects
from the context.

Concerning ways of organizing the world, East Asians tend to group objects on
the basis of similarities and on the relationship among the objects, whereas
Westerners tend to group the objects on the basis of categories and rules. Chiu
(1972) showed three images of objects (a cow, a chicken, and grass) to American
and Chinese children and asked them to make two groups. Chiu found that
American children grouped a chicken and a cow together because they are both
animals while Chinese grouped a cow and grass together because a cow eats grass
(Fig. 2). In the experiment judging similarity that Norenzayan and his colleagues
(2002) conducted, Korean students tended to associate a target image with Group
A which shares family resemblance, whereas American students appeared to
choose Group B based on the consistent property of a straight stem (Fig. 3).

A central idea to this research is summarized as "Holistic versus Analytic
thought." In their paper "Culture and Cognition" Nisbett and Norenzayan (2002)
proposed that cognitive processes differ according to Holistic and Analytic perspectives.
They stated that cultural differences in cognitive processes are tied to cultural

Fig. 2 Example of stimuli for categorization experiment (Nisbett 2003)

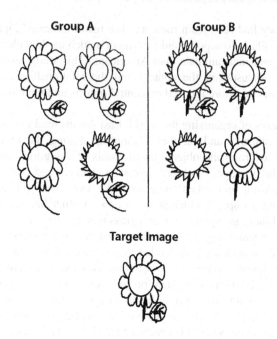

Fig. 3 Example of stimuli for similarity judgment experiment (Nisbett 2003)

differences in basic assumptions about the nature of the world (i.e., Holistic vs. Analytic). Holistic and Analytic reasoning was summarized as follows.

Holistic thought involves: (1) orientation to the context or field as a whole, including attention to the relationships between a focal object and the field; (2) a preference for explaining/predicting events on the basis of such relationships; (3) an approach that relies on an experience-based knowledge rather than abstract logic and the dialectical; 4) an emphasis on change, recognition of contradiction, and the need for multiple perspectives.

Analytic thought includes: (1) a detachment of the object from its context; (2) a tendency to focus on the attributes of the object in order to assign it to categories; (3) a preference for using rules about the categories to explain and predict the object's behavior; (4) inferences that rest in part on the de-contextualization of structure from content, use of formal logic, and avoidance of contradiction.

Cultural Cognitive Styles and Mobile Phone UI

Based on the theoretical background of culturally influenced cognitive differences mentioned in the previous section, which seem more closely related to the matter of communication known as "Human-Computer Interaction," Kim (2007) in her study aimed to illustrate how culturally different cognitive styles influence the information structure in the mobile phone interface by examining user performance and attitude toward the interface. She hypothesized that the user's performances and favorable attitudes would be enhanced when a menu structure works or looks like their cognitive style. More precisely the assumption was that Holistic thinkers would take and prefer a thematic menu approach, whereas Analytic thinkers would take and prefer a functional menu approach. For instance, to perform a task of setting a ring tone, the user may go through the "setting" menu in the main screen and find an option for ring tone. Alternatively, the user may find the same option under the "sound" menu in the main screen. Having the option under the "setting" menu is a menu structure, which is "functionally" grouped by the common function "setting". Having the same option under the "sound" menu is a menu structure, which is "thematically" grouped by the shared context (or theme) "sound." Considering that Holistic and Analytic thinkers categorize things differently, it was predicted that they would show different behaviors and attitudes toward certain menu structures due to their cognitive difference.

To verify this hypothesis, a prototype test and a cognitive style test were conducted with 30 Korean users from KAIST and 30 Dutch participants from TU Eindhoven. It was considered that their cognitive styles may not be reconciled with their culturally different cognitive styles, as was assumed. In other words, individual cognitive styles may be more salient compared to collective cognitive styles due to the small sample size. For this reason, each participant was asked to perform the cognitive style test so that the correlation between individual cognitive styles and individual performances could be revealed.

In the mobile phone prototype (an interactive prototype running in a desktop environment), the main screen of the mobile phone consisted of six menus (Call history, Messaging, Phonebook, Sound, Display, and Settings). The phone's setup was possible to change through thematic menus such as "Sound" and "Display" as well as through the "Setting" menu. For example, to set or change the wallpaper on the mobile phone, participants could start from the "Display" menu to select a certain picture from "My pictures" and then click "Set as wallpaper" from among the options in a context menu that popped up from the right side at the bottom. Participants were also able to change the wallpaper by accessing the "Setting" menu, entering "Wallpaper" in "Display," and finally selecting one picture from among a list of pictures (Fig. 4).

Participants were asked to change the ring tone (Task 1) and the wallpaper (Task 2) to a specific one for each task. After completing the two tasks, they were asked to perform the same tasks again using the other way. For example, if a participant changed the ring tone using the "Sound" menu during the first trial, the same participant would need to do the same task using the "Setting" menu within the second trial. This was to allow the subjects to experience and compare two different ways (thematic approach vs. functional approach) so that they were enabled to choose a preferred approach at the end of the test.

The cognitive style test was intended to discover whether an individual's categorization style is taxonomic or relational. One target picture and two alternative pictures were presented together and participants were asked to select the one alternative that best matches the given target picture as quickly as possible (Fig. 5).

Fig. 4 Two approaches for setting the wallpaper (Top: from 'Display', Bottom: from 'Settings')

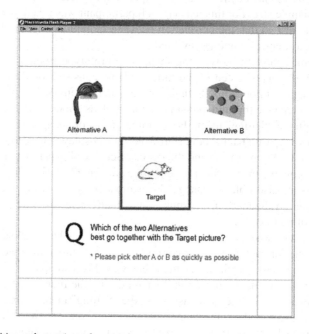

Fig. 5 Cognitive style test (sample screen)

The two alternatives were one that belonged to the same taxonomy as the target picture and one that shared a relationship with the target picture. For example, a picture of a mouse (or a rat) was presented as a target picture, and a squirrel and a piece of cheese were presented as alternatives. A mouse and a squirrel are both animals and so were considered to be in the same taxonomic category. A mouse eats cheese, thus the mouse and cheese were considered to share a relationship. The pictures remained on the screen until participants made their choices. Twenty six sets were presented in sequence.

Cognitive styles were found to be different according to the selected menus. Their categorization tendency was different between a group selecting the "Setting" menu and a group selecting the "Sound" menu while changing the ring tone. Such tendentious differences were also found for the changing of the wallpaper between a group selecting "Setting" menu and a group selecting "Display" menu. Categorization tendency also appeared to be different according to the preferred menus. In other words, the group that selected/preferred the "Setting" menu had a tendency to be more taxonomic (Analytic) than the group that selected/preferred the "Sound" or "Display" menu in both tasks.

Korean participants preferred a thematically grouped menu and Dutch participants preferred a functionally grouped menu. The categorization tendency of the Korean group was found to be more relational compared to the Dutch group, but the tendentious difference was not statistically significant. The sample size was not large enough to be generalized down to a collective cognitive style; for this reason, individual cognitive styles appear more highlighted than collective cognitive styles. However, a number of cultural psychological studies have showed such collective cognitive styles. Thus, the correlation between individual cognitive style and menu structure found in this research can feasibly be applied to a cultural level under the assumption that East Asians tend to make more relational groupings compared to Westerners.

This study shows the possibility of applying a culturally different cognition model into the interface architecture. Current structure of the interface appears universal across cultural areas. However, the findings in this research may be helpful to design an interface suitable to each cultural area based on the fact that the cognitive styles of East Asians and Westerners differ from one another. Given that mobile devices have a limited number of menus due to their small screen size, it is necessary to organize the limited number of main menus appropriately in order to offer logical and quick access to any command or option. This study suggests that menus can be organized in a different way depending on users' cognitive styles; hence, suggestions regarding structuring items in mobile phone are made available by this study.

The participants having a relational-holistic cognitive style performed the tasks using a thematic approach and preferred this approach in a situation where both approaches were available. Therefore, for East Asian users who are known to be more relational, it may be better to organize menus thematically so that they make more natural and efficient use of their devices. In the thematic structure, options are usually shown in the form of a context menu to offer contextual accessibility, an approach that suits the attributes of a holistic thinker. For example, it is possible to organize main menus with thematically grouped menus such as "Sound" and "Display" and put all tasks related to the theme together.

Participants with a taxonomic-analytic cognitive style performed the tasks using a functional approach and preferred this approach in a situation where both approaches were available. Therefore, for Western users who are known to be more goal-oriented, it may be better to organize menus according to goals or functions so that they feel certain of goal achievement. For example, it is possible to organize main menus with functionally grouped menus such as "Setting" and "Download."

Cultural Cognitive Styles and Web page UI

It is also important to consider the impact of culturally different cognitive styles on web page user interface. Web sites-the most popular medium of global communication-can potentially be visited by people around the world and people from different cultures employ different usage strategies on the web site. Cognitive style plays an important role in accommodating an individual's typical mode of perception, thinking, remembering, and problem solving in order to promote web usability.

Dong and Lee (2008) proposed a new approach to enhance the usability of web page by applying the culturally different cognitive styles in their study. They expected East Asians and Westerners to apply different viewing patterns and perception styles while browsing web page. To prove this assumption they conducted an eye-tracking experiment to observe and compare viewing styles of different cultural groups while viewing web page.

The prototype used in the experiment was designed by imitating a popular web site, Yahoo! The web page prototype was designed with the most basic web page elements and page layout. The clearly and neatly divided areas were designed to easily allocate eye movements data. Stylization of the design was restrained to limit distraction to the participants (Fig. 6). Prototypes with identical contents and layout, as well as identical page elements, were designed. Three different language versions of the prototype were provided in English, Chinese, and Korean.

14 American, 15 Chinese, and 12 Korean participants were invited to take part in the experiment. Participants were exposed to the prototype version in their native language, and they were asked to freely look at the web page without clicking on anything since the task was trying to let people show how they actually view a web page without a specific searching item so that their natural viewing pattern could be revealed. As soon as the prototype was shown on the display, the eye-tracking device was triggered by the experimenter to record the eye movements, and the recording was stopped after 30 s.

Each eye-tracking map from the three different national groups (Fig. 7) was marked in a chart according to two criteria of analysis. Criterion 1 was to analyze the participant's general reading style, whereas criterion 2 was to reveal the exact pattern behind that style. Observed viewing styles and patterns were codified and mapped for each national group in two radar maps (Figs. 8 and 9).

Figure 8 indicates that each group has a moderately different viewing pattern. For example, 7 out of 9 American participants tended to read the prototype page in

Fig. 6 English(left), Chinese(middle) and Korean(right) version of the prototype

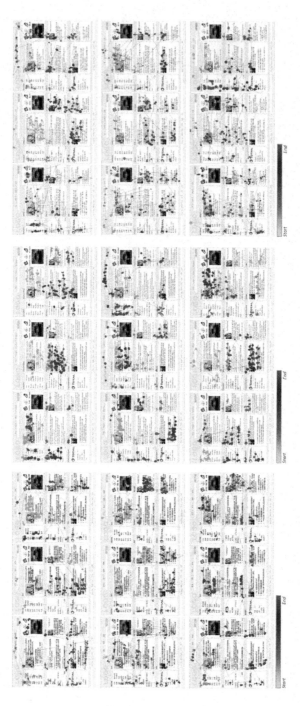

Fig. 7 English (left), Chinese (middle), and Korean (right) eye-tracking samples

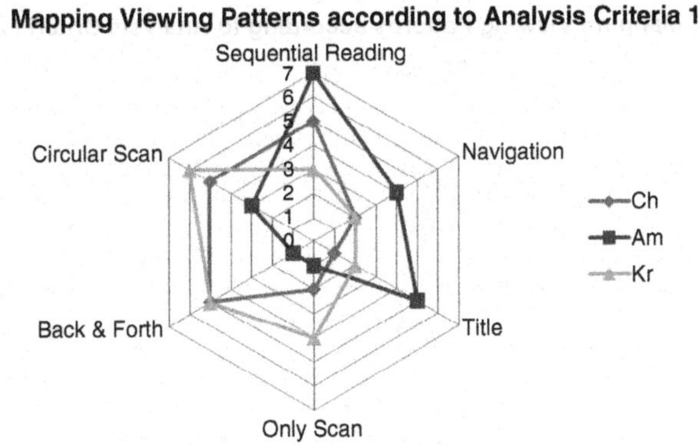

Mapping Viewing Patterns according to Analysis Criteria 1

Fig. 8 Mapping viewing patterns according to analysis criterion 1

sequential order, while only few Chinese and Korean participants showed sequential reading patterns. On the other hand, Chinese and Korean participants were more likely to scan back and forth between page contents, and they were more likely to scan the page in a circular pattern. A web page can be perceived as a package of different informative objects such as information items and/or information boxes, arranged on a field. Holistically minded people have the tendency to see the field as a whole. Hence, they employ a strategy to perceive the web page by scanning across all information objects. Scanning back and forth implies that Chinese and Koreans are not really reading carefully, but just randomly scanning the page. Analytically minded people, on the other hand, tend to detach objects from their background field. Those people tend to focus on each piece of information one by one; a behavior, which leads to a sequential reading pattern. Americans seldom scan without examining the details and rarely scan back and forth between contents. Americans are likely to focus on the page title and also likely to read the navigation, while few Chinese and Koreans do so. Analytically minded people are inclined to think in categories, so knowing what kind of categories the web site has would help them to perceive the web site.

Figure 9 illustrates that most Chinese and Korean participants applied a "0" shaped viewing pattern, while Americans rather applied a "5" shaped eye movement on the page. "0" shape implies that Chinese and Koreans tend to scan the whole page which is similar to the circular scan above. Most Americans show a tendency to read from the center to the periphery of the page. Other viewing patterns in Analysis Criteria 2 do not seem to be significantly employed by a certain group.

The present findings indicate that Holistically minded people and Analytically minded people have unique ways of perceiving a web page. The characteristics of perception reflect some aspects of Nisbett's proposition about cognition. It is suggested that the web page designer should be aware of the cognitive differences existing among Holistically minded people and Analytically minded people. Consequently, web page design must be carried out according to the target audiences'

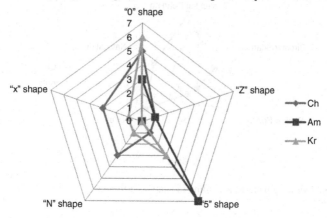

Fig. 9 Mapping viewing patterns according to analysis criterion 2

Table 2 Recommendations for web page design for different cultural group

Cultural groups	Recommendations
Holistic culture	In order to cater to people's way of browsing web pages, which involves obtaining an overall big picture of the web page by scanning the entire page, content design should show the whole context of the web site
	Since people tend to scan the whole page and show nonlinear scan patterns, the contents can be placed more freely on the page compared to when it is designed for Analytic culture
	When designing a web page, the harmony between the foreground and background as well as the relationship among all content areas should be taken into account. This guideline is derived directly from Nisbett's theory, while it is not proved by this study
Analytic culture	The web page design should be as clear and simple as possible. Major categories and highlighted contents on the web page may cater to people's usage. The web page layout should be clear enough to be read by users who focus on each information group
	Since people tend to employ sequential reading among areas and read from the center to the periphery of the page, the arrangement of all contents areas must be considered carefully
	Category title and navigation items should be named as clearly as possible since people tend to pay more attention to these items and gain an overall picture of the web site from them
	When designing web pages, efforts must be directed toward designing each content area. Independent content areas should be emphasized. This is directly from Nisbett's theory, while it has not been proved by this study

specific cognitive style in order to enhance perception and usage of the web page. This study further prepossessed several recommendations for web page design as shown in Table 2.

Design Method for Culture

We understand the importance of having design or user experience reflect cultural values and possible differences. However, understanding users properly in their cultural context should come first. In this part, we will introduce some of our studies on localized design methods for specific cultural groups and user research tools we invented to capture user behaviors and needs especially in their mobile context.

Localization of Design Methods for Different Cultures

Cultural Difference in Communication Pattern

Individualism versus collectivism is an idea that contrasts an individual who only cares for oneself and one's direct family members(I-conscious) to the one who emphasizes the importance of loyalty and unity for the group that cares for one(We-conscious) (Hofstede 1991). This idea is related to the communication pattern of the society's constituents and it can be explained in relation to Hall's (1977) "context" theories (Hofstede 2001). In Hall's culture theory, information during communication or in a message is a part of context. It is more or less defined by the degree to which the message or communication is internalized by an individual. In "high context cultures" most information is included in the context, and thus expressed less externally. In contrast, communication is direct, clear, and expressed externally in "low context cultures." Hofstede (2001) revealed that high-context communication occurs in collectivistic culture and low-context communication occurs in individualistic culture.

Some cross-cultural studies in cognitive psychology and creativity research explain that individualistic and collectivistic cultures have different attitudes toward discussion or argumentation because of their values and education systems. Richard Nisbett (2003) says that "lively discussion" is a part of the culture in individualistic countries, supporting academic activities and formulating social systems. People in individualistic countries learn to argue and persuade from childhood on and believe that problems can be solved through discussion.

Differences in Focus Group Interviews in East Asia and Europe

The degree of how much people care about a "positive face – the desire to be liked and approved by other people" (Ting-Toomey 1998) – can influence the degree of participation in different design methods where interaction between different individuals is required. In focus group interviews, participants are asked to talk about their personal experiences and subjective opinions on certain topics in a group.

When people care about their positive face, they may be afraid that their experiences or opinions might be "incorrect" or sound silly. These concerns could result in passive participation styles. Moreover, respective participants might be reluctant to present negative opinions and will have the tendency to preserve others' face, too. In consequence they might hold back disapprovals of any kind even though problems with products under evaluation were encountered or disagreements with other participants exist.

Chavan (2005) argued that people from collectivistic cultures tend to work around problems rather than to criticize them, while people from individualistic culture are likely to find problems and criticize. She claims that this difference may "corrupt" interview data when not carefully considered. In their comparative experiments on usability tests, Hall et al. (2004) revealed that a think-aloud protocol did not work well with people from collectivistic cultures, because the subjects felt uncomfortable to point out problems.

Lee and Lee (2007) explored cultural difference on participants' behaviors in focus group interviews and suggest how to conduct them in collectivistic culture. They hypothesized that people from collectivistic/high-context cultures will show less activeness of participation and weaker interaction among members than participants from individual/low-context cultures in group interviews, and conducted comparative experiments with participants from two cultures, the Netherlands and Korea, employing "focus group interviews."

Five engineering students in their early twenties (three males and two females in the Netherlands and two males and three females in Korea) were recruited in each country. In two focus group sessions in each country, the facilitator took a minimized role limited to giving topics and distributing turns in order to allow group-centered interaction and to minimize her influences on participants' interaction patterns. To elicit different kinds of speech styles such as storytelling or argumentation, the questions for the interviews included speaking of their own experiences of digital multimedia use, discussion of the products that were previously tested in individual usability tests, and the participants' desires for future products. Each session lasted about 110 min including a 10-min break. Each session was video-recorded for further analysis.

The analysis mainly aimed at comparing the degree of participation and interaction patterns among participants in two countries. To support comparison, Lee visualized the amount of participants' speech, besides describing observed findings. At first, she divided the interview time into 30 s interval units and highlighted those units every time each participant spoke (see Figs. 10 and 11). To see how they argue with each other, three categories were set into "questioning," "approval," and "disapproval" and the corresponding utterances were represented as three different types of arrows. The arrows start from a person reacting and head to a pointed person. Facilitator's utterances were also coded into four categories, such as "providing a topic," "pointing out a person," "asking volunteering," and "detail questioning," to map what kinds of facilitator roles are required according to participants' activeness and interaction patterns.

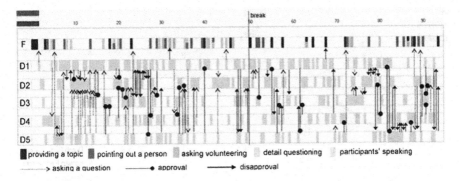

Fig. 10 Timeline analysis of the group interview in the Netherlands

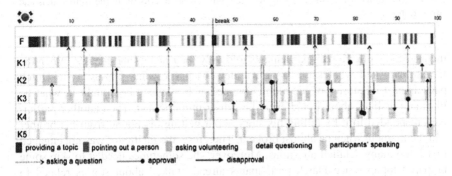

Fig. 11 Timeline analysis of the group interview in Korea

In Figs. 10 and 11, the number of highlighted areas represent the amount of speech and the number of arrows the degree of member-to-member interaction. Lee also expected to observe a change in the degree of participation and interaction over time. To easily compare the amount of speech and interaction as well as the difference of individual participation in a group, she calculated the number of highlighted time units and presented them as circular areas. Thus, the radius of the circle as shown in Fig. 12 is defined by the amount of highlighted units of Figs. 10 or 11, respectively. The number of member-to-member interactions was also presented as the width of lines according to each category.

Firstly, more speech was observed from Dutch participants than Korean participants, even though Dutch participants spoke in their second language. When the facilitator provided topics Dutch participants told "stories" and "anecdotes" related to the topics, while Korean participants tended to make short "answers" except for participant "K2". This tendency could already be observed when participants introduced themselves in the beginning of each session. For example, Dutch participants talked about their current studies or hobbies and, by doing that, broke the ice by

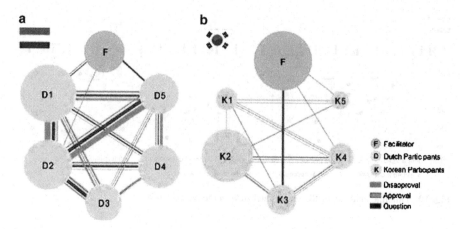

Fig. 12 Diagrams of the amount of speech and interaction patterns (**a**) in the Netherlands and (**b**) in Korea

themselves, while Korean participants told only their names and majors. When the facilitator asked what kind of digital devices participants possess, one Dutch participant told stories of his mobile phone, such as when he bought it, what he likes and dislikes about it and even the subscription he had. Then another participant responded to it by telling his story about getting his phone from his brother and the moment when he almost broke it. Therefore, the facilitator was not engaged to ask too many detailed questions. Moreover, she sometimes needed to skip some prepared topics since Dutch participants already talked about stories related to those topics.

However, in Korea participants answered relatively in short, for example, "I have a mobile phone and an electronic dictionary. I do not use an MP3 player." Then, the facilitator needed to ask "why" to know the reason for not using an MP3 player, and the Korean participant answered, "because I gave it to my mom." In effect, the facilitator was required to provide topics and ask detailed questions in Korea in order to elicit the information needed from participants.

Interactions among participants were observed to be considerably lower in Korea as shown in Figs. 10 and 11. On the other hand, Dutch participants showed lively discussion and member-to-member interaction during the whole session. They actively added opinions, asked questions, and showed approval and disapproval to other participants' utterances. It was observed that the turn-taking speed was faster in the Netherlands and, in fact, Dutch participants often interfered with each other, while this kind of interference seldom happened in Korea. In the Netherlands, simultaneous subgroup discussions sometimes happened naturally due to intensive argumentation. In contrast with Dutch participants, Korean participants seemed to "answer" the facilitator's questions rather than to "discuss" with each other. It was also observed that Korean participants tended to look at the facilitator while speaking while Dutch participants had many eye contacts with other participants. Even though the Koreans' interaction was passive at the beginning, it increased as time went by (Fig. 11). The degree of participation of each member in a group was less equal in Korea (Fig. 12).

The results of the comparative experiment show different behaviors in focus group interviews between two cultures. More active participation and member-to-member interaction was observed in the Netherlands, as hypothesized based on literature studies. Korean participants heavily relied on the facilitator while Dutch participants started active discussions voluntarily. Member-to-member interactions in Korea increased in the latter part of the interview. It is assumed that the participants became more accustomed with the discussion as time went by. If Korean participants need more time to get comfortable with the interview situation and other participants, ice breaking will play an especially important role for them.

The findings revealed that "instigation" and "motivation" for speech from participants and member-to-member interaction are more required in focus group interviews in collectivistic culture. This "instigation" and "motivation" can be facilitated by the moderator's skills, provided scripts and activities, physical environments, and so on. To explore how to facilitate "instigation" and "motivation" in focus group interviews in collectivistic culture, various tools can be applied in a session, such as pre-question cards, Mini-me dolls, bottle spinning game, and TV home shopping setting. Lee applied several of those tools in additional research and found that these tools provided "stimuli" which can boost participants' interests and motivation. Participants from collectivistic culture easily reflected themselves into an imaginary setting, for example, TV home shopping situation. This kind of role play and imaginary setting can play an important role to elicit active discussions, as it enables participants to adopt a rather indirect communication style.

Based on findings gathered from the empirical cases, Lee suggested some promising factors worth further development for deriving collective knowledge from collectivistic culture:.

• Foster sensitivity and motivation by providing playful props and activities.

Utilizing playful stimuli can allow participants from collectivistic culture to feel comfortable with the interview situation and provide them with motivation.

• Facilitate indirectness by providing imaginary roles and settings.

Participants from collective culture tend to adopt indirectness of their communication styles and get empowered in role playing and imaginary situations.

• Ice breaking is especially important for collective culture.

Participants from collectivistic culture seem to need more time to get accustomed to the interview situation and to interact with others. Try to open dialogues before the interview by pre-tasks or informal meetings. Playful props and activities will also help to break the ice in the beginning.

• Place tasks of evaluation and critiques in the latter part of the interview.Participants from collectivistic culture tend to be reserved in the early stage of the interview.

However, they become more active once they gain familiarity with the interview situation and other participants. Place tasks requiring criticism in the latter stage.

- Visualize respect for their participation and information.

To show approval and respect of participants' opinions will give them confidence and motivation.

Cultural Effects on Idea Generative Session

Generative session is a user research method that leads people to express their experiences by making a collage with given images; an approach particularly suitable to communicate latent knowledge which cannot easily be expressed explicitly. In generative sessions, images provided for the collage stimulate people's latent thoughts and needs and help to describe them. Therefore, the application of stimuli images plays a very important role for a successful creative workshop.

You (2009)) explored how to enhance the performance of generative sessions considering the fact that East Asians have the tendency to focus on the relationships of objects to context and to see the field as a whole, opposed to Westerners who tend to focus on the objects and detach an object from its context. Based on the cognitive difference in perception, she could make a hypothesis that cultural cognitive style – holistic (Eastern culture) and analytic (Western culture) – affects the way of using stimuli images and the result of generative sessions.

For the collage experiment, 125 stimuli images with central object and background were selected from magazines. Two sets of stimuli images were prepared – one with central object and background, and the other one with only central object and white background (Fig. 13). In total, 36 people were invited consisting of 19 Koreans and 17 Europeans. Participants were asked to describe their "photo-taking" experience by making a collage with one of the two stimuli image sets (one with central object and background, or the other with only central object), then presented his or her creation to the experimenter. The task was open-ended, and took around 1 h.

After the collage experiment, participants rated "how happy the central figure on each cartoon looks" on a 10-point scale in the facial emotion judgment test (Masuda 2008) which was to verify the participant's cultural cognitive style (Fig. 14). Of the 56 original cartoon sets of Masuda's experiment, 16 images were used: (a) two different central figures (Asian and Caucasian), (b) with two different expressions (moderate and intense happiness), (c) and peripheral figures with one of four different expressions (anger, sadness, happiness, and neutral). Each cartoon was presented in random order on a computer monitor.

The discrepancy of the Korean participants' judgment of matched images (a happy target and happy backgrounds) and that of mismatched images (e.g., a happy target and angry backgrounds) was significantly larger than with European participants. These results indicated that the Koreans were more influenced by the changes in background facial expressions than the Europeans. It also appeared that

Fig. 13 An example of stimuli images with background (Top), and with only central object (Bottom)

the Koreans and the Europeans have significantly different cognitive styles – Koreans were more likely holistic, whereas Europeans were analytic.

The performance of collage was evaluated by the richness of contextual information in a whole description. Content analysis was used to examine the participants' description. Table 3 shows topics extracted from collage and presentation. The frequency of each topic from each participant group was compared and significant difference was found especially in the frequency of describing "what to take – object."

The Korean participants were more affected by background than the Europeans and were induced to talk about contexts. It means that background of images was a means for the Koreans to describe contexts. Therefore, when context is important for research, background of images can be used to stimulate the participants' contextual memories. In addition, background contents should be diverse so as to extract people's various contexts. However, when context is not important for research, background on images should be minimized so as not to distract people's

Fig. 14 Happiness cartoon set (Masuda 2008)

attention for a task. On the other hand, the European participants tended not to be affected by background and they explained mainly what to take and fewer contexts than the Koreans. Thus, when context is important for research, more instruction for describing contexts or stimuli words like "when," "where," or "why" are needed to extract people's contextual memories. Image contents should be more varied than backgrounds.

The results also showed that the background of images stimulated more thoughts and feelings from the Koreans than from the Europeans. Therefore, when thoughts and feelings of Korean participants are important for research, background of images can be used to stimulate participants' thoughts and feelings. In addition, background content should be diverse so as to extract people's various thoughts and feelings. However, when thoughts and feelings of people are not important for research, background on images should be minimized to not distract the participants' attention for the task. On the other hand, European participants tended not to be affected by background. Thus, when thoughts and feelings of people are important for research, more instructions for describing thoughts and feelings or stimuli words like "I think that," "cute," or "conventional" are needed to extract people's thoughts and feelings.

Both the Korean and European sample mentioned "photo style-how to take" a lot. This showed that photo-style of stimuli images themselves stimulated people to talk about photo-style. Thus, to gain a certain sort of information from people, appropriate stimuli to describe the information are needed. In addition, not just image content but also the style can stimulate people's thought.

Table 3 Topics from collages and presentations

Category	Topic	Example
Description of experience	When	"Whenever I went to travel …"
	Where	"On a bus to Vegas, I saw endless mountains and foxes in a desert …"
	Who	"I asked my friends to take a photo …"
	What	"… took a photo of food …"
	Why	"To remind the memories with my friends …"
	How (photo-style)	"Fun photos that look like someone standing on the other person's palm …"
	How(which camera)	"… took a photo with a phone camera"
	How(how many to take)	"… took a hundred photos an hour"
	How(how skilled)	"I used to be a primitive when it comes to taking a photo"
Feelings and thoughts	About a photo	"Taking a photo has always been pleasant …""People say that a photo is the only souvenir after traveling …"
	About a camera	"There seem to be a lot of limits on a toy camera …"
	Needs	"On a beach, I had trouble taking a photo because of sea water …"
	Dreams	"If I had enough time and money, I could take a professional photo with DSLR …"
	About collage work	"I made this collage to describe how I bought a camera, and how I took up photo-taking as a hobby …"
Etc.	Etc.	"This pictures looks like Nepal, but that doesn't mean I've been there …"
	Not related to the experiment	"Lastly, I wanted to say something about myself. So … I attached this picture of eagles or aliens …"

Tools for Understanding the Invisibility of Culture

Another important issue of design methods related with culture and design is how to understand the invisible part of culture. Latent and tacit needs cannot be explicitly articulated because users take it for granted and are not even aware of it. The user observation is one of the most frequently used design methods for overcoming these difficulties. However, users using mobile devices are extremely difficult because users are continually moving and interaction with mobile device is too micro to be observed. Two tools were developed to facilitate the observation of users using mobile devices in HCIDL. MOA (Mobile Observation Analyzer) and Wi-Pro are introduced in the following section.

MOA (Mobile Observation Analyzer)

MOA was developed for understanding the user's behavior in a real-usage situation in order to identify tacit and latent needs. The key factors for success in this stage rely heavily on two issues: how to conduct user research as naturally as possible so that the user reveals his tacit or latent needs in an uninterrupted environment; how to understand users at different levels of activity so that a researcher has a systematic understanding of users without missing any critical aspect of their needs. MOA allows researchers to observe users from three points of views for exhaustive and comprehensive understanding of users: second point of view, first point of view, and third point of view (Fig. 15). First, MOA adopts the technology of a micro-wearable camera to understand the user's self point of view, what the user sees and interacts with at a very micro level. A very small video camera developed as a medical endoscope is embedded into the user's eyeglass frame. Wearing the eyeglasses as usual, without attracting other people's attention, the designer can get the video data of what the users see and can observe and record their interactions with mobile devices automatically and naturally (Fig. 16). Secondly, the shadow-tracking method is also implemented to understand a second point of view; here the researcher observes the user in close proximity, seeing the user's gesture of holding and carrying around the mobile device. The shadow-tracking method is a very typical observation technique. Finally, GPS technology is used for a third point of view, to observe the user's macro behavior, like the users' movement, rhythms, and position as they move about town.

MOA also has computer-aided video-annotating software as shown in Fig. 17 which allows a researcher to simultaneously view video clips of all three points of view. It allows a researcher to have a comprehensive understanding of the user's behavior from micro to macro level; understanding what the user saw, what they clicked on, during what motion sequence, and how they moved around. Its interface consists of four components: "tool bar," "video controller," "event table," and "editor." The tool bar manages all the software by providing access to basic menus like "Open," "Save," "Play," "Stamp," "Set Focus Window," and "Close." The video controller opens the video clips recorded in three different views of self, first, and

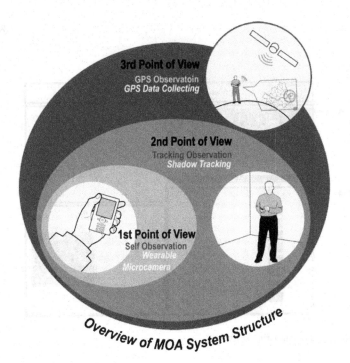

Fig. 15 MOA system structure

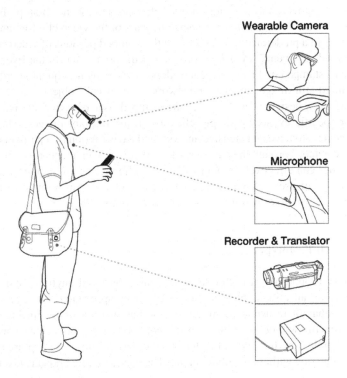

Fig. 16 Observation system with wearable camera

Tool Bar

Video
Controller
1, 2, 3

Event
Table

Editor

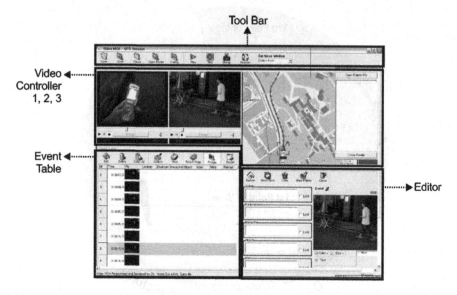

Fig. 17 MOA video annotating software

second, and controls "Play," "Pause," and "Stop" like on a VCR. While playing video clips, designers analyze various users' behaviors and use the "Stamp" function which allows him to stop and to record specific parts of the video clip for annotating user behavior in a predefined framework. All the stamped portions of video clips are to be recorded as "events" in "Event Table" in sequential order. In the Event Table all the events stamped in three video controllers are listed up in sequential order with time, captured still image, analysis frameworks like "user," "object," "action," etc. through which a designer can annotate the stamped user behavior. Designers can search for specific events by simply clicking on the relevant images. The editor allows designers to have an extensive analysis and a description of a particular event he or she selected. Through the analyzer and with all these elements mentioned thus far, a designer can effectively annotate and sort different data to capture insightful understandings of user behavior in a mobile environment. An example of the full user behavior scenario drawn from MOA is shown in Fig. 18.

Wi-Pro (Wish Prototyper)

People carry around and use mobile phones anywhere and anytime, and mobile phones become an inseparable part of the user's paraphernalia, like eye glasses. Obsessive behavior in using the mobile phone has made it unimaginable for the user to have a life without a mobile phone. People take it for granted as a necessity of life. A simple, low-fidelity tool called Wi-Pro was developed to capture a list of wishes of someone without a mobile phone. The user's mobile phone is taken away

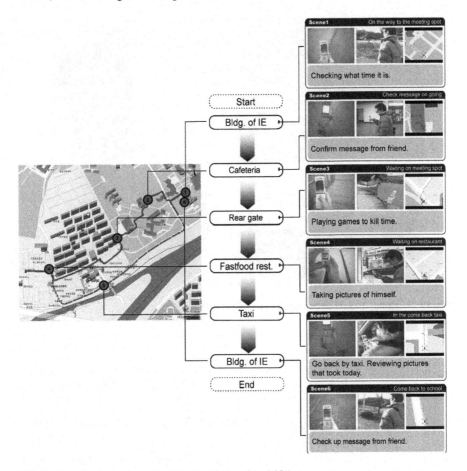

Fig. 18 Total scenario from user behavior observed by MOA

for one or two days and instead a fake one that is similar to a real mobile phone in shape with a folding cover is given, rather like a fake cigarette for people trying to quit smoking. People are so obsessed with smoking that they habitually put the fake cigarette to their lips even if it does not deliver nicotine. Similarly, users habitually take the substitute mobile phone out of their pocket even without any actual functions. A binding of Post-It notes inside the dummy mobile phone allows the user to write down their wishes – what they would want to do at that specific time if the mobile phone was real (Fig. 19).

While the user is playing with the dummy mobile phone, the user's actual mobile phone is analyzed with the user's permission to understand his use of the phone, for example, "how does the user personalize the menu" or "how does he organize addresses and other data."

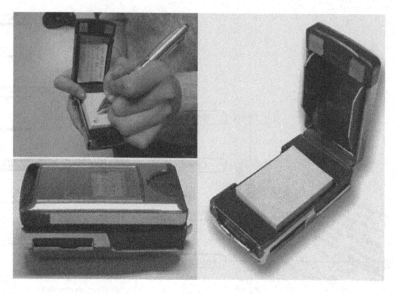

Fig. 19 A dummy mobile phone given to user for Wi-Pro

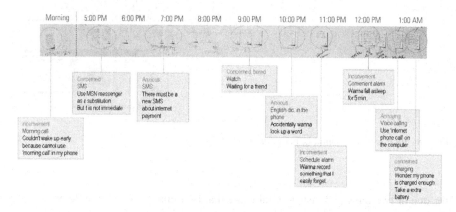

Fig. 20 An example of timeline analysis of user's wish notes from Wi-Pro

After 1 or 2 days of Wi-Pro, the user returns the fake mobile phone he used and on which he recorded his wishes. Upon retrieving the fake mobile phone, all the Post-its are arranged in a time sequence as shown in Fig. 20. All the wishes are analyzed in various ways, like frequencies of specific wishes, patterns over time, wishes in specific places, and so on. The user is invited to have a debriefing session and an in-depth interview about the wishes he expressed. This simple, low-fidelity method is very quick and effective in understanding the user's intense wishes and new ideas.

Conclusion

Due to rapid globalization culture becomes a very critical issue in design. Whereas visible elements like color and shape become more and more universal, invisible elements like people's conceptual models of product usage are still kept local to their culture. Moreover, the invisible part of a product such as user interface design and interaction design are becoming more important ever since product has become a knowledge-supporting tool. This tendency of nonvisualization is expected to be more accelerating as the way of interacting with product is resuming the more natural way of gesture like Wii from Nintendo. The people's natural behavior and gesture is one of the most culturally dependent elements and it will require a new dimension of study in cultural design. The more the invisible part of cultural design becomes important the more the localization of design methods is strongly required. Since invisible design problems can be dealt also only with invisible methods like observation and ethnography, design methods developed for observing people in the specific culture need to be customized in different cultures. This paper attempted to study design methods mainly in relation with Nisbett's theory but the study needs to be further expanded with other cultural dimensions like Hofstede's or Edward T. Hall's.

References

Chavan, A. L. (2005). Another culture, another method. *Proceedings of HCI International Conference.*

Chiu, L. H. (1972). A cross-cultural comparison of cognitive styles in Chinese and American Children. *International Journal of Psychology, 7,* 235–242.

Dong, Y., Lee, K. P. (2008). A cross-cultural comparative study of user participations of a Webpage: With a focus on the cognitive styles of Chinese, Koreans and Americans. *International Journal of Design, 2,* 19–30.

Hall, E. T. (1989). Beyond culture. New York: Anchor Books Editions.

Hall, M., de Jong, M., & Steehouder, M. (2004). Cultural differences and usability evaluation: Individualistic and collectivisitic participants compared. *Technical Communication, 51.*

Hofstede, G. (1991). Culture and organizations: Software of the mind. McGraw-Hill, London

Hofstede, G. (2001). Culture's consequences: Comparing values, behaviours, institutions and organizations across nation (2nd ed.). Beverly Hills: Sage.

Kim, J. H., Lee, K. P. (2007). Culturally adapted Mobile Interface Design: Correlation between categorization style and menu structure. *Proceeding of MobileHCI 2007, Singapore.*

Lee, K. P. (2001). Culture and its effects on human-interaction with design. Unpublished doctoral thesis, University of Tsukuba.

Lee, J. J., & Lee, K. P. (2007). Cultural differences and design methods for User Experience Research: Dutch and Korean participants compared. *Proceeding of DPPI 2007, Helsinki, Finland.*

Masuda, T. (2008). Placing the face in context: Cultural differences in the perception of facial emotion.

Masuda, T., & Nisbett, R. E. (2001). Attending holistically vs. analytically: Comparing the context sensibility of Japanese and American. *Journal of Personality and Social Psychology, 81,* 922–934.

Nisbett, R. (2003). *The geography of thought: How Asians and Westerners think differently and why.* New York: The Free Press.

Nisbett, R., & Norenzayan, A. (2002). "Culture and Cognition." Chapter for D. L. Medin (Ed.). Stevens' *Handbook of Experimental Psychology* (3rd ed.). New York: Wiley.

Rubin, J. (1994). *Handbook of Usability Testing*. New York: Wiley.

Ting-Toomey, S. (1998). Intercultural conflicts styles. A Face-negotiation Theory. In Y. Y. Kim & W. B. Gudykunst (Eds.), *Theories in intercultural communication*. Newbury Park, CA: Sage.

You, I. K. (2009). Cognitive style and its effects on generative session comparing Korean and European participants. Unpublished Master thesis of Industrial Design Department in KAIST.

Mobile Video in Everyday Social Interactions

Erika Reponen, Jaakko Lehikoinen, and Jussi Impiö

Abstract Video recording has become a spontaneous everyday activity for many people, thanks to the video capabilities of modern mobile phones. Internet connectivity of mobile phones enables fluent sharing of captured material even real-time, which makes video an up-and-coming everyday interaction medium. In this article we discuss the effect of the video camera in the social environment, everyday life situations, mainly based on a study where four groups of people used digital video cameras in their normal settings. We also reflect on another study of ours, relating to real-time mobile video communication and discuss future views. The aim of our research is to understand the possibilities in the domain of mobile video. Live and delayed sharing seem to have their special characteristics, live video being used as a virtual window between places whereas delayed video usage has more scope for good-quality content. While this novel way of interacting via mobile video enables new social patterns, it also raises new concerns for privacy and trust between participating persons in all roles, largely due to the widely spreading possibilities of videos. Video in a social situation affects cameramen (who record), targets (who are recorded), passers-by (who are unintentionally in the situation), and the audience (who follow the videos or recording situations) but also the other way around, the participants affect the video by their varying and evolving personal and communicational motivations for recording.

Introduction

Thanks to the video capabilities of modern mobile phones, video recording has become everyday activity for many people. Recording decisions are now often made spontaneously, as the recording devices are constantly available and naturally used in social situations without explicit planning. Internet access from mobile phones enables wide fluent sharing of captured material, even real-time. Acceptance

E. Reponen, J. Lehikoinen, and J. Impiö
Nokia Research Center P.O. Box 1000, 33721 Tampere, Finland

A. Marcus et al. (eds.), *Mobile TV: Customizing Content and Experience*,
Human-Computer Interaction Series, DOI 10.1007/978-1-84882-701-1_9,
© Springer-Verlag London Limited 2010

and habituation by the people are needed for video communication to become a common everyday activity and a constant customary part of social interaction.

In this article we discuss the effect of the video camera in the social environment, everyday life situations, and social interactions, based on earlier studies of ours, which were conducted to understand the needs and possibilities of mobile video. While this novel way of communicating via mobile video enables new social patterns, it also raises new concerns of privacy and trust between participating persons. We define the participating roles as cameramen (who record), targets (who are recorded), passers-by (who are unintentionally in the situation), and the audience (who follow the videos or recording situations). Further, we present the motivations for video recording and acceptability and transparency of it, regarding all defined roles of participants and habituation of the targets during the time. We also notice a two-way dependency between video recording and context. With video in everyday social interactions we not only mean the interaction via the video but also, equally importantly, the interaction in the physical recording place (primary context) and in the situations that follow (secondary context) (see also Reponen et al. 2007a).

We conducted user studies in Italy and Ireland, to better understand how people use their mobile phone video cameras in everyday situations (see also (Reponen et al. 2007b). In the study in Italy with 22 participants, our scope of interest included video-recording situations, as well as sharing and preserving videos. This article draws from the findings of the study. In addition, we also reflect on the findings from another study conducted with 24 participants during a weekend group-trip in Ireland, on mobile phone live video group communication (see also Reponen 2008).

Related Research

It is evident that digital photography has lowered the barrier for sharing; for example, in the area of still photography a user evaluation by Sarvas et al. concluded that as much as 89% of digital photos taken are shared at least once and most of the sharing is done within 3 days post-photography (Sarvas et al. 2005). Kindberg et al. (2005) discuss photographing situations and what is considered worth publishing and to whom. Their results suggest that people mostly take affective images which are then used for both social and individual needs.

Information and communication technologies are used for preserving our cultural knowledge for the future. For example, French philosopher Jean Baudrillard discusses notions of time (Baudrillard 1995) in a way which goes well with our findings. He observes two indications of human willingness to get rid of the limitations of linear time: Firstly, people want to capture everything and share it almost before it happened to have a feeling of living the situation; secondly, people want to record everything to be archived as a record of our culture. There is relatively little research about how people react to being targets of mobile phone video recording, but Huhtamo (2004) states as a media-archaeological notion that the threat of anyone being a target of a snapshot has always been noticed since the existence of photography, and the camera has a dehumanizing effect on the person carrying it. Huhtamo compares the situation to the discussions now taking place regarding-mobile phones and specifically to the emerging use of camera phones. Some earlier studies (see, e.g., Adams 1999; Adams 2000; Lehikoinen & Kaikkonen 2006) have shown that people do not tend to pay much attention to possible privacy threats, unless they have personally encountered invasion of privacy with regard to the information or multimedia content they have shared. A mobile video telephony study by O'Hara et al. (2006) suggests that key drivers for video communication in mobile contexts are sharing special occasions and showing things to talk about. Jacucci et al. notice that in large-scale events spectators experience the event together also in many other ways than watching (Jacucci et al. 2006) and that event information, media sharing, and awareness between group members are all important, media sharing being the most central (Jacucci et al. 2007).

Video Extends the Situation from Primary to Secondary Context

Mobile phone video camera affects the social context and we could say that social interaction will never be back to how it was before video communication possibilities were established. In this article we discuss social situations where video recordings are made and, conversely, what the effect is of the video recording on the social context. Limitations of time and place in interactions are diminishing due to the mobile video, because of its availability in new situations as well as new sharing possibilities.

When brought to situation, video camera at the same time brings the possibility of the context expanding from a primary to a secondary one (Fig. 1). By primary context we mean the immediate physical surroundings where people can experience each other and the event without technological devices. The physical location and common time are identifiers of the primary context. The extended situation which we call secondary context surfaces when material which was recorded in primary context is published and also sensed by someone, use of technology being a boundary between these (see also (Reponen et al. 2007a)). Video plays a role in interaction

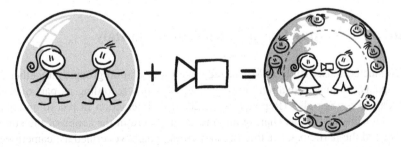

Fig. 1 Video camera extends the context from primary to secondary, from "a momentary bubble" to "the eternal globe"

in primary and secondary contexts as well as between these contexts. When the camera is present, there is always a possibility of capturing and sharing the material, a change for secondary context to arise, and thus more privacy concerns. A user study by Koskinen et al. reports that the photos taken of strangers are quite freely shared by friends (Koskinen et al. 2001). This makes primary context with a camera risky to persons who are in the photos by accident and/or who are not friends of the shooters. People within the primary recording context may be aware or unaware of the existence of the secondary context. Shared video has the special characteristic of broadening the context beyond the boundaries of physical senses; in a case of live video, enabling a phenomenon called telepresence. An early example of the real-time sharing was "Hole in Space" media art experiment, bi-directional video call between Los Angeles and New York by Kit and Sherrie (Galloway and Rabinowitz 1980). Nowadays that kind of experiment can be done even with mobile phones. Moreover, in the mobile domain even within one device, covering the whole chain from capturing to editing to sharing to consumption is already possible. The recorded material is also always easily available for use.

Because of camera phones, the possibility of expansion is now more often present in situations. Ever-better storing and sharing possibilities change the way people think about the recording situations because of the need for control over self-image. Sometimes, to understanding how the others see them, people take photos or videos about themselves just using the camera as a mirror (Reponen et al. 2007b). Even the possibility for secondary context affects the primary one but if the existence of the secondary context is seen as inevitable and the nature of it is known, the effect to primary context is specified. A video-camera-enabled mobile phone is an example of a device which makes the secondary context possible but also less sophisticated devices such as analog cameras and tape recorders have that potential, but they are slower. Secondary context has no boundaries; audience may exist in whichever volume, anytime and any place if there is the possibility for consuming the captured material. When compared to earlier capturing and publishing possibilities, the mobile phone makes the secondary context more probable. Rich communication between two or masses of people over time and space is easier than before. For example, via video sharing services like YouTube (www.youtube.com) and Qik (www.qik.com) the video may spread to large audiences in the secondary context.

Studying Everyday Use of Video Camera in Italy

We conducted a user study in Milan, Italy, with four natural groups, altogether 22 participants, aiming to examine how people use video recording as part of their everyday lives (See also (Reponen et al. 2007b)). Interaction in recording situations, subjects, as well as sharing and preserving were in the scope of the study. We noticed the participants acting in many roles, which we termed as: cameramen (who records), targets (who are recorded), passers-by (who are unintentionally in the situation), and audience (who follow the videos or recording situations).

In this article we refer to the study and present the participants' motivations and acceptance toward recording as a part of social interaction between defined roles in the video-recording context.

Participants were supplied with video camera phones for the time of usage period, and equipped with video-editing software and memory card readers for transferring the content to PCs. Each group was given also a small video camera for shooting DVD- or TV-quality video. Only delayed sharing of videos was supported in this study, real-time video sharing not being possible. Mobile phone subscriptions were provided for the participants. The participants were asked to use the mobile devices and the additional software as naturally as possible. Further, they were asked to send the created material to those people with whom they would communicate in their typical everyday life setting. The participants had a possibility to delete the most private material, if they wished, before they returned the devices.

The study produced two kinds of data about user behavior concerning video recording with a mobile phone. First, the interviews, which were recorded and transcribed, provided qualitative data. Second, all the multimedia material, including videos, still images, and messages that the participants produced was another set of qualitative and quantitative data.

Overall Findings

As results of the study we notice that video camera in the social situation affects peoples' behavior and interaction in diverse ways. In the following sections, we discuss separately the cameramen's, targets,' and audience's habituation and acceptance toward recording. Video-recording situations are usually dynamic by nature. The cameraman's role is always active because he selects the captured moments and views and decides about its use. Role of the target and audience may be passive, but most commonly it is active before they get familiar with being in front of the camera. We pay attention to targets' changing behavior in time and how the relations between participating persons and recording context affect the recording situation. The most passive role is enacted by passers-by, because they may even be unaware of the recording, likewise cameramen may be unaware of them.

Concerning delayed (non-real-time) videos, we found out that motivations for video camera usage can be divided into four areas. The first motivation concerns creating and using multimedia for preserving it for one's own use. Motivation comes clearly from cameramen themselves. We call this behavior (1) *for archiving one's life*. The other areas of recording behavior are related to communicative usage; two of them being connected to publishing for others via a communication device and self-expression, motivation coming both from cameraman and audience (2) *for sharing one's life*, and (3) *to enhance social presence*. The fourth usage behavior aims to affect the immediate social surroundings. Motivated by the cameraman, target, or generally the social context of that time, the video camera is used (4) *as a facilitator in group dynamics*.

Cameraman Archives and Shares

It has become more acceptable to record videos in everyday life situations, because of the mobile phone camera which can be carried all the time and used without explicit planning. Ad-hoc recording is now more convenient for the cameraman, both psychologically and physically and that is why recording is done more often than with traditional video camera.

Some participants of the study wanted to save all the pictures and videos which they took during the test period, whether good or bad in quality, and even create media-albums or diaries of the most important moments of their lives. The diary was seen as a very personal place for personal pictures and videos, and many participants mentioned a need for a protected and secured folder for their personal material. Some people collected memories by taking a picture of an item and saving it. For instance, one participant took a large amount of pictures of logos from advertisements, labels on clothes, etc. Another one photographed graffiti made by a famous graffiti painter. Also CD-covers, art, cars, and paintings were photographed in order to collect these items. This can be seen as a digital version of saving important memories in paper format such as special movie tickets or drawings between the pages of a diary. Motivation for this kind of "Archiving One's Life" activity comes purely from cameramen themselves but although participants did not mention it, these records could of course in the distant future be beneficial archives of the person for others. In these archives the videos can be thought to be very pure because they are for one's own use and there are not, in most cases, clear reasons for acted behavior. Because not much editing is done, hypothesis is that this content which is archived for one's own use, gives as realistic as possible a picture of the cameraman, his relation to others, and the recording context.

Although mobile phone video camera brings up new video recording themes, the old, familiar ones such as: people, pets, special occasions, and holidays still remain. New themes which derive from the always-with characteristics of the mobile phone video camera include: daily life (such as work, school, places, and activities), practical recordings (like notes), objects, celebrities, e.g., from television screen and magazines, or whatever is noteworthy.

Video Affects Target's Behavior

Joyful, slightly embarrassed, annoyed, and unresponsive responses toward being a target for recording were noticed in the study. In general, the attitude of the target persons toward recording and presence of the camera changed in 4 weeks in most cases from excitement to annoyance to ignoring (Fig. 2). We claim that adjusting to the camera makes targets less aware of it and thus feeling more safe and starting to act more natural way. Target's perception of privacy during recording depends on many things which are not unambiguous. The factors which define the target's attitude toward filming situation are: (a) *target's relation to the cameraman*, (b) *target's impression of cameraman's intentions* and (c) *the filming context*.

The presence of camera affects the social dynamics between the people. Additionally, the *"relation to the cameraman"* affects the target's response to the recording. If the target does not feel comfortable with the cameraman, use of the camera may be experienced as hostile, while close relationship between persons makes the situation more relaxed and the presence of the camera may even be ignored. Sometimes the camera strengthens the cameraman's position and puts the target into an interrogation. A good example of the relation between a cameraman and a target influencing behavior is a little girl recording videos of her big brother and grandfather. During 1 month, both targets' response was first very joyful, but before the end of the study, the brother's behavior turned to annoyance and further to ignorance while grandfather's behavior was still quite positive after 4 weeks (Fig. 2).

The target is in charge of his/her behavior in such situations but is not in charge of the camera and thus not in charge of the use of the recorded material. That makes the target's concerns for his/her privacy reasonable and self-evident. The sharing possibility raises some privacy concerns. The trust between familiar people in a primary context makes the recording situation more acceptable. The target usually has an assumption about the *"cameraman's intentions"* when recording starts. Publishing possibilities makes knowing these intentions of interest to the target; also other than sharing concerns affect the target's response based on the assumptions of these intentions. These assumptions characterize the attitude toward the cameraman. As an example of the intentions we mention a late teenager male participant filming his girlfriend in a flirtatious and cuddly style, and getting a similar response. In another case, when the cameraman acts as a reporter, the target immediately

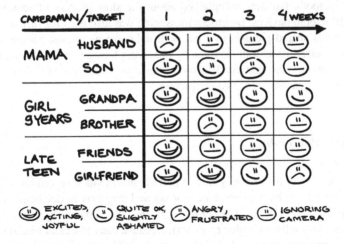

Fig. 2 The 4-week period with three cameramen and six targets visualized in the chart; the faces representing the moods of the targets

takes the role of an interviewee. The risk here is that if the cameraman's intentions are mis-assumed, the response can be unwanted.

The more familiar the *"filming context,"* the more open and natural is the response toward the cameraman; lots of anger, frustration, and affection have been noticed in the home environment. In the public context (such as a public place), the target's response is more acted and joyful. Emotions are caricatured, emphasized, and acted out in movie style when a camera is present. When being excited by the presence of a video camera, users tend to perform TV- or movie-like role plays; but with constant exposure to the video camera's presence this phase usually fades rapidly though.

Video camera has a big role as a *"facilitator in group dynamics"* in primary, but also in secondary contexts. In these cases the target of the recording can be in many cases thought to be the main motivation for starting the recording. We found a bi-directional correlation between the camera and the context. The presence of the camera in the social event shaped the way people behaved; the cameramen often interacted with others in order to make them talk to the camera and make the end result more collective while targets behaved the way they thought was desired. On the reverse side, the context and situation formulated the camera use. The study also showed examples of loosely planned, spontaneous short sketches that were made just for fun. Flirting is one example where the role of the video camera facilitates group dynamics. This kind of behavior was common especially in school environments. Some of the videos shot during the trial, show how one cameraman flirted with the targets by making jokes, flattering, and teasing them. In some cases the recording made the target flirt with the cameraman. A multimedia phone was frequently used as a tool for joking. As an example, a common activity for students was to take a picture of a friend at school, modify the face with image-editing tool, and send it via Bluetooth to friends in the class. This kind of activity made immediate feedback possible, but in some cases even required an immediate response. Generally, the younger participants appreciated the possibility of sharing pictures for free via Bluetooth, but they complained about the slow process of searching for available Bluetooth devices. Bluetooth messaging was also used for flirting. One of the participants shared pictures in a bar with unknown recipients. She recognized those who received Bluetooth message by observing how people used and handled their mobile phones and said that Bluetooth messaging made it easier to start a conversation with those who received her picture.

Surprising Passer-by

Passers-by are a very interesting group of participants in video-recording situations. They may be noticed by the cameraman or not and they may notice being recorded or not; surprise may concern either of those. In any case, a passer-by is not the main target or motivation for the video recording. Because there is a clear thread of unintentionally appearing in recorded content, the possible privacy concerns could be claimed being biggest for the passers-by. In most cases passers-by will never know the existing privacy thread if they do not notice being recorded. In our study, sometimes when participants recorded the social situation they discussed and made jokes with passers-by who were not meant to be recorded on the video but were anyway, at least for the audio. Because earlier study (Koskinen et al. 2001) tells us that trust between familiar people prevents sharing unwanted material about them, it can be assumed that cameramen do not pay much attention if there are some privacy threats for the passers-by who accidentally show in the video. Country-specific privacy protection regulations and laws for private and public spaces are something important to take the consideration though.

Importance of the Audience

For most cases the motivation for video recording comes from the existence of intended audience, for the possibility of the secondary context. Several participants expressed wishes to *"share their lives"* by means of photographs and videos. They sent photographs via MMS and e-mail and also showed them in face-to-face occasions on their phone displays. The shared material presented places, people, or activity that shaped peoples' lives. Some participants said that the photograph or the video clarified the message which the sender wanted to convey. In addition, pictures in a message strengthened expression of moods. Participants also wanted to share the results of their creative activity. For instance, a middle-aged housewife, who took about 40 video clips during the usage period, stated that *"I found my creativity when filming and editing the films"* and she was amazed how dramatically the atmosphere and mood of the film can be edited by only changing the background audio. Image-editing software was used for making simple modifications, such as frames, text boxes, or blurring of photographs, and also to add a personal touch to the pictures in order to make them more fun or more valuable. Pictures and videos in messages are extremely strong in *"enhancing feeling of social presence"* and togetherness when communicating with persons not present. This kind of activity took place mostly between couples and close friends. On many occasions these messages were responded to and sometimes they started a dialog. Because video captures the surroundings, including audio, it conveys social presence. Due to the fact that in that time MMS supported video transmission poorly, the participants who were familiar with PC usage sent videos via e-mail. Benefits of the possibility to share the captured multimedia content included: *"real time," "immediate," "spontaneous," "message is polite," "it's like a gift," "feeling of being connected and reachable."* Having the material created on a mobile phone and thus always available was also considered as a big benefit. Sharing raised concerns such as need to control the spreading of content to the secondary context. Participants felt that the rich information in MMS sometimes revealed more of their situation than they desired. Editing seemed to be done to prevent that. We noticed that the material which was intended to be shared was edited more often than the material aimed for personal use.

Live Video Experiment in Ireland

To bring up real-time mobile video viewpoints for this discussion of mobile video in everyday social interactions, we refer to a mobile phone live video group communication experiment which we conducted with 24 participants in Ireland during a weekend group trip to Dublin, which was an unfamiliar city for the participants (See also (Reponen 2008). We wanted to better understand possibilities of live video in the area of mobile phone communication and study people's behavior in live video streaming situations in the mobile context and group communication, in all roles. Results are collected via field observations, a questionnaire, and group discussions.

Live videos in this experiment were one-directional. Cameramen streamed video live from mobile phone to the defined web pages and the audience followed the videos from the Internet with their mobile phones. To enable easy group communication with text messages, participants were asked to define a phonebook-group into their phonebooks, for fast and easy group SMS sending for whole group. They were also guided to create in advance a text message template for announcing upcoming live videos with link to the sender's live video web site and send that before each live video stream sending action. People self-organized into dynamic subgroups and everyone had the possibility to send and follow videos from a mobile phone or to take part in sending as a member of a group. Videos were shared on the public Internet page but the intended audience was the experiment participants and as an extra, a few persons who wanted to follow the trip videos from home. As a simultaneous task, the participants shared separate videos on YouTube, but that part of the experiment is only very briefly referred to, in the form of comparison comments.

Main Findings

Live video enriched the interaction inside the traveling group and it was generally considered as a nice addition. Videos where some participants were acting as television-like commentators or interviewers were liked the most. This live audio and/or video commentary helped audience understand the context such as location, event, and situation. To announce their upcoming live videos, participants either used a general message just to share the time and live video web link or define more specifically the intended content or location. The fastest way to send an alarm message and video was to use readymade default notification message. Default messages were used in sudden situations, while specific ones were for static or planned situations. Live videos were one-directional but interaction was gained by answering to the live video with SMS. Text feedback which was not the defined task in the experiment but used naturally, was considered very important, giving a feeling of two-way communication.

Twelve **cameramen** would in the future like to share the live videos with familiar people, six with everyone, and three persons would not like to share them at all.

Greetings, events, parties, travel, and unexpected or exiting situations are considered as possible contexts for sharing. Ten of the saved 33 videos were taken outdoors (park, beach, and street). From the indoor videos six were taken in bars, five at airports, three at museums, two hotels and two videos were recorded on buses. Because the experiment was made on a trip, home and work locations were not included. Outdoor videos were often recorded on the move, which gives an intense first-person view and feeling. Indoor videos are more static, moving only the camera. On the move videos last usually longer, showing mostly walking and talking groups, and showing and commenting on the surroundings. Indoor videos typically concentrate on interviews, greetings, and showing people, special events such as music gigs and museums or bar conversations and joking.

In live video experiment seven participants clearly liked and five did not like at all when they noticed being **targets** on live video. Five persons ignored being on video and two persons commented that they hoped not to say anything stupid while they are on live video. Most of the videos had clear posing acts and a fun, comic mood. This resulted from the short use period (See also (Reponen et al. 2007b)) and leisure characteristics of the trip. Even though knowing the possible audience is important, just like in the Milan study, also the action of recording in a group situation has a certain value in shaping the group dynamics. This in some situations lowers the influence of the audience and makes the target the main motivation for the recording.

Some **passers-by** mentioned going away from the scene every time when they notice video recording started nearby, because they do not want to be part of the video. Generally passers-by are not much aware, nor worried about recording. Likewise, the cameramen are not largely interested in passers-by. In the future, if the everyday video recording and sharing becomes more common and the material is available and easily accessible to anyone, the role of the passers-by may be more discussed.

In the future, eight of the participants would like to be on **audience** of videos by familiar people, five of the participants would like to follow videos by people with common interests, five by anyone, three by celebrities, and one by professionals. The most popular (nine votes) context for following live video was the bar, a place for leisure and interaction. Three participants considered vehicles as the best watching environment because of spare time, two wanted to see videos anytime, and two requested a place where they can hear the audio well. Watching the videos together evoked feelings and interactions in the subgroup and was considered fun.

Live and Delayed

There are similarities and differences between use of live and delayed video. Among the Ireland experiment participants, 16 clearly answered preferring following live videos while only five preferred watching videos later and 13 preferred sending live videos versus five liked to share videos delayed. Generally, the participants did not put as much requirements for live video as for delayed video because real-time video is almost not thought to be a video but a virtual window between locations, giving information about what is happening now, while delayed videos are considered most useful if they contain interesting content and/or good technical quality. Based on our experiment we notice that live video is mostly context-oriented while stored, delayed video focuses more on content. Real-time video is useful in immediate social interactions, while delayed video can be used in less instant but still rich and powerful communication. Since the participants of the Italy study commented even videos which are shared delayed by MMS being *"real-time"* and *"immediate,"* it seems to be that, in peoples' minds, being live or real-time is not always counted in seconds but in hours. Continuous live video enables the most natural interaction between primary and secondary context though as far as good enough technical quality is offered.

Based on observations during the studies (Reponen 2008; Reponen et al. 2007b), we make assumption that saving of videos induces different threats than real-time video, and there are different risks in terms of privacy. Risk with saved videos has the possibility for wide and uncontrollable audience in the secondary context while real-time sharing has a risk of an uncontrollable cameraman, target, and passers-by in the primary context. The risk of live video could also be called risk of uncontrollable content, because of no preview chances for the cameraman or the target. Live video has the possibility of becoming also a delayed video if saved; then both live and delayed sharing risks relates to it.

In real-time sharing, it was considered very useful by the audience if someone acted as a commentator or interviewer in the video recording scene. The commentator focuses on camera and context, clarifying the situation, paying attention to the audience, the familiar way as from television. The commentary helped in understanding the context, while only following the natural discussion between people on video was not enough to get the audience to understand the picture. In the Italian study, commentary, that is, talking to camera was used mostly in videos which were intended for facilitating the group dynamics, cameraman often acting as television style interviewer and also in videos which were used for enhancing social presence between people.

Summary

In this article we have presented new possibilities and threads of mobile video (See also Reponen 2008; Reponen et al. 2007a; Reponen et al. 2007b). There are many forms of mobile video in addition to the traditional video call between two mobile phones, which can be utilized in everyday communication. Video affects the social interactions in the primary and secondary contexts, by which we here mean the recording scene and the video following situation, and between these two. Separate roles of cameramen, targets, passers-by, and audience are recognizable. Camera's impact on the behavior of the present persons in primary context is evident, e.g., by the posing acts. In between the primary and secondary contexts, achieving the feeling of togetherness beyond the boundaries of shared physical location or shared time is noticed. In secondary-context interaction, the video affects group dynamics, for example television, giving a common focus, or bringing a virtual participant into the interaction. We suggest that the more people get used to the cameras around, the less attention they pay to them and in time become almost unaware of them. This seems to lead to less artificial behavior and lower concerns regarding publishing and privacy loss. The target's behavior in the primary context where the camera is present depends on the situation and on the relation to the cameraman and changes in the course of time; in most cases it starts with joy and turns to ignoring.

We found out during the Ireland live video experiment that although videos were one-directional, communication was two-directional. To create a desired interaction state, apart from live video, other communication methods, mainly SMS, were also used. Live videos are good for instant communication and context awareness while delayed videos are used more for sharing content. That is the reason why users set less quality requirements for live than non-real-time video content. In the group communication context, participants liked commentary in live videos because it helped understanding context. Television-like behavior was witnessed also in delayed videos. Sharing and following live video is in most cases, based on the Dublin live video study, preferred over a delayed one. Videos would mostly be shared between familiar people for greetings, events, and special situations, but possible use cases were not limited to those.

Mobile video is used for expanding group dynamics, preserving material for one's own use or sharing it with others to enhance social presence or to share one's life with familiar of unfamiliar people, even real-time. Mobile video has an effect on social interactions not only in crossing the boundaries of physical place or time but also in the recording situation in the primary context and following situation in the secondary context.

Discussion

With this article we want to present possibilities and raise thoughts and questions about video in everyday social interactions. When mobile phone video is in scope, we can not only talk about technology or user interface, but we need to take into consideration the heavy impact of video on people and society. Many technological challenges, such as battery consumption, are to be solved though. Preserving captured material for one's own use or enhancing personal interaction with familiar people is possible, but there is also potential to get a large unknown audience, caused by the various and wide-sharing possibilities of mobile video. This gives mobile video the chance to become an almost television-like medium which is traditionally not private or interactive in its nature but more like mass media. Numerous social media services with video-sharing capabilities as well as activities in the area of interactive television predict the fading boundaries between television and the Internet. Video has potential in everyday social interactions as well as more traditional use of it, for example in television, film, and video conferencing. Mobile phone video clearly introduces new levels to interaction and communication.

References

Adams, A. (1999). The implications of users' privacy perception on communication and information privacy policies. *Proceedings Telecommunications Policy Research Conference*. Washington, DC.

Adams, A. (2000). Multimedia information changes the whole privacy ballgame. *Proceedings of the Tenth Conference on Computers, Freedom and Privacy*, pp. 25–32.

Baudrillard, J. (1995). Lopun illuusio. Galilée. Gaudeamus Kirja. Helsinki 25.

Galloway, K., & Rabinowitz, S. (1980). *Hole in Space*, from http://www.ecafe.com/getty/HIS/index.html. Accessed 23 November 2008

Huhtamo, E. (2004). Pockets of plenty: An archaeology of mobile media. *Proceedings ISEA 2004*, pp. 24–27.

Jacucci, G., Oulasvirta, A., & Salovaara, A. (2006). Active construction of experience through mobile media: A field study with implications for recording and sharing. Personal and Ubiquitous Computing journal (online). Springer.

Jacucci, G., Oulasvirta, A., Ilmonen, T., Evans, J., & Salovaara, A. (2007). CoMedia: Mobile group media for active spectatorship. *In CHI 2007, ACM Press*, pp. 1273–1282.

Kindberg, T., Spasojevic, M., Fleck, R., & Sellen, A. (2005). I saw this and thought of you: Some social uses of camera phones. *Proceedings of CHI 2005, ACM Press*, pp. 1545–1548.

Koskinen, I., Kurvinen, E., & Lehtonen, T. -K. (2001). Mobiili kuva, Edita/IT Press, Helsinki, pp. 80–81.

Lehikoinen, J. T., & Kaikkonen, A. (2006). PePe field study: Constructing meanings for locations in the context of mobile presence. *Proceedings of the 8th Conference on Human-computer Interaction with Mobile Devices and Services MobileHCI '06*, pp. 53–60.

O'Hara, K., Black, A., & Lipson, M. (2006). Everyday practices with mobile video telephony. *In CHI 2006, ACM Press*, pp. 871–880.

Reponen, E. (2008). Live@Dublin – Mobile Phone Live Video Group Communication Experiment. In: EuroITV2008, Proceedings. Springer.

Reponen, E., Huuskonen, P., & Mihalic, K. (2007). Primary and secondary context in mobile video communication. Personal and Ubiquitous Computing Journal (online). Springer.

Reponen, E., Lehikoinen, J., Impiö, J. (2007). Mobile phone video camera in social context. In HCI International 2007, Proceedings Vol. 2, LNCS_4551. Springer.

Sarvas, R., Oulasvirta, A., & Jacucci, G. (2005). Building social discourse around mobile photos – A system perspective. *Proceedings Mobile HCI 05, ACM Press*, pp. 31–38.

Does Mobile Television Enhance a New Television Experience?

Bram Lievens, Eva Vanhengel, Jo Pierson, and An Jacobs

Abstract Television has become a common – and often a dominant – practice in the everyday life of people. A transition to a mobile environment seems natural – as industries like to believe. But is this really so? To what extent will mobile television have the same position as well as the same practices as the traditional television set? Our research has identified that the affordances of mobile television are quite different. In this chapter we will first identify those affordances and then we will investigate whether these also lead to a new practice of watching television.

Introduction

Mobile voice communication is nowadays a widespread service in large parts of the world and is still increasing in other parts. It is even surpassing voice communication via fixed lines in an increasing number of countries. However, in order to stay profitable, due to growing competition, these companies are looking for additional, new sources of income, preferably services that take more bandwidth in order to generate sufficient turnover. In this regard the industry has been introducing all kinds of new mobile services and applications. This is supported by the technical opportunities the current generation of mobile phones offers. Today, mobile phones are no longer just devices to make phone calls, but have become complete multifunctional devices for taking photos, recording movies, navigating in a city (via GPS), and offer many other functionalities (Lievens et al. 2007).

In this sense the mobile phone has become a platform that – besides voice communication – is invading many more spheres of our everyday life while being

B. Lievens (✉), E. Vanhengel (✉), J. Pierson (✉) and A. Jacobs (✉)
Vrije Universiteit Brussel (VUB), Studies on Media, Information and Telecommunication (SMIT), Interdisciplinary Institute for BroadBand Technoloy (IBBT), Pleinlaan 2, 1050, Brussel
e-mail: bram.lievens@vub.ac.be
e-mail: eva.vanhengel@vub.ac.be
e-mail: jo.pierson@vub.ac.be
e-mail: an.jacobs@vub.ac.be

A. Marcus et al. (eds.), *Mobile TV: Customizing Content and Experience*,
Human-Computer Interaction Series, DOI 10.1007/978-1-84882-701-1_10,
© Springer-Verlag London Limited 2010

in (semi-) public settings than before. Within the everyday practices of people, watching television seems to be one of the last forms of media consumption that has not extensively been deployed on the mobile phone.

Although people can, of course, already experiment with mobile (broadcast) television via a 3G mobile broadband subscription, this is still a highly expensive solution and is not widely adopted in most of the European countries. However, the European commission recently decided to promote DVB-H (Digital Video Broadcasting for Handhelds) as the main standard for mobile broadcast television. This should further the broadcasting of television signals to all kinds of handheld devices using this standard, without the need for an expensive continuous telephone connection. With policy and industry aligned, it would seem that a widespread take-up of mobile television in Europe is about to happen. The reasoning is: People already watch a lot of television, so why would they not want to watch television in other places than at home. But is this really so? The expectations of governments and telecommunication businesses are quite high, but do television audiences really want to have access to television at any time and any place?

In this chapter we investigate to what extent mobile television finds a place in the everyday life practices of people: How do users integrate the mobile television application in their daily activities? To what extent are the current television practices being transferred to a mobile environment? Do the affordances of mobile devices enhance or counteract the mobile television experience?

Conceptual Framework

The development decisions regarding mobile television technology are inspired by how people watch television in everyday life. Developers and operators assume that as many people enjoy watching television, they will replicate this behavior at other times and other places than at home. In that regard the expectations on mobile television are, certainly in the beginning, quite high. In July 2006 Juniper Research predicted that broadcasting mobile television would draw a revenue of $11.7 billion by 2011. This would be three times more than the streamed services at that time (Juniper Research 2006).

This technological deterministic vision differs from more constructivist perspectives on technology development. The latter argue that technology is an artifact shaped through the interaction with a wide range of social forces (linked with societal, historical, political, and cultural trends) leading to intended and unintended consequences (Au 1998; MacKenzie and Wajcman 2005). As technology is socially co-constructed, it is important to acknowledge the interpretative character of technology as well as the wider context in which the technology is being developed and used (Pinch & Bijker 1987; Klien & Kleinman 2002). Also, Dourish (2006) acknowledges the interdependent character. He argues that technology and the everyday context cannot be separated from each other, as they are mutually constitutive. This means that technology only exists by means of its use.

Therefore, two concepts are important: the affordance of a technology and the practice of that technology.

The first concept, affordance, was introduced by Gibson in the late 1970s to identify the perceivable possibilities for action, meaning what – in the case of Gibson – the environment has to offer to someone. Norman (1988: 9) defines this concept as: "the perceived and actual properties of the thing – primarily those fundamental properties that determine just how that thing could possibly be used." This implies that an affordance is not only shaped by the fundamental properties of an object but that this affordance at the same time identifies that object. This is a rather unidimensional, static, and object-deterministic vision. Vyas et al. 2006 argue that – in line with social constructivism – the affordance of an object is the relationship that is socially and culturally constructed by the users and the artifact in the everyday environment. Dourish (2001: 118) sees this as "a three-way relationship between the environment, the organism and an activity."

McGrenere and Ho (2000) distinguish three fundamental properties of an affordance. First, it only exists by the action capabilities of a person. Second, it is independent to a person's ability to perceive it. Third, an affordance is fixed and does not change when a person's need or goals change.

Based on the concept of affordance one could argue that the interaction and therefore the uses of the object are predefined. But in reality we see that new technologies, services, or applications are often used in a different way than foreseen. This is not only because the affordance of this technology enables alternative and atypical use, but it also stresses that there is an interaction between the user and the technology. This interaction can be defined as a practice. Reckwitz (2002) defines a practice as an emphatic term that describes the whole of the human action, whether or not related to a certain object. But although this definition refers to a dynamic process, a practice is often perceived as a routinized type of behavior (Reckwitz 2002).

In this paper we first identify the affordances of mobile television. Second we investigate to what extent these affordance codetermine the practice of mobile television. Will the new affordances of mobile television also lead to new practices of watching television?

Method

The findings within this chapter are based on the results of the interdisciplinary MADUF research project ("Maximize DVB Usage in Flanders") conducted between September 2007 and April 2008. The objective of this project was to generate an optimal model for providing mobile television services in Flanders (Belgium) via DVB-H and developing a proof of concept to be tested extensively by users. Our role in this project was, on the one hand, to evaluate and validate this mobile service and, on the other hand, to investigate the experience of mobile television. For this we set up a "living lab." A living lab can be described as an experimentation environment in which technology is given shape in real-life contexts and in which (end) users are considered "co-producers" (Pierson & Lievens 2005).

By introducing this DVB-H technology in the natural environment of the user, we were able to investigate different dimensions of mobile television in an everyday setting. In practice this means that a DVB-H setup was implemented specifically for the project. This setup covered the whole area of Ghent, a middle-sized city in the center of Flanders and offered about 12 TV-channels and ten radio-channels (including the most popular regional public and commercial channels).

In total, 70 users participated in the living lab, divided over three consecutive phases. The participants were selected based on purposeful sampling techniques (Sandelowski 1995). Not only maximum variation, where we wanted to cover a broad spectrum of participants, but also phenomenal variation was applied. For the latter, specific selection criteria within the domains of mobility, viewing behavior, and ICT skills were taken into account. All the respondents (working and living in one city – the city of Ghent) received a DVB-H-enabled mobile phone (Samsung P940) or a specific DVB-H receiver (special designed Option Globetrotter) on their portable computer during the full period of a single research phase, which lasted for 2 months. This approach enabled a comparison between different types of user groups, but also to look at the differences in TV-viewing between mobile phones and portable computers.

Each phase contained a multi-methodological approach, following the four main living lab phases as identified by Pierson & Lievens (2005). It starts with a contextualization of the respondents. In the next phases diaries as well as in-depth interviews and focus group interviews were used. Each research phase ended with an exit measurement to compare the different data and to identify possible patterns.

Although it was our objective to conduct three similar research phases in order to compare the data, we had, due to the technological limitations, to adjust each research phase (Fig. 1). In the first research phase we focused on the mobile users: people who have their mobile phone always with them, some people who already have used 3G. In total 20 mobile phone users participated in this phase. All of them received a DVB-H-enabled phone. In the following phase 30 respondents participated: 20 people received a DVB-H mobile phone, ten people received a DVB-H card that makes it possible to receive DVB-H on their portable computer. The focus in this phase was on youngsters as well as on those people we believe had a lot of in-between free-moments. In the third and last phase again another 20 mobile

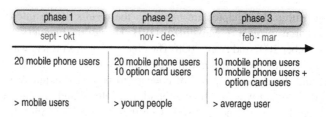

Fig. 1 Overview of different research phases

television users participated in the trial: ten people where equipped with only the DVB-H mobile phone. The other ten people received both the DVB-H mobile phone and the DVB-H card for their portable computer. The selection criteria this time needed to be simplified because it was very difficult to gather people with the preconceived criteria formulated in the second phase.

During the living lab we focused on the specific usage of mobile television as well as on the affordances and practices. In that regard not only the basic who, what, when, and where were investigated, but also the context in which people use their mobile phone or portable computer to watch television. These findings were then compared with existing practices of "traditional" television behavior.

Usage of Mobile Television

There has been already a lot of research conducted on mobile television and on DVB-H in particular (see a.o. Södergård 2003; Mason 2006; Maki 2005; Lehtola & Mokka 2002). To some extent our research is similar to those projects. It is of no surprise that some of our findings are in line with the results of those researches:

1. **Short sessions.** Mobile television users like to use their mobile phone or portable computer within short, spare moments while waiting, eating, driving… Those short sessions often last no longer than 10–15 min. In fewer cases we noticed that mobile television is also used as a prolongation or substitution for their traditional television. These situations are rather rare and occurred only when the main television set in the living room is occupied or in those places where there is no other television in the neighborhood. When it is used as a substitution people watch longer on their mobile television but mostly in a case of necessity. Apart from this mobile television is also used as background while doing something else.

2. **Home usage.** Although mobile television provides the ability to watch television everywhere, it turns out that most of the respondents use their mobile device at home. In addition, but clearly less often, they also watch at work or in the car, tram, bus, or train. The same applies for other public spaces like restaurants, snack bars, the library, and cafés. The essence of a mobile device is that it is portable so it can be used wherever and whenever you want. Nevertheless, we have experienced that people mainly watch mobile television at home. The "mobile" aspect of the device is not seen as such. The mobile aspect is more often used at home: moving over mobile television from the kitchen into the bedroom, into the bathroom or the work place. In addition mobile television is also a nice recreation at work. In more restricted situations, mobile television is also used "on the road," while waiting for the tram or bus, a friend or while traveling by car for example.

3. **Evening TV.** Mostly people watch television on their mobile in the evening. In some specific cases they had a viewing session during midday (mostly to watch

the 13 h news). Opposite to other studies we almost see no activity in the morning. This can be partly explained by the fact that in Flanders we do not have a tradition of morning-TV. In the mornings only some child-related programs (like cartoons) are being offered. Besides we noticed that the programs they watch on a mobile phone or portable computer are often the same as those watched on traditional television (Fig. 2).

4. **Sporadic use.** The frequency of use of mobile television is quite low, especially compared to traditional television. Where the latter is used on a daily basis, people watch mobile television very sporadically. The usage is linked to certain moments and contexts, e.g., during free moments. But even at those moments mobile television is not used that often. An important element here is that people simply forgot they had the possibility to watch.

5. **Individual use.** Mobile television, in contrast to viewing at the *traditional* television, is an individual activity. People do not sit and watch mobile television broadcasts with others. This is mainly due to the fact that the mobile phone is perceived as an individual device, as well as the limited screen size. Only in very specific situations, like when regular television screen is not available and people

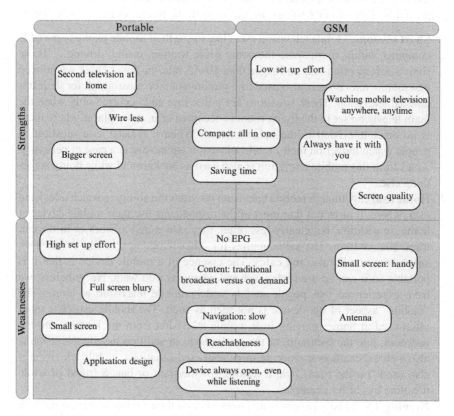

Fig. 2 Strengths and weaknesses of mobile television for a portable computer and mobile phone

desperately want to see a television show, they will sit close to each other to stare at the mobile screen. But this practice is rather unique.

Mobile Television: A Single Practice or Multiple Practices?

As television is a fully domesticated technology, people have, over time, created a very specific practice. A classic way of typifying this practice is the notion of "couch potato," introduced in the 1980s. This was trademarked by cartoonist Armstrong in 1980 (Moss 2006), where the metaphor refers to the passive, inactive audience members in their couches just absorbing television content. When comparing this practice with watching television on the mobile device we do see a significant difference. This is for the following reasons:

1. **Mobile television is not a television experience.** As mentioned above, watching television is a lean-back activity targeted to get an optimal "relaxing" experience. The big screen, a surround system, etc., are all technologies that enhance that experience. Mobile television cannot generate such an experience. Therefore, it is almost impossible for the respondents to watch certain type of programs (like movies, series, etc.). Because of this, mobile television is used in a rather functional way, in the sense that it is used as a time-killer, when people have nothing to do during a short period. This situation determines in a strong way the practice. It is seen as a gadget that is practical during senseless, but often necessary, short moments in everyday life. For this and also related to the affordances of mobile devices watching television is often not perceived as watching television, but doing something on a mobile device (on the same level as checking an sms or your agenda) .

2. **Mobile television as snack-TV.** As mentioned above, the viewing sessions on mobile television are quite short (mainly 5–10 min). This is because mobile television is mainly used as a time-killer. People do not know the broadcasting scheme by heart – except for their favorite programs. Therefore, during the short period of time that they have available, they have to quickly browse through the different channels to see what is on. Often going through these channels is the only thing they can do during that period. Only when something strikes their eye do they stick to that program. Mobile television is in this sense reduced to snack-TV.

3. **Mobile television and the need for easy content.** The fact that people watch mobile television for short periods does not immediately imply the need for alternative TV-formats like the mobisode. We noticed during the project that there is a preference for existing types of short programs (which last maximum 25–30 min) where people could easily tune in. The television news is a good example of such a program, both on a computer and a mobile phone. It is not only quite short, but it also gives the opportunity to easily watch a specific part even though you do not have the opportunity to follow the whole program.

4. **Mobile television as an individual experience.** Television is often a social activity. The whole family is gathered in the living room around the television set. In this setting people interact with each other, e.g., having discussions on the program. This is definitely not the case for mobile television. Despite this social aspect of television, we see that watching mobile television in public spaces is an individual activity. This is not only due to the limitations of screen size, but mainly because of the fact that the mobile device is perceived as a personal device. This individualism is so strong that even regular contextual factors are perceived as disturbing. For example, some of the respondents find that watching television in public spaces is too difficult because it is too noisy for an optimal experience.

5. **Mobile television and multitasking.** In contrast to regular television behavior where watching television is often the only activity, we have noticed that mobile television is to a large extent used in combination with other activities that are performed simultaneously. In those situations the respondents have referred to mobile television as an enhanced radio-player, meaning that it is reduced to a background or wallpaper functionality (Fig. 3).

Traditional Television Habits Die Hard

The elements above illustrate that watching television on a mobile device leads to a specific practice. Although it is different from the traditional television practice, we see that (for the time being) the latter does influence people in their mobile practice. The current television practice can be seen as a kind of reference point. Because of the fact that television is, in a way, domesticated in our everyday life, it has become an important part of this life. This routine is currently also influencing the usage of mobile television. Traditionally, people watched television in the evenings and were not in the habit of watching during the day. This is also reflected in the current broadcasting scheme, e.g., in Flanders there is no morning programming. All broadcasting is focused on prime time and therefore in the evening where we see that it has been used the most frequently.

In the few cases that people did watch television during daytime, they were confronted with advertisements or commercial quiz-games. This is perceived as extremely annoying. They would switch their mobile phone or portable computer off to do something else.

> You are watching and all of a sudden the commercials starts. You never keep on watching those commercials. It takes at least 10 min and if you have to watch for 10 min on your mobile phone I prefer to close it. (Mark, male, 42 years)

Besides also as a result of the broadcasting scheme and the daily practice, these programs are often watched at home. As mentioned above, mobile television is mostly used at home during those moments that they already had foreseen watching television in their daily routine. To illustrate the impact of the fact that, currently,

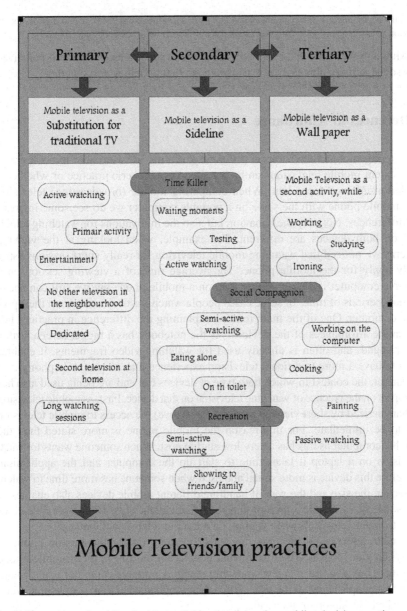

Fig. 3 Three ways of mobile television activities that determine mobile television practices

watching television is domesticated in the daily routine some of the respondents stated that after the first experimental weeks of having mobile television they simple forgot they had the possibility to watch television on their mobile device as they only think of watching television during the evening.

In the beginning it is very pleasant en spectacular to show the mobile television to friends, but soon your interest is gone. You don't have a lot of time to use it. (Ralph, male, 34 years)

Although we know that even with mobile television, television is still perceived as a social activity, this does not always mean that people watch together.

Differences in Affordance

By offering mobile television on different platforms we were able to compare to what extent mobile television can be perceived as a generic practice or whether it is platform/device-dependent. When comparing mobile (broadcasting) television on a mobile phone with the same on a portable computer we do see some interesting differences. Not only the behavior, but also the motivations for watching television on both devices are different. For example, when looking at the viewing patterns we noticed that watching mobile television for really short sessions especially apply for the mobile phone. The average time of a viewing session on a portable computer is clearly higher than on a mobile phone but we still can speak of short periods of time. In some cases people watch for over an hour on their portable computer. One of the main reasons explaining the difference in practices lies within the affordances of the devices. As the notebook has a bigger screen size, a better sound, and often is already used for watching video fragments, it enables users to have a more traditional television experience than on a mobile phone.

Further, the context in which both type of devices can and are being used also has an impact on the practice of watching television on that device. First, as mobile television is characterized by short viewing sessions (see above) the access to mobile television should be immediate. For this reason the mobile phone is more suited than the portable computer as this has a very low startup cost. When someone wants to watch television on a laptop it takes time to start up the computer and the application. Therefore this device is more suited and used when someone has more time to watch. Moreover, the size and the way of handling different mobile devices also enables or limits the use of mobile television in specific situations, e.g., using a portable computer to watch television when waiting on a tram or a bus is not that easy.

Finally, and maybe the most important element is that the mobile phone is always in your pocket. This means that people not only have their mobile phone with them but also that it is always within reach. A portable computer is not something that people carry all the time. Often this is a planned action, people plan when they take their laptop on the road.

The Impact of Affordances on Mobile Television

We have already stated a number of times that the affordances of mobile devices determine the mobile viewing practices and the overall experience. The perception of people regarding mobile television is that it is something that can be used where you want and whenever you want. In addition, it is essential that mobile television also offer adjusted content so that people can watch whatever they want.

The existing affordances means that mobile devices are still being perceived as devices for which they were initially designed: a mobile phone is a device to communicate (making/receiving phone calls or sms); the portable computer is a "professional" device used for work. And although devices have been evaluated over time, this primary function is still dominant in the practice of the device.

The affordance of mobile devices depends on technological abilities. Related to mobile television there are three main technological aspects that have a big impact on the practice and experience of mobile television:

1. Screen size. The screen size of the mobile phone is often seen as too small for long watching sessions, although the quality of the video resolution of DVB-H has been rated quite high by every single respondent.

> I think the screen is too small. I've you become a little bit older you can't see that well anymore. (Nicole) I think the same way; the screen is too small to watch television. For a couple of minutes it is ok, but I'm not going to watch mobile television for four hours (Tony).

The ideal screen size is a trade-off between two opposites. On the one hand, people want their mobile device to be as portable as possible, resulting in small devices. On the other hand, they want to have the best experience, which requires a big screen. As the primary function of the device is still the main criterion, better portability is more preferred.

> Now it fits in my pocket. [...] A bigger screen would make the mobile phone more heavy and I think it would not fit in my pocket anymore. (Walter, man, 28 years)

The people who had the possibility to use a portable computer, their way, argued that the screen was more similar to a traditional television and especially practical at home at places where they do not have a television or for example at work.

2. On-demand. An important element of using DVB-H as a core technology for television is that it only enables broadcasting. The technology does not support or enable any interactivity. This is perceived as a major barrier as this implies that on-demand services are not possible. Because mobile devices are more and more moving toward interactivity (via Internet application) the expectations of a new technology is that it should also embed such functionalities. For mobile television this is crucial as we saw that people only watch very short periods and during that time they would like to see what they want. This is only possible when interactivity and an on-demand feature are enabled. Especially those people who already have experienced interactive digital television – that embeds those possibilities – expect that a new technology like mobile television would offer the same comfort.

> I would like to use it like my regular digital television. I would like to have the opportunity to select those programs I really like to watch. Now I'm dependant on the current broadcast scheme, but if you are used to watch interactive television at home.... For example, I was watching 'Blokken' (a very popular Flemish quiz in prime-time) but that moment I rather preferred watching something else. (Sabine, female, 42 years)

3. Coverage. Besides the screen size and the content that disturbs watching mobile television practices, it is absolutely necessary that there is a global coverage both outdoors as well as indoors. During our project many users experienced a lot of issues with indoor coverage. Because of this people would not be motivated anymore to switch on their mobile for watching television. The outdoor coverage cannot be limited to a certain area and needs to be strong enough to be used while being on the move, e.g., when traveling by train or car.

> I was looking to a program but a switched it off on the moment that it felt out. I can remember that the screen blocked and that I said to my boyfriend 'This is not easy to watch.' (Alice, woman, 26 years)

To enhance coverage, mobile phones were equipped with an antenna that could be pulled out if needed. But although this could increase the quality of the receiving signal, people were not using it. They found that the antenna was something outdated and vulnerable, and too noticeable. Especially because of the latter aspect it was not used in public spaces, as people were afraid of the reactions of others.

Three Main Mobile Television Activities

Above we have argued that (a) the affordances of mobile devices influence strongly the practice of mobile television, (b) that there are some commonalities identified in mobile-viewing practice, (c) that despite these commonalities there is no generic mobile television practice as this is slightly different for specific mobile devices, and (d) that the traditional viewing patterns are still dominant in such a way that they shape mobile-viewing practice. Based on these findings we have identified three ways of mobile television practices, which strongly relate to traditional viewing.

First, mobile television – in some cases – can be a primary activity. This means that people use their mobile television as "substitution" for their traditional television. This is mainly the case in exceptional situations where there is no other television available and that people really want to see a certain program. Therefore people use their mobile devices to intentionally watch a specific television program. During this activity watching television is the main activity, meaning that the main attention is focused on television. The cases of mobile television as a primary activity mainly occurred when the regular television set was not available, e.g., when someone else was watching television in the living room, the mobile television was used as a substitute for this TV-set in order to still watch the programs they really wanted to see at that time. Only then we saw that it was used as a shared screen, meaning that more than one person was watching the same mobile television screen.

> The first Sunday I watched CSI (a popular detective series) on the mobile phone, together with my wife. Close to each other. Because we moved house and we had no television connection yet, we watched together, close to each other. (Patrick, man, 39 years)

This type of activity, which is in line with traditional viewing patterns, is identified as "television in the front" (Lievens et al. 2007) and only takes place in case of "emergency." People will always prefer their traditional television over mobile television because of the bigger screen and the context wherein they can watch their favorite program, thus sitting on a couch in the co-presence of others (as a joint activity). One specific case, for example, refers to the students who do not have a television in their student flat. For them having the possibility to watch television when they really want to, mobile television – preferably on their portable computer – is perceived as a good alternative.

> It is true. You don't need an extra television set as you can always watch. In my student flat it is ideal. (Annabel, female, 23 years)

Second, mobile television can be a secondary activity. This means that people while performing another primary activity (e.g., waiting on a bus, doing the dishes), at the same time, watch mobile television. When watching television is not the prime activity, not only is attention less, but also the usage is determined by the primary activity. This secondary activity often takes place when people want to fill in waiting moments. Because of this, mobile television is then seen as a time-killer, as a practical solution to pass senseless, often short, moments. For example, mobile television is used while waiting for the tram or bus. The prime activity here is waiting for the bus; in practice this means that people will not only watch television, but also constantly look around to see whether the bus has arrived. Once the bus arrives, the activity of watching television is stopped because they have to get on the bus. Mobile television in this sense can be seen as a sideline activity. We even noticed that mobile television was used while watching the regular television screen in the living room.

> I had to pick up my son at school and I was a bit to early. [...] I never watch a specific program. When I watch television it is mainly because I was bored [...]. (Yvan, male, 33 years)

> I used it during waiting moments. I had to go to the doctor and used it while I was waiting. Instead of taking a lot of books with me or reading some magazines in that are always available in the waiting room, I liked to watch television on my mobile phone. (Edward, male, 51 years)

Third, and finally, watching mobile television can also be a tertiary activity. This means people use the television functionality on their portable computer or mobile phone as a wallpaper when performing other activities. The attention for television is even less than in the secondary activity. Where in the latter people still looked at the screen, in this type of activity the mobile television is reduced to a radio functionality. In the project, people used their mobile television as a background while doing other things like working on the computer, cooking or painting. During this activity they had no need to watch the screen, but the television became a companion. For this tertiary activity, music channels, discussion programs, and news programs were very popular as they are easy to tune into and there is no explicit need to watch the screen.

> It is something I always do at home: instead of turning on the radio I switch on the tv an chose a music channel, but I don't watch it the whole time. It's basically as background:

you quickly watch, but you are doing other things the same time. Or, you are doing something in the kitchen or the bathroom. For me it is a substitute for the radio: I never turn on the radio at home. (Els, female, 34 years)

The secondary activity, where it is used to enlighten waiting or unpleasant moments in the primary activity, applies the most in the case of mobile television. This is also related to the existing affordances and practices of the mobile phone in general. People are already using their mobile phone during primary activities to check sms or to make a quick (nonfunctional) phone call. Mobile television is in that sense perceived as just another application (next to games, calendar, photo-camera, or Internet). This means that mobile television is not being equated with watching television. Even in the very rare cases where mobile television acts as a substitution (and then being a primary activity) it is being perceived as doing something on the mobile rather than as 'watching television'. It is this kind of perception that currently guides the actual practice of mobile television.

Conclusions

The results of the Maduf project confirm earlier findings on the usage of mobile television via DVB-H. People watch mobile television not that often. And if they watch they do this mostly at home, in the evenings, and often for a short period.

But our research also clearly indicates that watching broadcasting television on a mobile device has its own practice. This practice is characterized by five main elements. First, people are not able to get the same television experience as in their normal setting. Second, mobile television is considered as snack-TV mainly to pass time. Third, it is necessary, because of this snack-TV idea that the content is not only easy to access, but also easy to tune-in to. Fourth, in contrast with traditional television, mobile television is a personal activity. People watch the mobile television screen alone, without others that are co-viewing.

And finally, fifth, watching mobile television is mostly done in combination with other (for the users, more important) activities. These are the elements that determine the current practice of mobile television.

But this practice is also substantially influenced by the affordances of the current technology (related to the device or platform). First the affordances of current television (certainly for what concerns interactive digital television services) and the dominant surrounding habits still strongly influence the mobile practice. A lot of the existing practices are being transferred to the mobile one. People still watch mainly at home, and the same programs. Further, the expectations of the user are that mobile television, perceived as a new technology, would at least hold the same functionalities. Second, also the type of mobile device determines the practice of how mobile television is being used. DVB-H on a mobile phone is not used in the same way than on a portable computer. The affordances of each device are responsible for different viewing practices. The mobile phone, mainly because of the screen size and the context in which it is used, is more for snack-TV and as a secondary activity. Mobile television on the portable computer – because of the bigger screen, better audio, etc. – is more used as a substitution for the regular television set. For this it is also more suited as primary activity. Third, currently there are still a number of technological limitations on DVB-H that do not enable to benefit of the true affordances of mobile television. The exact trade-off between portability and a large screen to enable a real television experience is not yet in balance. There is the need for interactivity in order for people to watch what they want whenever they want it. There is need for a better coverage, both indoor and outdoor, so that people can watch wherever they wanted and by so mobile television becomes really mobile.

For what concerns mobile television we can distinguish three types of mobile television activities based on the level of attention. The attention is the highest when mobile television is used as primary activity, but using mobile television as a primary activity is seldom the case. Because of the affordances as well as the current practices we see that mobile television is mostly being used as a secondary activity. This means that is used as a complementary activity while performing another primary activity. Mobile television is currently perceived as just another application on people's mobile device and not as a new television experience. This means that mobile television, as a practice, is competing with all of the other mobile applications and services that are available (of which some are already domesticated in a firm way). Next to that, mobile television is – in some cases – used as wallpaper, as a kind of a companion. During this tertiary activity mobile television is often not more then a plain radio set.

Therefore the optimistic assumptions and forecast by the industry and telecom operators on mobile television, via DVB-H in particular, need to be nuanced and placed into perspective. The current practice of mobile television does not reflect the affordances that it intrinsically has. In order to do so, not only a number of technological issues need to be tackled, but also the mindset of people has to change in order to break through the old habits: mobile television is not an application you use on your mobile, but is watching television which accidently happens through your mobile. Only then one can fully benefit from mobile television as a new way of recreation.

Acknowledgments This paper is the result of research performed within the Maximize DVB Usage in Flanders (Maduf) project, a joint research project of the Interdisciplinary Institute for Broad Band Technology (IBBT) and several industrial partners. The research was conducted by Nokia Siemens Networks, Belgacom, Telenet, Option, Proximus, Scientific Atlanta, and VRT in cooperation with the IBBT research groups: Catholic University of Leuven (CUO and ICRI), the University of Ghent (IBCN, WICA, MMLab and MICT), the Free University of Brussels (ETRO and SMIT) and IMEC (DESICS). Within this project IBBT-SMIT was responsible for the qualitative user research.

References

Au, K. (1998). Social constructivism and the school literacy learning of students of diverse backgrounds. *Journal of Literacy Research, 30*(2), 297–319.
Dourish, P. (2001). Where the action is: The foundations of embodied interaction (p. 245). Cambridge: MIT Press

Dourish, P. (2006). Implications for Design. CHI 2006 (April 22–28, 2006). Montréal, Québec, Canada

Juniper Research. (2006). Mobile TV. Watch it grow (2nd ed.). Century House, Priestley Road, Basingstoke, Hampshire RG24 9RA

Klien, H., & Kleinman, D. (2002). Social construction of technology. *Science, Technology & Human Values, 27*(1), 28–52.

Lehtola, S., & Mokka, S. (2002). First steps of mobile digital television: State of the art and first user impressions. Research Report TTE5-2002-18, VTT Information Technology, from http://www.vtt.fi/tte/

Lievens, B., Van den Broeck, W., & Pierson, J. (2007). The mobile (R)evolution in everyday life: A cross border between public and private sphere. In *Conference Proceedings of Mobile Media 2007, Sydney, Australia*, July 2–5.

MacKenzie, D. A., & Wajcman, J. (2005). Introductory essay: The social shaping of technology. In D. A. MacKenzie & J. Wajcman (Eds.), *The social shaping of technology* (2nd ed., pp. 3–27). Maidenhead: Open University Press.

Maki, J. (2005). Finnish mobile TV Pilot: Results, Research International Finland Presentation, from http://www.mobiletv.nokia.com/dowload_counter.php?file=/pilots/finland/files/RI_Press.pdf

Mason, S. (2006). Mobile TV-results from the DVB-H trial in Oxford. EBU technical review, April 2006 1/7.

Moss, J. (2006). Couch potato: Life as a fulltime television watcher. Voice of America, August 20, 2006, from http://www.voanews.com/specialenglish/archive/2006-08/2006-08-20-voa1.cfm

Norman, D. (1988). *The design of everyday things* (p. 95). Basic Books: New York.

Pierson, J., & Lievens, B. (2005). Configuring living labs for a 'thick' understanding of innovation. In *Conference proceedings of EPIC 2005 (Ethnographic Praxis in Industry Conference)*, pp. 114-127. NAPA (National Association for the Practice of Antropology).

Pinch, T., & Bijker, W. (1987). The social construction of facts and artifacts: Or how the sociology of science and the sociology of technology might benefit each other. In W. Bijker, T. Hughes, & T. Pinch (Eds.), *The social construction of technological systems: New directions in the sociology and history of* technology (pp. 17–50). Cambridge: MIT Press.

Reckwitz, A. (2002). Toward a theory of social practices. *European Journal of Social Theory, 5*(2), 243–263. London: Sage.

Sandelowski, M. (1995). Focus on qualitative methods: Sample size in qualitative research revisited. *Research in Nursing and Health, 18*, 179–183.

Södergård, C. (Ed.) (2003). Mobile television – technology and user experiences. Report on the Mobile-TV Project. Espoo 2003, VTT Pulbications 506, VTT Technical Research Centre of Finland, p. 273.

Vyas, D., Chisalita, C. M. & van der Veer, G. (2006). Affordance in interaction. In *Proceedings of the 13th Eurpoean conference on Cognitive ergonomics: Trust and control in complex socio-technical systems, Zurich, Switzerland*, pp. 92–99.

Part III
Innovation Through Conceptual and Participatory Design for Mobile Multimedia Systems

An Ambient Intelligence Framework for the Provision of Geographically Distributed Multimedia Content to Mobility Impaired Users

Dionysios D Kehagias, Dimitris Giakoumis, Dimitrios Tzovaras, Evangelos Bekiaris, and Marion Wiethoff

Abstract This chapter presents an ambient intelligence framework whose goal is to facilitate the information needs of mobility impaired users on the move. This framework couples users with geographically distributed services and the corresponding multimedia content, enabling access to context-sensitive information based on user geographic location and the use case under consideration. It provides a multi-modal facility that is realized through a set of mobile devices and user interfaces that address the needs of ten different types of user impairments. The overall ambient intelligence framework enables users who are equipped with mobile devices to access multimedia content in order to undertake activities relevant to one or more of the following domains: transportation, tourism and leisure, personal support services, work, business, education, social relations and community building. User experience is being explored against those activities through a specific usage scenario.

Introduction

Interestingly, as the amount of content about tourism, leisure, and transport services that is available on the Web increases, its use is limited on behalf of mobility impaired (MI) users due to lack of appropriate tools. The MI user group includes all those users that encounter one or more physical or cognitive disabilities that affect their capability to move from one location to another. The user groups are classified on the basis of functional limitations. For the categorization of various

D.D. Kehagias, D. Giakoumis and D. Tzovaras
Centre for Research and Technology Hellas, Informatics and Telematics Institute, Greece

E. Bekiaris
Centre for Research and Technology Hellas, Hellenic Institute of Transport, Greece

M. Wiethoff
Technical University of Delft, The Netherlands

A. Marcus et al. (eds.), *Mobile TV: Customizing Content and Experience*,
Human-Computer Interaction Series, DOI 10.1007/978-1-84882-701-1_11,
© Springer-Verlag London Limited 2010

impairments the codes provided by the International Classification of Functioning, Disability and Health (ICF) were applied. According to these, ten MI user groups are identified: (1) Cognitive Impaired, (2) Wheelchair Users, (3) Communication Disabled, (4) Hearing Impaired, (5) Upper Limb Impaired, (6) Lower Limb Impaired, (7) Physiological Impaired, (8) Psychological Impaired, (9) Upper Body Impaired, and (10) Vision Impaired.

In a typical scenario of use, where users request information on their mobile devices in order to navigate themselves from one point of interest (POI) to another, users forfeit search facilities that take into account their impairments. The main reason for this is because existing information is not adequately marked up. In order to enable facilities such as the aforementioned ones for MI users, the existing information should be appropriately annotated.

In general, users who plan a new trip or those who are moving are especially interested in getting access to several tourism-related information resources. In most common cases travelers access desired content by performing manual search through a typical Web browser, but this is useful only at a pre-trip stage. When it comes for the users on the move to exploit available information on the Internet, a more sophisticated and automatic way of discovering information is required that will exploit properly annotated data and services that meet the specific needs of MI users.

In this chapter we introduce ASK-IT, an ambient intelligence framework that supports the needs of MI people and enriches their sociability through geographically distributed Web services and available content, rendered on mobile devices. This framework allows users that are equipped with an appropriate mobile device to retrieve relevant content from specific community building services, as well as to navigate themselves inside a specific geographical region and access specific POI. By using the mobile device, the user experiences possibilities far beyond the ones provided in the context of mobile TV.

A large number of Web services today offer on-line access to desired content through suitable software interfaces, thus solving interoperability problems between heterogeneous and distributed Internet-based applications. Today, searching for Web services involves keyword search in Universal Description, Discovery, and Integration (UDDI) registries. This practice is inefficient and unreliable because it does not support service discovery based on service capabilities and specific user needs. We are particularly interested in infrastructures that enable efficient service discovery in order to assist MI travelers.

In order to enable automated discovery and delivery of existing Web services and enlarge access to them by MI users we exploited the use of ontologies in the context of our ambient intelligence framework. Our developed infrastructure supports seamless ontology-based search and retrieval of content that serves MI user needs. By using a set of specific tools, existing service providers may register their content and services within our ontology and make them visible to all registered users.

In the next section, we refer to similar tools and popular approaches that exist today in the context of ambient intelligence assistive technologies. We then describe the ambient intelligence framework that supports the mobility of users with functional limitations. At first we briefly describe the procedure adopted for the user requirements elicitation that results in the specification of user information needs and the corresponding services. After this, a description of the ASK-IT environment is provided in terms of its architecture and functionality. Finally, we present a set of services and a typical demonstration scenario of usage, in which users are involved in social and community building activities by exploiting the provided nomadic context.

Related Work

In general, work that is relevant to ASK-IT could be identified across three dimensions. In the context of the ambient intelligence framework presented in this chapter, an ontology has been developed in order to support search and retrieval, based on the specific attributes of MI users. Thus, the first dimension concerns applications and techniques for the realization of ontology-based search and retrieval, as well as the use of ontologies for annotating the information needs of MI users. The second dimension concerns related work in the area of semantic Web service tools, which provide the means for the semantic annotation of Web services. The third dimension refers to projects with relevant target groups, as well as those that share goals similar to the ones addressed in the ASK-IT project. These projects typically include applications, designed in order to support social activities through nomadic contexts.

Ontology-Based Search and Retrieval

Several ontology-based infrastructures have been developed recently. Most of them involve the use of ontologies to enable search and retrieval capabilities in a particular domain of interest. For instance, Ramachandran et al. (2006) use an inference engine to submit queries to an ontology about atmospheric data in a manner similar to ours. In particular, they use Web services and the Simple Object Access Protocol (SOAP) to enable querying to the inference engine. Our ontological framework has also adopted this approach in terms of the technology it uses to make the ontology accessible by other applications. In Hübner et al. (2004) an ontology and a set of interconnected and semantically unified geographic information resources can be searched using a similar Semantic Web enabled search engine. Although many tools have been developed that enable Semantic Web search capabilities of Web services, our approach introduces for the first time a framework that deals with the information needs of MI users on the move.

The development of the ontology was originally motivated by the fact that MI users needed to be provided with services that address the specificities introduced by the various types of impairments, defined in ICF classification. Up to then, the main research efforts related to the use of ontologies for supporting MI user needs were mainly focused on the user–computer interaction and accessibility issues related to Web navigation.

For instance, Yesilada et al. (2004) introduce a semi-automated tool that supports travel and mobility of visually impaired users. This tool transforms existing Web pages, by the use of a travel ontology, in order to extract information that may be interesting to the user. Thus, it enhances navigation capabilities on behalf of visually impaired users.

Work in by Karim and Tjoa (2006) provides an ontology to enable mapping between various impairments and attributes of user interfaces (UI). This enables improved access to personal information systems by enabling user interfaces adapted to user needs, through a custom application, called SemanticLIFE. The ontology covers many MI user attributes in a manner similar to ours. Although advanced use cases, such as trip planning, can be realized, the main focus remains on the UI customization according to user impairments.

In addition to the aforementioned approaches that focus on the attributes of MI users, noticeable efforts exist about the creation of ontologies for generic use. These are applied on similar application domains as the ones involved in our ontology, such as traveling and accessing tourism and leisure information, but without addressing the distinct attributes of MI users. Typical examples of such ontologies include travel ontology (Choi et al. 2006) and tourism and leisure (Tomai et al. 2005) among others.

Semantic Web Service Tools

In ASK-IT we use ontologies to semantically annotate Web services. Semantic annotation of Web services produces service descriptions that are adequate for service advertisement but they hide the details of service invocation. The implementation of the functionality that an ontology-based service definition provides may require the aggregation of a number of existing and on-line available Web services.

Many tools have been developed that support the automatic synthesis and invocation of Web services. The majority of them provide adequate UI for semi-automatic and automatic Web service composition. Such a tool is the Web Service Composer that allows the user to compose a sequence of Web service workflows and invoke Web services annotated in DARPA[1] Agent Markup Language for Services (DAML-S) (Sirin et al. 2003). Another tool, called WSDL2OWL-S (Paolucci et al. 2003) converts Web services descriptions from the Web Service Description Language (WSDL) to the Web Ontology Language for Services (OWL-S). The barrier that such tools introduce is that they require special technical

---

[1] Defense Advanced Research Projects Agency

expertise that is usually absent on the most service providers side. On the contrary, the ASK-IT framework enables inclusion of existing services to the ontology through an easy-to-use Web-based interface.

A recent proposal submitted as a World Wide Web Consortium (W3C) recommendation (Akkiraju et al. 2005) introduces WSDL-S, an effort to enhance WSDL expressiveness by adding semantics to it. Although promising, this effort lacks wide support by existing tools.

Relevant Projects

Many EU-funded projects have been launched in the area assistive technologies. Such projects are implemented as ambient intelligence frameworks, focusing on specific assistance scenarios and on top of smart environments to support the cooperation of heterogeneous device ensembles. One project in this category is EMBASSI that creates a smart environment within a living room scenario, within automobiles and terminal systems (Herfet et al. 2001). In PERSONA (http://www.aal-persona.org/), the main goal is the development of a scalable open standard ambient assisted living technological platform to support a broad range of services for the elderly. As within our framework, PERSONA deals with the development of an ambient intelligence, content aggregation system of agents, based on a common ontology about the transport domain.

Other well-established examples are the Easy Living from Microsoft (Brumitt et al. 2000), the Interactive Workspaces project (Johanson et al. 2002) developed at Stanford University, the Intelligent Classroom (Flachsbart et al. 2000) at Northwestern University, or the OXYGEN project (Oxygen Project 2005) at the Massachusetts Institute of Technology. These are typical examples of smart environments that involve the use of mobile devices and delivery of services to the end-users.

The Ambient Intelligence Framework

Target Groups and User Requirements Elicitation

In ASK-IT, special care has been taken so that the overall framework functionality reflects real-user information needs. For this purpose, a user requirements elicitation process was conducted in collaboration with user representatives, experts, and stakeholders. A special methodology has been designed for capturing the user information needs (Sommer et al. 2006). This applies the principles of two well-known psychological theories, *Action* and *Activity* theory.

Action theory provides a general framework for describing human behavior in working environments, which can be applied to any type of goal-directed human behavior (Riva 2005). A hierarchy of actions and operations to achieve a certain goal is structured, which is composed of different levels of organization. The action process as a whole is hence organized by sequential action patterns. Subsequent actions operations are controlled by personal goals and sub-goals. Figure 1 shows an example of such a hierarchical structure of actions of a person who arrives at a hotel by car. Decomposing complex goal-directed actions in this manner enables the identification of specific support needs of users with different types of functional limitations with sufficient detail.

One shortcoming of the Action theory is that it ignores the social context of the environment to which it is applied. On the other hand, Activity theory allows the description of the minimal meaningful context into which an action is defined. The most important elements of the context are the objective of the activity, the subjects involved, the available tools and the division of labor, the set of rules under which the action takes place, and the community in which the subject takes part (Frese and Zapf 1994).

The combination of the two theories results in a context-based representation of the interaction between users and the environment, with a succession of activities and a hierarchy of actions and operations. This representation allows the structured definition of content requirements as needed for the new tourist information services to be specified. For each user group, relevant requirements were specified in the form of a matrix. Table 1 presents an extract of the matrix for the second user group (wheelchair users).

The ASK-IT ontology, as well as the user requirements are derived as the result of this methodology, in order to be up-to-date with respect to the real-user information needs. The ontology provides a formal way for describing the various information needs of MI users. The supported functionality is tailored to meet the special needs of the ten user groups defined according to the ICF classification.

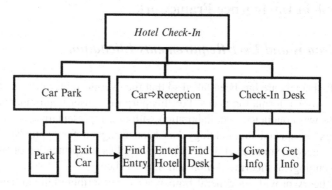

Fig. 1 Example of a hierarchical-sequential action process: A person traveling by car arrives at a hotel

Table 1 An extract of the wheelchair users matrix for tourism and leisure activities

Activity	Action	Attribute	ValueType	ValueLimit
Facilities: Getting in	Accessing entrance	Stairs	Boolean Yes/no	
		Thresholds	Boolean Yes/no	
		Height of thresholds	Mm Integer number	Maximum 20 mm
		Width of doors	Mm Integer number	Minimum 850 mm
		Ramp	Boolean Yes/no	Yes, if stairs

Architecture and Functionality

Adopting an architectural model similar to the client-server model, the ASK-IT ambient intelligence framework is divided in two main subsystems, the Server Side and the Client Side. The Server Side is responsible for the integration of the services that provide data and content, whereas the Client Side includes all modules that are responsible for handling interaction with users and manipulating data and content received upon request from the Server Side. The communication between these two subsystems is utilized through the exchange of messages between software agents. Several types of agents reside in both the Server and the Client Sides of the framework.

Server Side Architecture

The ASK-IT Server Side is comprised of a set of modules that implement the basic infrastructure for supporting alignment of existing services in the Repository, as well as their access, storage, and maintenance in collaboration with the other modules. The Repository is implemented as a software module and storage facility integrated into the Server Side.

Figure 2 depicts the interoperations occurring between the basic modules of the Server Side, as well as any external actors or any other layer components. The Data Management Module (DMM) aims at developing an automatic mechanism for aggregating information originated from multiple service content providers, as shown in Fig. 2. The end-user requests, through a UI docked on the Client Side subsystem, (desktop application, mobile phone, PDA), a specific service through a personal user-agent, which in turn requests the service from a broker agent after being translated into a machine-readable format. The actual role of the DMM is to listen to the request, decompose it, perform ontology-based search for the appropriate services and finally return the requested information back to the user.

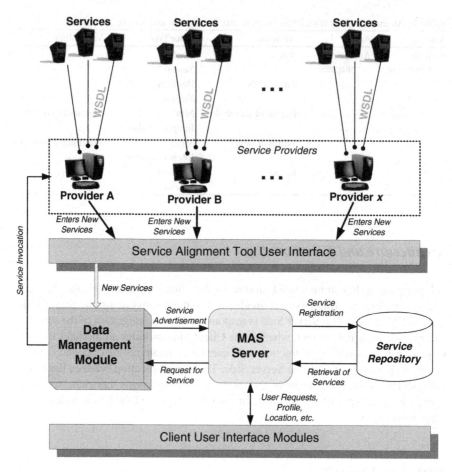

Fig. 2 Data management module and interacting modules

The main parts of the Server Side architecture involve:

1. *Web Services and Service Providers.* All content required to be rendered on the end-user device (client–user interface modules) is produced by a set of registered Web services. These are connected to a set of corresponding providers who are responsible for the creation, maintenance (e.g., update), and public availability of Web services. Access to services is realized through a set of Web service interfaces. In practice, these interfaces implement the SOAP protocol and are based on the WSDL that describes services on the provider's side.
2. *The Service Alignment Tool User Interface,* which provides a Web-based front-end to the DMM and the Service Repository. The primary goal of this tool is to provide a common interface to all interested service providers that intend to align their services within the repository of ASK-IT supported services. In this way, service providers make their services visible in the repository so that any interested party may search for them and request their invocation.

3. *The DMM* that supports the following operations:

- Receives a user request for a particular type of services. User request is passed indirectly to the DMM through the Multi-Agent System (MAS) server that hosts a set of software agents that interoperate between the DMM and the Client Side of ASK-IT. The agents notify the DMM about the details of the user request received by the Client Side.
- Performs a refinement process in order to identify the service provider that best suits the needs of the requesting party.
- DMM is also responsible for indexing all available (registered) services, and supports categorization of real services according to the conceptual elements defined in the ontology.
- When requested by the MAS, the DMM performs invocation of real Web services, establishing direct content to the service providers hosts and returns the requested content to be delivered to users through the Client Server layer. The DMM is equipped with the necessary mechanisms that provide physical access of available services and retrieval of associated content.

4. *The Service Repository* enables services advertisement in order to make them visible by the agents of the MAS, and also accessible through an ontology-based search and retrieval mechanism. It includes ontological descriptions of the available services and provides a physical means for their storage. It operates as a middleware between the Service Repository and the existing Web services. It manages service advertisement to the MAS, as well as storage of service definitions in the Repository.

5. *The MAS server* operates as the main software infrastructure that hosts the software agents of the Service Side. Agents operate as user representatives that act in a goal-oriented manner in order to fulfill a set of user-specific requirements. The MAS is implemented using the Java Agent Development Environment (JADE) and application programming interface (http://jade.tilab.com). It includes an arbitrary number of dynamically created software agents, according to the number of concurrently processed user requests. These agents capture the user requests for services. They also perform an ontology-based search in the Service Repository about the content that is required to be obtained from the available Web services in order to fulfill the exact needs of a specific use case currently in progress, with respect to the profile of the involved user. Finally, the agents are responsible to return the right content to the Client Side that delivers it on the end-user application.

Client Side Architecture

The ASK-IT Client Side architecture, which is depicted in Fig. 3, supports content rendering on Personal Digital Assistant (PDA), as well as other portable devices (e.g., mobile phones). It is an architecture based on the functionality offered by the OSGi[2]

---

[2]OSGi stands for Open Service Gateway initiative, now an obsolete name.

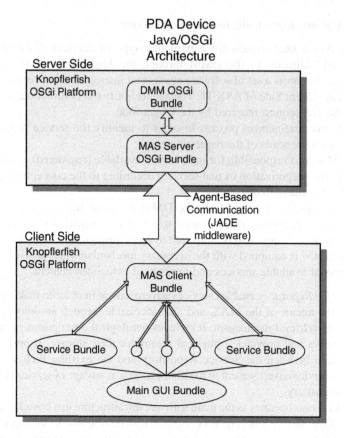

Fig. 3 Client architecture

framework and on the ambient intelligence features offered by software agent technology. Within the ASK-IT project, client applications for personal computers and Symbian-based mobile devices have been developed as well, which however share the same agent-based architecture. The only difference concerning these implementations resides on the technologies used during the development process.

The PDA version of the ASK-IT Client Side subsystem is designed for Windows Mobile 2005+ operating system. The overall functionality in this case is based on the IBM J9 Java Virtual Machine (WEME). The UI of the PDA application is exclusively based on the Java Advanced Windowed Graphics (AWT) application programming interface, due to the restrictions imposed by the Connected Device Configuration (CDC), with which the J9 platform is compatible. The corresponding configurations for Symbian-based mobile devices include the Connected Limited Device Configuration (CLDC), version 1.1 and the Mobile Information Device Profile (MIDP), version 2.0 configurations.

One of the basic features of the OSGi framework is that it builds any software system as a set of OSGi bundles, where each bundle represents a part of the overall system source code. A bundle can be seen as a *black box*, with concrete inputs and outputs. Each bundle exports a description of the functions it offers to a common OSGi bundle context (using Java interfaces). Thus, it allows other bundles to access and exploit the functionality of any other bundle registered in the same bundle context.

The ASK-IT Client Side consists of a large number of OSGi bundles. These can be classified in two main categories: (a) the main client bundles and (b) the core ones. The first category includes the bundles that provide the overall functionality of the ASK-IT client application, whereas the second includes those bundles that provide supportive operations. The most important bundle among the core ones is the *ASK-IT GUI Main Core* bundle. Its role is to export all interfaces that belong to the main bundles to the common OSGi bundle context, a functionality that facilitates bundle-to-bundle communication.

In ASK-IT, the OSGi framework functionality is enabled via one of its implementations, known as *Knopflerfish OSGi R4* (Knopflerfish OSGi 2008), that runs on top of the Java virtual machine. This is an open source implementation of the *OSGi service platform release 4* (OSGi Service Platform 2008). It acts as a container within which the main and core bundles are running. The Client Side is also implemented as an OSGi platform, where the main client bundles reside.

The Client Side architecture takes into consideration the various services that Server Side can provide to the users. Each service supported in ASK-IT provides its functionality via a suitable end-user interface. Services are also represented by *service bundles* (Fig. 3). These can be used either in stand-alone mode, or in conjunction with other service bundles, in order to provide composite services. The service bundles provide the link between the user and the ASK-IT Client Side. They handle actual user interfaces upon request. In particular, the service bundles provide appropriate UI through which users request the invocation of services in a seamless manner.

As illustrated in Fig. 3, the main graphical user interface (GUI) bundle is the one that controls the overall Client Side functionality from the user's perspective. This launches the activation of all other Client Side bundles. Through this, the UI provided by the service bundles are placed and shown to the user.

Geographically Distributed Content and Services

Within the ASK-IT project, a large amount of geographically distributed content is offered to the end-users through a number of integrated services. The user requirements elicitation process determines the services that should be supported in ASK-IT in order to fulfill the information needs of MI target users. These services are implemented as Web services offered by various providers throughout Europe. Several types of services are integrated in ASK-IT, and for each one of them there is typically more than one provider-specific implementation. Different service providers may be located in different countries, thus making it possible to seamlessly provide location-aware information to the end uses.

In addition, ASK-IT deploys a mechanism that supports the retrieval of content from services that best suits the user profile. This operation is performed by the Server Side that selects among services of the same types the one that fulfills the user needs in the best way. The selection is based on various criteria to ensure maximization of the provided quality of service (QoS). For instance, when the user searches for a specific type of POI (e.g., restaurants) the search mechanism gives priority to that POI that had been confirmed in previous search.

In particular, a user-agent constantly monitors user's choices and preferences. For instance, if the user is always interested in specific types of POI when invoking the POI Search service, this information will be stored in the device, through appropriate Client Side bundles. On future calls of the mapping service, whose operation is to display maps on the PDA device, the user-agent will take specific care in order to show to the user favorite POI. Other information, which is taken into account in the user profiles includes the type of user impairment. Moreover, the user application provides service ranking capability on behalf of the users, thus resulting to the provision of more personalized services.

ASK-IT Service Models

The ASK-IT Data Management Module organizes the integrated services in the form of *service models* and corresponding operations offered by each model. The definition of these models is the result of the user requirements elicitation process conducted in the beginning of the project. The following service models are defined within ASK-IT:

- *Geo-coding*. Within this model a number of different services that can provide the coordinates of a specific address (or vice-versa) are integrated.
- *Mapping*. The ASK-IT Mapping service model integrates a number of services that provide mapping-creation capabilities.
- *POI Search*. This model integrates a number of services that provide information about POI throughout Europe. Since the accessibility of POI is an important issue in ASK-IT, the returned POI are accompanied with their accessibility status concerning the supported user groups.
- *Route Calculation*. Within this model various services with route calculation capabilities (multimodal, outdoor, indoor, etc.) are integrated and offered to the end-users.
- *Traffic Events*. This model integrates services that return information about traffic events that are happening inside a specific region.
- *Bus Info* service model integrates a set of services that return information about bus stops, lines, and routes.
- *Social Events*. The model integrates services that offer information about social events occurring in cities throughout Europe.

- *E-Working.* Within this model, a set of services concerning e-Working relevant operations, such as e-mail downloading and documents reading are integrated.
- *E-Learning.* This model integrates Web services about e-Learning. It covers services related to on-line courses.
- *Emergency.* Given the fact that ASK-IT pays special attention to vulnerable user groups, the Emergency service model integrates services that can request for help (e.g., call for an ambulance) in case of emergency.

Sociability and Mobile Community Building Services

One of the aims of the ASK-IT project is to encourage the creation of mobile communities among impaired people. Sociability can be achieved within the ASK-IT nomadic context through proper integration and intelligent utilization of the supported services. The ASK-IT ambient intelligence framework offers services that provide various types of multimedia content. As it was expected, the research that took place within the ASK-IT project for the analysis of the user needs indicated that these services, either by stand-alone use or in collaboration with other, enhance the way that MI people form new mobile communities or join existing ones. This section outlines the sociability-support services offered in ASK-IT.

Sociability-Support Services

Within ASK-IT, user sociability is enhanced through a set of new capabilities provided to the users. Among the various supported services, two of them relate to community building and social activities most than the others. These are the e-Learning and the Social Events service models.

E-Learning

The ASK-IT e-Learning service model defines a set of services that cover the needs of users wishing to attend e-Learning courses. By this model, users can register and follow a large number of courses, despite their location, simply by using a mobile device. Apart from the most obvious learning capabilities, these services offer to the users the possibility to communicate with other students attending the same courses. In this manner, users enhance their sociability, as they become members of a group with people that share the same interests. This communication is by all means encouraged by the ASK-IT framework, as it provides services that support the exchange of various types of messages between co-students or students and tutors of the courses. Rich multimedia content and hyperlinks may be also exchanged between users of the same group.

Social Events

Another very important service model toward user socialization is the one that provides information about social events. Within this model, a set of integrated services are offered from the Server Side to the users, through the end-user application UI, in order to inform them about potential social events taking place nearby and on specific times. These services enhance user socialization, as they encourage people to meet with each other and share their interests.

As in most of the ASK-IT conceptual models, in the social events service model, there are a number of different integrated services offered by different providers from various cities among Europe. In order to take advantage of this feature, the requests for content related to social events trigger the invocation of the most appropriate service. This is mostly offered by the provider who is located closest to the geographic location of interest.

By default the end-user client application notifies in advance the user on a real-time basis about various types of social events currently taking place in the user surrounding area. Furthermore, it offers the capability to search for social events taking place in other locations and on different times as well. Whereas the content offered by the sociability-support services can vary from provider to provider (some events may offer additional information such the e-mail address of the contact person), the social events returned by the ASK-IT framework are always accompanied by information on the accessibility status of the venue, according to the group to which the user belongs. Multimedia content such as venue photos are also displayed on the mobile devices in order to make the social events even more attractive to the sceptic users.

An additional way to enhance user sociability is via the *push-info* functionality. If the user enables the *push-info* option, the framework takes into account user preferences about which types of social events the user thinks are interesting. Thus, when an event of such a type occurs at an accessible venue close to the user current location, a real-time notification is posted to the user. This is a very useful function to provide real-time info to the user, while on the move.

Integration of Social Events and Info-Mobility Services (POI Search and Route Calculation)

User sociability may be also enriched through the integration of the Social Events services and other info-mobility services. Apart from informing the users about social events, the client application also graphically displays on the portable device the route to the venue where the social event is about to take place. As soon as the users are notified about existing social events, they have the option to invoke the route calculation services that returns the route from their current location to the social event place. This operation is implemented by the synergy of three Client Side service bundles, namely: Social Events, POI Search, and Route Guidance. This cooperation of the three bundles is handled by the service orchestration mechanism that makes the combination of the different services transparent to the end-user.

User Experience

In this section a usage scenario is presented as an example of preliminary user experience on the ASK-IT ambient intelligence framework. This usage scenario demonstrates the aforementioned collaboration between the ASK-IT Social Events, POI Search and Route Guidance service models. Before proceeding, we need to outline some of the assumptions about the following demonstration. First, we assume that we are in Hamburg, Germany. The users use the ASK-IT client application on their PDA device in order to initially request information about social events of interest.

As shown in Fig. 4, after the invocation of the Social Events service the user is presented with a list of the social events that are taking place in Hamburg. Behind the scenes, before the invocation of the Social Events service, a set of other functionalities were activated by the ASK-IT ambient intelligence framework. These are performed in the following steps:

1. The Client Side retrieves the user coordinates from the GPS sensor located on the PDA device.
2. The user coordinates are transformed to a specific address through the ASK-IT Geo-coding service.
3. The user address is given as input to the ASK-IT Social Events service model, together with the current date.

Fig. 4 Social events service invocation results

4. The Server Side selects the Social Events service that would return the best results; it invokes it, receives the results, and returns them to the client application in the form of agent communication messages, exchanged between the Server and the Client Side agents.

After users receive the list of the returned results, they select to view the details of one of them. Figure 5 depicts the result of this action. At this point, information about the social events is presented to the user, like the name of venue, its address, etc. Users, who are interested in participating in this event, may request to be guided there.

The Client Side of the ASK-IT ambient intelligence framework invokes the client application's POI Search module that retrieves information about the venue, at which the event is taking place. The information returned by this module is depicted in Fig. 6. At this point the user can request further information, such as venue pictures, as shown in Fig. 7, or a map of the venue surrounding area.

In the next step users can request to be guided to the specific POI via the Route Calculation service. This service returns the route as a set of segments drawn on a number of maps that guide users to the event location. The specific user impairment, type is taken into account in order to provide accessible routes (Fig. 8 and 9).

For this purpose, the Client Side invokes the Route Calculation module, by providing the following inputs: the current address of the user location, which is received as the starting point and desired the destination point, i.e., the name of the

Fig. 5 Information about a social event

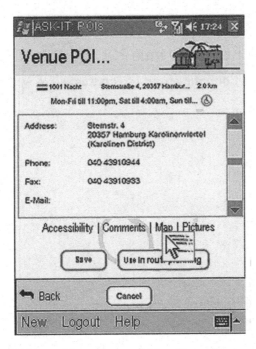

Fig. 6 Information about the social event's venue (Point of interest)

Fig. 7 Information about the social event's venue (Point of interest)

Fig. 8 The user is guided to the social event's venue

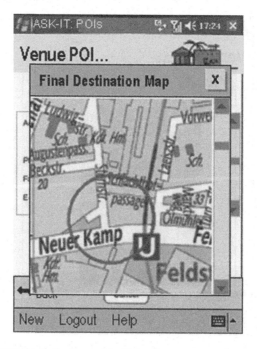

Fig. 9 The user locates the destination point of interest

venue at which the specific event of interest is taking place. The result by the invo-cation of the Route Calculation service is shown in Fig. 8.

The returned map shows additional information such as a set of directions that guide the user where to go. Apart from the textual representation of these direc-tions, users may be given audio instructions that are activated through a text-to-speech mechanism. The directions, along with the maps, constantly change, as the user moves from one map to another. Additional interactive content displayed on the user application includes accessible POI located in the active map area, e.g., restaurants (Fig. 8). Finally, users follow the provided directions in order to arrive at the desired destination and attend the social event. The application notifies users when they reach the desired destination by a displayed circle around the requested POI, as shown in Fig. 9.

Summary and Conclusions

In this chapter we introduced the ASK-IT ambient intelligence framework, whose unique feature is that it serves the needs of MI people by offering a set of geo-graphically distributed services and relevant multimedia content. The MI users are divided into ten groups in agreement to the ICF classification. Through ASK-IT users are able to exploit a set of new capabilities and enrich their sociability, by being offered specific services in various domains.

The architecture of the ASK-IT technical infrastructure is separated into two different subsystems, namely the Server and the Client Side. This architecture allows users to receive the results of their request in a seamless and totally transpar-ent manner. The Server Side is equipped with all the necessary tools and infrastruc-ture that enable search and retrieval of content through real invocation of Web services. The architecture is open to new service providers located at geographi-cally distributed locations, thus supporting users in various traveling scenarios and providing them with location-aware services. The goal of the presented infrastruc-ture is to realize a set of typical activities that are trivial for non-impaired users in the domain of transport, tourism, and leisure. Moreover, it targets to enrich user sociability, by offering a range of possibilities and scenarios of use. The most rep-resentative of them include various activities to support e-learning, notification on events which the user is interested in, as well as route planning and the provision of info-mobility services, based on social events and user preferences.

From the description of the above cases, it is shown that users are able to exploit new opportunities in order to enhance their sociability and enforce their community building activities. This is one of the most valuable contributions of the presented framework because it confronts one major social problem, i.e., the community isolation that people with disabilities often encounter. Through e-learning scenarios of use, these people are able to shape groups of classmates and people with similar interests. This is a major step toward the enhancement of the MI user sociability.

Moreover, the ambient intelligence infrastructure that virtually surrounds the user on the move, offers notification services about social events of user interest. The Social Events service model exploits capabilities far beyond those met in a typical notification tool. It brings rich multimedia content to users, such as maps, venue pictures, audio and textual descriptions of the events under consideration, etc. Thus, the user is encouraged to participate in various types of social events (meetings, leisure activities, parties, etc.) and meet other people with or without disabilities. The social events, about which the users receive notifications, match a set of user preferences and conform to each user's impairment type (e.g., the event takes place at a venue accessible by wheelchair users). A typical scenario of use, based on preliminary user experience, as the one described in the previous section, provides an example that shows how sociability can be achieved in the provided nomadic context.

References

Akkiraju, R., Farrell, J., Miller, J., Nagarajan, M., Schmidt, M., Sheth, A., & Verma, K. (2005). Web service semantics – WSDL-S, W3C Member Submission, from http://www.w3.org/Submission/WSDL-S/. Accessed 4 January 2008

Brumitt, B., Meyers, B., Krumm, J., Kern, A., & Shafer S. (2000) Easy living: Technologies for intelligent environments. In *Proceedings of International Symposium on Handheld and Ubiquitous Computing*, 12–29.

Choi C., Cho M., Kang Young, E., & Kim P. (2006). Travel ontology for recommendation system based on Semantic Web. In *Advanced Communication Technology (ICACT-2006). The 8th International Conference, IEEE Press*.

Flachsbart, J., Franklin, D., & Hammond, K. (2000). Improving Human-computer interaction in a classroom environment using computer vision. *In Proceedings of the Conference on Intelligent User Interfaces, ACM Press, New York*.

Frese, M., & Zapf, D. (1994). Action as the core of work psychology: A German approach. In M. D. Dunnetee et al. (Eds.), *Handbook of Industrial and Organizational Psychology* (Vol. 4; pp. 271–340). Consulting Psychologists Press Palo Alto (1994)

Herfet Th, Kirste Th, Schnaider M (2001) EMBASSI – Multimodal assistance for infotainment and service infrastructures. Computers&Graphics 25(4):581–592

Hübner S, Spittel R, Visser U, Vögele TJ (2004) Ontology-based search for interactive digital maps. IEEE Intelligent Systems 19(3):80–86

Johanson B, Fox A, Winograd T (2002) The interactive workspaces project: Experiences with ubiquitous computing rooms. IEEE Pervasive Computing Magazine 1(2):67–74

Karim, S., & Tjoa, A. M., (2006). Towards the use of ontologies for improving user interaction for people with special needs. In *Computers Helping People with Special Needs, Springer Berlin/Heidelberg*.

Oxygen Project. (2005). Massachusetts Institute of Technology, from http://www.oxygen.lcs.mit.edu/Overview.html. Accessed 4 January 2008

Paolucci, M., Srinivasan, N., Sycara, K., & Nishimura, T. (2003). Towards a semantic choreography of Web services: From WSDL to DAML-S. In *Proceedings of the International Conference for Web Services, (ICWS 2003)*.

Ramachandran, R., Movva, S., Graves, S., & Tanner, S. (2006). Ontology-based semantic search tool for atmospheric Science. In *Proceedings 22nd International Conference on Interactive Information Processing Systems for Meteorology, Oceanography, and Hydrology, Atlanta, GA*.

Riva, R. (2005). The psychology of ambient intelligence: Activity, situation and presence. In G. Riva, F. Vatalaro, F. Davide, & M. Alcaniz (Eds.), *Ambient Intelligence* (17–33). IOS Press Amsterdam.

Sirin, E., Hendler, J. A., & Parsia, B. (2003) Semi-automatic composition of Web services using semantic descriptions. In *Proceedings. Workshop on Web Services: Modeling, Architecture and Infrastructure (WSMAI), ICEIS Press.*

Sommer, S. M., Wiethoff, M, Valjakka, S., Kehagias, D., & Tzovaras, D. (2006). Development of a mobile tourist information system for people with functional limitations: User behaviour concept and specification of content requirements. In *Lecture Notes in Computer Science* (Vol. 4061), *Springer, Berlin.*

Tomai, E., Spanaki, M., Prastacos, P., & Kavouras, M. (2005). Ontology assisted decision making a case study in trip planning for tourism. In *On the Move to Meaningful Internet Systems, Springer, Berlin/Heidelberg.*

Yesilada, Y., Harper, S., Goble, C., & Stevens, R. (2004). Screen readers cannot see (ontology based semantic annotation for visually impaired Web travellers). In Koch, N., Fraternali, P., & Wirsing, M. (Eds.), *Web Engineering – 4th International Conference, ICWE 2004 Proceedings (LNCS 3140), Springer, Berlin.*

Knopflerfish OSGi. (2008). An open source OSGi platform, http://knopflerfish.org/. Accessed 21 October 2008

OSGi Service Platform. (2008). Release 4 Home Page, from http://www.osgi.org/Release4/Javadoc. Accessed 21 October 2008. Accessed 21 October 2008

Creativity in Interactive TV: Personalize, Share, and Invent Interfaces

Radu-Daniel Vatavu

Abstract This chapter tries to induce changes in the way we think about interfaces and currently interact with television today. Either in the comfort of our home, in public shared spaces, or on the go via personal mobile devices, interaction should be intuitive, simple, and undemanding. This chapter is a quest for creativity and invention, it is about bringing new ideas into current interaction paradigms as well as shifting the way we see TV interfaces today. Technology has been available for quite a while now providing mechanisms that allow us to play, record, store, archive, and stream TV-related information, but the way we interface such complex systems and mechanisms is still bound to dozens of buttons on one or more remote controls. When groups of people need to interact simultaneously with today's TV set, the interface barrier immediately appears with all its inherent frustrations: lack of control at the desired time and no immediate availability of the interface; single-viewer and single-task interfacing; and limited or burdensome options for viewing, archiving, and sharing. The ultimate goal of this chapter is to encourage creativity in TV interface design with focus on today's available and affordable technologies such as video cameras and computer vision, computer graphics, and projection equipment all under the same principle: keep the interaction as simple and intuitive as possible and add just a bit of fun to it to make it really captivating.

Introduction

Interactive television has known many advances in the past decades with respect to technology, concepts and business models, services provided and, last but not least, interfaces and interaction techniques (Cesar et al. 2006b; Cesar et al. 2007; Jensen 2005; Jensen 2008; Lekakos et al. 2007; Lugmayr et al. 2004; Tscheligi et al. 2008).

R.-D. Vatavu (✉)
Research Center in Computer Science, University "Stefan cel Mare" of Suceava, 13, University Street, 720229, Suceava, Romania
e-mail: vatavu@eed.usv.ro

A. Marcus et al. (eds.), *Mobile TV: Customizing Content and Experience*,
Human-Computer Interaction Series, DOI 10.1007/978-1-84882-701-1_12,
© Springer-Verlag London Limited 2010

Advances in technology allowed many television environments to be available today starting with the home scenario where family and friends watch programs together up to the on-the-run consumer playing streaming television on personal mobile devices (Cui et al. 2007; Oksman et al. 2007; Vangenck et al. 2008). Each environment comes with its own features and limitations for which efficient interaction techniques must be developed.

Of a particular importance we still find the home environment where families and friends gather in order to watch, comment, and enjoy television shows, movies, news broadcasts, or live sports transmissions for which they share the same interest. Although collaborative TV watching has evolved and may be achieved at remote distance via Internet streaming media and instant messaging applications, the home environment has a particular feature which makes it rather unique: it is able to support and encourage on-site socialization and human bonding. The home environment still represents the main place for social interaction, an important area (perceived as such) for socializing between family members, friends, and neighbors as investigations on home trends do report (Bernhaupt et al. 2007; Obrist et al. 2008).

Another interesting feature worth mentioning for home environments is that although the static scenario is predominant (usually fixed large screens as Fig. 1 illustrates the classic view of a living-room home environment), mobile TV has equally entered the home space by the use of secondary mobile screens which provide more control and less limitations (Cesar et al. 2008; Cruickshank et al. 2007; Cui et al. 2007; Robertson et al. 1996). Mobile TV was found popular in the home space even when large screens were present due to the fact that viewers had low control over what was being watched, negotiation was usually involved with regards to the interface (the remote control), or simply privacy- and comfort-related motivations were reported (Cui et al. 2007).

The most important fact to note in present-day home environments is that the global experience is a shared one: all the viewers share the same viewing transmission. However, when we look at the interaction part we find the exact opposite: the interface being reduced to the traditional remote control which by itself proves very

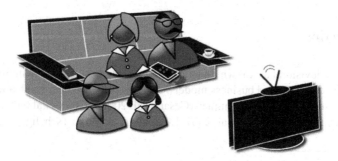

Fig. 1 Commonly encountered home environment with family and friends watching television together. Although the viewers share the same transmission, the interface is limited with respect to this sharing part: lack of control at desired time, negotiation may occur, the interface is temporarily owned

limited with respect to the sharing part. Although the viewing experience is shared among the group, the control part of the interface only allows one-viewer-at-a-time interaction which drastically limits the interaction with respect to the sharing part of the viewing experience. The interface device may be viewed as temporarily blocked or temporarily owned by the other viewer at one particular time.

The main goal of this chapter is to encourage creativity in TV interface design. This goal is motivated and supported by the various advances in technology such as computer graphics, computer vision, and artificial intelligence, sensing and smart sensors, projective and novel displays. The technological advances allow acquisition, recognition and interpretation of speech, gestures, and body actions which can be embedded in the design of the interface and interaction techniques. Viewers may prefer engaging in dialogs or simply uttering single-word commands they are familiar with; may prefer pointing directly at the TV or performing familiar postures or gestures; would enjoy a personalized remote; or combine the remote, speech, pointing and gestures into a multimodal interface. The best environment to test and play with technology is at home where sensors and cameras can be hidden away transforming thus into pervasive technology. Also, people seem not to realize the now ubiquitous technology surrounding them which becomes part of the physical environment (Bernhaupt et al. 2007; Haddon 2006). Figure 2 illustrates a novel representation of the home environment where (as limited by imagination) everything is turned into an interface: mobile devices, coffee tables, living room objects, toys, etc. The goal is to induce creativity in design.

Before diving into technology, we briefly discuss several requirements which may be drawn for new generation of creative TV interfaces as Fig. 3 illustrates:

- Interfaces should be simple and intuitive. Although this statement sounds general and the goal may appear as idealistic, simplicity may be found in gestures

Fig. 2 Vision for novel TV interactions where interfaces are ubiquitous: mobile devices, coffee tables, everyday living-room objects, toys may be sensed and tracked by various sensors and installations for the purpose of interaction

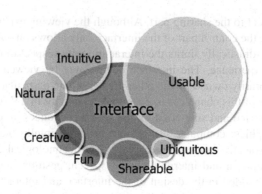

Fig. 3 Requirements for novel creative TV interfaces: intuitiveness, naturalness, and usability of the interface should be merged with a bit of creativity and fun-to-use; shareable and ubiquitous interfaces extend further the design requirements

(we use gestures every day in order to interact with and manipulate real-world objects or to convey information), speech, and interpreting human actions while intuitiveness may be achieved by using familiar objects to play the role of the interface.

- The interface should not require learning, memorization, or recalling commands (should not add cognitive load or require training to master). Multifunctional remote controls are especially found complex to be used for household members which leads to old and new remote controls coexisting even when they perform the same functions. Viewers complain about complexity, large number of (as perceived unusable) remotes with the effect of only few buttons actually used (Bernhaupt et al. 2007).

- The interface should be shared among the group. Lack of sharing leads to lack of control at desired time, negotiations, or interfaces that become owned or blocked by one viewer for a given amount of time. It should be noted that a shared interface does not necessarily translate into every viewer having their own personal interface with conflicts easily foreseen but instead it relates to the property of the interface to be immediately available and instantly shareable among the group (e.g., the coffee table (Vatavu et al. 2008) is a shared wide-area, immediately available interface).

- The interface should possess a dimension of fun that makes the interaction process captivating. The dimension of fun is usually introduced by novel user-friendly technologies. It is interesting mentioning that studies conducted on interaction techniques that use the remote control (Bernhaupt et al. 2007) found children drawing out their desired remote control which should have a funny and cool shape. The interaction cube of Block et al. (2004) was designed with this very idea of fun in mind: humans are described as playful and creative explorers of their environment and hence good design has to address these basic needs too without compromising the effectiveness of a tool.

- The interface does not have to respect a given format (e.g., the remote control cloned into the DVR, CD, and other remotes) but instead designs should be creative and use familiar and everyday objects as the interface – coffee tables, pens, coffee cups, etc. This also relates to humanizing the interface which has the effect of reassuring users who may be unfamiliar with technology (Roibs et al. 2005).

Besides these requirements, care must be taken with regards to several specific elements when designing novel multimodal TV interfaces with respect to general human–computer interface design. The TV home environment differs with respect to the traditional computer scenario (Ibrahim & Johansson 2002):

- There is a distance of several meters between the installed TV screen and the viewers which impacts the format of the information to be displayed with respect to text and graphics size and their amount.
- TV output combines both video and audio information, hence feedback should be considered accordingly (e.g., audio feedback could be disturbing when superimposed over broadcasted transmission)
- Television is about fun and entertainment with family and friends enjoying shows and transmissions; hence, the interface, interaction techniques, and feedback provided should be designed in accordance with this general feeling of relaxation and recreation.

Novel Input Technologies

We continue by discussing the technologies available today that allow acquisition, recognition, and interpretation of human input such as speech, gestures, and body actions as they are perceived as natural, intuitive, and familiar forms of interaction. Relevant references from the literature are provided with respect to such interfaces being designed to control TV or media devices found in the home environment.

Speech in the Interface

Speech is a natural and effortless way to issue commands which makes it a good candidate for interfacing the TV set. It was found that viewers prefer uttering verbal commands or engaging in dialogs while comfortably seated in their living-room context rather than performing menu manipulation via the remote control (Ibrahim & Johansson 2002). Also, the considerable advances in automatic speech recognition and natural language processing have motivated designers to consider speech as an input technique (Berglund & Qvarfordt 2003; Ceccaroni et al. 2005; Fujita et al. 2003; Ibrahim et al. 2001; Nakatoh et al. 2007; Portolan et al. 1999; Wittenburg et al. 2006).

There are two main approaches for using speech recognition in the interface. The first one is to recognize a limited set of predefined commands (Nakatoh et al. 2007) for channel selection (via the channel number or the name of the broadcaster), volume control or category search (e.g., locating a TV program category with a simple single-word utterance such as "soccer"). Simple utterance commands work well with high recognition accuracy rates and allow for saving time by performing quick menu selections (shortcuts). There are also disadvantages that come tied with this approach: the vocabulary needs to be consulted prior to usage (no free speech) and viewers need to memorize fixed words and phrases which add cognitive load; not all the synonyms (as perceived by users) may work; the vocabulary is limited. The second approach is to develop dialog-based systems which use unrestricted syntax or vocabulary (Wittenburg et al. 2006). They are complex to design and implement; although, they may prove better at handling recognition errors due to engaging viewers in dialogs via guiding questions.

Speech acquisition is achieved by embedding a microphone into the remote control which is usually redesigned in order to present fewer buttons (see Fig. 4). Speech comes therefore as a complementary or alternative input technique that augments the remote control.

The main challenges with speech remotes are related to error rates, environmental noise and speaker variations. Recognition errors can cause irritation, frustration, and implicitly low performance, hence error resolution strategies must be employed (Berglund & Qvarfordt 2003). Displaying an n-best list with potential word alternatives that match the viewer's utterance was found as a good option to improve interaction (Berglund & Qvarfordt 2003). Speech input is effective especially for performing quick menu selection via shortcuts instead of completing the various menu steps (Ibrahim et al. 2001), this being a general motivation of using speech to achieve efficiency in interaction (Martin 1989). Also, speech was suggested to accompany and complement the remote control as viewers subjectively prefer the remote being already familiar with it. Spoken natural language combined with visual output was found preferable for TV applications (Ibrahim & Johansson 2002).

Fig. 4 Speech input is achieved by embedding microphones into the remote control. Special care is needed with regards to recognition accuracy, speaker variation, and environmental noise filtering. Speech comes as complementary rather than alternative interaction

Gestures Acquisition, Recognition, and Interpretation

Controlling TV with the bare hands via pointing, signs (postures) and motion gestures is very intriguing and consequently gestures have been tackled before and investigated in the context of interfacing the TV set (Freeman & Weissman 1995; Kohler 1998; Lenman et al. 2002; Vatavu et al. 2008). Gestures are popular and place themselves in a privileged position when it comes to interfaces as they play an important part in our lives including art, science, music, dance, allowing us to work, communicate, express feelings, and enhance and accompany speech. Using gestures is something we have been training for all our lives, are still in the process of learning, and we make use of them according to our personalities, jobs, social situations and events, most of the time without even realizing it. The naturalness and familiarity of gesturing are revealed even more by the fact that blind people gesture as they speak just as much as sighted individuals do, even when they know their listener is also blind (Iverson & Goldin-Meadow 1998). Gestures express ideas, feelings, and intentions, sometimes replacing words and enhancing speech. They convey information and are accompanied by content and semantics. Various psycholinguistic studies have been conducted in what concerns the understanding of gesture communication and they provide an excellent starting material for gesture studying and understanding (Kendon 1986; McNeill 1992). Also, representations of gestures as commands for human–computer interaction have been investigated as well (Vatavu & Pentiuc 2009) (Fig. 5).

Gesture acquisition and recognition have been investigated by several interested research communities (computer vision, pattern recognition, human–computer interaction) and currently represent very active fields of research. When dealing with gestures as human input there is always the quest for the ideal technology to use (technology that would not importunate, burden, or distract from the actual interaction process) as well as for the right gesture vocabulary. With regards to technology, video cameras, tangible and accelerator-based devices need to be considered. The second challenge that arises is the interaction part. For example, what is the best gesture to use when switching on and off the TV set? Should the same gesture be used for switching on and off or should we have different gesture

Fig. 5 Gestures are used in order to manipulate objects, express feelings and intentions, and to convey information

commands with appropriate meaning? What does the "best" gesture mean? A command may be preferred by one user while at the same time be regarded as awkward to perform or totally inappropriate for another. Is there a standard gesture vocabulary or should users have the possibility to define their own commands? Should the system adapt to viewers by learning new sets of commands? Do viewers prefer defining new commands, etc.? Many questions arise from just the simple idea of controlling the TV set via gestures and there are works in the literature that report on various advances.

To begin with, a decision must be made with regards to the gesture acquisition technology and scenario and so far, video-based acquisition of gestures seems to be the preferred approach (Freeman & Weissman 1995; Kohler 1998; Lenman et al. 2002; Vatavu et al. 2008). The main advantage that comes with vision gesture acquisition and which provides the comfortable feeling of natural interaction is the fact that the technology is non intrusive and does not require users to wear additional equipments or devices. Users may interact freely with the system with no need for wearing or interacting via an additional device that may distract, restrict, or burden the natural movement (e.g., wires more or less heavy attached to gloves or hand-wearable trackers, glove sizes that may be a bit small or large). Of equal importance, vision-based solutions are relatively inexpensive compared to trackers that exhibit a price range from several hundreds to tens of thousands of dollars.

Current research prototypes that make use of computer vision techniques in order to detect and recognize hand gestures perform in sometimes very complex environments. Freeman and Weissman (1995) use hand posture recognition combined with visual feedback of the hand position on the TV screen. Seated on a couch, users manipulate a graphical icon of a hand on the screen. The authors demonstrate a TV-set control application using the template-matching technique with only one posture used: the open hand facing the video camera. A hand icon on the computer screen follows exactly the movements of the user's hand. The system thus exploits visual feedback: users see the icon hand on the screen so they know how much to move their hands. The command is triggered when the user holds up the open hand which determines the TV set to enter the control mode. Closing the hand leaves the control mode. Various graphical controls are adjusted using movements of the hand. The problems the authors address are how to provide a rich set of commands without training or memorizing complicated gestures and how to achieve command recognition in a complex visual environment. There are many possible commands to give the television (e.g., "mute," "channel 37," "louder") yet no universal set of hand signals to specify all of them. Voice is not appropriate for channel surfing nor for changing parameters by incrementers such as volume control. Activating TV menus and performing selections are also reported by Lenman et al. (2002) with similar working prototypes. The scenario seems popular and is illustrated in Fig. 6; however, it must be noted that it comes with several drawbacks.

The ARGUS system (Kohler 1998) was designed to control home appliances (TV included): users point toward a device and control its standard functions such as power on/off, volume up/down, play or stop via hand gestures. The focus is on object identification, prediction of motion using Kalman filtering and visual input

Fig. 6 Gesture acquisition scenario: viewers sit comfortably in front of the TV set while a video camera monitors gestures. Although popular among researchers, this scenario comes with several drawbacks such as: privacy and intimacy issues, complex background to analyze, gestures performed in mid-air which induces fatigue for long-term interactions

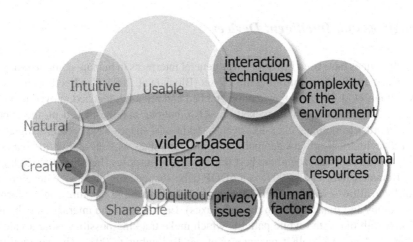

Fig. 7 Additional constraints for video-based gesture interaction that come on top of the general requirements for novel TV interfaces

without the need of markers attached to the human body. Two cameras are installed in a room monitoring an interaction area where several devices are located. The user points toward a device and the system confirms intention by audio feedback. Selection is achieved by bowing the thumb finger which simulates a click event. Several gestures are defined for multiple devices (VCR, TV, CD player, etc.) in order to control their various functions.

Additional constraints come with video-based gesture interaction as illustrated in Fig. 7, constraints that must be handled on top of the requirements for novel TV interfaces. First of all, one major disadvantage of all the above gesture-based interfaces is that having a video camera permanently facing and monitoring the viewers

while they sit in front of the TV set may issue problems and freights with regards
to intimacy and privacy. Viewers may feel uncomfortable while knowing that one
or more video cameras are facing toward them monitoring their every movement.
Another important issue as noted in Lenman et al. (2002) is represented by the fact
that the current setup with subjects seated facing the TV and performing gestures
with their arms in mid-air is not suitable from the articulatory and muscular systems
point of view causing inconvenient interactions due to fatigue settling in. In the end
it must be noted that the environment is generally complex, thus problems also arise
from the complexity of the scene to be analyzed by computer vision algorithms:
crowded scenes with multiple objects and colors lead to difficulties in hand tracking
with immediate effect on the entire system performance. Care thus must be taken
when designing video-based interfaces for gesture acquisition and maybe a shift in
scenario paradigm is needed (Vatavu et al. 2008).

Tangibles and Intelligent Devices

Tangible cubes have been investigated as general interfaces in human–computer interaction and applied for controlling the TV set (Block et al. 2004; Van Laerhoven et al.
2003; Tahir et al. 2007) as they can be grabbed and released, touched, moved in 3D,
rotated, twisted, shaken, or knocked on. Also, buttons may be placed on the cube
faces in order to simulate click-like events. Additional shapes have been investigated
such as cylindrical artifact geometries of different sizes as well as hybrid shapes;
however, the cube was found the best for interaction purposes (Ferscha et al. 2008).

ARemote (Tahir et al. 2007) is a 6DOF cube-shaped tangible device developed
in order to allow selections from TV channel lists by using 3D gestures (in the form
of rotations and translations on the three axes). Each side of the interaction cube is
marked with black and white patterns which make tracking possible using a video
camera and the ARToolKit package (Kato & Billinghurst 2004). The interaction
techniques are based on crossing and scrolling operations. Horizontal (X) and vertical (Y) movements control the position of an on-screen cursor while Z-axis rotations allow for scrolling at various speeds. A horizontal list may thus be scrolled to
the left or right using Z-axis rotations until the desired channel appears in the current view after which its selection is achieved via a quick vertical movement.
Another interaction technique is to have all the channels displayed on the screen
and to use the XY position of the on-screen cursor in order to perform direct selection: a channel is selected when the cursor crosses it.

Block et al. (2004) propose a tangible cube device with gravity sensing and wireless communications embedded (Van Laerhoven et al. 2003). A 3D representation
of the cube is displayed on the TV screen with streams rendered on each face.
Viewers may zap channels intuitively by performing cube rotations, thus triggering
changes in the channels displayed on the faces of the virtual cube. At one moment
up to three streams are simultaneously displayed. Once the cube is put down the TV
channel that is currently facing the viewer is displayed in full screen. As soon as

Fig. 8 Tangible devices such as special designed cubes or everyday objects such as toys may be used in order to map movements and rotations to shortcut commands for interfacing the TV-set

the device is grabbed again the 3D virtual cube interface is re-activated. The playful cube design includes an amount of fun as the authors put it: humans are described as playful and creative explorers of their environment and hence good design has to address these basic needs.

Tangible devices have the advantage of allowing physical shortcuts for the most frequently used commands (Ferscha et al. 2008) (see Fig. 8). Horizontal rotations may be mapped to volume control while flipping the cube triggers channel switching. Cube shaking has been used as a shortcut for navigating to the home menu (Ferscha et al. 2008).

Several unusual interfaces have also been reported such as affect-input devices (Jackie et al. 2007) or even plush toys (Kawasaki et al. 2005). The concept of using plush toys or general everyday objects is that they are more familiar and appealing than special designed devices such as the remote controller. Also, plush toys are especially pleasing to children. The plush toy of Kawasaki et al. (2005) is tracked using a video camera. Grabbing the toy and holding it in front of the TV (and the video camera) triggers the start of the recognition process. Translation movements of the plush toy horizontally or vertically may be mapped to different actions such as controlling the volume or turning the TV on/off.

Practical Study: Interactive Coffee Tables

We continue by discussing a practical study of coffee tables (Vatavu et al. 2008) which may be turned into wide-area immediately available shared TV interfaces. The design principles behind the interactive coffee tables are found in the requirements illustrated in the introduction section for novel creative interfaces: interaction should be shared and immediately available to all viewers; techniques should be simple to perform, should not add cognitive load or require training; fun if possible; use everyday objects (TV viewing rooms usually have a coffee table).

Vision, Design, and Technology

The vision for interactive coffee tables is illustrated in Fig. 9. Viewers are watching TV gathered around the coffee table whilst a video camera is monitoring the surface of the table on which there is a separation between interactive and noninteractive regions. TV interfacing is achieved by placing and moving hands inside the interactive region. Delimitation between interactive and noninteractive areas on the tabletop is needed in order for the table to still maintain its basic functionality (that of a coffee table) allowing objects to be placed or hands to rest in the noninteractive regions without accidentally sending TV commands.

The current design illustrated in Fig. 9 splits the tabletop into two regions: the interactive part in the middle (farther away from users so that hands placed in the middle should be intended not accidental) and a noninteractive part around the sensitive region up to the borders of the table. It must be noted that this design is not by all means unique and others may be imagined and set up in accordance with the default number of viewers, preferred usage, or location of the coffee table in the living room. Vatavu and Pentiuc (2008) propose several designs for space partitioning on the surface of the coffee table.

Detection of hands above the tabletop is achieved using image-processing techniques as Fig. 10 illustrates. Background removal and color detection are followed by grouping filtered pixels into binary large objects (Gonzalez & Woods 2007) for which simple shape parameters such as area, width, and height are computed.

Fig. 9 Vision for interactive coffee tables: all the viewers may interact with the TV set using the same wide-area interface via simple hand movements on top of the video-sensitive area of the table. The interactive area is depicted in the center of the table with a darker color

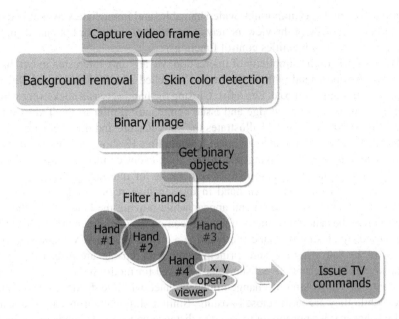

Fig. 10 Image processing flow: acquired video frames are filtered for skin-like color pixels and background is removed; the results merge into a binary image for which binary large objects are identified; object parameters such as width, height, and area are used to filter hand candidates; each hand is classified into open or close, associated to a viewer and its location mapped to the TV screen; commands are issued according to context when hands are closed

The approach is simple and fast and gives good and accurate results if a good contrast between the coffee table and the skin color can be arranged. Discrimination between the two hand postures (open and closed) is achieved by inspecting the shape parameters as extracted by the image-processing techniques. The area, width, and height of the hand-open posture are greater than the ones associated to the hand-closed posture, hence a fixed threshold allows for gesture classification. It must be noted that dedicated techniques have been reported in the computer vision literature for detecting and tracking hands in complex scenarios such as Caetano et al. (2002), Cho et al. (2001), Kolsch & Turk (2005) but they involve complex implementations not always accessible to HCI practitioners. The presented approach is easy to implement, allows for immediate testing, and gives real-time processing.

Interaction Techniques for a Shared Wide-Area Immediately Available Interface

By visually designating interaction sensitive areas on the coffee-table surface, television control may be achieved via hand movements across the surface which may be performed by any of the viewers at any time. The interface is thus simple, intuitive, fun, and very important, wide-shareable, and immediately available to all the participants. Any of the viewers may at any time place one or both hands in the interactive area which entitles control functions.

With regards to the simplicity of interaction, we are only interested in two hand postures: the open hand with all the fingers stretched and the hand closed with all the fingers maximum-flexed, i.e., a fist. Closing the hand acts as a click event which enables viewers to acknowledge and issue commands similar to the TAFFI interface (Wilson 2006). Figure 11 illustrates the click gesture and the interaction techniques that make use of one or two hands while Fig. 12 shows a few snapshots of the system running. By making use of the click event combined with the hands locations on the table, several distinct commands for interfacing the TV may be implemented. Placing one open hand in the sensitive region of the coffee table makes the channels selection menu appear while moving the hand across the surface triggers the same movement of a hand icon on the TV screen. Menu selection is achieved by closing the hand (performing a click). General TV menu selection may work by following the same principle. When two hands are placed inside the sensitive region, their relative distance is exploited for modifying the value of various controls. The volume is changed in accordance with the distance between the hands while they are in the closed posture. Similar sliding controls can be considered whenever it is appropriate to map the distance between the hands to a relative change in the value of a parameter.

Due to the wide table size and viewers being positioned at its various sides the interface becomes shared: different viewers may place their hands in the interactive area at the same time. User detection may be achieved by tracking each hand since it first entered the interactive area. The side it entered the area identifies the user sitting at the corresponding side of the table. Different users may have different

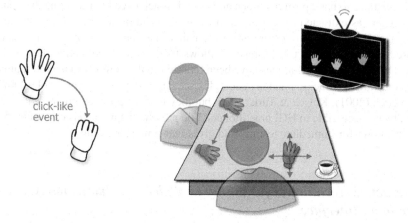

Fig. 11 Interaction techniques at the coffee table. *Left*: hand open followed by hand closed generates a click-like event in order to acknowledge and issue commands (such as menu or list selection). *Right*: viewers control hand icons on the TV screen

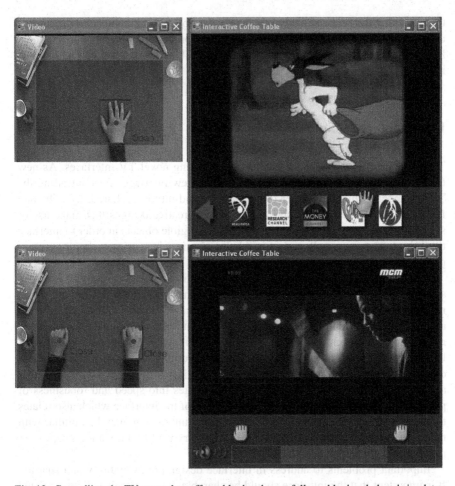

Fig. 12 Controlling the TV set at the coffee table: hand open followed by hand closed simulates click-like events for selecting TV channels from a horizontal list (*top*); two closed hands control the amount of volume in accordance with their relative distance (*bottom*). Left figures show snapshots taken from the video camera while right figures illustrate TV capture screens

colored hand cursors displayed on the TV screen and control may be performed simultaneously (for example, one viewer may browse channels while another lowers down the volume; several viewers browse and change the channels they are watching in a picture-in-picture viewing mode).

Moving the interaction to the coffee-table space instantly removes the problems and issues discussed for video-based gesture acquisition interfaces. First of all, it must be noted that the interaction process is not fatiguing any more even for long-term interactions as the hands comfortably rest on the surface of the table and are not held in mid-air. The video camera only monitors the coffee table and not the viewers, which alleviates the privacy issues. When it comes to recognition accuracies and resources needed for processing the video information, the important fact to note is that the scene to analyze is far less complex being reduced to the surface of a table (of usually one single color). Instead of processing images of an unknown living-room scenario, the coffee table scene to analyze is much simpler and known in advance.

Discussion and Conclusions

This chapter tried to address creativity in designing novel TV interfaces. As new technologies become more and more available, new interfaces for controlling the TV set appear which are easier to use, natural and intuitive, shared, friendly, and fun. The chapter surveyed such innovatory and creative designs that make use of speech, gesture, special designed or real-world tangible objects in order to interface the TV set. These were all made possible by advances in sensing technology, computer vision, and artificial intelligence techniques.

It is questionable whether the best interface is the natural one that employs speech, gesture, and body movements or if tangibles which require hands-on manipulation are the way to go. As often is the case, multimodality might be the answer, where speech or gesture come at the right moment (when it feels right or natural) to complement tangible interaction. Dealing with human input is still challenging yet good results may be obtained with careful design (e.g., the coffee table completely shifts the interaction space from vertical to horizontal with the great advantage of scene simplicity that further translates into speed and robustness of processing). Questionable also is the universality of the interface which also relates to multimodality: viewers have preferences when interacting, may be familiar with tangibles not just yet willing to change, or may very well find it natural to speak or point.

Important problems to address in interface design are availability and sharing. It is important that the interface should be sharable; however, this is tightly related to the time needed for the interface to become available. Instant availability assures a sharable interface although much depends on the context and location where the interaction takes place (e.g., the coffee tables are shareable and immediately available due to their wide size). When handling simultaneous sharing of the interface conflicts may occur and it is important to design preventively in order to minimize the need for negotiation.

The dimensions of playful use, fun, and consequently related excitement when using novel technologies give just a bit of something extra to the interface. Children in particular but grownups too transform into playful explorers of the possibilities offered by a creative interface; hence, a good design should suit this extra need as well. The dimension of fun, without compromising usability, leads to enthusiasm and eagerness to try and test as well as to the desire for more and eventually may lead to accepting the interface. Looking for interfaces that are fun to use may prove challenging; however, good starting points may come from asking children (Bernhaupt et al. 2007) or interaction techniques may be developed watching how children intuitively feel the need to interact when introduced to novel physically interactive environments (Bobick et al. 2000; Pinhanez et al. 2000).

Finally, the quest for creativity was the goal of this chapter and a new perspective for innovatory interfaces was sought to be induced. Left alone, technologies, recommendations, and specifications of what a good interface should be or look like, previous practices or surveys of existing designs, the new generation of TV interfaces will just have to have that bit of sparkle that will produce a shift in paradigm from the way we see TV interactions today.

References

Berglund, A., & Qvarfordt, P. (2003). Error resolution strategies for interactive television speech interfaces. In *Proceedings of International Conference on Human-Computer Interaction (INTERACT '03), Zurich, Switzerland, September 1–5, 2003, IFIP, Amsterdam*, pp. 105–112.

Bernhaupt, R., Obrist, M., Weiss, A., Beck, E., & Tscheligi, M. (2007). Trends in the living room and beyond. In P. Cesar, K. Chorianopoulos, & J. F. Jensen (Eds.), *Interactive TV: A shared experience, 5th Conference on Interactive Television, EuroITV 2007, LNCS 4471, Springer-Verlag*, pp. 146–155.

Block, F., Schmidt, A., Villar, N., & Gellersen, H.-W. (2004). Towards a playful user interface for home entertainment systems. In *Proceedings of the European Symposium on Ambient Intelligence 2004, Springer*, 207–217.

Bobick, A., Intille, S., Davis, J., Baird, F., Pinhanez, C., Campbell, L., Ivanov, Y., Schutte, A., & Wilson, A. (2000). The KidsRoom. *Communications of the ACM Special Issue on Perceptual User Interfaces, 43*(3).

Caetano, T. S., Olabarriaga, S. D., Barone, D. A. C. (2002). Performance evaluation of single and multiple-gaussian models for skin color modelling. In *Proceedings of the 15th Brazilian Symposium on Computer Graphics and Image Processing*, pp. 275–282.

Ceccaroni, L., Febrer, A., Hernndez, J. Z., Martnez, E., Martnez, P., & Verdaguer, X. (2005). Using AI to make interactive television more usable by people with disabilities. In *Proceedings of First International Conference on Home automation, Robotics and Remote Assistance for all (DRT4all), Madrid, Spain*.

Cesar, P., Bulterman, D. C. A., & Jansen, A. J. (2006). An architecture for end-user TV content enrichment. In *Proceedings of EuroITV 2006, Greece*.

Cesar, P., & Chorianopoulos, K. (2006). Interactive digital television and multimedia systems. In *Proceedings of the 14th Annual ACM International Conference on Multimedia, Multimedia '06. ACM Press, New York*.

Cesar, P., Chorianopoulos, K, & Jensen, J. F. (Eds.) (2007). *Interactive TV: A Shared Experience*, Eu-roITV 2007, LNCS 4471. Springer-Verlag.

Cesar, P., Bulterman, D. C. A., & Jansen, A. J. (2008). Usages of the secondary screen in an interactive television environment: Control, enrich, share, and transfer television content. In M. Tsche-ligi, M. Obrist, & A. Lugmayr (Eds.), *Changing television environments* (pp. 168–177). EuroITV 2008, LNCS 5066, Springer-Verlag.

Cho, K. –M., Jang, J. –H., Hong, K. –S. (2001). Adaptive skin color filter. *Pattern Recognition, 34*(5), 1067–1073.

Cruickshank, L., Tsekleves, E., Whitham, R., Hill, A., & Kondo, K. (2007). Making interactive TV easier to use: Interface design for a second screen approach. *The Design Journal, 10*(3).

Cui, Y, Chipchase, J., Jung, Y. (2007). Personal TV: A qualitative study of mobile TV users. In P. Cesar, K. Chorianopoulos, & J. F. Jensen (Eds.), *Interactive TV: A shared experience* (pp. 195–204). *5th Conference on Interactive Television, EuroITV 2007, LNCS 4471, Springer-Verlag*.

Ferscha, A., Vogl, S., Emsenhuber, B., & Wally, B. (2008). Physical shortcuts for media remote controls. In *Proceedings of the 2nd International Conference on Intelligent Technologies for Interactive Entertainment*, pp. 1–8.

Freeman, W. T., & Weissman, C. D. (1995). Television control by hand gestures. In *Proceedings IEEE International Workshop on Automatic Face and Gesture Recognition, Zurich.*

Fujita, K., Kuwano, H., Tsuzuki, T., Ono, Y., & Ishihara, T. (2003). A new digital TV interface employing speech recognition. In *Proceedings of IEEE International Conference on Consumer Electronics*, pp. 356–357.

Gonzalez, R.C., & Woods, R.E. (2007). Digital image processing (3rd ed.). Upper Saddle River, NJ: Pearson Prentice Hall.

Haddon, L. (2006). The contribution of domestication research to in-home computing and media consumption. *The Information Society Journal, 22*, 195–203.

Ibrahim, A., & Johansson, P. (2002). Multimodal dialogue systems for interactive TV applications. In *Proceedings of the 4th IEEE International Conference on Multimodal Interfaces 2002 (ICMI'02), Pittsburgh, USA*, pp. 117–122.

Ibrahim, A., Lundberg, J., & Johansson, J. (2001). Speech enhanced remote control for media terminal. In *Proceedings of EuroSpeech '01* (Aalborg, Denmark, September 2001). *International Speech Communcation Association, Bonn, Germany*, Vol. 4, pp. 2685–2688.

Iverson, J. M., & Goldin-Meadow, S. (1998). Why people gesture when they speak. *Nature, 396*, p. 228.

Jackie Lee, C. -H., Chang, C., Chung, H., Dickie, C., & Selker, T. (2007). *Emotionally reactive television.* In Proceedings of ACM IUI'07, pp. 329–332.

Jensen, J. F. (2005). Interactive television: new genres, new format, new content. In *Proceedings of the 2nd Australasian Conference on Interactive Entertainment, ACM International Conference Proceeding Series* (vol. 123), Creativity & Cognition Studios Press, Sydney, Australia, pp. 89–96.

Jensen, J. F. (2008). Interactive television – A brief media history. In M. Tscheligi, M. Obrist, & A. Lugmayr (Eds.), *Changing Television Environments* (pp. 1–10). *6th Conference on Interactive Television, EuroITV 2008, LNCS 5066, Springer-Verlag.*

Kato, H., & Billinghurst, M. (2004). Developing AR applications with ARToolKit. In *Proceedings of the 3rd IEEE/ACM international Symposium on Mixed and Augmented Reality* (Nov. 02–05, 2004). *Symposium on Mixed and Augmented Reality. IEEE Computer Society, Washington, DC*, pp. 305–305.

Kawasaki, Y., Igarashi, T., Ajioka, T., & Honda, I. (2005). Vision-based Gestural Interaction Using Plush Toys. In *Proceedings of ACM UIST'05.*

Kendon, A. (1986). *Current issues in the study of gesture. The Biological foundation of gestures: Motor and semiotic Aspects* (pp. 23–47). Hillsdale: Lawrence Erlbaum.

Kohler, M. (1998). Special topics of gesture recognition applied in intelligent home environments. In I. Wachsmuth, & M. Frohlich (Eds.), *GW 1997. LNCS (LNAI)* (Vol. 1471; pp. 285–296). Heidelberg: Springer.

Kolsch, M., & Turk, M. (2005). Hand tracking with flocks of features. In *Proceedings of IEEE Conference on Computer Vision and Pattern Recognition, CVPR'05.*

Lekakos, G., Chorianopoulos, K., & Doukidis, G. (Eds.) (2007). *Interactive digital television: Technologies and applications.* EuroITV 2006, IGI Publishing.

Lenman, S., Bretzner, L., & Thuresson, B. (2002). Using marking menus to develop command sets for computer vision based hand gesture interfaces. In *Proceedings of the 2nd Nordic Conference on Human-Computer Interaction, ACM Press, New York*, pp. 239–242.

Lugmayr, A., Niiranen, S., & Kalli, S. (2004). *Digital interactive TV and metadata.* Springer-Verlag: Future Broadcast Multimedia Series: Signals and Communication Technology.

Martin, G. L. (1989). The utility of speech input in user-computer interfaces. International Journal Man-Machine Studies, 30(4), 355–375.

McNeill, D. (1992). *Hand and mind: What gestures reveal about thought.* Chicago, IL: University of Chicago Press.

Nakatoh, Y., Kuwano, H., Kanamori, T., & Hoshimi, M. (2007). Speech recognition interface system for digital TV control. *Acoustical Science and Technology*, 28(3) (special issue on applied systems), pp. 165–171.

Obrist, M., Bernhaupt, R., & Tscheligi, M. (2008). Interactive TV for the home: An ethnographic study on users' requirements and experiences. *International Journal of Human-Computer Interaction*, 24(2), 174–196.

Oksman, V., Noppari, E., Tammela, A., Mkinen, M., & Ollikainen, V. (2007). Mobile TV in everyday life contexts individual entertainment or shared experiences? In P. Cesar, K. Chorianopou-los, & J. F. Jensen (Eds.), *Interactive TV: A shared experience. 5th Conference on Interactive Television, EuroITV 2007, LNCS 4471, Springer-Verlag*, pp. 215–225.

Pinhanez, C., Davis, J., Intille, S., Johnson, M., Wilson, A., Bobick, A., & Blumberg, B. (2000). Physically interactive story environments. *IBM Systems Journal*, 29(3/4), pp. 438–455.

Portolan, N., Nael, M., Renoullin, J. L., & Naudin, S. (1999). Will we speak to our TV remote control in the future? In *Proceedings of the HFT'99 Conference.*

Robertson, S., Wharton, C., Ashworth, C., & Franzke, M. (1996). Dual device user interface design: PDAs and interactive television. In *Proceedings of the SIGCHI Conference on Human Factors in Computing Systems: Common Ground, CHI '96, ACM, New York*, pp. 79–86.

Roibs, A. C., Sala, R., Syed Ahmad, S. N. A., & Rahman, M. (2005). Beyond the remote control: Going the extra mile to enhance iTV access via mobile devices & humanizing navigation experience for those with special needs. In *Proceedings of 3th Conference on Interactive Television, EuroIT.*

Tahir, M., Baily, G., & Lecolinet, E. (2007). ARemote: A tangible interface for selecting TV channels. In *Proceedings of the 17th Annual Conference on Artificial Reality and Telexistence, ICAT'07, ACM Press*, pp. 298–299.

Tscheligi, M., Obrist, M., & Lugmayr, A. (Eds.) (2008). *Changing television environments.* EuroITV 2008, LNCS 5066, Springer-Verlag.

Van Laerhoven, K., Villar, N., Schmidt, A., Kortuem, G., & Gellersen, H. (2003). Using an autonomous cube for basic navigation and input. In *Proceedings of the 5th International Conference on Multimodal Interfaces, ICMI'03, ACM Press, New York*, pp. 203–210.

Vangenck, M., Jacobs, A., Lievens, B., Vanhengel, E., & Pierson, J. (2008). Does mobile television challenge the dimension of viewing television? An explorative research on time, place and social context of the use of mobile television content. In M. Tscheligi, M. Obrist, A. Lugmayr (Eds.), *Changing television environments* (pp. 122–127). EuroITV 2008, LNCS 5066, Springer-Verlag.

Vatavu, R. D., & Pentiuc, S. G. (2009). Multi-level representation of gesture as command for human computer interaction. Computing and Informatics, Slovak Academy of Sciences, Bratislava, accepted, to appear in 2009

Vatavu, R. D., & Pentiuc, S. G. (2008). Interactive coffee tables: Interfacing TV within an intuitive, fun and shared experience. In M. Tscheligi, M. Obrist, & A. Lugmayr (Eds.), *Changing television environments* (pp. 183–187). *6th Conf. on Interactive Television, EuroITV 2008, LNCS 5066, Springer-Verlag.*

Wilson, A. D. (2006). Robust computer vision-based detection of pinching for one and two-handed gesture input. In *Proceedings of the 19th Annual ACM Symposium on User interface Software and Technology* (Montreux, Switzerland, October 15–18, 2006), *ACM, New York*, pp. 225–258.

Wittenburg, K., Lanning, T., Schwenke, D., Shubin, H., & Vetro, A. (2006). The prospects for unrestricted speech input for TV content search. In *Proceedings of the Working Conference on Advanced Visual interfaces* (Venezia, Italy, May 23–26, 2006), *AVI '06. ACM, New York*, pp. 352–359.

Part IV
Understanding the Context: Data Gathering, Requirements and Evaluation Methodologies

Content for Mobile Television: Issues Regarding a New Mass Medium Within Today's ICT Environment

Dimitri Schuurman , Lieven De Marez, and Tom Evens

Abstract The industries of mobile and television technologies are heading toward convergence in the shape of mobile television. Content is assumed to be a main key factor for the success of this ICT innovation as a possible new mass medium. As most trials to date tend to be sponsored by strategic stakeholders and have a technology-driven approach, we aimed for a more user-centric research methodology within MADUF, Flanders' mobile TV trial. To this end, a meta-analysis on mobile TV user studies was carried out, a panel of 35 experts was surveyed and a user study with 405 respondents was conducted. Within this chapter, we present a SWOT-analysis for possible content on mobile TV, based on all previous research results.

Introduction: Mobile Television, Another Convergence Exponent

Mobile and television technologies are probably among the most prominent industries in the converging Information and Communication Technology (ICT) environment today (Ahonen & O'Reilly 2007: 75–93). Mobiles have already converged with cameras, radios, mp3, personal digital assistants (PDA) and gaming technologies, and digitalization has also brought the realm of TV into new territories with the advent of IPTV (Internet Protocol Television) and digital television. Today, many providers believe that television itself is headed for convergence with mobile technology and services.

Mobile manufacturers and service providers have recently had to cope with saturating markets. Because many countries in Asia and Europe have reached a mobile subscription rate close to (or even over) 100% penetration (Netsize 2007: 10), mobile operators are entering a new phase in which not only the number of new subscribers is low, but the average revenue per user (ARPU) is also declining

D. Schuurman, L. De Marez, and T. Evens
MICT, Ghent University, Korte Meer 7-9-11, 9000 Gent, BELGIUM

A. Marcus et al. (eds.), *Mobile TV: Customizing Content and Experience*,
Human-Computer Interaction Series, DOI 10.1007/978-1-84882-701-1_13,
© Springer-Verlag London Limited 2010

(Andersson 2005: 3). Operators therefore need to find new sources of revenue. Many operators[1] are counting on broadcasting mobile TV becoming their newest "cash-cow" and providing an opportunity to create a new kind of "mobile multimedia." This evolution would enable the operators to increase the ARPU by opening up the market potential of media industries (Södergard 2003: 15; van den Dam 2006: 1; Urban 2007: 48).

On the other hand, traditional television business models are challenged by the fragmentation of public, and proliferation of new, video and TV broadcasting technologies. For the television industry, mobile television would mean a new distribution channel for their content (Urban 2007: 48) and the possibility of reaching new audiences (Södergård 2003: 3) and the traditional evening peak-time audience at other times of the day (Digitag 2005: 10).

Clearly, the convergence of mobile services and television might be considered the "logical next step." One illustration of the providers' belief in mobile television as the new exponent of convergent media is the recent proliferation of trials and commercial rollouts. One of the first commercial trials took place in Berlin as early as 2004. From 2005 onwards, most European countries followed this example. Some of these trials included user and market research,[2] but most focused only on testing transmission technology.[3] Technology-oriented mobile television trials also occurred outside Europe, again testing transmission protocols. In Belgium, a pilot-project was started in 2006[4]: "Maximizing DVB-H Usage in Flanders" (MADUF).

Despite the common-sense necessity of more user-centric research and development, the user is still too much overlooked in today's mobile television trials. Because content was "king," or at least was one of the most important determinants in the success or failure of many other new media technologies such as HDTV, SACD, CD-I, WAP, and so on (Bouwman et al. 1994: 31; Wallace 1999: 25), content will undoubtedly also be a decisive factor in the success of mobile television. However, most of the trials so far lack research into what makes up compelling mobile content, or at least what kind of content will be needed for a successful introduction of mobile television. In other words, the current wave of trials is not sufficiently user-centric. When preparing for the MADUF Flemish mobile TV trial, we aimed at a solid basis for a more user- and content-centric approach by incorporating a meta-analysis of the trial results and the results from an expert panel and user survey.

---

[1] For example, Vodafone, Telefonica, Orange, Bouyges, SFR, etc.

[2] Finland: Finnish mobile TV pilot group (2005); Holland: Konijnenberg (2006); Spain: Mestre (2006); France: Médiamétrie (2006); UK: Mason (2006)

[3] For example, Rai Turin trial, Italy: Morello (2006); France, TDF trial: Pauchon (2006).

[4] This project was carried out under the wing of the IBBT and included some of the most important media and telecommunications companies in Flanders (e.g., Telenet, Belgacom, VRT, and Siemens). The data in this paper are the result of research we conducted in this project. The MADUF project studied the possibilities of mobile television using DVB-H technology and ran from January 2006 to March 2008.

Mobile Television

Few people will have difficulty understanding the "mobile television" concept that represents the convergence of two of the most widespread technologies. Television is literally going mobile: detaching itself from a fixed location, consumable at any time and place on a mobile device (Södergård 2003: 15), thus enabling a true personalization of the viewing experience (van den Dam 2006: 2). Mobile television had of course already existed as a rather marginal technology based on analog terrestrial transmission. Technological innovations now offer digital image quality and the possibility of reception on a consumer device that people always tend to carry with them: their mobile phone. These two benefits mean mobile television can be considered as a new and innovative technology, whereas the analog mobile television should be seen as an early predecessor.

There are essentially three ways in which live streams and on-demand programs can be delivered to mobile handsets. The first is via the mobile network itself (e.g., UMTS), secondly, by satellite (e.g., DBS), and thirdly, by terrestrial digital TV (e.g., DVB-H[5], DMB, etc.). Due to issues concerning bandwidth and high costs (Feldmann 2005: 65–68; Carey 2006: 123) the first option has in many cases ceased to be viable, at least in terms of live streaming. DBS television reception is a technology used for moving vehicles such as ships, trains, aircraft, and cars, but it is not suitable for reception on a small mobile device (cf. Hules et al. 2005; Lee et al. 2003; Price 2003; Wang & Winters 2004). In the range of mobile terrestrial digital TV on offer, various competing technologies (DVB-H, T-DMB, MediaFlo, etc.) have emerged and are contending for commercial use.[6] The introduction of commercial broadcast services, in Italy for example, seems to be the precursor to a broader development in this field (Strohmeier 2006: 4). Research conducted by Informa (2005) predicts that DVB-H will be the leading technology for mobile television. Most European trials made use of DVB-H technology, and this is also the chosen transmission technology for the Flemish MADUF trial.

Before elaborating on mobile television (broadcast), it seems appropriate to put "mobile television" in context. Some authors (Carey 2006; Feldmann 2005; Goggin 2006) consider mobile television to be one of the many mobile services. Vesa (2005: 6) provides a useful distinction between the various typologies of mobile services, each with its own basis for categorization, and uses them to formulate a typology of mobile services consisting of three broad categories of services: conversation, content services, and data access. The first is subdivided into mobile voice (e.g., voice calls, push-to-talk) and person-to-person messaging (i.e., non-voice conversation services such as SMS, MMS, e-mail, chat, and instant messaging).

---

[5] DVB-H is the mobile extension of the DVB-T transmission protocol

[6] For more technical information regarding these technologies, we can recommend the following papers: Sieber & Weck (2004); Kornfeld & Reimers (2005); Scheide (2005); Faria (2005); Pekowsky & Maalej (2005)

The second, mobile content services, includes SMS- and MMS-based content services, browser-based content services, and downloadable applications. The third category is called mobile data access, and refers to various kinds of transfer methods available for the use of the mobile services described in the two previous categories (e.g., GSM data, GPRS, CDMA, EDGE, UMTS, etc.) (ibid. 7–8). As this typology does not mention any sort of mobile TV, we can place it both in the second category (i.e., mobile TV as a content service) and in the third category, mobile data access. In the latter case we refer to the technological aspects of mobile broadcast TV (e.g., technologies such as DVB-H, DBMS, MediaFLO, etc.).

Other authors see mobile television as "television going mobile." From this perspective, mobile television becomes more than just a mobile service: it is regarded as a new and distinct mass medium. Wood (2006) distinguishes five general reasons why one consumes media: identity-building, sharing an experience with others, entertainment, information, and multitasking. He states that each of these "reasons" should be fulfilled in order to achieve a successful mass medium. Orgad (2005) mentions the following six benefits for mobile TV: (1) flexibility, independence and a sense of security, and "belonging"; (2) enhanced personal and intimate viewing experience; (3) seeking time and location-sensitive information; (4) filling empty time; (5) do-it-yourself – creating personal content; and (6) mobile intimacy, networking, fandom, and enhancing one's intimate relationships. In this view, it can be argued that mobile TV should be considered as a new mass medium with its own content and usage modes. Ahonen & O'Reilly (2007: 80–86) explicitly state that mobile television should be seen as the seventh mass medium, with capabilities that exceed the other six.[7]

Importance of Content

The first requirement for a successful technology is that it functions well. This explains the focus on performance in technological development processes and the majority of mobile TV trials, and the lack of user-centric research and range of content. As is the case with most disruptive technologies, the first consideration for mobile broadcast TV has to be technological. Indeed, a new technology is doomed to fail if it cannot deliver a stable and user-friendly product (i.e., easy to learn and easy to use). For mobile TV, this turned out well in many of the trials whose sole purpose was to test the feasibility of the chosen technology and to assess whether "Mobile TV could be done" (Carlsson & Walden 2007). In most cases, the content shown on the available channels was not subject to research of any kind, but simply provided some existing linear TV channels.

---

[7] The six other mass media, according to Ahonen & O'Reilly, are: print, recording, cinema, radio, TV, and Internet

However, the success of a new technology such as mobile TV ultimately depends on more than the technological factor alone. Nolan and Keen (2005) distinguish several other factors such as the competition between rival standards, the absence of regulatory frameworks, and the absence of clear-cut spectrum allocation (particularly in Europe). Even when these are taken into account, we still confine ourselves to the critical criteria for success, on the macro level of supplier-related factors.

Hence, it is of the utmost importance that new technologies also take account of the user-centered factors on a micro level. Failures of such recent technologies as WAP and CD-I and the "battle of standards" for VCR (VHS vs Betamax) or the latest generation of DVDs (HD-DVD vs BluRay), show that the availability of desirable content has possibly become one of the most crucial factors in the success of a new technology (Wallace 1999). The adage "content is king" thus still prevails, especially in such an essentially top-down medium as television.

Content is thus a major issue that must be tackled in order to ensure a user-centric product range for mobile television, but this question only arises when the "chicken and the egg" problem is resolved (Bouwman & Christoffersen 1992: 169; Bouwman et al. 2002: 102–103). Initially, when they are introduced, many innovations face the problem of the availability of suitable and attractive content. Content producers are not willing to invest in often expensive new content (e.g., HDTV) while there is still no certainty of a large enough consumer base. On the other side of the coin, the consumer hesitates about adopting the new technology if he is unsure whether there will be enough satisfactory content available. If these two processes coexist, the result is that media suppliers are not willing to take any risks because of the slow uptake of the new technology, while the absence of attractive content provides the consumer with a good reason not to adopt the new technology.

In this article we shall try to offer the reader a counterweight to the technology-centric view of mobile television (trials), and shall concentrate on the different types of content and the strategies suppliers can offer if they want to reach as large an audience as possible.

Content Going Mobile

To explain why the media and content industries are eyeing the mobile channel, Andersson (2005: 9) distinguishes three main drivers.

Firstly, there is the drive to go digital and, more generally, the fact that the world is becoming connected. This endeavor can be seen from two angles: not only from that of the supply side (a "push" view) but also from that of the demanding consumer (pull). The latter can be ascribed to the desire of contemporary consumers to receive "any content, always, anywhere and anyhow." This global trend toward digitalization has necessitated all kinds of content producers to adapt their business models and to broaden their range. However, while Andersson confines this idea solely to the Internet, we need to acknowledge the bigger picture. The challenge is to meet the customer's need to obtain media content not only from the Internet, as Andersson contends, but also from other and newer channels such as mobile media.

This has resulted in a converging ICT environment where each individual service is offered by various technologies (De Marez & Paulussen 2006: 235). This digitalization has resulted in a shift from the traditional layer model of ICT to a so-called vertically intertwined layer model (Felder & Liu 1999: 111; Van Dijk 1999: 9). The traditional layer model describes the relationship between (1) the physical infrastructure, (2) the services that transport the signals via the physical infrastructure from sender to receiver, (3) the services end-users consume, and (4) the end-user (Bouwman et al. 2002: 54). Whereas in a traditional layer model every service had its corresponding infrastructure and transport service, thus clearly resulting in vertical integration, digitalization has resulted in an ecosystem where one can no longer perceive a direct link between "medium" and "type of information." With this in mind it is only logical that content providers try to make their audiovisual content available on as many platforms as possible and thus guarantee a wide audience. Traditional TV has already migrated to DTV and IPTV, which freed the viewing experience from the constraints of "time." With the advent of mobile TV, watching TV is now also becoming dissociated from "place" and the pursuit of convergence seems almost to have been achieved.

According to Andersson (2005: 10), the second driver of mobile content is the need for interactivity. Kronlund (2006) distinguishes three reasons why interactivity is such an important feature of mobile TV for the various media players, including the regular consumer. First of all, interactivity is an appropriate stimulator of mobile TV use for the average consumer (cf. also Orgad 2006). The appeal of interactivity lies in the additional services that can be accessed, such as shopping by mobile TV or playing along with a program. Because the mobile phone itself is a communication device, a feedback channel is already at hand (Steinbock 2005). Mobile programs could be adapted to make use of these communication possibilities. By giving the consumer the opportunity to participate actively, the system will be used for a longer period. Secondly, interactivity thus means additional traffic and revenues for operators and improved positioning with regard to the TV industry and content providers (Johansen 2006). Thirdly, for content suppliers and aggregators, interactivity can enhance the "stickiness" of their program formats, which in turn is favorable to their advertising revenues.

Initially, interactivity can be introduced relatively simply: voting by means of a simple SMS message. Later, fully interactive program formats can be worked out, which in turn can generate additional revenue. These extra earnings may prove vital to traditional telecom operators who risk losing their market share due to dwindling voice revenues because their customers are watching TV on their mobile instead of calling or texting. The main challenge will be the development of mobile content formats that make use of this interactivity in a way that is attractive to the end-user.

The third driver distinguished by Andersson (2005: 10) is the need for personalization and marketing. Evolving on the personalizing trend, with the use of personal ringtones and wallpapers as the most obvious result, mobile TV fits into the trend toward demarcating a personal territory within the public sphere (cf. also Orgad 2006).

Since different forms of advertising are a significant part of the general content range, advertising cannot be neglected when analyzing mobile content. It is expected that advertising will be an important source of revenue alongside subscriptions and a means to make content cheaper for the end-user. Mobile TV offers clear benefits to advertisers, as customers can even be reached when they are on the move. However, the scope of this paper does not permit us to go into further detail on the subject of advertising.

Three Different Content Paths

In the remainder of this paper, we shall draw up a typology of mobile TV content, which will be further elaborated on in terms of content types and program formats on the basis of the literature and our empirical research.

Generally speaking, we can distinguish three possible ways of offering consumers mobile TV. Firstly, regular television images (i.e., linear programming) can be shown by means of a mobile device. Secondly, the viewer can be offered TV content tailor-made for his mobile. This can then be divided into two categories. When the content derives from existing TV programs, we speak of repurposed content. When entirely new content is generated for mobile viewing, we speak of mobile-specific content.

Simulcasting Linear TV

The easiest, and therefore also the least expensive, way of providing content for mobile TV is by transmitting a regular linear TV feed. This technique also is called retransmission, simulcasting, or migrated content (Ok 2005; Orgad 2006). It suffices to reformat the feeds of existing TV channels and to compress them. These channels are transferred as a whole to the mobile medium, without altering the content. Here, the difference between regular TV and mobile TV is limited to two aspects.

Firstly and rather obviously, customers can see TV on the go, instead of actively "going to" the information (Groebel 2006). This place-shifting of familiar TV content is attractive to the end-user, as he already "knows" the content. As was the case in the Finnish mobile TV trial, viewers seem primarily attracted by well-known brands and programs (Finnish Mobile TV Pilot Group 2005).

Secondly, there is the difference in screen size (Orgad 2006). This brings us to the biggest disadvantage of linear transmission: the fact that the programs are made for a large screen. The viewing comfort on a small portable screen is much less.

The fact that end-users watch linear programs on a less comfortable screen is what van den Dam (2005) calls the "must see" function for mobile television: die-hard fans of a particular TV show want to watch "their" show at any cost, even if it means lower quality.

Hence, it is doubtful that a mere simulcast will be a good strategy. This would only allow a degree of place-shifting of the regular TV experience, and only in the absence of a regular TV set. Mobile television remains nothing more than a substitute for the regular TV viewing experience.

However, according to the research firm A.T. Kearney, watching linear TV on phones is exactly what users want to do. A.T. Kearney polled consumers on three continents. When presented with content options ranging from unique video composed specifically for handsets, to repurposed content and to basic TV streaming, consumers overwhelmingly opted for what was familiar, choosing the brands and programming they see on their TV (Fitchard 2005). Andrew Cole, head of A.T. Kearney's telecom and media practice, commented: "The mass media content that you and I love is what people want to see on their phones. They essentially want to see their cable TV channels on their handsets. They want the familiar."

When the place-shifting of familiar (linear) content is the only benefit of mobile TV, it is to be considered as no more than another mobile service (cf. supra). However, this reaction can be perfectly explained by referring to the seminal Marshall McLuhan (1964). As early as the 1960s he proposed the following: "The content of a new medium is an old medium." Back then, he already had realized that when a new medium is introduced, it will always be used in the same way as an older, already familiar medium. The new possibilities of a medium will not at first be recognized or acknowledged. Metaphorically speaking, we are heading for the future looking backwards (de Boer & Brennecke 1995: 92). For example, when TV was first introduced, it was thought of and used as radio with pictures or as an outlet for films. Other interpretations of the concept of television (i.e., medium-specific programs), were not developed until later. McLuhan (1964) used another cogent metaphor: the horseless carriage syndrome. The new medium is considered in terms of the old medium, just as the car was seen as a carriage, but without a horse. In the case of mobile TV, this means that if mobile TV develops into a new mass medium, content that exploits the full possibilities of the new medium will follow. Merely simulcasting linear television cannot suffice.

Repurposed TV

In the case of repurposed mobile TV, existing content is recycled for the mobile medium with minimal adaptation. So in our definition the repurposing is limited to formal and technical factors. In other words, repurposed programs basically have the same content as their regular TV counterparts but are split up into smaller segments or are cropped to better suit the smaller screens of mobile devices. In the latter case, there is software that separates out the foreground and background. The part of the screen identified as "background" is reduced in pixels to save bandwidth. The image is also reduced in size by zooming in on the areas identified as "foreground" (Yoshida 2006). A good example is a newscast split up into individual items where the image zooms in on the reporter's head.

Because mobile TV is still in its infancy, this is the path many mobile TV suppliers are inclined to follow. The biggest advantage of repurposing existing content is that it is better suited for mobile viewing. Nolan & Keen (2005: 68) even say that one of the main conclusions of early trials and studies is that there is a need to repurposing broadcast television. Repurposing existing TV content thus combines the best of both worlds: it recycles well-known brands with proven quality, and it adds this to a better viewing experience that results from the adaptations to the form the content appears in (e.g., cropping screen size, etc.).

These adaptations, although only in form, imply a certain cost, but nonetheless remain a lot cheaper than developing original mobile-specific content: "Made-for-mobile video content can cost several hundred thousand US dollars per series. ... Repurposing content – editing down existing shows to fit the mobile screen – is significantly cheaper. A lot of companies use interns to do the editing, and costs are about US$50 per minute at the low end and US$500 per minute at the highest" (Coffman & Schulze 2006).

It is striking that some authors (Ahonen 2006; Mittermayr 2006; Orgad 2006) consider the repurposing of existing content to be an intermediate phase in anticipation of the moment when enough mobile programming will be made. Again, we can refer to McLuhan's ideas on new media and their initially limited content. However, in this respect it is another aspect that dominates. As the number of mobile TV viewers is still rather limited, it is too early to invest in one specific type of content, because it is still unknown which type will attract the most viewers. The content suppliers prefer to play it safe and rely on content derived from existing brands and concepts. Only when there is more clarity about the potential market for the technology and the desired content, can programs be adjusted to these markets. However, waiting to see which way the wind blows can prove risky. Content producers wait to distribute mobile formats until they are certain about the future market potential, but in the meantime potential customers postpone the purchase of a mobile device as long as they are not sure about what is on offer.

Mobile-Specific Content

Unlike the two previous categories, the third category of content adapts to all the requirements of the new medium, formally and technically as well as in terms of content. Advocates of mobile-specific content say that this type of content is a necessary final step in the evolution of mobile television. The smaller screen, shorter usage duration, noisier usage environment and so on should eventually lead to a new visual grammar, expressed in mobile-specific content (Orgad 2006).

Besides the obvious disadvantage of the high production cost inherent to brand-new content, the lack of existing brands can prove another hindrance to a broad content range (cf. the previously mentioned challenge of which comes first, content or customers). Another possible limiting factor is that a lot of content suppliers show anticipatory behavior when it comes to new content for mobile devices due to the remaining lack of clarity in business models. After all, it is important to know who is entitled to the revenue flows. Currently, it seems that only mobile service operators are making money out of mobile TV. Traditionally, these groups are not very keen on redistributing their revenues to other parties such as content providers. It is doubtful that this attitude will remain justifiable. Once the trials are finalized and turned into full commercial use, a fair description of the different roles and matching revenue flows will be necessary (Hart & Milanesi 2006). However, early mobile TV services have already shown that content specifically designed, tailored, or easily repurposed for the mobile TV space is particularly attractive to consumers (ibid. 68). They mention short-form programs such as rolling news, 30-min documentaries/programs, and "Mobisodes."[8] They further argue that there is an especial need for content which can serve cyclical "snacking" behavior. They think that nomadic users will dip in and out of the service every now and then throughout the day.

We will devote some attention to one type of mobile-specific content: user-generated content (UGC). Holt (2006) distinguishes three kinds of user-generated content: laissez-faire, gatekeeper, and community content. The first is the basic form of UGC where everything within the legal guidelines is shared with everybody. In the second type of UGC a gatekeeper is the intermediate factor between the content creator and viewer and exerts some editorial power. He will act as a sort of moderator and the more intensively and thoroughly he operates, the better the quality of the program (Portu 2006). According to Holt (2006) the two first types of UGC are granted only a short life. This kind of user-generated content will not go beyond what he calls "girls lifting their sweaters and boys lighting their farts." It is doubtful that the public will be enthralled with this kind of content for very long. A brighter future may then be in store for a third type of user-generated content called community UGC. This type of content requires more commitment from the user, automatically resulting in more compelling content. A nice example of community UGC is SeeMeTV. This initiative by the British mobile operator Three is conceived as a "customer-content channel." Users upload their own videos to a mobile portal, where other users can watch these videos for a small charge (Goggin 2006). Uploaders are paid for each video other users watch.

Case Study: Flanders

As stated above, content is an important factor in mobile TV. This applies when estimating the potential adoption of mobile TV as well as when tackling the issue of who makes the first move, which content suppliers have to deal with. This paper therefore repeats empirical research on these content-related issues that

---

[8] Mobile spin-offs from familiar linear TV series (e.g., 24, Lost, etc.)

was conducted as part of the Flemish mobile TV trial. We also conducted empirical research for this purpose. Our main research questions can be summarized as follows:

- What are the strengths and weaknesses of general (linear) content types for mobile TV?
- What opportunities and threats can be identified for repurposed and mobile-specific content?
- How do these strengths, weaknesses, opportunities, and threats compare to the three main drivers identified for mobile TV-content: place-shifting, interactivity, and personalization?

To answer these questions, we followed a threefold research methodology, involving the following three steps:

1. A meta-analysis of **user studies**, conducted within various **mobile television trials**.
2. **Expert panel survey**: initial contacts with experts in the field showed that in the current early stage of the product life cycle, a lot of information that is not yet available in official reports can be obtained from personal conversations. To this end, a panel of mobile television experts[9] was put together. About half the experts were questioned face-to-face,[10] while the remainder were questioned in an online panel survey. The questionnaire was identical in the two cases. Thirty-five international experts eventually agreed to take part in the survey.[11]
3. The findings from the previous two research stages provided us with the necessary input to construct a **user survey**. In the course of a month, a representative sample of 405 Flemish people was surveyed. The respondents were asked about the content types they would like to see on mobile television. They also had to give a score to a set of 12 specific content formats.

All this enabled us to compare and analyze information and results gathered from previous trials, an expert panel, and a user survey.

---

[9] The expert panel consisted of two types of experts: people who worked for a company or organization that participated directly in a mobile TV trial (trial experts) and a number of experts who were not involved directly in a mobile TV trial, but had proven their expertise by recent publications on mobile TV (non-trial experts).

[10] Some of them were visited, while others were met at conferences (e.g., IBC 2006, Amsterdam and Mobile Entertainment Market 2006, London)

[11] Firstly, the experts were asked to compose a top and bottom five of the most and least promising content types for mobile television. They were also asked to elaborate upon the strengths and weaknesses of the content types at hand. Finally, the experts were asked about the opportunities and threats of the different content types when used as repurposed or mobile-specific content.

Results

General Content Types

Trial results (Finnish Mobile TV Pilot Group 2005; Mason 2006; Mestre 2007; Médiamétrie 2006) point out that news, soaps,[12] and sports are clear winners in every country. This "**content triumvirate**" appears to have a universal appeal among mobile television viewers, satisfying the need for information (news) as well as entertainment (soaps) and benefiting from the "anytime, anywhere" live aspect (sports). Music was very popular in the UK and in France, but scored much less in Finland and Spain. This content type is closely associated with younger viewers, and has a less universal appeal than the "triumvirate." A bright future is also predicted for adult content on mobile TV (Holt 2006), but lack of this content type in the trials (except for The Netherlands, cf. Konijnenberg 2006) provides no evidence to support this claim.

In our expert survey, all participants were given a list of 16 content types. They were asked to rank the five most promising (MP) content types for mobile television. Subsequently, they were asked to list the five least promising (LP) content types.[13] The highest-ranked content type was granted five points, the second four, and so on. The results can be found in the table below (Table 1).

Table 1 Most and least promising content according to the expert panel

MP genres	Score	LP genres	Score
1. News	120	1. Films	77
2. Sports	85	2. Documentary	59
3. Music	57	3. Discussion	44
4. Soap	41	4. Lifestyle	30
5. Adult	36	5. Children's programs	26
6. Cartoons	24	6. Gaming channels	24
7. Radio	20	7. UGC	21
8. Other entertainment	18	8. Radio	17
9. Reality	13	9. Reality	15
9. Lifestyle	13	10. Music	14
11. Gaming channels	10	11. Soaps	13
11. Children's programs	10	12. Cartoons	12
13. Documentary	6	13. Other entertainment	10
13. Films	6	14. Sports	7
15. Discussion	4	15. News	2
16. UGC	3	16. Adult	1

---

[12] We use the term "soaps" to indicate soaps and series

[13] By asking the experts to list a top five of the least promising content types, we also forced them to consider the weaknesses of the content types, which is necessary in order to arrive at a strengths-weaknesses-opportunities-threats (SWOT) analysis

Experts clearly regard **news** as the most promising content type for mobile television and consider a mobile-specific or at least repurposed format as the best way to serve the information needs of the consumer and benefit from the mobile medium. A looped format was often suggested (cf. also Orgad 2006; Carlsson & Walden 2007: 7–8). Experts see the appeal of **sports**, the second MP-content type, in the "live" aspect that can be experienced "anytime, anywhere." Most sports would benefit from repurposing because of the smaller screen. Experts explain the high score of **soaps** by referring to their loyal community of fans. Linear transmission would already be able to fulfill a considerable number of needs as it allows fans to watch their favorite soap "anytime, anywhere." However, repurposed content can create added value for the fans by establishing a synergy between mobile and regular television, for example by broadcasting summaries or extra content on mobile television, or by allowing user interaction.

According to the experts, the hegemony of the content triumvirate will be challenged by **music**. Music videos come in a short format that is suited for mobile consumption. They are very popular among youngsters, so linear transmission might work. This content type also lends itself perfectly to some kind of interactivity (voting, user discussion, etc.), as already demonstrated in the Berlin trial (cf. infra, Sattler 2006). Personalization could be achieved by offering artist-related ringtones, wallpapers, and other mobile phone utilities.

Experts consider **adult content** as a promising niche that might play an important role in the adoption process, as this content type benefits the most from the personal nature of the mobile TV medium. If some user-interactivity was added, Orgad's reason for use – "boosting love life" – (2006) could become a reality.

Programs that require too much attention or are too long (films, documentaries, and discussion programs) are clearly considered unsuitable for mobile television. Experts regard lifestyle programs as unpromising because of their laidback, "couch potato" nature. User-Generated Content (UGC) seems to be a content type that confuses experts. It gets the lowest ranking as MP content, but comes in only seventh as LP content. However, quite a few authors predict a bright future for UGC in mobile television (cf. Holt 2006; Ahonen & O'Reilly 2007: 85; Orgad 2006).

Experts are also polarized in the case of radio, with a seventh place as MP content and an eighth place as LP content.[14] Some experts indicate high potential for radio in DVB-H technology, even as a possible substitute for FM. However, other experts think that radio has nothing to do with mobile "television."

In the user survey, a broader range of program categories was used. The results of the most desired content types can be found in the table below (Table 2).

At first sight, the most eye-catching difference is the appearance of film in the top five. While experts think this is the least promising genre for mobile television, potential users indicate they are definitely interested in watching films on mobile television. This confirms the findings in some of the user trials (Lloyd et al. 2006;

---

[14]Radio was only available in 5 of the 11 trials from which data was used in this study

Table 2 Most promising content according to the user survey participants

MP genres	Score	MP genres	Score
1. News	6101	14. Live events	774
2. Series	1922	15. Lifestyle programs	758
3. Music	1864	16. Sports background	614
4. Film	1861	17. Reality shows	464
5. Soaps	1520	18. Daily life shows	442
6. Sports	1516	19. Children's programs	362
7. News background	1409	20. Visual radio	300
8. Quiz	1276	21. UGC	281
9. Documentary	1182	22. Show programs	266
10. Comedy	1165	23. Erotic programs	84
11. Talkshows	1116	24. Porn	82
12. Live sports	1040	25. Sex talkshows	72
13. Cartoon	949		

Mason 2006; Rauch & Geissler 2005; Sattler 2006; Kim 2006) that users might watch mobile television in longer sessions than initially expected.

In parallel with the opinion of the experts, music also ranks high among the users surveyed. Music can thus definitely be seen as a serious contender for the content triumvirate. It is also remarkable that sports news ranks only sixth. The low score for adult content, occupying the last three places, seems unrealistic. As some experts said during the open interviews, respondents tend to underreport their preference for this content type. Adult should definitely be regarded as a promising content type, but other methods of estimating the potential of this content type have to be found (such as logging the content watched in user trials, cf. Konijnenberg 2006).

Repurposed and Mobile-Specific Content

A meta-analysis of the trials and additional information provided by the trial experts revealed that hardly any repurposed or mobile-specific content was tested during these trials. In Finland, two UGC channels[15] were tested. They turned out to be a failure, in the absence of both content submitted and viewers. The Dutch trial included a glamour channel[16] with gossip and paparazzi items in a looped format (Konijnenberg 2006). The channel was slightly more successful, but the sparseness of additions to and refreshment of the program loop caused rapidly declining viewer rates. The trials in Oxford and Paris included two commercial channels

---

[15] Indicatv and Snaditv

[16] HollywoodTV

specialized in mobile-specific content such as short films and comedy clips.[17] The Berlin trial included an interactive music channel.[18]

In order to get a better view of possible repurposed and mobile-specific content, "wild ideas" revealed by the expert survey were used to compose a list of 12 repurposed or mobile-specific program formats (new or existing). Here is a brief introduction to these 12 formats:

1. Visual newsflash: When a specific news item is broadcast on TV (breaking news), a signal is given to the user so he or she can immediately watch the images (push news-service).
2. Traffic TV: A channel devoted to traffic problems, with images (some live) and information on traffic jams and other traffic-related subjects.
3. Visual radio: A radio station that provides additional visual information such as traffic updates, music-related information, live images from the studio, competitions, etc.
4. Event TV: A TV channel devoted to a specific event (e.g., a music festival, a major exhibition) with highlights, interviews with artists, information on the program, live images from the different stages, etc.
5. Mobile-specific film: Short films tailor-made for mobile television.
6. Sports highlights: The user is kept up to date on sporting events (e.g., a football game) by updates with game highlights.
7. Summaries: Summaries of soaps and series that can be watched when one has missed an episode or when one wants to refresh one's memory before watching a new episode.
8. Get close to…: A program that shows a day in the life of a music group with footage by a professional film crew and by the band itself. The viewer can interact with the band members by sending images or voting with the mobile device.
9. Mobisodes: Short programs based on well-known series (e.g., 24, Lost) and which feature new story lines, additional characters, etc.
10. Free channel overview: A free channel where famous faces give an overview of what is being broadcast on the other channels.
11. Soccer addicts: A program consisting of user-generated content presented and commented by a host.
12. Extra imagery: Extra content from well-known television shows (e.g., Big Brother, Temptation Island) that has not been broadcast before. This can include interviews with candidates, bloopers, etc.

Interest in these formats was measured on a five point interest scale[19] in the user survey. The results are shown in the table below, ranked from high to low (Table 3).

It is striking that only four items out of 12 show a mean score higher than the neutral value of 3.00. This means that the overall interest in repurposed and

---

[17] ShortsTV and SFR TV

[18] VIVA+ Get the Clip

[19] 1: not interested, 2: hardly interested, 3: neutral, 4: interested, 5: very interested.

Table 3 Repurposed and mobile-specific types according to users

Interest in repurposed and mobile-specific programs	
Visual newsflash	3.80
Traffic TV	3.27
Visual radio	3.08
Event TV	3.01
Mobile-specific film	2.98
Sport highlights	2.76
Summaries	2.66
Get close to...	2.30
Mobisodes	2.27
Free channel overview	2.25
Soccer addicts	2.14
Extra imagery	2.09

mobile-specific programs is quite low among the people surveyed. Clearly, the visual newsflash is most popular, followed by traffic TV. Visual radio and event TV score hardly any higher than the neutral 3.00. Mobile-specific film is the first "entertainment" format on the list, but even that scores less than the neutral score. Program formats associated with well-known "brands" such as summaries, mobisodes, and extra imagery show remarkably low scores. The UGC-format "Soccer addicts" is also quite sharply rejected by the people surveyed, as is the case with the mixed reality/UGC-show "Get close to ..."

These results show that the possible end-user sees the potential for mobile TV mostly as an informative medium, allowing the mobile TV user to get breaking news and traffic updates anytime, anywhere. In fact, both functions are quite closely associated with the concept of "visual radio," as breaking news and traffic updates are now mainly delivered by radio. In other words, the survey participants show most interest in mobile TV as a "visual radio" that offers up-to-date information anytime, anywhere, with the addition of images.

There is significantly less support for the idea of mobile TV as an addition to linear television. This may indicate that the end-user (in Flanders) sees mobile TV as radio with added images rather than as TV going mobile. However, more research on this subject is necessary.

Discussion

When analyzing the most wanted and watched content types for mobile TV, the content triumvirate of news, sports, and soaps seemed very popular in trials amongst experts and in our user survey. These three content types are able to satisfy the need for information/updates (news and sports) as well as the need for entertainment (soaps and sports). Music and adult content were identified as the two main alternatives to this triumvirate. Music seems to be able to allow mobile TV to be used as a background medium, while adult content benefits most from the fact that mobile TV is seen as a truly personal medium.

Experts regard prolonged content that demands attention and linear narrative content as less suited to mobile television, films being the most striking example. Nonetheless, our user study revealed that there is considerable interest in even longer content such as films. The prominent role that some authors (Holt 2006; Ahonen & O'Reilly 2007: 85; Orgad 2006) assign to UGC is clearly not top-of-mind in either the end-user or the mobile-TV experts surveyed. Even when UGC was proposed in the form of easily comprehensible formats ("Soccer addicts" and "Get close to") with links to popular regular content genres (sports and music), the survey participants remained largely uninterested. The failed experiment during the Finnish trial (cf. supra) also points in the same direction.

Based on our user survey, repurposed or mobile-specific content with an information value seems to have the greatest chance of success. The low scores of the program formats associated with linear TV programs emphasize the notion that mobile TV is considered more as radio with images than as television going mobile.

When taking into account all the information derived from our research, including the SWOT exercises done by the experts, we are able to distinguish some general tendencies that apply to mobile content in general. These can be summarized in a SWOT table. The "strengths" and "weaknesses" refer to existing linear content shown on a mobile screen, whereas the "opportunities" and "threats" indicate the possibilities for repurposed and mobile-specific content (Table 4).

One of the most obvious strengths is the fact that **mobile TV is an easy innovation concept** to understand, as most people are familiar with both TV and mobile technology, and one can access the familiar, linear content on a mobile device. The main benefit for the viewer lies in the fact that he can access the familiar linear content **live, anytime, anywhere**. One of the most recurring arguments is that it is best

Table 4 SWOT analysis of content for mobile TV

General SWOT	
Strengths	**Weaknesses**
Mobile TV is an easy concept	Not suited for small screen
Live anytime, anywhere	Long programs
Non-linear structure/clips	Demanding too much attention
Short programs/items	Begin-Middle-End (narration)
Auditive-dominant programs	No specific benefits
Opportunities	**Threats**
Short programs/items for time-killing	High production costs
Highlights/update function	Willingness to pay
Background medium/visual radio	Communication device
Personal device	Battery power
Extra material (behind the scenes)	Competition from other media
Interactivity/cross-media applications	

if this content is short: **short programs** or **item-based** programs from the linear offer should be best suited for mobile viewing. The same goes for programs that have a **non-linear structure**, such as music **clips**. The latter example also incorporates another strong point for the content of mobile TV: **audio-dominant programs**.

The most commonly given weakness for linear content on mobile TV is the fact that it is **not suited to a small screen. Long programs, programs demanding too much attention** and programs with a clear **Begin-Middle-End** structure are supposed to be especially uncomfortable to watch on a small, portable screen.

Last but not least, when linear programs only are transmitted, there are **no specific benefits** for the end-user apart from the place-shifting of familiar TV content.

The main opportunities can be split up according to the usage goals that can be fulfilled. **Short programs and items**, possibly in a looped format, seem best suited for **time-killing**. **Extra material** can be broadcast when the aim is to offer the consumer familiar **brands**. The **visual newsflash** format and other informative formats can serve as an **update function**. The **visual radio** concept seems best suited to allowing mobile TV to be used as a **background medium**.

Possibly one of the most characteristic opportunities for mobile TV is the fact that it is considered a very **personal device**. It can be assumed that adult content, adapted to the screen size, will be the content type that benefits the most from this personalization. Another widely acclaimed opportunity is the possible **interactivity** arising from the fact that the receiving device is a mobile phone, which also paves the way for **cross-media applications**. This last opportunity might lead to the most innovative formats, but apart from a few voting applications, hardly any content has been developed or tested in this respect.

The main threat for repurposed and mobile-specific content is the **high production costs** (cf. supra). This is largely connected to the fact that it is still an open question whether consumers will show any substantial **willingness to pay** to make up for the high costs.

Furthermore, the opportunity for interactivity may also be a threat for mobile TV. The mobile phone is still primarily a **communication device**, and too much interference by mobile TV of the normal communication functions should be avoided. This applies especially to the threat of **battery power**. When mobile TV consumes all the energy, the device cannot be used for its initial purpose: calling and texting.

The last identified threat is **competition** with **other media**. Mobile TV will have to offer some clear advantages when compared to the other media available, otherwise end-users will see no reason to adopt the new technology.

Conclusion

The literature on mobile TV revealed two main attitudes toward this new technology. Some considered it as merely another mobile service, where others saw mobile TV as a possible new medium. We elaborated on this distinction by looking at the content side of mobile TV, which resulted in a threefold typology of possible content paths: linear retransmission, repurposed content, and mobile-specific content.

If mobile TV were to offer nothing more than the content already available on the consumer's regular TV set, the only benefit for the end-user would be the place-shifting of regular TV content, and this with a substantial loss of viewing comfort. If this were the case for mobile TV, it might indeed be seen as no more than another mobile service. However, content that includes repurposed and mobile-specific content would enable mobile TV to carve out its own niche as a new and distinct medium.

What this content should look like is still subject to much discussion. In the current study, we carried out a meta-analysis of user trials, surveyed a panel of experts in the field of mobile television and carried out a representative user study. However, the results should not be seen as decisive, but rather as an exploratory starting point for more user-centric research, which in our opinion is "key" for successful ICT innovations.

Both experts and users tend to agree that linear content should be an essential part of the content. Overall, the content triumvirate of news, sports, and soaps seems indispensable. Music and adult content seem to have sufficient strong points for mobile viewing. In the case of repurposed and mobile-specific content, the user study revealed that mobile TV is seen more as an extension of radio than as "TV going mobile." Users tend to prefer informative content formats that have more in common with radio to content formats based on linear TV programs.

However, many issues remain unresolved. It remains unclear how repurposing has to be done and how one can make appealing mobile-specific content. Thorough scientific research with a user-centric approach seems to be the path to follow. Despite the limitations of our own research, we have tried to pave the way for this kind of research by providing a theoretically built framework for a typology of (mobile) content. This should enable further investigation on the subject of mobile television and its content.

References

Ahonen, T. (2006). "Tomi Ahonen says it's time to grasp mobile's hidden power," *Mobile Communications Europe*, URL (consulted June 2006), from http://app.adestra.com/accounts/tfinf_telecoms_media/files/projects/project_224/MCE424.pdf

Ahonen, T., & O'Reilly, J. (2007). *Digital Korea*. London: Futuretext.

Andersson, C. (2005). *Mobile media and applications, from concept to cash: Successful service creation and launch*. Chichester: Wiley.

Bouwman, H., & Christoffersen, M. (1992). *Relaunching videotex*. Dordrecht/Boston/London: Kluwer.

Bouwman, H., Hammersma, M., & Peeters, A. (1994). CD-I, marktkansen en belemmeringen. *Enige noties betreffende de mogelijke acceptatie van CD-I, Massacommunicatie, 22*(1), 27–40.

Bouwman, H., Van Dijk, J., Van den Hooff, B., & Van De Wijgaert, L. (2002). *ICT in organisaties. Adoptie, implementatie, gebruik en effecten*. Amsterdam: Boom.

Carey, J. (2006). Contents and services for next generation wireless networks. In J. Groebel, E. M. Noam & V. Feldman (Eds.), *Mobile media: Content and services for wireless communications* (pp. 115–130). Mahwah, NJ: Lawrence Erlbaum.

Carlsson, C., & Walden, P. (2007). *Mobile TV – To Live or Die by Content.* Paper presented at the 40th Annual International Conference on System Sciences (HICSS'07), Hawaii.

Coffman, C., & Schulze, J. (2006). *Getting into mobile TV and video: Financing, producing and distributing TV and video content.* London: Informa Telecoms & Media.

De Boer, C. & Brennecke, S. (1995). *Media en publiek : theorieën over media-impact.* Amsterdam: Boom.

De Marez, L., & Paulussen, S. (2006). De internationale ICT-sector. De informatiesamenleving is een convergentiesamenleving. In D. Biltereyst (Ed.), *Internationale communicatie.* Ghent: Academia Press.

Digitag. (2005). *Television on a handheld receiver – broadcasting with DVB-H,* from http://www. digitag.org/DTTResources/DVBHandbook.pdf

Faria, G. (2005). *DVB-H: Digital TV in the hands!* White paper, Teamcast.

Felder, S., & Liu, P.-W. (1999). New Pricing Models in the Context of Convergence. *Communications & Strategies, 34* (2), 109–133.

Feldmann, V. (2005). *Leveraging mobile media: Cross-media strategy and innovation policy for mobile media communication.* Physica-Verlag: New York.

Finnish mobile TV pilot group. (2005). *Finnish Mobile TV: key results on the Finnish DVB-H trial.* Presentation.

Fitchard, K. (2005). *TV wars go wireless.* Telephony, 246(18), 24–27.

Forum, London, October 30, 2006.

Goggin, G. (2006). *Cell phone culture: Mobile technology in everyday life.* New York: Routledge.

Groebel, J. (2006). Mobile mass media: A new age of consumers, business, and society? In J. Groebel, E. M. Noam, & V. Feldman (Eds.), *Mobile media: Content and services for wireless communications* (pp. 239–252). Mahwah: Lawrence Erlbaum.

Hart, T., & Milanesi, C. (2006). Mobile TV: Beyond the Hype, from http://www.gartner.com/teleconferences/attributes/attr_151877_115.pdf

Holt, M. (2006). UGC: The Third way [Electronic Version]. *Telecoms.com.* Retrieved 21/03/07 from http://www.telecoms.com/itmgcontent/tcoms/expertview/articles/20017355677.html.

Hules, F., Streelman, G., & Yen, H. (2005). A direct broadcast satellite reception system for automotive OEMs *IEEE Antennas and Propagation Society International Symposium (IEEE Cat. No. 05CH37629), 1B,* 80–83.

Johansen, T. (2006). Mobile TV: The business model – talking pictures. *European Communications,* (summer), 16–18.

Kim, H. (2006). T-DMB Service of Korea. Presented on Mobile Content Industry.

Konijnenberg, G. J. (2006). MIPTV Cannes 2006: Innovative mobile TV. Presentation on MIPTV Cannes, April 7.

Kornfeld, M., & Reimers, U. (2005). *DVB-H – the emerging standard for mobile data communication* [EBU Technical Review, January 2005].

Kronlund, J. (2006). Interactivity in mobile TV, assessing the market impact of DVB-H successful strategies for the launch & roll-out of mobile broadcast. London.

Lee, J. M., Choi, W. K.; Pyo, C. S., & Choi, J. I. (2003). Ku-band active array antenna for mobile DBS reception. *9th Asia-Pacific Conference on Communications (IEEE Cat. No.03EX732), 3,* 869–872.

Lloyd, E., Maclean, R., & Stirling, A. (2006). Mobile TV – results from the BT Movio DAB-IP pilot in London [EBU Technical Review].

Mason, S. (2006). Mobile TV – results from the DVB-H trial in Oxford [EBU technical review, April 2006].

McLuhan, M. (1964). *Understanding media: The extensions of men.* New York: McGraw-Hill.

Médiamétrie. (2006). "Synthèse De L'étude Médiamétrie Pour Bouygues Telecom Sur L'expérimentation Télévision Sur Mobile," URL (consulted April 2007), from http://services-mobiles.typepad.com/services_mobiles/files/M_diam_trie_TV_sur_mobile.pdf

Mestre, A. (2007). Business models and opportunities: DVB-H in Spain, *DVB World 2007* (Dublin: 2007).

Mittermayr, H. (2006). Media on the Move: Mobility and mobile TV – some of the options, presentation at IBC, 09/09/06, from http://qedsessions.metacanvas.com/ibc2006/session/saturday_9_september/Herbert%20Mittermayr.mp3

Morello, A. (2006). *DVB-H development in Italy*. Presentation on Broadcast Mobile Convergence (WIMA 2006), Monaco, 02/02/2006.

Netsize. (2007). *The Netsize guide. Convergence: Everything's going mobile*. Paris: Netsize.

Nolan, D., & Keen, B. (2005). *Mobile digital television: The coming handheld revolution*. London: Screen Digest.

Ok, H. R. (2005). *Cinema in your hand, cinema on the street: The aesthetics of convergence in Korean mobile (phone) cinema*. Paper presented at the Conference on Seeing, Understanding, Learning in the Mobile Age.

Orgad, S. (2006). *This box was made for walking... How will mobile television transform viewers' experience and change advertising?* London: Department of Media and Communication London School of Economics and Political Science.

Pauchon, B. (2006). *Broadcast services towards mobile devices*. Presentation on Broadcast Mobile Convergence (WIMA 2006), Monaco, 02/02/2006.

Pekowsky, S., & Maalej, K. (2005). *DVB-H architecture for mobile communications systems*. RF Design, 36–42.

Portu, S. (2006). *Presentation*. Paper presented at the Mobile Content Industry Forum 2006.

Price, D. (2003). The telco video holy grail. *CTE-The Cable Communications Quarterly, 25*(4), 37–40.

Rauch, C., & Geissler, J. (2005). MobileTV in Germany: bmco Case Study, *Vodafone R&D*, URL (consulted April 2007), from http://www.vodafone-rnd.com/competence/docs/MobileTV-in-Germany.pdf

Sattler, C. (2006). *Results of mobile TV pilots – a survey*. Berlin: BMCO Forum.

Scheide, R. (2005). FLO technology brings multimedia content to mobile devices. *News from Rohde & Schwarz, 3*(187), 48–49.

Sieber, A., & Weck, C. (2004). What's the difference between DVB-H and DAB – in the mobile environment [EBU Technical Review, 299].

Södergård, C. (2003). *Mobile television: Technology and user experiences* (Report on the Mobile-TV project). Espoo: VTT Technical Research Centre of Finland.

Steinbock, D. (2005). *The mobile revolution: The making of mobile services worldwide*. London: Kogan Page.

Strohmeier, R. (2006). *How can we create an innovative climate in Europe for mobile television?* "Driving Mobile Television" high level seminar, part of the DVB Project, Brussels, 20/09/2006.

Urban, A. (2007). Mobile Television: Is it just a hype or a real consumer need? *Observatorio Journal, 1*(3), 45–58.

van den Dam, R. (2006) *Primetime for mobile television: Extending the entertainment concept by bringing together the best of both worlds*. New York: IBM Institute for Business Value, from http://www-935.ibm.com/services/us/gbs/bus/pdf/ibv-ge510-6275-02.pdf

Van Dijk, J. (1999). *The network society. Social aspects of new media*. London/Thousand Oaks/New Delhi: Sage.

Vesa, J. (ed). (2005). *Mobile services in the networked economy*. London: Idea Group.

Wallace, A. (1999). Box of delights. *Cable and Satellite Europe* (May), 84–85.

Wang, J., & Winters, J. H. (2004). An embedded antenna for mobile DBS. *IEEE 60th Vehicular Technology Conference, Wireless Technologies For Global Security* (Vol. 1–7; pp. 4092–4095).

Wood, D. (2006). *DVB-H gives television wings*. Powerpoint Presentation.

Yoshida, J. T. (2006). Technique alters high-end video for mobile TV [Electronic Version]. *EETimes Online*. Retrieved 28/03/2007 from http://www.eetimes.com/showArticle.jhtml?articleID=183700613

Different Attitudes Concerning the Usage of Live Mobile TV and Mobile Video

Koji Miyauchi, Taro Sugahara, and Hiromi Oda

Abstract The usage of live mobile TV and mobile video devices is increasing in Japan as well as in other countries. We conducted a user study in the summer of 2007, in the Tokyo area of Japan, with 11 participants, in order to understand through qualitative interviews when, how, and why people were using such devices. In this chapter, we present several findings from this user study, which reveals the different attitudes concerning the usage of live mobile TV compared with that of mobile video. These findings consider the following points. (1) Usage on commuter buses or trains, (2) usage at home, (3) usage related to experience sharing, and (4) interest of live mobile TV users in mobile video, and interest of mobile video users in live mobile TV. This chapter also proposes some ideas to improve user experience with mobile TV and video, and compares the results of our user study with those conducted in Finland, Korea, the USA, and the UK.

Introduction

Many products enabling the enjoyment of mobile TV [1] and/or mobile video are emerging in the market. Examples of such products include HP iPAQ, Apple Video iPod and Sony PSP. Various cell phones have both TV and video functions nowadays.

The "1seg" service (a mobile terrestrial digital audio/video/data broadcasting service in Japan) was officially started in April, 2006. The bandwidth of one channel of terrestrial digital broadcast in Japan (ISDB-T) is divided into 13 segments.

K. Miyauchi, T. Sugahara and H. Oda
Hewlett-Packard Laboratories Japan, Hewlett-Packard Japan, 3-29-21, Takaido-Higashi, Suginami-ku, Tokyo, 168-8585, Japan
e-mail: koji.miyauchi@hp.com taro.sugahara@hp.com hiromi.oda@hp.com

[1] This chapter uses "mobile TV" to denote "live mobile TV" where there is no misunderstanding

A. Marcus et al. (eds.), *Mobile TV: Customizing Content and Experience*,
Human-Computer Interaction Series, DOI 10.1007/978-1-84882-701-1_14,
© Springer-Verlag London Limited 2010

HDTV broadcast occupies 12 segments, and the remaining (13th) one segment is used for mobile broadcasting. The name "1seg" is derived therefrom. The shipment of cell phones with 1-seg functionality enjoyed rapid growth in the market of TV-enabled cell phones (JEITA 2008b). This situation can be seen in Table 1.[2] The cumulative shipment of 1-seg-enabled cell phones in August, 2008 was 41 million units, which was about 24 times more than that in August, 2006. The percentage of the monthly shipment of 1-seg-enabled cell phones was 85% of all cell phones in August, 2008, which had been only 8.3% in August, 2006.

The greater Tokyo area of Japan has a population of 34.5 million [3] in 13,557 km^2 (Statistics Bureau, Ministry of Internal Affairs and Communications 2000). This implies very high population density (about 2,500 people per square kilometers). People in the Tokyo area spend about 51 min commuting each way (NHK Broadcasting Culture Research Institute 2006). In the morning and evening, many people move between their homes and offices using public transportation such as buses and/or trains.

Under these circumstances, we conducted a user study on the usage of mobile TV and video devices in Tokyo, Japan in August, 2007. This was a qualitative user study in order to understand when, how, and why people were using these devices, and its aim was not to get statistical results such as "30 percent of people liked comedy". Rather, we sought to identify the issues from different types of users and devices.

Although we expected similar usage of mobile TV and video devices at first, sharp contrast was found between the usage of mobile TV and those of mobile video. This chapter presents several findings from the qualitative interviews, compares those findings between mobile TV and video related to the following points, and proposes some ideas to improve user experience with mobile TV and video.

1. Usage on commuter buses or trains
2. Usage at home
3. Usage related to experience sharing
4. Interest of mobile TV users in mobile video, and interest of mobile video users in mobile TV

Table 1 Shipment of 1-seg-enabled cell phones

Year-month	Shipment (in 1,000 unit)	Cumulative Shipment (in 1,000 unit)	Shipment percentage to all cell phones (%)
2006–08	239	1,736	8.3
2007–02	1,120	4,960	22.7
2007–08	1,467	13,242	36.7
2008–02	2,948	25,869	61.5
2008–08	1,774	41,468	85.1

[2] This table was created using the data from JEITA (2008a; 2008b)

[3] This number is the summation of the population of Tokyo and surrounding three prefectures in 2005 (Tokyo: 12.6 million, Kanagawa: 8.8 million, Saitama: 7.1 million, Chiba: 6.1 million)

Besides presenting the above findings, comparison, and proposals, we compared the results of our user study with those conducted in Finland, Korea, the USA, and the UK in order to position our user study among related works. This chapter was extended based on Miyauchi et al.(2009; 2008).

Structure of this Chapter

We overview our user study in Section "Design of the User Study." Then, we introduce the findings from our user study. In Section "Usages of Mobile TV Devices," we explain the findings from mobile TV users, and in Section "Usages of Mobile Video Devices," the findings from mobile video users. After introducing findings, Section "Discussions" discusses the usage of mobile TV and video devices, and presents some ideas to improve user experience with mobile TV and video. Section "Previous Work" introduces several previous works, and compares the results of our user study with the ones conducted in other countries. Finally, we conclude our user study, and present some future directions in Section "Concluding Remarks and Future Directions."

Design of the User Study

Participants

We collected volunteers who owned a TV or video-enabled portable device and used it at least once a week. They were required to be either an employee of our company or a family member who was living with an employee. We received 27 applications and chose 11 people taking into consideration age, mobile devices they owned, and usage frequency. The volunteers' ages ranged from 14 or more years. Table 2 shows the distribution of the participants by age.

As Table 3[4] shows there were six mobile TV users and six mobile video users. One person used his device for both functions. The table also shows seven people

Age range	Number
14–25	2
26–35	3
36–45	4
46+	2
Total	11

Table 2 Age of participants

---

[4]"MobaHo!" in Table 3 is a mobile satellite digital audio/video broadcasting service

Table 3 Types of used mobile device

Device type	Usage (TV/video)	Number
Cell phone (with 1-seg function)	TV	4 (1 also used for mobile video)
Cell phone (analog TV)	TV	1
MobaHo! Receiver	TV	1
Cell phone as mobile video	video	3 (1 also used for mobile TV)
Video iPod	video	2
PDA	video	1

Table 4 Usage length in months

Usage length in months	Number (TV)	Number (video)
1	1	1
2–3	2	0
4–5	2	0
6–11	0	0
12–24	1	5

were using a cell phone with mobile TV or video functions. Most mobile TV participants used their device less than half a year, while most mobile video ones used more than 1 year, as you may see in Table 4. The difference in usage length might reflect the fact that 1-seg service started about 1 year before this user study. About half of the participants used their device less than three times/week, while the other half used their device more than seven times/week. They used commuter vehicles[5] for about 20–90 min each way.

Method

We used the same method as in O'Hara et al. (2007) and Vorbau et al. (2007) as much as possible in order to compare our results with theirs. We had a meeting with the participants to explain the purpose and schedule of the user study, and asked them to keep a diary for 3 weeks in August, 2007. They were asked to write down any activities they undertook related to mobile TV or video experiences (e.g., "watched a baseball game" or "looked for an interesting TV program") including date, place, circumstance (e.g., "on the train from work" or "while cooking not to miss good scenes") and device used. A diary image is shown in Fig. 1.

---

[5] This chapter uses "commuter vehicle" to denote the public transportation such as bus or train to commute

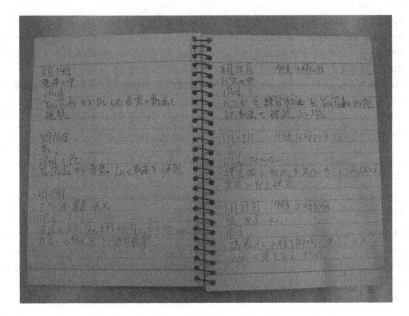

Fig. 1 A sample diary image

After keeping a diary for 3 weeks, we had a one hour interview with each participant individually. Their diaries were used in the interview mainly to recall the scenes where they used their device. In each interview, we spoke with the participants so that they could explain in more detail about the circumstances and motivations of the episodes written in the diary. We used notebooks, a digital voice recorder, a mini disc recorder or a video recorder to record each interview with whichever means the participant permitted us to use. The diary notebooks were collected after the interviews for analysis. Each participant was given a 5000 JPY book coupon as a token of our gratitude after the interview.

Usages of Mobile TV Devices

Mobile TV on Commuter Vehicles

Most mobile TV participants watched TV programs when riding on commuter vehicles, especially in the evening. There were some conditions which determined whether to watch TV with their device.

1. Existence of good TV programs. Variety shows were the most popular contents among our participants, and more programs of variety show were broadcast in the evening.

2. Seating availability. They had more opportunities to be seated in the evening because the number of commuters in a bus or train became smaller than in the morning. Seating availability was important in enjoying mobile TV as it facilitated the act of holding the device.
3. Relaxed atmosphere. Some participants also required a relaxing atmosphere. They felt relaxed when they sat, when the vehicle was not too crowded, and when they felt a sense of freedom after work. In the interview, they commented:

> I don't want to watch TV when I stand on the train. I would like to watch it relaxing on a seat (M, 36–45).[6]

> ... I don't watch TV on crowded trains, as I don't feel like watching because I am not comfortable (F, 26–35).

4. Duration before getting off the vehicle. When they had to take out and put away their device in a short time, they did not choose to use their device. This was because they felt busy, and it took a little time before they could view a clear and stable picture after they turned their device on (some explanation in Section "Reception Status of Live Mobile TV Programs").

> [I watch TV] when I have more than 15 minutes If I don't have more time, I don't want to watch it (M, 26-35).

When participants took a crowded train, especially in the morning, they did not watch TV with their device, but they slept, read a book, played games, exchanged e-mails, listened to music or radio, or just stood. What they did might depend on the degree of crowdedness of their commuter vehicles, and the existence of interesting TV programs. These behaviors were just the same as other passengers.

> For one thing, I have no TV programs good to watch in the morning. [... omit ...] I either read a book, sleep, or play a game on a train in the morning (M, 36–45).

A variety show consists of multiple short acts such as musical performances and comedy skits, which is suitable for a program on a commuter vehicle. They could start viewing midway through a program and enjoy some acts before getting off. Some of them also watched a drama on commuter vehicles, which was usually about an hour long, and it was usually longer than their riding time. They did not mind if they could not watch a whole drama, because they recorded the drama which they really wanted to watch with the video recorder at home. They did not watch TV seriously via the mobile TV device, but it provided light entertainment.

> There are multiple acts in one variety show, and it is enough to watch some acts. In that sense, a variety show is a content suited to '1seg' (M, 36–45).

> I don't mind if I cannot watch the whole drama, because I record it at home (M, 14–25).

---

[6] We use 'M' for male and 'F' for female. The pair of numbers indicate the range of age

Most mobile TV participants searched for interesting TV programs by turning on and changing channels without checking TV guides. They seemed to have no specific TV programs in mind to watch. It is interesting to note that this behavior matches that of traditional TV viewers in the early evening (Taylor & Harper 2002), where they said that "programs were chosen in a highly unplanned fashion by 'surfing' through the channels until something appealing was found."

I watch a TV program which happens to be broadcast when I turn it on (M, 36–45).

Several participants enjoyed TV programs such as variety shows as well as news and sports programs with subtitles even without sound. Some participants did not like earphones. The additional step to take out earphones from somewhere might be inconvenient, because they did not use earphones for usual usage (talking and e-mail). It seemed that sound was not necessary for the light entertainment by mobile TV on commuter vehicles.

I often choose a program which I can enjoy without sound, for example, a variety show, or one which I can enjoy midway through the program (F, 26–35).

When I view TV without sound, subtitles appear on the display. I can read the words of a commentator in a baseball game a little after each play. [... omit ...] I have no problem without sound (M, 26–35).

A business trip has a different features from that of commuting. Some participants commented that a business trip was a good opportunity to enjoy mobile TV. If it was not a rush hour when they traveled, they could often sit down and had enough time to watch TV. A business trip brought them good conditions to enjoy TV with their mobile device in a relaxed situation. In fact, it could satisfy three out of four conditions which were listed at the head of this section, except the first one, the existence of good TV programs to watch.

When I go to Haneda Airport, I always use a bus, a limousine. It often takes more than an hour. I can watch a whole drama, mainly when I return [to Tokyo] (M, 26–35).

The mobile TV participants desired light entertainment on commuter vehicles with as little effort as in just turning on their mobile TV device after work. There were several conditions to determine to use their mobile TV device. A business trip gave them better conditions than commuter vehicles, and was another opportunity for them to enjoy mobile TV.

Mobile TV at Home

We found that some participants did not use their mobile TV device at home, because they preferred to use a traditional TV set. We also found some examples of participants using their mobile TV device to watch a different program whilst in the same room as other family members, when the traditional TV set was already being used. Moreover, some participants used their device when they were using the toilet.

Besides these typical usages of mobile TV devices, we found some active viewings rather than a micro-break usage. One participant took her device anywhere in the house where she did not have a TV set (for example, kitchen, toilet) so that she did not miss good scenes. When she was watching a music program, and wanted to sing along with the songs, she took her device with her to another room and sang along whilst listening with the built-in speaker.

> When I am at home, when I am cooking or in the toilet, [... omit ...], I take it around the house to watch the scenes which I don't want to miss. When it is noisy or it may annoy other family members, I take my device to another room and watch it to practice singing a song (F, 26–35).

As is often the case with Japanese houses, air-conditioners are installed in a room-by-room basis, and there are some rooms without an air-conditioner. One participant commented that the room where she had a traditional TV set had no air-conditioner, and the bedroom had an air-conditioner but had no TV set. She was not satisfied with the quality of the mobile TV, but she used her device to enjoy watching TV programs in her air-conditioned bedroom on a very hot day. We regard her activities as a positive attitude about watching TV with her mobile device.

> Because the room where we have a TV set doesn't have an air-conditioner, I use my cell phone in the [air-conditioned] bedroom, although it is a little difficult to watch (F, 26–35).

Another participant used his device when he and his wife were eating dinner in the dining room where they had no TV set. They put his device on the power-charging cradle between them on the dining table. They used the built-in speaker to listen to sound. This is one of the social and sharing experiences with the mobile device, rather than simple passing of time.

> Because we have no TV set in our dining room, we use my cell phone [with TV function] to watch TV as an alternative method (M, 36–45).

This participant had once used his mobile TV device in bed before this user study. He commented that he used his device, because he had to stay in bed and he had no traditional TV set in the bedroom. He also mentioned that he would not use his device now that he had a traditional TV set there. When he wanted to watch TV in a situation without a traditional TV set, he used his device otherwise he did not, because he preferred to watch TV with a large display.

> I have ever used my mobile TV device in the bedroom. [... omit ...] I couldn't move because of the pain in my waist, so I often watched TV with my cell phone, then. [... omit ...] But now I will use a new traditional TV set which I bought for the bedroom (M, 36–45).

With the above examples, we considered that people were not satisfied with the quality of their mobile TV device, but they made use of their device actively when they wanted to watch TV in a more convenient location in their houses. The mobile TV participants seemed to make use of the portability of their device to compensate for the lack of time-shift capability of live TV programs. It is interesting to point out that we could not find any evidence that usage of mobile TV device in the bedroom was common in Japan. This is quite different from the results of other studies in the USA and the UK (see Section "User Study on Mobile Video in the USA and the UK").

Experience Sharing via Mobile TV

We found some examples in the interviews when a participant was in a restaurant or cafe with his/her friends and they used the device (1) when they had no topics to talk about at hand, or (2) to show the mobile TV to friends, sometimes proudly. A participant went to a cafe with her friend, and talked for a while, but after some time, she found that she wanted to search for some topics to talk about. She turned on her mobile TV, and showed her friend something interesting. This is a kind of searching for a topic to talk about and a kind of social activity to help them continue their conversation.

> There was one time when I watched a TV program with a friend together with my cell phone when we were at a cafe and had nothing to talk about at hand. I said to her, 'now there is a TV program like this' (F, 26–35).

Because the 1-seg service started about a year before this user study was conducted, it was not so common to have a cell phone with 1-seg function, then. A participant showed his cell phone to his friends in order to show them how clearly TV can be watched. His cell phone provided a topic and worked as a kind of social medium.

> [I showed my mobile TV] to boast of it [to my friends] when we were at a beer garden. I showed it the other day. I show it to them because many people don't know how clearly I can view TV with this. I often do so (M, 26–35).

Recently, many cell phones have been equipped with more and more functions. Some cell phones work as a commuter pass or electronic purse. One participant already used such cell phone, but several were anxious about the situation when they lost or changed their phone to a newer one. According to a consumer behavior survey (Economic and Social Research Institute 2008), the average usage years of cell phone by Japanese people is 2.9 years, and two of the reasons to buy a new cell phone are a trouble in the old cell phone (33.6%), and an upgrade to an advanced product (42.5%). The above participants presented their fear about the credit information included in a broken cell phone, or were worried about abuses of electronic money included, when they lost their cell phone.

> I don't feel attractive to a cell phone with electronic purse function. [... omit ...] I feel strong worries about the credit information included in the former cell phone, when I change my phone because of its trouble (M, 36–45).

> I am not interested in electronic purse at all. I am afraid of its lost. Because I have ever lost my cell phone before, I don't want to add such function (F, 26–35).

Reference (Matsuda et al. 2006) reported that a cell phone in Japan had once been used as a public medium in a workplace or a department, but it changed to a private one in the 1990s. In this user study, it was not so often that the participants lent their mobile TV device, especially cell phone, to other people. A cell phone includes private information such as telephone numbers, e-mail addresses and e-mail texts. Cell phone owners might have a call while they lent their cell phone to others. Recently, some cell phones even work as a commuter pass or electronic purse. These conditions made them regard a cell phone and similar device as a personal device, and people began to hesitate to ask other people to lend it.

> If I am asked to lend my mobile TV device, I will, but I have never been asked yet. ... Oh, no, I can't! Because it also works as telephone (M, 26–35).

> I can lend my mobile TV device where I am. [... omit ...] There may be a call while lending. In that sense, I can lend it only in front of me (F, 26–35).

The mobile TV devices worked not only as a tool for entertainment, but also as a kind of topic source and social medium to communicate with others. Mobile TV participants regarded a cell phone as a personal or private device, and some cell phones even worked as electronic money. These made it difficult for them to lend their cell phone to other people, which was one of the different points from other user studies (see Section "User Study on Mobile TV in Korea").

Reception Status of Live Mobile TV Programs

Several participants complained that they often experienced noise or interruptions. They tried to rotate the antenna, changed the channel, and waited for 30 seconds to a few minutes. If they were on commuter vehicles, they knew the locations where the condition would recover. But in other places, they gave up watching. They also had to wait for 2–10 s before getting a clear view when changing channels. They felt this duration was long.

> I often suffer from interruptions. Then I try other channels. If the others are not good, I return to the original channel and wait for a while. I give up if it doesn't recover after about 30 seconds (F, 26–35).

> Whenever I change the channel, I am forced to wait for a while. It is not convenient (M, 36–45).

The quality of mobile TV is important to distribute pay contents to consumers. We asked the participants whether or not they spent money on 1-seg TV programs if they could view pay contents with their mobile TV device. Our participants showed disapproval toward paying money. The reasons we found from the interviews were as follows:

1. What they watched was the same content as traditional TV which was free of charge. They could not agree to pay money for 1-seg TV programs for their mobility.
2. They used the mobile TV devices for passing time or light entertainment. They stopped watching if they had to pay for it. We could see this attitude in one participant's comment.

> I am using it [mobile TV] just because I can watch easily and free of charge. For me, this is not an indispensable item of my life (M, 26–35).

3. As explained above, the viewing quality was not good enough because of noise or interruptions.
4. If people pay money for content, they would like to use it effectively. For example, they would like to watch it multiple times, and watch it with different devices.

One participant was worried if the contents for 1-seg receivers could not be watched clearly with other devices, especially with a traditional TV.

5. It was not clear that they could watch the pay TV programs as scheduled. Time-shift capability is necessary to use pay contents. Video-on-demand will be an option to realize this desire.

At the time of this user study, mobile TV participants often experienced noise and interruptions, and it took a little time to view clear picture after they turned their device on or changed channels. This inconvenience may affect the spread of pay contents in the future.

Interest of Mobile TV Users in Mobile Video

Although some mobile TV participants had a cell phone with both TV and video functions, with the exception of one user, they did not often use the video function. They knew video preparation including downloading, format-conversion, and compression required time. It seemed that they did not like the time-consuming preparation for video contents. A participant who had a cell phone with both TV and video functions commented that she viewed video contents only when she was handed a memory card of video contents by her friend, and she did not prepare video contents by herself. This does not always imply that mobile TV users are less technology-oriented people. One of them used Sony PSP and LocationFree [7] to watch recorded TV programs at a different place from where they were recorded. He commented that content transfer to a memory card was inconvenient, and that home electronics appliances were more convenient.

Honestly, I don't know how to prepare for video contents. I don't want to watch it if I have to do so (M, 26–35).

I don't like to record video contents or transfer them from PC. I view it only when someone hands a memory card to me (F, 26–35).

I don't want to watch video contents then [on the train], I like watching TV. It is inconvenient if I have to transfer the contents to a memory card (M, 36–45).

Several participants expressed their desire to record and watch live TV programs with one device. Considering battery consumption, existence of entertainment programs at night, and that they suffered noise and interruptions while viewing (see Section "Reception Status of Live Mobile TV Programs"), the TV program recording with a mobile TV device will be limited to the one on the battery-charging cradle at home at night. The video-on-demand style service will be another option. NHK (Nippon Hoso Kyokai, "Japan Broadcasting Corporation" in English) has just begun "NHK on Demand" service in December, 2008 (NHK (Japan Broadcasting Corporation) 2008), which distributes video contents of its archive. Observation on the consumers' movement toward this service is required for a while.

---

[7] Sony LocationFree was used to send recorded contents to his PSP via the Internet

A new product may have this function, I hope I can also record TV programs [with the same device] (F, 26–35).

When I record a TV program with a cell phone, I am afraid I cannot record it if I don't have a good reception. It is no use to set the recording time if I don't know the reception status. When I record a program, I guess I have to keep it in a fixed place... Well, I won't record a TV program with it [a mobile TV device] (M, 26–35).

Our mobile TV participants had no interest in mobile video, because they did not like to spend much time on time-consuming video content preparations. Although some of them were interested in a device with which they could record and watch TV programs by one device, there seemed to be some conditions to enjoying this function.

Usages of Mobile Video Devices

Mobile Video on Commuter Vehicles

Half of the mobile video participants watched video contents on commuter vehicles in the mornings, and all did in the evenings. The number of commuters in a vehicle was one of the conditions to determine the usage. Those who watched videos in the morning could be seated, or rode on a train which was not so crowded that they could put their bag on the train floor. The other half of our mobile video participants did not use their mobile video device in the morning commuter vehicles. The main reason was the difficulty of holding the mobile device when they had to hang on to a strap with one hand and hold a bag with the other hand. We already saw what mobile TV users did on a crowded commuter vehicle in the morning in Section "Mobile TV on Commuter Vehicles." The mobile video participants also did similar activities in a crowded commuter vehicle.

Well, [when the train is crowded,] I am just standing (M, 36–45).

When I am standing on the train, I listen to audio programs most of the time (M, 46+).

We found that there were three types of contents which the participants enjoyed. They were news (including news commentaries), entertainment, and business or self-development related content. Four out of six participants viewed or listened to news or news commentaries. One participant recorded a news program on TV ("World Business Satellite" by TV Tokyo) of one hour at night and watched it the next morning. Some participants did not subscribe to any "paper" newspapers. So we could see it as a replacement of the newspaper. As for entertainment, some participants enjoyed drama, comedy, or animated cartoon.

Although news and entertainment were viewed, several participants also viewed contents which were useful for self-development or for their business. They viewed English lessons, programs for science and technology, hobby related contents, and videos for sales promotion. One participant even created the contents which contained recordings of his golf swing and swimming style in order to check his condition. These content categories and behaviors suggested that mobile video users had specific purposes and made use of their commuting time for them.

> English programs are convenient. Their length is suitable. [I learn] English conversation or English words. A program for English words is 2 or 3 minutes long (M, 46+).

> My hobbies are golf and swimming. [... omit ...] I took golf lessons and reviewed my golf swing and swimming style. I made video contents of my performance (M, 36–45).

Mobile video users prepared video contents in consideration of their available time. Multiple participants reduced the length of the contents by fast-forwarding the contents or skipping unnecessary parts such as commercial breaks. Another participant who transferred to multiple trains on his way to his office prepared video contents according to each riding duration, that is, he prepared shorter contents for a short ride, and longer contents for a long ride. These usages and preparations were useful to adjust the content length to their commuting time, or to repeat the necessary parts. The mobile video participants' behaviors suggested active viewings for their purposes on commuter vehicles.

> Well, I view the content [a news program] by fast-forwarding. The playing speed is about twice the normal speed (M, 26–35).

> Because animated cartoons are about 25 minutes long, I move the cursor to skip unappealing parts (M, 36–45).

> I often watch short contents then [on a short ride]. I mean, I watch some contents such as English words which are a few minutes long. I spend 45 minutes ride for a longer content (M, 46+).

As mobile TV users, mobile video users viewed video contents on their business trip. A long-distance travel provided an opportunity to enjoy video contents. In many cases, they had better conditions than everyday commuter vehicles, because they could take a reserved seat, stay in a larger space in a train or airplane, and have enough time to view a whole content. The categories of the contents ranged from entertainment such as animated cartoons to self-development. Compared with the mobile TV participants, mobile video participants did not have to mind the existence of the contents to watch.

> I go on a business trip once or twice a month. I take a train for about two hours, or one and a third hours. [... omit ...] I watch video during the travel. [... omit ...] I watch video of my golf swings, cultural programs [English lessons] and animated cartoons then (M, 36–45).

As the above examples suggest, mobile video participants seemed to have some specific purposes such as self-development, and they tried to use their commuting time for them. Generally speaking, they viewed mobile video actively on commuter vehicles. A business trip gave the participants good conditions to enjoy mobile video as well as mobile TV.

Mobile Video at Home

Most participants did not use their mobile video device at home. Actually, they did not like to watch contents with a small display. Many of their contents came from video recorders or PCs (Internet, CDs, or DVDs). If they could use a video recorder or PC with a larger display, they did not use their mobile device. When some participants arrived home, that was the first time they relaxed after work and self-development on commuter vehicles. A desire to relax caused them to use a device with a larger display which they preferred, and not to use their mobile device.

> Well, I have never viewed [video contents with my mobile video device] at home. Actually, I use a PC and video recorder [instead] (M, 26–35).

Some participants always put their device on the power-charging cradle at home. Power charging might be necessary for them so that they can view contents with confidence on the commuter vehicles the following day.

> I seldom watch video contents at home. When I come home, I put it on the fixed place [on the power charging cradle], and I won't touch it any more [until the next day] (M, 46+).

The mobile video participants might prepare for video contents mainly to watch on the commuter vehicles, not for watching at home. English lessons, science and technology, or other contents related to self-development were not appropriate to relax at home. And some participants did not watch repeatedly many contents including news and English lessons (words and short phrases). Once they watched contents on commuter vehicles, they would not watch them at home. They watched new content every day.

> I rarely watch contents again. [...omit...] Once watch, I delete them soon (M, 46+).

Only one participant commented that he used his device at home. He played a musical instrument, and he had to practice it in his room while viewing music video contents. Because he had no PC in his room, he had to use his Video iPod there. His behavior could be regarded as a hobby or entertainment, but also we could consider that he practiced the instrument to become a better player, that is, not just as passing time. He explained that:

> I listen to music contents outside, and view them at home. In my case, I use it [Video iPod], connect it to the speakers, and practice the instrument viewing the contents with sound (M, 14–25).

Some participants commented that they used their device for private use and when they were alone. They had some family members at home, so the situation did not match this policy. The details are described in Section "Experience Sharing via Mobile Video." This is another reason why they did not use their mobile video device at home.

Contrary to the behaviors on commuter vehicles, the mobile video participants seemed to want to be relaxed with a larger display after work and self-development on commuter vehicles. They did not often use their mobile video device at home.

Experience Sharing via Mobile Video

Most mobile video participants commented that they used their mobile video device when they were alone. They seemed to have an opinion that the mobile video device was a product which a person enjoyed by himself/herself when he/she was alone. It was rare to exchange video contents with another person. One participant told us that he did not send contents, but taught URL (Uniform Resource Locator) of contents to others. In Section "Interest of Mobile TV Users in Mobile Video," we saw an example of a mobile TV participant who had a cell phone with both TV and video functions that she had some experiences to view video contents stored in a memory card, only when she was handed the memory card by her friend. Another participant prepared video contents from DVDs (movies, animated cartoons, or educational contents for children) in order to let his child view them in his car. He connected his Video iPod to a 7-inch display in his car. It is true that he prepared video contents for his child, but it is difficult to consider that he intended to share contents with his child. Although we could regard the above types of behaviors as experience sharing, those could be considered passive ones at most.

> I have no chance [to send contents to others]. If I do so, I don't send contents, as most of the contents are from the Internet, I teach their URLs (M, 46+).

> I take my child to a swimming pool by my car, [... omit ...] I let my child view 'Shrek2' [stored in my Video iPod] from home to the pool (M, 46+).

We asked some of them what they would do if they met up with an acquaintance on a train. The typical answer was:

> When I meet up with somebody on the train, I will stop viewing. I use it when I am alone (M, 46+).

From social points of view, they could not continue watching video contents for some reasons.

1. Manners when they met up with an acquaintance: Watching video implied that they paid more attention to their video content than to the acquaintance. They might feel this was not polite.
2. Disapproving looks from other passengers: They also could not watch video contents together for fear of getting disapproving looks from other passengers. We did not observe a trend of multiple people watching mobile TV or video with a small display together on a public transportation in Japan, except young people, especially high school girls. They required some special reason in order to do so.

They also had some reasons related to personal viewpoints.

1. Privacy in content selection: Because content selection was a type of private information, they might feel it was difficult to show the contents to others.
2. Lack of common tastes or interests: It was not probable for them to know the acquaintance's tastes or interests in video contents. In order to let the other person

watch a video content, the participant must know the tastes or interests of that person.

3. Lack of good contents to watch together: It was not probable for them to have any proper contents to watch together, either, because they prepared the contents mainly according to their own purposes, not for watching together.

A few participants had experiences where they viewed videos together with other people. The following examples presented that experience sharing via mobile video could be possible under the above conditions.

• A participant recorded a song which his friends had talked about, and took it to the place where they were having a drink in order to introduce the song to his friends. They had a common interest in the song, and the participant prepared for it.

  I recorded it [the song] with it [my cell phone], and I showed it to others while we had a drink next day (M, 36–45).

• A high school student participant introduced his experience where he used his friend's device to view the comedy programs collected by his friend. We expect they knew their tastes well, because they were friends from the same school.

  My friend sometimes lets me view parodies of an animated cartoon. I laugh at the sight of it on my friend's device (M, 14–25).

• Another participant had some experiences where he showed his device to others soon after he purchased his device. It is natural for those people to have some common interest in watching video contents with a new mobile device that the participant had just bought.

  Well, this device is used for personal use. [But] I had several cases where I showed it to other people in order to let them know how video could be enjoyed, only during the first month after I bought it (M, 26–35).

Just like the participants who used a cell phone with TV function, mobile video participants who used a cell phone with video function commented that they could not lend their device to others, because their cell phone included privacy information such as telephone numbers and e-mail texts. As we considered above, mobile video device also had privacy information about what kind of contents they had in their device. It became even more difficult to lend their cell phone to others when those phones worked also as a commuter pass or electronic purse. On the other hand, a participant who used Video iPod commented that he could lend it to others, but he had never been asked to do so. His iPod had no function of telephone or e-mail exchange. If there was no problem in privacy information, people could lend it to others, but actually, there was nobody who asked the device holders to allow him/her to use it.

  Well, I cannot do so [lend it to others]. It [my cell phone] is actually money, commuter pass, and more, a telephone and a tool to send and receive e-mails (M, 26–35).

  Yes, of course, I don't mind it [lending my iPod to others]. But actually, I have never lent it. [... omit ...] I have never been asked to do so. (M, 46+).

For the mobile video participants, it was difficult to watch video contents with others. It was because of social requirements, privacy matters, lack of knowledge of the other persons' tastes or interests, and the preparation of contents. However, we could also observe some examples of sharing experiences with their device, when under proper circumstances. Lending a device was also difficult for a participant using a cell phone with mobile video function, just as mobile TV participants who used a 1-seg-enabled cell phone.

Video Content Preparation by Mobile Video Users

Compared with the case of mobile TV, mobile video viewings have more steps such as searching for contents, collecting the contents, format conversion, copying to a mobile device, and arranging the collected contents. From the interviews with the participants, there were several content sources, such as the Internet, TV programs, DVDs or CDs, and contents recorded by their video recorders. Some examples of the content sources were introduced in previous Sections "Mobile Video on Commuter Vehicles" (case of traditional TV news program, and case of a digital video recorder), and "Experience Sharing via Mobile Video" (case of DVDs).

We did not find any participants who spent much time on content search. Because most participants used their device for a year or more, the contents which they watched were fixed to some degree. One participant used iTunes to select contents, and he picked up contents from only a few categories. Another participant used YouTube[8] to search for contents by giving detail conditions, so he did not need to spend much time searching.

> I don't spend much time [searching], because iTunes gives well categorized content groups, I look into the categories of my tastes and the most popular 10 contents, and the like. I look up contents from only those two (M, 46+).

Our participants had complaints about time-consuming downloading and format conversion, but those who made these processes automatically while they slept had no problems. They just started the process using their PC, and did other things such as visiting web sites, reading e-mails, and going to other rooms.

> Actually, conversion by DivX[9] requires time. After I start the conversion [by PC] at home, I don't touch it. I always start at night, and the conversion is finished by the morning (M, 36–45).

> I think it probably takes about 30 minutes [to convert the format]. As I have made this process automatic, I only have to copy the converted files to a mini SD memory card in the morning (M, 26–35).

---

[8] http://www.youtube.com/

[9] 'DivX' is a software to convert file formats

The lengths of the contents which our participant viewed ranged from a few minutes of the ones related to English learning or introduction of technologies and new products, 15 min of the sales promotion videos, to 30 min of the ones related to news commentary or animated cartoon. We asked them the ideal length of video content. We observed there were two groups. One group liked a shorter content of a few minutes to 5 min, or a long content with multiple shorter parts in it. The other liked 15–30 min. People who enjoyed English lessons or comedy skits preferred shorter contents, and those who viewed hobby-related contents or news tended to like longer contents. The former participants watched various contents in a short time, and the latter needed a whole content of such length.

> A few minutes is a little too short. I like contents of five minutes or so. [... omit ...] Even though a content is long, for example, 30 minutes long, I like the one which I can stop watching at every 5 minute on the way (M, 46+).

> Ideally, I like a comedy skit of two minutes or less. Anyway, when I laugh with my friends, it is fun to view various short ones. But about music contents, I don't have any preference on their length (M, 14–25).

There were no participants who used pay contents on their mobile devices. They explained some reasons. Some participants did not think it was worth paying money for the video contents of low resolution. Another participant already enjoyed many free contents. He had no time to view pay contents, and he was afraid about the cost if he had to pay for all those contents. Some participants commented that they would pay for music contents, because they had good quality. These comments implied that mobile video participants were not so satisfied with the quality that they could be willing to pay for them.

> I may pay for the contents to watch by my PC, but I won't pay for the contents to watch by my Video iPod. [... omit ...] But I will be able to pay at maximum 100 JPY for a piece of music (M, 46+).

> These [the contents I watch] are all free of charge. I cannot continue enjoying if I have to pay for them, because the amount is so much. [... omit ...] I am already enjoying free contents. I don't have enough time to watch pay contents as well (M, 46+).

One Video iPod holder wanted to view the video contents which he had recorded with his video recorder when his child took part in some events. But he did not view those contents on his Video iPod, because he had no convenient way to copy the contents from a compact flash card of his video recorder to his Video iPod. Another participant pointed out that there was a lack of easy connectivity with the mobile video device and other consumer appliances such as a DVD recorder. He was also anxious that recorded contents of 1-seg TV programs could not be viewed clearly with other devices. These desires are important not only to promote the use of mobile video devices, but also to spread the use of pay contents, because people have a desire to view the same content on different devices from traditional TVs to mobile devices (Vorbau et al. 2007). People may consider it worth paying for the contents, if they can view them not only on a traditional TV but also on their mobile devices.

> I once wanted to do so [watch video taken with my video recorder], but now, I don't. [... omit ...] There may be some convenient tools [to transfer contents from a compact flash card to my iPod] in the world, but I don't have one. It requires time in searching for one. That's why I don't do now (M, 46+).

Although video content preparation for mobile device requires time, our participants did not mind spending some time on it by making the process as simple as possible. After using their device for a year or so, their viewing style became routine to some degree, so they did not spend much time searching for contents. We could not find any participants who paid for mobile video contents. We found some problems in connectivity of mobile video devices with other devices.

Interest of Mobile Video Users in Mobile TV

About half of the participants showed no interest in viewing live TV programs on their mobile device, while some of others expected to buy a cell phone with 1-seg function or to have a mobile TV device as a precaution in the case of disasters. They commented that they could get enough news from the Internet, it was doubtful that their favorite TV programs were broadcast when they could view them, or the previous analog mobile TV could be used only in limited areas.

> I don't think that a cell phone with [live] TV function is important as a mobile device to view [live] TV programs. I hope to have it as a precaution in the case of disasters. It is not certain that I will be able to view my favorite programs when I am available. So I think it is better to have a mobile device as a machine to view the contents which I record (M, 36–45).

This user study was conducted when 1-seg-enabled cell phones were not used widely. Recently, more and more cell phones have begun to have the 1-seg function, and the mobile video participants may use one in the future. There may be an opportunity for them to try one, and change their mind toward mobile TV.

Discussions

Usage Comparison on Commuter Vehicles

One of the important findings in this user study is that there were different attitudes concerning the usage of mobile TV and video devices. We introduced usage of mobile TV and video devices on commuter vehicles in Sections "Mobile TV on Commuter Vehicles" and "Mobile Video on Commuter Vehicles". Many mobile TV participants viewed entertainment programs, especially variety shows on the evening commuter vehicles, only when they could be seated and when the vehicles were not too crowded. They searched for TV programs by turning on and changing channels without TV guides. In contrast, several mobile video participants viewed

Fig. 2 Arranging the findings with cards (these cards were used in another user study)

contents for self-development such as English lessons or business-promotion videos related to their jobs as well as entertainment. They did not mind spending some time on content preparations that require much effort, which many mobile TV participants were reluctant to do.

These facts imply that the mobile TV users wanted to relax with light entertainment after work with as little effort as turning on their device. On the other hand, the mobile video users tried to make good use of the commuting time for specific purposes such as improvement of their English skills. The mobile video users might want to use their commuting time in order to get the most of the cost of content preparation. When comparing the two groups of people, there were differences in desires for the mobile devices behind the differences in the contents they viewed, preferences for content preparations, and the usage of the commuting time.

Usage Comparison at Home

We found a general tendency for both mobile TV participants and mobile video ones to prefer to use a larger display to watch TV or video contents at home. But Section "Mobile TV at Home" presented some findings that mobile TV participants aggressively used their device to enjoy watching TV programs in a convenient location in their homes. It seemed that their mobile TV devices compensated time-shift inability of live TV programs by virtue of their portability.

In contrast, all mobile video participants except one person did not use their device at home. Their commuting time was the "self-development" time for some participants. They seemed to want to be relaxed with a larger display at home after work, so they did not touch their device until the following day.

Usage Comparison Related to Experience Sharing

Sections "Experience Sharing via Mobile TV" and "Experience Sharing via Mobile Video" presented some different attitudes between mobile TV users and mobile video ones related to experience sharing. The mobile TV participants used their device as a topic source, or to let their friends know how TV could be viewed with their mobile TV device. They used their device as a social method to promote communications. Because this user study was conducted when it was not so common for people to have a 1-seg-enabled cell phone, some mobile TV participants presented their device to illustrate how people could enjoy TV with their mobile device. The number of this type of experience sharing will decrease after more and more people begin to use a 1-seg-enabled cell phone. One mobile video participant commented that he showed his device to others only during the first month after he had bought it. His experience supports this expectation.

Watching a video content together was more difficult than watching a TV program together. The former requires a few more conditions.

(1) Preparation: Mobile TV users did not have to prepare any contents. They just had to turn on and change channels to find a good TV program to watch together. But mobile video users had to prepare the contents before they left home. It was not so probable for them to have some proper video contents to watch together, and to know other people's tastes or interests beforehand.

(2) Privacy in content selection: What video contents one prepares in his/her device is considered private. Mobile video users faced some risk of privacy disclosure to other people if they watched video contents together. So, the experiences of watching together were limited to intimate circles or the situation where they watched a specific content which all of them were interested in. Mobile TV users had less or no risk on this point. What they chose were TV programs which were provided by TV broadcast stations, not selected by themselves. It would not be a serious privacy problem in choosing a TV program.

Although we found some examples in experience sharing from interviews of both mobile TV and mobile video participants, experiences of watching video contents together required more conditions than those of watching TV together.

Interest of Mobile TV Users in Mobile Video, and Vice Versa

We saw in Section "Interest of Mobile TV Users in Mobile Video" that mobile TV participants knew that the video content preparations require time, and that they did not like to spend much time on it. We found in Section "Interest of Mobile Video

Users in Mobile TV" that multiple mobile video users did not have preferences or interests to use mobile TV. There seemed to be two groups of mobile device users, who had quite different opinions.

The mobile video participants prepared their video contents with as little effort as possible such as during the night (see Section "Video Content Preparation by Mobile Video Users"). If the mobile TV participants know how to prepare video contents with ease or if they have some video-on-demand services whose contents they can receive while they do not use the device (sleeping time or working hours, for instance), there may be an opportunity for them to start enjoying video contents with their mobile device.

The 1-seg service started about a year before this user study. More and more cell phones are equipped with 1-seg function recently, as we have seen in Table 1 in Section "Introduction." Some mobile video participants will begin to use this type of cell phone after this user study, and may change their minds toward mobile TV.

Although mobile TV users and mobile video users appeared to represent two different groups, this situation may change in later user studies because of the widespread 1-seg-enabled cell phone (that is, cell phone with both functions), or if easier methods to prepare mobile video contents, or new video-on-demand services will be introduced in the future. NHK (Japan Broadcasting Corporation) started a service of this type ("NHK on Demand") in December, 2008 (NHK (Japan Broadcasting Corporation) 2008). We would like to watch consumers' movement toward this service.

Proposals to Improve User Experience with Mobile TV and Video

Here we present some ideas which may be used to improve user experience with mobile TV and/or mobile video.

- Display apparatus: In order to use a mobile device in a crowded vehicle, consumers may need a hands-free device. One example is a glass-like device, which we wear in front of our eyes, and listen to sound through bone conduction. Another example is a display on a wrist-band. In this case, we need earphones, or we use subtitles without sound. If we can make use of mobile TV/video devices even in a crowded vehicle, we are able to view the contents more regularly, which is one of the desirable features for self-development.
- Improvement of broadcasting conditions: Mobile TV participants suffered from noise and interruptions when they watched mobile TV. Reduction of noise and interruptions is important to promote pay mobile TV programs or to sell mobile TV devices with recording function. People will not feel it is worth paying for if TV reception condition is not clear enough, and people may feel anxious about the quality of the recorded contents, when they use a device with which they can record as well as watch TV programs.
- Summarizing TV/video content: We cannot expect that the length of content matches our available times such as our commuting times. Some participants skipped the contents or viewed them by fast-forwarding in order to view the

necessary parts in a limited time. We may apply summarization technologies to TV/video contents in order to adjust the length of contents to a specified length. Then, people become able to choose the contents with the desired details.

- TV/video programs suitable for mobile TV/video devices: There were several participants who used their mobile TV devices without sound. Traditional TV programs are produced under the condition that they are watched with sound. Researches on the contents without sound may bring about some chances to invent new and proper contents for mobile devices. In this study, most mobile TV users did not use their device on commuter vehicles in the mornings. One of the reasons was the lack of TV programs to watch. There is a space here to devise a genre of TV programs good to watch in the morning vehicles. Mobile TV users need the same contents as traditional TV programs to enjoy familiar contents as they usually do. But at the same time, it is desirable to have programs for mobile TV which are not broadcast for traditional TV (Cui et al. 2007). We may pick up baseball games as one candidate. In Japan, not all baseball games are broadcast for traditional TV. People may want to watch those games which cannot be watched on traditional TV. As one participant suggested in Section "Interest of Mobile Video Users in Mobile TV," a news program concerning disasters is another candidate. We will be able to get necessary information when we are outside our home or office.

- Labor-saving way to prepare video contents: Compared with TV viewings, video viewings on mobile devices require that we do extra work such as searching, downloading, format-conversion, and copying to the mobile device. This was a barrier for the mobile TV participants to use their device as a mobile video one even though they used a device which also had video function. It is convenient to have some easy ways/tools to define and execute basic routines for preparation of mobile video contents. These days, there are many products with both mobile TV and mobile video functions. If the cost of video contents preparation is reduced, people may use both functions according to their situation, where they need light and easy entertainment, and where they want to do some work for their personal purposes with recorded video contents.

Previous Work

Everyday practices of traditional TV were reported by Taylor and Harper (2002). Specifically, they reported highly disengaged viewings and TV channel hopping in the early evening. Similar behavior patterns were also observed for mobile TV users on the evening commuter vehicles. Mobile TV devices seemed to extend people's TV hours in the early evening toward the commuting time from office to home.

Various aspects of cell phone usage in Japan were reported by (Okada & Matsuda 2002; Matsuda et al. 2006). They studied multiple phenomena on the cell phones from social and cultural points of view. We learn how Japanese people use cell phones from these books including e-mail exchanges which might be derived from the days of text messaging by pagers in 1990s. Reference (Matsuda et al. 2006) also mentioned to cell phones with camera function. Our work adds other findings on cell phones with mobile TV or video functions, and on the usages by commuters in Japan.

The usage of cell phones with 1-seg function was reported by (japan.internet. com 2006; Yano Research Institute Ltd 2006). These reports were based on web inquiries of quantitative approach just after the introduction of 1-seg services in 2006. They reported that cell phones with 1-seg function were used to watch news at night. Our study is a qualitative research which can be a complementary work to them by adding several findings comparing the usages of mobile TV devices with those of mobile video ones.

The works by Knoche & McCarthy (2005) and Knoche et al. (2005) reported design requirements for mobile TVs, such as the required bandwidth for different types of content, and assessment of image resolution and bit-rate requirements for displaying on mobile devices. They asked four people in the UK 12 questions in regard to design requirements for a future mobile TV interface (Knoche & McCarthy 2005). They also conducted a user study with 128 participants to examine different image resolutions and encoding bit-rates (Knoche et al. 2005). Their works were related to video-on-demand or MobiTV style mobile TVs, and technological challenges, while our study is related to mobile TV to grasp the states of mobile TV usage in everyday practices.

There are already several user studies on the usage of mobile TV or video devices. For example, Södergård (2003) conducted a user study on the mobile TV in Finland, and Cui et al. (2007) conducted one in Korea. Reference (Repo et al. 2004) conducted a user study on the mobile video in Finland, and O'Hara et al. (2007) and Vorbau et al. (2007) conducted one in the USA and the UK. These works deal with either mobile TV or mobile video. Our work deals with both mobile TV and mobile video, and we were able to compare the usages of those two devices at the same time. The above studies are compared with our study in the following subsections.

User Study on Mobile TV in Finland

Södergård (2003) conducted a large-scale user study on the mobile TV using a prototype system in Finland in 2002 and 2003. A total of 81 people took part in this study. Every user used the system at WLAN (Wireless Local Area Network) hotspots for 4 weeks. They used either a PDA (Personal Digital Assistant) or tablet-PC including HP Jornada and HP iPAQ.

They found that people normally watched short programs or pieces from longer programs. Our results indicate that the participants did not intend to watch short programs, but our participants preferred to watch variety shows, which consisted of several short performances. This feature is similar to "pieces from longer programs" in their study.

They also explained that the typical contexts of usage were when their participants were waiting for something or passing time. In our case, our participants mainly used their device on commuter vehicles as entertainment tools during their commuting time. At home, our people used their device for passing time, but we also found some cases where their behaviors could be considered as active viewings, for example, so as not to miss good scenes or for a social tool with their family members when they had dinner.

User Study on Mobile TV in Korea

Cui et al. (2007) conducted a user study on the live mobile phone TV in Seoul, South Korea in September, 2005. TU Media (South Korean telecommunications operator) started the first commercial live mobile TV service in May, 2005. Their study was conducted about 4 months after the introduction of the first mobile TV service, while our study was done about a year after the 1-seg service started. Eight people took part in their study. The average age was 24.1 years. Seven participants were not married and six of them shared their apartment with their parents. These facts suggest that most of the participants were young people. The participants of our study were a little older and most of them were householders. From the point of participant attributes, their study and ours supplement each other.

They found that motivations of their participants to use mobile TV devices included a desire to kill boredom, novelty (a desire to be the first), staying up-to-date with popular events, and playing games. A desire to kill boredom and a desire to be the first were not so strong in our participants. Our participants had desires to have a relaxing time with TV programs on commuter vehicles after work. The ages and occupations of the participants might be reflected in these findings.

Their participants seemed to enjoy TV programs in their room at home without any control from their parents. In our study, there were two high school students, and they sometimes used their mobile device in their room. One participant used his device when a traditional TV in the living room was already being used, or when he wanted to use it while studying. The other participant used his Video iPod in his room and practiced his music instrument while viewing video contents. But we could not observe that they were worried about the control by their parents, or that they watched mobile TV or video contents in their room to run away from the control by parents. In these findings, we could observe some cultural or social differences in the house management between Korea and Japan. Korean parents might have stronger control over their children.

They pointed out the cultural differences in TV sharing and device lending between Korea and Japan. They also mentioned that Japan has a culture of individualism. We found some kinds of device sharing where some participants showed their device to their friends to let them know the TV or video capability or other purposes (see Sections "Experience Sharing via Mobile TV" and "Experience Sharing via Mobile Video"). Some participants also commented that they could lend their device where the participants had control of them. It is true that they also commented that they could not lend their device to other people. Although some sociological studies may be required, at this time, we consider this a privacy problem, not individualistic culture. Telephone numbers and e-mail texts were included in their devices, or they might have a call while lending their cell phone to another person. Some of our participants' cell phones also worked even as commuter pass or electronic money.

User Study on Mobile Video in Finland

A user study on cell phones with video capability was conducted by Repo et al. (2004). Thirteen people took part in this study. Ten Nokia cell phones were distributed to the participants for a week (three were shared with a member of the same household). The participants were asked to keep a diary during the week.

They found two kinds of contexts in mobile video usage. One is when they were alone and wanted to avoid boredom or pass time. The other one is when they were with a few people and enjoyed contents such as karaoke or cartoons together. Some of our participants used their mobile video device for entertainment, and viewed video with others together on some occasions. But we also found usages for self-development, for example, English lessons or business-promotion videos. People (employees of an IT-industry company in Japan) wanted to use commuting time for their particular purposes with some effort of preparing video contents included. In this sense, our study extends their work in finding other reasons or motivations to use mobile video devices.

User Study on Mobile Video in the USA and the UK

O'Hara et al. (2007) and Vorbau et al. (2007) conducted a user study on the mobile video in the USA and the UK, which was a model of our user study. Twenty-eight people took part in the user study, 13 from the UK and 15 from the USA. They used the diary method of 3 weeks, and had a 60–90 min qualitative interview with each participant individually. We adopted the same method as much as possible. By comparing results of their study and ours, we expect to make clear the differences between the USA/UK and Japan.

They looked into their findings from a social point of view. This is a special point of this study from other works. O'Hara et al. (2007) introduced an example explaining how a teenage girl used her Video iPod in the living room before dinner. She did not watch TV in the living room so often because her brother did, while she used a computer instead. They pointed out that this was a moral order of control over the main TV. She did not go to another room to watch TV either, because she needed to be in the shared space of the house while waiting for dinner. This might be required of family members in England. In other words, she was in the living room watching mobile video as per the social expectation.

They found that comedy was the most popular genre on their participants' device. Some of our participants enjoyed comedies or animated cartoons which had similar features as light entertainment. But, our participants also used their device for self-development or work (English lessons, new product information, swimming-style training videos, practice of musical instrument, business-promotion videos, etc.). This difference might derive from the differences in commuting style. More Japanese employees in the Tokyo area might use public commuter vehicles than in the USA and the UK. Our mobile video participants made use of their commuting time for some "useful" purposes aggressively in a sense.

They pointed out that many participants, especially younger ones, considered the search for video contents to be entertainment, and the technologies to find valuable contents served as kudos among friends. This was not found in our study at all. Several of our participants seemed to have definite purposes, and many of them used their device in some fixed way after using it for more than a year. This may explain why our participants did not need to spend much time on the search for video content.

In their study, many participants used their mobile video device in bed. This type of behavior was not often found in our participants. Most of our mobile video participants preferred a larger display, so they decided not to use their mobile device at home (see Section "Mobile Video at Home"). One participant had once watched his mobile TV in bed before this user study, and bought a traditional TV set for the bedroom later (Section "Mobile TV at Home"). He commented that he used his mobile device because he had to stay in bed, and he had no TV set in the bedroom, then. He also commented that he would not use his device in the bedroom, now that he had a traditional TV set there. Our study did not reveal any evidence that viewing mobile TV/video in the bedroom was common in Japan.

Concluding Remarks and Future Directions

We reported our qualitative user study on the usage of mobile TV and video. This user study was conducted in the Tokyo area of Japan in the summer of 2007. The participants of our user study were 11 people, who were employees of Hewlett-Packard Japan, or a family member of an employee of the company. In this chapter, we introduced our findings from the interviews with the participants, compared the usage of mobile TV and video, proposed some ideas to improve user experience with mobile TV and video, and compared our results with some user studies conducted in other countries. We found some contrasts between the usage of mobile TV and that of mobile video. They are:

1. On commuter vehicles: Mobile TV users wanted light entertainment, while mobile video users wanted to make the most use of commuting time for their specific purposes.
2. At home: Mobile TV users tried to use their device aggressively to watch TV programs in a convenient location, while mobile video users wanted a relaxing time with a larger display. Most of them did not use their mobile video device at home.

3. Experience sharing: Mobile TV users could watch TV programs together with other people more easily than mobile video users. This was because mobile TV users did not need any content preparation, and they did not have to mind privacy problems in content selection.
4. Interest of mobile TV users in mobile video, and vice versa: The two groups of mobile device users seem quite different currently, but this situation may be changed in the future.

We can think of several directions for further research and development. One approach is to apply our findings to the development of new products or services. This chapter presented some ideas in Section "Proposals to Improve User Experience with Mobile TV and Video." Another is to conduct a quantitative study to examine the hypotheses from our user study. We can measure the range of application of those hypotheses by statistical results. A third is to conduct another qualitative user study. The situation of cell phones has been changing drastically. It will be interesting to conduct another qualitative user study to catch this changing status. More and more cell phones have both mobile TV and mobile video functions in Japan. People may change their way of using cell phones in the future.

We hope that this chapter reveals some findings to people who are interested in the state of the usage of mobile TV and video devices.

Acknowledgments The authors thank the volunteers of this user study for their cooperation.

References

NHK Broadcasting Culture Research Institute: National Time Use Survey 2005 (in Japanese) (2005). *'NHK' is Japan Broadcasting Corporation. Survey on how Japanese people use their time everyday* (Report, NHK Broadcasting Culture Research Institute, Tokyo, Japan), from http://www.nhk.or.jp/bunken/research/life/life 20060210.pdf

Cui, Y., Chipchase, J., & Jung, Y. (2007). Personal TV: A qualitative study of mobile TV users. In P. Cesar, K. Chorianopoulos, & J. Jensen (Eds.), EuroITV 2007, no. 4471 in LNCS. Heidelberg, Germany: Springer.

Economic and Social Research Institute, Cabinet Office, Government of Japan. (2008). *Table 9 of Consumer Behavior Survey of Japan in March* (in Japanese), from http://www.esri.cao.go.jp/jp/stat/shouhi/2008/0803shouhi.hmtl

japan.internet.com. (2006). *Macromill investigated the trends of the users of 1seg-enabled cell phones (in Japanese)*, from http://japan.internet.com/allnet/20060605/3.html, Dated 2006-06-05T18:00

JEITA. (2008a). *The shipment of the mobile phones (in Japanese). JEITA means 'Japan Electronics and Information Technology industries Association,'* from http://www.jeita.or.jp/japanese/stat/cellular/2008/

JEITA. (2008b). *The shipment of the receivers for terestrial digital TV broadcasting (in Japanese). JEITA means 'Japan Electronics and Information Technology industries Association,'*from http://www.jeita.or.jp/japanese/stat/digital/2008/

Knoche, H., & McCarthy, J. D. (2005). Design requirements for mobile TV. In *MobileHCI '05: Proceedings of the 7th international conference on Human computer interaction with mobile devices & services* (pp. 69–76), *ACM Press, New York, USA*. DOI http://doi.acm.org/10.1145/1085777.1085789

Knoche, H., McCarthy, J. D., & Sasse, M. A. (2005). Can small be beautiful?: assessing image resolution requirements for mobile TV. In *MULTIMEDIA '05: Proceedings of the 13th annual ACM international conference on Multimedia* (pp. 829–838), *ACM Press, New York, USA*. DOI http://doi.acm.org/10.1145/1101149.1101331

Matsuda, M., Okabe, D., & Ito, M. (2006). *Personal, portable, pedestrian: Mobile phones in Japanese life* (1st ed.) (Japanese Translation), Kitaoji-Shobo, Kyoto, Japan. ISBN4-7628-2532-8, Japanese translation of ISBN0-262-59025-5, MIT Press.

Miyauchi, K., Sugahara, T., Oda, H. (2009). Relax or study? A qualitative user study on the usage of live mobile TV and mobile video. ACM Computers in Entertainment 7(3), 1–20. DOI http://doi.acm.org/10.1145/1594943.1594955

Miyauchi, K., Sugahara, T., & Oda, H. (2008). Relax or study?: A qualitative user study on the usage of mobile TV and video. In M. Tscheligi, M. Obrist, & A. Lugmayr (Eds.), EuroITV 2008, no. 5066 in LNCS (pp. 128–132). Heidelberg, Germany: Springer.

NHK (Japan Broadcasting Corporation). (2008). *NHK on Demand: Broadband access to NHK programs - at any time*, from http://www.nhk.or.jp/nhk-ondemand/english/index.html

O'Hara, K., Mitchell, A. S., & Vorbau, A. (2007). Consuming video on mobile devices. In *CHI 2007: Proceedings of the SIGCHI conference on Human factors in computing systems* (pp. 857–866), *ACM, New York, USA*.

Okada, T., & Matsuda, M. (2002). Understanding mobile media (in Japanese) (1st ed.). Yuhikaku, Tokyo, Japan. ISBN4-641-28070-3.

Repo, P., Hyvönen, K., Pantzar, M., & Timonen, P. (2004). Users inventing ways to enjoy new mobile services – The case of watching mobile videos. In *HICSS 2004: Proceedings of the 37th Annual Hawaii International Conference on System Sciences* (p. 40096.3). IEEE Computer Society, Washington, DC, USA.

Södergård, C. (2003). *Mobile television – technology and user experiences* (Report on the Mobile-TV project). Report VTT Publications 506, VTT Information Technology.

Statistics Bureau, Ministry of Internal Affairs and Communications. (2000–2005). *Table 1. Population, Population Change . Area and population density, information on the 2005 population census of Japan*, from http://www.e-stat.go.jp/SG1/estat/Xlsdl.do?sinfid=000000036BBC

Taylor, A., & Harper, R. (2002). Switching on to switch off: An analysis of routine TV watching habits and their implications for electronic programme guide design. *usableiTV, 1*(3), 7–13.

Vorbau, A., Mitchell, A. S., & O'Hara, K. (2007). My iPod is my Pacifier: An investigation on the everyday practices of mobile video consumption. In *HotMobile 2007: Proceedings of the Eighth IEEE Workshop on Mobile Computing Systems and Applications* (pp. 29–33). IEEE Computer Society, Washington, DC, USA. DOI http://dx.doi.org/10.1109/HOTMOBILE.2007.1

Yano Research Institute Ltd. (2006). *The study on the viewing style of 1seg-enabled cell phones (in Japanese)*, from http://www.yano.co.jp/press/pdf/169.pdf, Press release on 2006-08-03

User Experience Evaluation in the Mobile Context

Marianna Obrist, Alexander Meschtscherjakov, and Manfred Tscheligi

Abstract Multimedia services on mobile devices are becoming increasingly popular. Whereas the mobile phone is the most likely platform for mobile TV, PDAs, portable game consoles, and music players are attractive alternatives. Mobile TV consumption on mobile phones allows new kinds of user experiences, but it also puts designers and researchers in front of new challenges. On the one hand, designers have to take these novel experience potentials into account. On the other hand, the right methods to collect user feedback to further improve services for the mobile context have to be applied. In this chapter the importance of user experience research for mobile TV within the mobile context is highlighted. We present how different experience levels can be evaluated taking different mobile context categories into account. In particular, we discuss the Experience Sampling Method (ESM), which seems to be a fruitful approach for investigating user TV experiences.

Introduction

Currently, the mobile phone is the most likely platform for mobile TV but PDAs, portable game consoles, and music players are attractive alternatives (Knoche et al. 2007a; Knoche & Sasse 2007b). Many users have expressed a desire to access entertainment on the move in order to stay up-to-date with favorite programs or breaking news, to participate in interactive shows, or simply to pass some time. We understand TV in general and mobile TV in particular as enabler for both an individual and a shared viewing experience, especially used for killing time, fighting loneliness, staying up-to-date, browsing content, and getting information (Jumisko-Pyykkö et al. 2008a). Mobile TV provides this experience to people at places where other possibilities to watch TV are unavailable. Therefore, it is essential to understand these places and the corresponding context for supporting the user experience (UX).

M. Obrist, A. Meschtscherjakov and M. Tscheligi
HCI & Usability Unit, ICT&S Center, University of Salzburg, Sigmund-Haffner-Gasse 18, 5020 Salzburg, Austria

A. Marcus et al. (eds.), *Mobile TV: Customizing Content and Experience*, 195
Human-Computer Interaction Series, DOI 10.1007/978-1-84882-701-1_15,
© Springer-Verlag London Limited 2010

Although mobile TV field trials around the world revealed the popularity and potential for mobile multimedia services (Schmidt-Belz & Jones 2006; Serco 2006), there are still a number of usability and UX challenges open. The current research in interactive mobile TV focuses mainly on personalization, video-on-demand, EPG, and on shifting the experience of traditional TV services to mobile TV (Saleemi et al. 2008). Serco Usability Services has proposed a first set of design guidelines for mobile TV products (Serco 2006). By investigating how users react to mobile TV products through a series of independent research studies. However, there is still a need to investigate user requirements for providing a seamless and attractive UX of mobile services, especially with regard to novel developments toward mobile 3D TV and videos (Jumisko-Pyykkö et al. 2008a).

In particular, there is a need for a better understanding of the context of use in order to steer the development of TV services and content. Furthermore, also the right methodological approach to explore user experiences in this context has to be found. A thorough understanding of UX has significant potential for shaping a user's interaction with complex systems. "In understanding how interaction shapes experience, time plays an important role in consciousness and in designing actions so that users like not just the outcome of the actions but the feeling of executing them" (Ardito et al. 2007). Moreover, interaction experiences between people and artifacts can be investigated for different contexts on the visceral, behavioral, and reflective levels (Norman 2004).

In this chapter we will focus on these challenges. First, a detailed overview on the field of UX is provided with a special focus on mobile user experience. Second, we will especially highlight how to approach and investigate UX in the mobile context. In particular, we describe our experiences evaluating mobile devices and services with the experience sampling method (ESM). ESM is a known method applied on mobile devices, but its full methodological potential is not yet explored, especially not for multimedia and mobile TV applications. Finally, we will report some initial insights on an ESM study performed on an IPTV platform.

Understanding User Experience

Since it became clear, that a number of product qualities go beyond the instrumental aspects of product use and usability, UX research has evolved (Karapanos et al. 2008; Buxton 2007; Hassenzahl & Tractinsky 2006). Currently there is no agreed and unique definition of UX among the researchers in the field of Human-Computer-Interaction (HCI). However, there are a variety of different meanings associated with UX (Law et al. 2008; see also COST Action MAUSE Group http://www.cost294.org/).

In this section we provide an overview on UX research that seeks to define and understand the concept of UX itself. In particular, we address UX in the mobile context toward a better understanding of mobile user experience.

Approaches to Define UX

The concept of seeing technology in terms of experience was originally introduced by McCarthy and Wright (2004). Since then several attempts have been made to describe the concept of UX (e.g., Alben 1996; Forlizzi & Battarbee 2004; Arhippainen & Tähti 2003; Hassenzahl 2003, 2004; Kankainen 2003; Law et al. 2009).

Overall, UX has a dynamic nature, due to the ever-changing internal and emotional state of a person and due to differences in experience made during and after an interaction with a product (Law et al. 2009). UX ranges from traditional usability aspects like learnability, flexibility, and robustness to aesthetic values, and even more complex concepts (Arhippainen & Tähti 2003). Holistic approaches define UX as an experience being more than just the sum of some factors. Although definitions like "a user's experience is a result of a motivated action in a certain context" (Kankainen 2003) might be easier to understand, it is more difficult to make the concept operational and measurable in empirical research.

A more concrete definition of UX was provided by Hassenzahl and Tractinsky (2006). They define UX as a consequence of a user's internal state (predispositions, expectations, needs, motivation, mood, etc.), the characteristics of the designed system (e.g., complexity, purpose, usability, functionality, etc.), and the context (or the environment) within which the interaction occurs (e.g., organizational/social setting, meaningfulness of the activity, voluntariness of use, etc.).

When approaching UX it is also essential to look beyond static aspects and to investigate the temporal aspects of UX (seeing UX as based on the past and developing over time). The investigation of UX over time has gained more attention within UX research recently (Karapanos et al. 2008).

Levels of UX

Regarding the temporal dimension of UX, Donald Norman (2004) states that interaction happens on three different levels. The visceral level is the first impression of a product through its appearance. At this level people do not think about it, and feelings occur automatically. Spontaneous judgments – if we like or dislike a product – take place. At the behavioral level people use and experience a product. They appraise its functions, find out how well the functions fulfill their needs, and how easily the product can be used. At the reflective level consciousness takes part in the process. People understand and interpret things; they remember past experiences and use their experiences for future actions.

In reality these levels do not occur separately, but influence each other over time. In addition to Norman we see another level as important, namely the pre-experience level (see Fig. 1). Prior to the visceral level people also have pre-experiences with similar devices/services. Brand images, advertisements, and friends may have an influence, raise expectations, or lead to a skeptical attitude. This is especially true for mobile phones and even more for mobile TV. On the one

Fig. 1 Levels of UX over Time

hand, mobile phones have become widespread tools. Even infants experience the use of mobile phones, when watching their parents or other people. On the other hand, pre-experience as a dimension for UX is not only important to consider within one domain but also when services are transferred from one domain to another. Concerning mobile TV one has to keep the fact in mind that most people have experiences in watching traditional TV. Bringing TV to mobile devices has to take this fact into account.

UX for Mobile TV

UX in the mobile TV environment has become an area of high relevance in the academic world and of increasing interest for the industry as has been shown at conferences like the first international conference on designing interactive user experiences for TV and Video (uxTV 2008). Even though different approaches for understanding UX for mobile TV exist (e.g., Jumisko-Pyykkö et al. 2008a), a detailed understanding is still missing. Recent research focuses mainly on navigation design for UX (Cooper 2008) or on the production process for mobile TV (Engstrom et al. 2008).

Although the above-described approaches represent a first step toward defining a unified vision of UX, there is still a lack of more dedicated research for the mobile multimedia TV field, especially considering the context as a major factor influencing UX.

The Mobile Context

When producing a new service or device, it is essential to pay attention to the context in which the interaction with the device may actually be placed. The context affects the way people perceive the device and how it is used. The term "context" has manifold meanings within various academic disciplines. Bradley and Dunlop (2005) provide a multidisciplinary overview on the understanding and modeling of context.

In HCI, several definitions of context have been proposed during the past years (e.g., Shilit & Theimer 1994; Rodden et al. 1998; Lieberman & Selker 2000). In our research we follow one of the most comprehensive definitions of context, which is provided by Dey and Abowd (1999). They define context as "any information that can be used to characterize the situation of an entity. An entity is a person, place, or object that is considered relevant to the interaction between a user and an application,

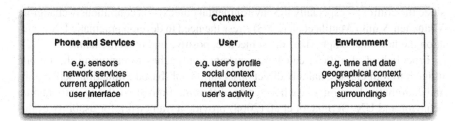

Fig. 2 Primary Context Categories

including the user and applications themselves." They also suggest dividing context into primary context parameters, namely location, identity, activity, and time.

Not surprisingly, there have also been many classifications of context with a special focus on mobile devices. Huuskonen (2005) proposes three primary categories and several subcategories for mobile phone applications (see Fig. 2). Firstly, the environment includes the geographical environment, other things around (e.g., people, devices and things), other phones in the pocket, the physical environment, time and date, and other available services in the environment. Secondly, the phone and services include sensors, network services, current application, and the user interface (e.g., screen size, the use of headphones). Thirdly, the user includes the user's profile, the social, the mental, and the physical context of the user, as well as the user's activity. In addition we have to be aware of the fact that the context, in particular for mobile devices, is constantly changing. It is therefore not enough to measure environmental context parameters once but whenever significant changes occur.

Jumisko-Pyykkö and Hannuksela (2008b) have listed several areas such as vehicles (e.g., public transportation, private cars), waiting halls or lounges, workplaces, homes, and cafes as relevant environmental context factors for mobile TV. Studies have revealed that people do not watch mobile TV during short journeys, and they favor text over video in noisy environments. Audio is the medium preferred when people are in motion, whereas text and video are the most pleasant media when people do not move (Jumisko-Pyykkö & Hannuksela 2008b). Moreover, Södergård (2003) report that mobile devices are particularly used in the public sphere. The use of mobile TV applications is therefore characterized, on the one hand, by mobility and, on the other hand, by waiting and so-called idle moments.

These examples show that the different context categories have to be taken into account when designing mobile TV applications.

Evaluating User Experience in the Mobile Context

Evaluating UX is challenging since it is not only dependent on the system but also on the user and the environmental context in which the interaction happens. Evaluating UX for mobile devices and applications is even more challenging since the context – especially the environmental context – is continuously changing. Väänänen-Vainio-Mattila et al. (2008) stress the need to develop pragmatic UX evaluation methods that emphasize "the subjective, positive and dynamic nature of UX."

Froehlich et al. (2007) categorize current approaches to capturing the mobile usage into four classes, namely direct observation, lab-based evaluation, self-report, and automatic logging – each offering different, limited visibility into human behavior and UX. Bernhaupt et al. (2008) provide a framework for usability evaluation methods for mobile applications, already including methods going beyond traditional usability practices. They describe four main categories: (1) user testing methods like thinking-aloud protocols, log-file analysis, user observation either in the laboratory or in the field; (2) inspection-oriented methods like heuristic evaluation and cognitive walkthrough; (3) self-reporting and inquiry-oriented methods like diary studies, ethnographic studies, (video) observations, contextual inquiries, interviews, questionnaires, and probe studies; and (4) analytical modeling like task model analysis and performance models.

This classification can be applied to UX evaluation of mobile TV applications. But to get a comprehensive view of the UX when interacting with mobile devices and services, a triangulation of different methods seems to be suitable.

Investigating Each Experience Level

We have outlined that UX happens on different levels (see Fig. 1). To capture the UX over time each level can be evaluated separately using different methods and combinations of methods.

The *pre-experience level* might be explored by using inquiry-oriented methods like interviews and questionnaires prior to the first usage of the mobile TV application. At this level contextual information can be explored through context scenarios, storytelling as well as within co-design and co-creation sessions as part of a user-centered design approach. Using scenario-based creative techniques, proved to be relevant for the mobile context in our previous research (e.g., Beck et al. 2008). Moreover, cultural probing is very useful to explore users' expectations and current experiences in a real-life context, in particular when the context itself is not easily accessible, such as the private home context (see Obrist et al. 2008; Bernhaupt et al. 2007).

The *visceral level* is best inspected by observing the users while experiencing the mobile device or service for the first time. Observational techniques combined with thinking-aloud techniques are appropriate to capture users' emotions when passing through the "out of the box" experience. Thereby, it has to be considered in which context this experience is made: in a private or public context (e.g., home versus shop) or in which social context (e.g., alone, with friends, colleagues). When addressing mobile services on this level, focus group or workshop settings are applicable in order to capture UX.

The *behavioral level* is the most challenging one to evaluate. It is on this level that the experience happens. To get a comprehensive understanding of the UX, the usage of mobile TV services has to be captured over a longer period. A promising method, which we have already applied in some mobile studies, is the experience sampling method (ESM) (Larson & Csikszentmihalyi 1983).

Finally, the *reflective level* is again best evaluated using questionnaires and interviews. At this level users tell about their experiences with the system. UX on the reflective level is dependent on all prior levels and changes over time.

Approaching the Behavioral Level with ESM

As mentioned above, the most challenging level in evaluating UX is the behavioral level, as it is the level where the interaction between the user and the device or services in a specific context happens. With regard to the mobile context, most contextual factors are changing on the behavioral level; therefore it is challenging to address them in the evaluation.

ESM on mobile devices has gained a lot of attention, especially since people are used to carrying mobile devices with them most of the time (e.g., Intille et al. 2003; Froehlich et al. 2007). Computerized experience sampling involves the use of mobile devices on which the sampling software is installed. It collects information about both the context and content of the daily life of individuals by asking the user to answer open and closed questions at several random, predefined, or event-triggered points throughout the day for a certain period of time.

This method enables the researcher to collect in situ user experiences over a longer time period without entering the field himself or herself. Although, one of the disadvantages of ESM is that it disrupts the user's activity, requiring the user to stop the current activity and answer questions. Therefore, Intille et al. (2003) propose the use of image-based experience sampling, where photos and short video clips are captured and can provide rich contextual information to the designer. This method variation seems to be highly relevant for mobile TV evaluations. Further evaluations related to the mobile context also consider context-aware experience tools as well as the combination and triangulation of different in situ methods (Intille et al. 2003).

In the case of mobile TV the mobile device itself can serve as the provider of the questions and collector of the answers. Contextual information of the phone or service as well as environmental contextual information can be sensed through the mobile device itself. This contextual information can also be used to trigger questions at the moments when the interaction happens or soon after it. Terminating a mobile TV application for instance might be used to trigger a set of question. The contextual information can be used manifold. Firstly, it can be logged and analyzed to gain insights on usage behavior. Secondly, it can be used to serve as the trigger for ESM questions and therefore tailor the study to question regarding UX of mobile TV. This has the advantage that the user is only prompted, when he actually uses these applications and therefore minimizes the burden for the user. Thirdly, the logged contextual data can be brought into relation to the answers users give.

Related to mobile TV, we see a potential for ESM studies for evaluating UX, in particular considering the opportunity for audiovisual-inspired sampling. For another TV-related application, namely for an IPTV (Internet Protocol Television) platform, we have already gathered some initial experiences using ESM. The main intention behind the implementation of ESM on the TV integrated into the interactive IPTV application (as part of the European CITIZEN MEDIA project www.ist-citizenmedia. org), was to collect some real-life user feedback on the provided interactive services, but also to investigate the applicability of the sampling method for a TV environment. First results showed that the test participants liked the idea of getting questions directly through the TV (at least under the condition that they can cancel the survey). Many participants stressed the advantage of getting questions immediately after doing something, and not some days or weeks later. Moreover, it was pointed out that it is a good method to address a different variety of people using the TV. A more detailed analysis of the revealed data is still going on. However, we are convinced that ESM is a comfortable, easy, and straightforward way to collect user feedback in a TV-related context. Overall, the technical development and implementation should not be underestimated as well as the research setup itself (defining the right questions and frequencies for asking questions, etc.).

With regard to the evaluation of UX on mobile devices we have developed MAESTRO, a toolkit for experience sampling, which is capable of logging behavior and capturing the user's experiences during mobile device handling. We have designed and implemented MAESTRO to give the researcher the possibility to dynamically orchestrate experience sampling studies for evaluating usage behavior of mobile devices and services such as mobile TV. The ESM tool was for instance used to explore users' emotional attachment towards mobile devices and services (see Meschtscherjakov 2009).

Conclusions

Even though several studies beyond usability and toward user experience in the mobile context have been conducted, there are still necessary steps to be taken to have a clear evaluation approach addressing in particular user experience for mobile TV. To capture experiences throughout all the levels where it happens (namely pre-experience, visceral, behavioral, and reflective level) a mixture, of different methods seems to be appropriate. Especially the experience sampling method shows the capabilities to fit best the methodological challenges, as revealed from our research in mobile and TV-related contexts.

Acknowledgments: We would like to thank all who enabled our research on user experience (e.g., the CITIZEN MEDIA project funded by FP6-2005-IST-41).

References

Alben, L. (1996). Quality of experience. *Interactions, 3*(3), 11–15.

Ardito, C., Costabile, M., Lanzilotti, R., & Montinaro, F. (September 3, 2007). Towards the evaluation of UX. In *Workshop "Towards a UX Manifesto" at the International Conference HCI 2007, Lancaster, UK*, 6–9.

Arhippainen, L., & Tähti, M. (2003). Empirical evaluation of user experience in two adaptive mobile application prototypes. In *Proceedings of the International Conference on Mobile and Ubiquitous Multimedia, Norrköping*.

Beck, E., Obrist, M., Bernhaupt, R., & Tscheligi, M. (2008). Instant card technique: How and why to apply in user-centered design. In *Proceedings PDC2008*.

Bernhaupt, R., Weiss, A., Obrist, M., & Tscheligi, M. (2007). *Playful probing: Making probing more fun*. INTERACT 2007, 10–14 September 2007, LNCS 4662, 606–619. Heidelberg: Springer.

Bernhaupt, R., Mihalic, K., & Obrist M. (2008). Methods for usability evaluation of mobile applications. In J. Lumsden (Ed.), *Handbook of Research on User Interface Design and Evaluation for Mobile Technology, IGI global* (pp. 745–758).

Bradley, N., & Dunlop, M. (2005). Toward a multidisciplinary model of context to support context-aware computing. *Human-Computer Interaction, 20*(4), 403–446.

Buxton, B. (2007). Sketching user experiences: Getting the design right and the right design. San Francisco, CA: Morgan Kaufmann.

Cooper, W. (2008). The interactive television user experience so far. *Proceedings of the 1st International Conference on Designing Interactive User Experiences for TV and Video, Silicon Valley, USA* (October 22–24, 2008). UXTV '08, ACM, New York.

Dey, A., & Abowd, G. (1999). Towards a better understanding of context and context-awareness. Technical Report, from ftp://ftp.cc.gatech.edu/pub/gvu/tr/1999/99-22.pdf

Engstrom, A., Esbjornsson, M., Juhlin, O., & Perry, M. (2008). Producing collaborative video: developing an interactive user experience for mobile tv. *Proceedings of the 1st International Conference on Designing Interactive User Experiences for TV and Video, Silicon Valley, USA* (October 22–24, 2008). UXTV '08, ACM, New York.

Forlizzi, J., & Battarbee, K. (2004). Understanding experience in interactive systems. In *Proceedings of the 5th Conference on Designing Interactive Systems: Processes, Practices, Methods, and Techniques, Cambridge, MA, USA* (August 1–4, 2004). DIS '04, ACM, New York, 261-268.

Froehlich, J., Chen, M., Consolvo, S., Harrison, B., & Landay, J. (June 11–14, 2007). My experience: A system for in situ tracing and capturing of user feedback on mobile phones proceedings of MobiSys? San Juan, Puerto Rico.

Hassenzahl, M. (2003). The thing and I: Understanding the relationship between user and product. In M. Blythe, C. Overbeeke, A. Monk & P. Wright (Eds.), *Funology: From usability to enjoyment* (pp. 31–42). Dordrecht: Kluwer.

Hassenzahl, M. (2004). The interplay of beauty, goodness and usability in interactive products. *Human Computer Interaction, 19*, 319–349.

Hassenzahl, M., & Tractinsky, N. (2006). User experience – a research agenda. *Behavior & Information Technology, 25*(2), 91–97.

Huuskonen, P. (2005) Interaction through non-interaction. Interaction through non-interaction: Context awareness and distributed applications. *Keynote speech at Applied Spoken Language Interaction in Distributed Environments (ASIDE2005), Aalborg, Denmark*.

Intille, S. S., Rondoni, J., Kukla, C., Iacono, I., & Bao, L. (2003). A context-aware experience sampling tool. In *Proceedings of CHI'03, Posters: Computer everywhere, Florida, USA*, 972–973.

Jumisko-Pyykkö, S., & Hannuksela, M. M. (2008b). Does context matter in quality evaluation of mobile television? In *Proceedings of 10th International Conference on Human Computer Interaction with Mobile Devices and Services (MobileHCI 2008)*, 63–72

Jumisko-Pyykkö, S., Weitzel, M., & Strohmeier, D. (2008a). Designing for user experience: What to expect from Mobile 3D TV and video? In *Proceedings uxTV 2008 conference, Silicon Valley, USA.*

Kankainen, A. (2003). UCPCD: user-centered product concept design. *Proceedings of the 2003 conference on Designing for User Experiences, ACM Press, San Francisco, California.*

Karapanos, E., Hassenzahl, M., & Martens, J. -B. (2008). User experience over time, Work in progress. In *Proceedings CHI 2008, ACM, New York, USA,* 3561–3566.

Knoche, H., Papaleo, M., Sasse, M. A., & Vanelli-Coralli, A. (2007a). The kindest cut: Enhancing the user experience of mobile TV through adequate zooming. *ACM Multimedia 2007 conference,* (23–29 September), Augsburg, Germany.

Knoche, H., Papaleo, M., Sasse, M. A. & Vanelli-Coralli, A. (2007a). The kindest cut: Enhancing the user experience of mobile TV through adequate zooming. In Proceedings of the 15th international Conference on Multimedia (Augsburg, Germany, September 25–29, 2007). Multimedia'07. ACM, New York, 87–96.

Larson, R., & Csikszentmihalyi, M. (1983). The experience sampling method. In H. T. Reiss (Ed.), *Naturalistic approaches to studying social interaction. New directions for methodology of social and behavioral sciences* (pp. 41–56). San Francisco, CA: Jossey-Bass.

Law, E., Roto, V., Vermeeren, A. P., Kort, J., & Hassenzahl, M. (2008). Towards a shared definition of user experience. In *CHI '08 Extended Abstracts on Human Factors in Computing Systems, Florence, Italy* (April 05–10, 2008). CHI '08, ACM, New York, pp. 2395–2398.

Law, E. L., Roto, V., Hassenzahl, M., Vermeeren, A. P., and Kort, J. (2009). Understanding, scoping and defining user experience: a survey approach. In *Proceedings of the 27th international Conference on Human Factors in Computing Systems* (Boston, MA, USA, April 04–09, 2009). CHI '09. ACM, New York, NY, 719–728.

Lieberman, H., & Selker, T. (2000). Out of context: Computer systems that adapt to, and learn from, context. *IBM Systems, 39*(3–4), 617–632.

McCarthy, J., & Wright, P. (2004). Technology as experience. Cambridge, MA: MIT Press.

Meschtscherjakov, A. (2009). Mobile attachment – emotional attachment towards mobile devices and services. In *MobileHCI09: Proceedings of the 11th International Conference on Human-Computer Interaction with Mobile Devices and Services (supplementary proceedings).* Accepted for publication.

Norman, D. A. (2004). *Emotional design: Why we love (or hate) everyday things.* New York: Basic Books.

Obrist, M., Bernhaupt, R., & Tscheligi, M. (2008). Interactive TV for the home: An ethnographic study on users' requirements and experiences. *International Journal of Human-Computer Interaction, 24*(2), 174–196.

Rodden, T., Cheverst, K., Davies, K., & Dix, A. (1998). Exploiting context in HCI design for mobile systems. *Workshop on Human Computer Interaction with Mobile Devices,* from http://www.dcs.gla.ac.uk/~johnson/papers/mobile/HCIMD1.html

Saleemi, M. M., Björkqvist, J., & Lilius, J. (2008). System architecture and interactivity model for mobile TV applications. In *Proceeding of 3rd ACM International Conference on Digital Interactive Media in Entertainment and Arts (DIMEA 2008), ACM.*

Schmidt-Belz, B., & Jones, M. (2006). Mobile usage of video and TV. In *Proceedings of 8th conference on Human-computer interaction with mobile devices and services 2006,* 291–292.

Serco. (2006). Usability guidelines for Mobile TV design. *Internet,* from, http://www.serco.com/Images/Mobile%20TV%20guidelines_tcm3-13804.pdf

Shilit, B., & Theimer, M. (1994). Disseminating active map information to mobile hosts. *IEEE Network, 8,* 22–32.

Södergård, C. (2003). Mobile television – technology and user experiences report on the mobile-TV project (Rep. No. P506). VTT Information Technology.

Väänänen-Vainio-Mattila, K., Roto, V., & Hassenzahl, M. (2008). Towards practical user experience evaluation methods. *Proceedings of the International Workshop on Meaningful Measures: Valid Useful User Experience Measurement (VUUM), Reykjavik, Iceland* (June 18, 2008). IRIT, Toulouse, France.

Part V
Context and Sociability in Mobile Interactive Multimedia Systems

Social Properties of Mobile Video

April Slayden Mitchell, Kenton O'Hara, and Alex Vorbau

Abstract Mobile video is now an everyday possibility with a wide array of commercially available devices, services, and content. These new technologies have created dramatic shifts in the way video-based media can be produced, consumed, and delivered by people beyond the familiar behaviors associated with fixed TV and video technologies. Such technology revolutions change the way users behave and change their expectations in regards to their mobile video experiences. Building upon earlier studies of mobile video, this paper reports on a study using diary techniques and ethnographic interviews to better understand how people are using commercially available mobile video technologies in their everyday lives. Drawing on reported episodes of mobile video behavior, the study identifies the social motivations and values underpinning these behaviors that help characterize mobile video consumption beyond the simplistic notion of viewing video only to kill time. This paper also discusses the significance of user-generated content and the usage of video in social communities through the description of two mobile video technology services that allow users to create and share content. Implications for adoption and design of mobile video technologies and services are discussed as well.

Introduction

The consumption of video-based media is an integral part of everyday life. On average, people spend several hours each day consuming video-based material whether they are watching it, talking about it, or simply reading about it. The activity can be focused or unfocused, solitary or social. Video accompanies different parts of our lives, such as when we have breakfast, eat dinner, relax for the evening, go out for a drink, and even when we go to sleep. It can inform us and mediate our social and emotional states. Video can be part of the backdrop to particular periods of people's

A.S. Mitchell, K. O'Hara and A. Vorbau
Hewlett-Packard Labs, 1501, Page Mill Rd. MS 1181, Palo Alto, CA 94304

A. Marcus et al. (eds.), *Mobile TV: Customizing Content and Experience*,
Human-Computer Interaction Series, DOI 10.1007/978-1-84882-701-1_16,
© Springer-Verlag London Limited 2010

lives and special occasions. It evokes key memories both personal and shared, cementing intimate relationships between friends and families. Video can bring people together for shared viewing. Talking about, displaying, swapping, and sharing video content are all vehicles through which identity, group bonds, and membership are developed. Video-based media is also consumed in different environments, thus shaping the social activities that occur there. For example, plasma screens in bars can both be a distraction from social engagement (e.g., watching the TV instead of talking) or can be the focus of particularly strong group bonds (e.g., watching a sports match in the pub).

How we consume video-based content and integrate it into our personal and social lives is determined by the technologies through which we experience it: how content is distributed, rendered, purchased, organized, shared, chosen, listened to, interacted with, and repurposed. This relationship between technology and how people consume video can be illustrated by looking at some key technical shifts over the years and the resulting social phenomena. Consider, for example, the effects of introducing VCRs into the home environment. These created a shift away from the organizing structure of the TV schedule, giving people the opportunity to view content at more convenient times. VCRs also encouraged new ways for the prerecorded content to be distributed and accessed, for example, through the rental and purchasing of prerecorded video content. These ways were also rich with social possibilities – for example, how a video collection comes to be an expression of identity, how video content could be lent or given to friends, how renting a video could be the basis for a social occasion, etc.

With the advent of digital video technologies, we are seeing even more dramatic shifts in the ways that video-based content can be produced and consumed, how it is delivered to devices (e.g., broadcast vs. download vs. tangible storage media vs. Bluetooth, etc.) and how it is copied, exchanged, organized, chosen, controlled, and manipulated by both individuals and groups.

One particular shift in recent times, of concern to us in this chapter, has been the emergence of technologies and services designed to support mobile video consumption. Device manufacturers, telecommunication operators, and media broadcasters are making enormous investments in these capabilities with dedicated mobile video and TV devices, content delivery services, and content. These and other such services are changing the landscape of video content delivery and pose an interesting challenge to the more traditional broadcast companies. As well as published content, there are also more and more opportunities for user-generated video content. In particular, the current generation of camera phones allows such capabilities to be ubiquitously carried around – changing when and where such recordings can be made, viewed, and shared in social groups. Likewise, social network sites and other web 2.0 technologies are changing the context within which user-generated mobile video on mobile phones is made (Grossman 2007). Other technologies are emerging which support the sharing of user-generated content in social networks. We will discuss examples of such video creation and sharing technologies and factors which may influence adoption of video in social communities.

The shift from fixed video consumption practices to mobile usage does not simply result in a transfer of the same experience to a greater range of places. Rather, as we have seen with social studies of portable MP3 players and mobile phones, the mobile form factor profoundly changes the ways in which people orient toward these technologies and content as well as how these artifacts become integrated into people's everyday lives (Bull 2000; Bull 2007; du Gay & Hall 1997; Kirk et al. 2007; Knoche et al. 2005; Logan et al. 1995; Palen et al. 2000; Rode et al. 2005). We would expect similar shifts to happen in line with these growing possibilities for mobile video distribution and consumption, resulting in a new range of solitary and social behaviors around video consumption. Our concern in this chapter, then, is to explicate these changing behaviors. Rather than taking the perspective that it is just TV on the move, our aim is to understand what is particular about the mobile video experience and what are the social properties of mobile video that shape these experiences. How do people consume mobile video both published and user-generated to achieve particular social effects?

History of Social Video

There are numerous social studies of television in the literature. Of these, perhaps the most extensive is Silverstone's study of television and everyday life (Silverstone 1994). While this offers some pointers to everyday behaviors with regards to TV, much of the analytic concern is above what is practical from a design perspective – being concerned more with societal significance of the TV. Of greater relevance to our concerns here are the more design-oriented social studies of TV/video consumption whose analytic concerns are more with the details of everyday practices and their relationships with particular TV/video technologies (Black et al. 1994; Brown & Barkhuus 2006; Logan et al. 1995; Mateas et al. 1996; O'Brien et al. 1999; Rode et al. 2005; Taylor & Harper 2003). A number of important issues arise in these studies. For example, Taylor and Harper in their ethnography of TV in the home highlight the ways in which TV viewing in the home gets structured and, in particular, how different modes of viewing relates to the wider social context in which TV gets consumed. Early parts of the evening, for example, can be characterized by a relatively passive and indiscriminate viewing behavior – part of the ritual of coming home that allows people to "switch off" from the relative stresses and strains of the workday. Mid-evening viewing, by contrast, is characterized by a more selective viewing with a greater emphasis on social and communal viewing whereby the family sits down to watch TV in order to "be together." Late-evening viewing is characterized by more individual content preferences and done after household chores are complete and children are in bed.

The social organization of the household and its relationship to TV is also an important theme in O'Brien et al.'s (1999) ethnography of a set-top box (STB) device in the home (TV, Internet, etc.). A key insight of this study concerns the household as a distributed system. So while the TV/STB in the living room did promote some of the social functions of togetherness, the concentration of functionality into the set-top box in the living room did not allow for a natural distribution of activities across different people and spaces in the house where appropriate. As we shall see later, this theme plays a part in the motivations underlying everyday practices with mobile video.

Another point to draw from these studies concerns methods for distributing content. The study by Barkhuus and Brown (2006) is illustrative here in its look at practices around video downloading and the social motivations behind this activity relative to broadcast content. A critical point here is control over content choice. Control is not simply about what one wants to watch at a particular time but brings a host of other important social values associated with content ownership, such as the importance of content collection and the ability to share this with others. The study also highlights the need to consider the whole TV life cycle; not just the viewing experience but the activities that happen around this, e.g., viewing program guide, etc. These methods again have bearing on the different practices emerging around particular types of mobile video devices.

The above studies offer important insights that help understand aspects of mobile video consumption within a broader ecology of video consumption practices. But, they do not offer insights into the unique qualities of mobile video. Much of the work on mobile video has been largely technological in its focus, or it has focused on particular aspects of usability such as video quality preferences or navigation issues (e.g., Knoche et al. 2005; Stockbridge 2006). While important in their own right, these studies do not address our concern with everyday behaviors with mobile, its integration into people's lives, and its relationship to the places where people use it. A few key studies have attempted to do this. First, Södergård reports on an extensive study of a mobile TV prototype in Finland (Södergård 2003). In the study, participants were given a prototype device, either an iPAQ or Tablet PC, on which they could view content from three Finnish TV channels over WLAN. The study highlights the value of TV anytime (being released from TV schedule) and anywhere for people. It also begins to highlight some interesting characteristics of people's mobile viewing behavior, such as the predominance of very short viewing periods (of the order of a few minutes), sometimes listening rather than viewing, and that favored content was different from traditional TV. It also reports some of the different places where people viewed TV such as the home or at the bus stop. In terms of understanding mobile video, the study makes a good start but the analysis often stops a little short, describing behaviors but not really exploring the social context and motivations associated with the behavior.

We get some more sense of social motivations and relationship to place in the study of Repo and colleagues (2003, 2004). In their week-long study, they gave participants video-enabled mobile phones with access to a small amount of content streamed from a Finnish TV channel. Of interest in the study is their discussion about video-viewing behavior in public spaces. Drawing on Goffman's notion of "face" they highlight three strategies for managing face: averting disturbance by avoiding irritation to others around, adjusting to signaled disapproval, and purposeful aggressive behaviors to deliberately draw attention. In addition, the study starts to point out ways in which mobile video comes to be enjoyed as part of a shared experience rather than just alleviating boredom for an individual – a theme which we explore further in our study. This study, though, is only a starting point for our understanding. The authors indeed call for further research, acknowledging the limitations of their own study in terms of the narrow focus on the mobile phone, small range of content type, limited period of use of the technology, and content delivery mechanism (namely streaming video).

Taken together, these studies begin to offer us some insights. However, further research is necessary to really understand the contextual factors and social motivations shaping practices as they are enacted and given meaning in everyday life. We aim to address some of these shortfalls by conducting a study that focuses on what people are doing in everyday life with a range of their own mobile video devices. By looking at these existing practices, we are able to understand how people have assimilated mobile video into their everyday lives and characterize further the "social circumstances" of use and relationship of use to particular places and situations.

Study of Everyday Practices with Mobile Video

Understanding the new solitary and social behaviors that have developed around video consumption is integral to continued innovation in the area of mobile video. In an effort to divulge some of the mystery behind mobile video usage, we conducted a study of current mobile video consumers. We gathered information about the circumstances of how and when users watched mobile video as well as their overall preferences regarding mobile video and any unmet needs. We also looked at more focused details such as how users accessed, stored, organized, shared, and created video-based content that they consumed on a mobile video device. In the following sections we provide a description of our investigation, an analysis of our data, as well a discussion on technology recommendations and potential areas of opportunity in the mobile video space.

Evaluation

The only requirements for our volunteers were that they own a video-enabled portable device and that they use the device for watching video at least once a week. We broadcast a request for volunteers via e-mail. Participants were pre-screened for the study by either a phone conversation or by answering a series of questions via e-mail. Our participants owned and used a variety of devices. The Apple Video iPod was the most common device used in the study, which reflects its relative popularity in the consumer market. Participants also used Sony Playstation Portable (PSP) devices, video-enabled Archos devices, HP iPAQ handhelds, and video-enabled mobile phones. We excluded the use of laptop-only mobile users since we chose to focus on purely hand-held mobile viewing experiences.

Some factors which may affect mobile video usage such as the use of public transportation and the availability of media services differ widely from country to country (Stockbridge 2006). Therefore, we chose participants from both the USA and the UK to see if any geographic trends emerged. Our final participant group consisted of 28 volunteers (13 from the UK and 15 from the USA), both male and female, ranging in age from 14 to 47. The aim here was not to create the basis for statistical comparisons across different types of users and devices (which would not be appropriate with such a sample size). Rather, in such an exploratory study, the aim was to provide opportunities for issues particular to different types of users and devices to be highlighted. Each participant was compensated with a gift certificate at the completion of their interview valued at 50 British pounds or US$50.

At the start of the study, each participant was given a small diary notebook and asked to record their mobile video experiences for a 3-week period. We asked them to record the date, circumstance (e.g., "on the train home from work" or "waiting for my mom to pick me up from practice"), and activity (e.g., "watching Family Guy" or "looking for free videos on iTunes") for every mobile video episode they had during the given time period. See Fig. 1 for the instructions included in the diary notebook, and see Fig. 2 for an example page from a single diary entry of one of our participants. We encouraged them to record not only when they watched mobile video, but also when they performed other related activities as well, such as searching for or purchasing content. At the end of the 3-week diary period, we met with each participant individually for a 1-h interview. Some of the younger partici- pants were interviewed in pairs if they had a friend who was also in the study in order to help them be more comfortable and communicative in an interview setting. During the interview, we had participants talk through their diary entries with us and discuss in more detail the circumstances and motivations of each experience. Each interview was either video-recorded or audio-recorded to ensure accuracy in quoting the participants, and we kept their diary notebooks for further review.

Analysis

Recorded diary episodes highlighted how mobile video was being consumed in a huge variety of places, including buses, cars, trains, airport lounges, work cafeterias, people's desk in the office, cafes, the gym, the hospital, on the walk to school, and the school playground. As we shall see, it also started to inhabit places where one expects to find other forms of fixed televisions and video consumption devices such as in the home and at friends' houses. Mobile video was consumed at different times during the day and for a range of durations. Earlier prototype studies of mobile video had suggested that viewing episodes on mobile devices were typically short (e.g., Södergård 2003). There was some consistency here with some partici- pants not watching mobile video for long periods of time because of the small

Please include the following for each entry:

- ◆ Date
- ◆ Time
- ◆ Location
- ◆ Device
- ◆ Action Performed

Example Diary Page

9pm Wed

Waiting for friends in downtown

Palo Alto

Video iPod

watching 'Law & Order'

or

Monday morning

on the train from Guilford to

Bristol

Audiovox smartphone

browsing for new content and then

downloading Rocketboom and

watching two episodes

Fig. 1 Diary instruction page (Vorbau et al. 2007)

screen size. However, a more accurate characterization of behavior was that viewing episodes were determined by the range of different content length available relative to standard broadcast TV, and perhaps more importantly, the practicalities of the particular circumstances where it came to be viewed. In this respect and in contrast to the earlier prototype-based studies, we saw how people watched a range of different content, both published and user-created, from short 30 s clips and 5 min Podcasts through to 30 min TV shows and movies. Mobile video allowed people to utilize different time periods for particular purposes.

How people were incorporating mobile video into their everyday lives and routines was of particular significance to us. Similar behavior patterns were observed in each country; therefore, we will not compare or contrast results by geography. For some of the participants it remained a novelty, but for many it became something that was routinely used. It was fitted into daily habits as individuals and as members of friends and family groups for particular social effect. In exploring this, we take a look first at some of the individual usage of mobile video as well as

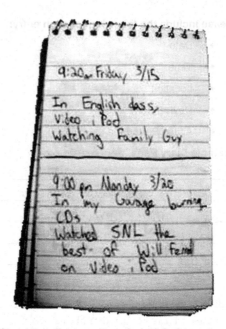

Fig. 2 Actual diary entry page (Vorbau et al. 2007)

mobile video content choice, then we move on to consider the social and collaborative aspects of its consumption.

Individual Viewing

Solitary viewing was the predominant form of consumption of mobile video. *"Passing time"* was unsurprisingly cited as one reason for this behavior, but a deeper look at the episodes revealed important social factors underlying this seemingly solitary behavior. Many of these viewing episodes took place in shared or public settings, such as the workplace or waiting spaces where other people were around. Over and above simply passing time, then, the consumption of mobile video in these settings was used as a way of managing relationships with others around.

Managing Solitude

Consider, for example, the routine use of mobile video during lunch breaks at work by several participants. For these, lunch was spent alone rather than shared with other colleagues. Having lunch alone in the cafeteria was, socially speaking, mildly uncomfortable. Watching mobile video allowed people to appear purposeful rather than alone in these contexts. Alternatively, some participants avoided the cafeteria and lunched alone at their desks. However, it was still important for them to have a lunch break. Being immersed in the audio-visual experience of mobile video allowed them to claim back their own time and space, blocking out sights and sounds of a shared workspace.

Disengaging from Others

Watching mobile video in shared settings was also used to avoid possibilities of social engagement. A good illustration of this can be seen in an episode recorded by one of the young male participants. For the school run each morning and evening, his parents car-pooled with another family. This meant that he shared the car's back seat with the children from the other family. Because they were younger than he was, he found them a little irritating. Watching video on his PSP with headphones was his way of avoiding engagement with them in the close confines of the car. To a similar effect he also showed them the Simpson's to keep them quiet.

> I held it up and they were watching it and I thought 'oh blimey if it's like £200.00 to keep them quiet. I will pay it any day'. I just sat there and thought 'watch it please'. I held it so they could all see it. Best car journey home ever really.

Controlling the acoustic environment in these shared spaces was another motivation. For example, a young male participant described being driven to school by his dad. His dad played music in the car which our participant did not like, so he would watch mobile video with headphones to *avoid* listening to his dad's music.

In public transport situations, we saw mobile video usage for some similar kinds of reasons. As well as managing the boredom of these journeys, mobile video with headphones was used to create a private space and manage what Bull (2000) calls the close proximity of unknown others within these public spaces. Of course, people used other technologies and content to do this such as MP3 players. But video was particularly useful here since it demands visual attention too, allowing further disengagement from unknown others.

Choosing to use mobile video in these spaces and circumstances (as opposed to adopting other strategies such as listening to music with headphones or reading) was contingent on a number of factors that characterized these spaces. Unlike the Repo study (Repo et al. 2003, 2004) the concerns here were not with disturbing people with sound since the devices were typically used with headphones in these spaces – indeed an important part of the privatizing function of these devices. Rather, they seemed to relate to the ability to be settled and undisturbed in these spaces. To illustrate some of these factors consider an example from a participant who regularly took the bus to and from work:

> Taking the bus [to work] takes between 45 minutes and an hour. In the morning I would come by bus sometimes or with a colleague – in the evening I would go back by bus – but that is when I was watching most of the content. There is less sunlight [in the evening] plus the bus is busier during the morning. If I was sharing the seat with someone – I don't know why – maybe you don't feel comfortable or something – you need more space to expand yourself. It's easier to listen to music – I have an MP3 player with me sometimes – probably just because I have the headphones already connected to it. At the bus stop I sometimes watch things but if there are many people around I don't watch it because there is no where to sit.

As we see from this quote, the time of his journey was sufficient for him to get into a piece of content. This contrasted with other participants who routinely took journeys of 5–10 min and who did not view video because the journeys were too short to justify the effort. At times when the bus was particularly busy (e.g., on the morning commute) he avoided watching video because of the difficulty getting comfortable and settled with other people around. Sharing a bus seat with others made it awkward to get his mobile video device out and hold it. At these times, it was simpler and more convenient to listen to music since the device could remain in his bag or pocket. At night, when the bus was less busy he could get sufficiently settled to watch video on his iPaq.

Of particular importance about these transport experiences is that they are made up not just of single places but rather a system of places that people have to transition between. For example, people move from bus stop to the bus and back off again, or from train platform to the train and off onto the destination platform. At the airport, this is even more complicated as people move from queues at the check in desk through to the departure lounge (punctuated by trips to the shops or toilet) onto the gate and finally onto the plane. The transitions between these places both by participants themselves and the people around them play a significant role in their ability to be settled, shaping these mobile video experiences, and even decisions to watch video at all.

Let us consider the bus example again. At the bus stop, it was important to maintain attention on whether the bus was arriving or not. This demanded visual monitoring which competed for attention with the video viewing. Even on the bus, the experience was a little distracted in the sense that people would look up from the screen to look around at people to see those getting on and off and to monitor where the bus was, as described in the following quote:

> The content I was watching you are not always looking at the screen – you sometimes look around to see what is in your environment so you continue listening to it – the plot. It's the environment forces you – you are less into it than you would be at home. You are looking at people coming on to the bus or looking where you are – its only maybe a glimpse but its not like being at home in front of your TV.

This was not a problem, merely a characteristic of the experience, but it tended to impact the participant's choice of content. They would watch things they described as *"throw away,"* something that could be *"easily put down,"* or where continuity could be maintained through the audio.

Managing Transitions Between Spaces

Form factor also played a key role here, with smaller form factor devices allowing participants to better manage transitions between different spaces. For example, the PSP has a slightly larger form factor relative to the iPod or iPAQ, and thus it would be carried in a bag rather than a pocket. Having to take a device out of the bag to watch then put away again to make a transition to a different space created a sufficient effort burden for people not to bother getting it out in places where they are waiting for only a short period of time such as a train platform. However, even with these smaller devices, watching video in itself was often much less conducive than listening to audio for dealing with the transitions between spaces because audio did not require the same kind of stop–start behavior that the visual attention of video demands. One could continue listening to music while moving from platform to train, or from bus stop onto the bus, or from departure lounge seat to the shops.

Sharing the Experience

Watching Together

While much of mobile video viewing behavior was characterized as solitary viewing (albeit often in the presence of other people in public and shared spaces), an important feature of people's behaviors with mobile video concerned shared viewing episodes. On a purely practical level, there were certain pragmatic difficulties with shared viewing of these devices and typically it would be limited to small groups of two or three people. Sharing the audio on some devices was also difficult. For example, with the iPod there is no internal loudspeaker available, so people would do things such as use one headphone ear bud each and cup the ear buds in their hands to try and amplify it or simply not bother with the sound at all. With other devices such as PSP and mobile phones, the built-in loudspeaker would be used (though in noisier environments of certain public spaces this too was sometimes a poor experience). While identifying these practical limitations lends itself to potential design opportunities, also of significance is why such behaviors happen in spite of the practical difficulties. There is value in such behaviors that needs understanding.

Looking more closely at these episodes we see that mobile video creates interesting new opportunities for social occasioning. What is important here is how the devices allow specific pieces of content to be carried into new social contexts. It is within particular social contexts that the content on these mobile video devices could be made meaningful. In one episode, for example, a group of four boys were at school and used a PSP in order to watch the film "Shaun of the Dead." The film was their collective favorite; something they had *"all seen about ten times before"* and something that they would not be allowed to watch in adult company. The group had retreated to the graphics room because *"not many teachers go in there"* and gathered round the PSP. What was notable about their viewing was that they did not watch the film continuously. Rather, they fast forwarded to the *"funny bits"* in the film in order to watch those. They would each call out different scenes to forward to, have discussions together about which were the good bits, and comment as the scenes played. This behavior was more than simply passing the time. Rather, they were enacting their friendship through suggestions, agreements, and disagreements about scenes and expressing something about their tastes as individuals and as group members. The device mobility allowed this to play out away from the presence of inhibiting authority figures they would find at home and in more public parts of the school.

In another episode, we see how sharing specific types of content was part of belonging to a group or community based around a specific interest. The participant in question belonged to a gang of skateboarders. The gang would congregate in a particular part of the city where other skaters skated. At the end of one particular day, they went to a local coffee shop to continue *"hanging out."* While there, three of the group gathered round a video iPod to watch professional skateboarding videos together. Again we see here how these particular pieces of content were being made meaningful within a particular social context. Watching the videos was a resource for expressing their identity as skateboarders to the others in the group. They also used the videos to discuss good places to go and skateboard. Of significance here is that this group was organized around the particular location and vicinity where they all skated. This is not something that would take place in each others' homes because their homes were not the places where they interacted as a group. It was the mobility of the device and content that created the opportunity for being part of this social context.

Some participants also used mobile video as a way of spending time with their children. We noted earlier how parents would sometimes give their device to their children to watch, but there were also examples of watching mobile video together with their children. On occasions, they would also sit and watch the cartoons together. This kind of shared experience was a much more active form of viewing than the passive experience of simply handing the device over. It was a way of brokering conversation and of spending time together. As one participant noted:

> He asks questions as we are watching Felix the Cat or Dora the Explorer and I'll answer them.

On other occasions, sharing mobile video was used as a resource for shared decision making and planning about social occasions. For instance, one couple while waiting for their children to finish playing at a local leisure center decided to think about what to do on an upcoming evening when they had a babysitter available. They downloaded to their phone several trailers of currently showing movies and watched them together in order to discuss whether there was anything worth them going to see.

> The kids were running round and playing and very happy and my wife and I were talking about going to the cinema on Wednesday night because we had a babysitter to look after the children. We didn't know what was on at the cinema so thought why don't we just look on the myview.com website and see what films were on. We downloaded some film previews – the Weather Man and Walk the Line and a couple of. We were able to play them and see the different scenes but it was so loud in there with all the kids and things that we couldn't actually hear the volume. So we ended up ignoring the volume – and we were talking over it – oh this looks funny or this looks good. We concluded we didn't want to see the Weather man.

Showing Video to Others

Sharing mobile video was not just about watching things together but also about *showing* things to other people for particular purposes (e.g., Södergård 2003).

There were several episodes in which participants showed personal content such as family videos using their mobile devices.

> This is the type of file [video of the family on PSP] that I want to be able to have with me – it's more family, It's not … for me. I'm sure there is a market out there for people who want to download the next CSI but …

An important feature of this behavior was that people were putting and keeping certain pieces of content on their mobile devices specifically for this purpose. It is not just that the content happens to be on the device and then comes to be appropriated for these collaborative practices. For example, one participant described keeping his holiday videos on his phone (as opposed to just downloading them to his PC) for a certain time period after the holiday because he knew that people would ask him how the holiday went.

> It stays on there for a while during the period when people are still asking me whether I had a good holiday – I can then show them the videos when they ask.

Similar behavior was also seen with published content. One couple kept documentaries recorded from the TV on their mobile device. The point of keeping the content was not to watch it themselves but rather to show particular bits to friends whenever they visited their friends' homes. The content would form the basis for discussion between them – part of the ongoing socializing of a visit to a friend's house. Another female participant would keep certain pieces of content on her device after watching it because she wanted to show her friends who would be interested. Through the act of showing chosen content, she demonstrates her own interests and understanding of what her friends find cool.

The motivations for having mobile video content on these devices extend beyond the obvious notions of having stuff available to watch. What became apparent from our interviews was the value of simply *having* content on the device, in particular for the younger participants. As has been seen in research on music, content collections can be an important way of representing aspects of identity or provide clues about the identity of others whose collections you are viewing (Brown & Sellen 2006; O'Hara & Brown 2006; Silverstone 1994). Video content collections on these mobile devices had similar properties. Several younger participants spoke of how they would just browse through their friends' devices to see what was on there.

> People just look through your videos just to see what you have got. When we are just sat somewhere people will look through your videos to see what you have got – just anywhere when you are sat around bored – have a look at the phone.

The social motivations here are intimately bound up with the methods of content distribution to the device. Keeping content on the device that has been specifically chosen by the user (as with download models of distribution) has different social consequences relative to content distribution based on streaming TV services. Downloading afforded a sense of ownership bringing different social values. For example, two high school students scoured file-sharing networks like LimeWire, searching for "*.m4v," the file extension for iPod-compatible videos. They also searched Google Video because the site has the option of downloading videos in iPod and PSP formats. The search for content for these participants was not just a necessary and tedious task, but instead was perceived as a game and even a social activity that could be enjoyed with friends.

Opportunities for humor were another motivation for showing mobile video content. A good example of this was the use of the mobile phone to show highlights from the Premiership football by one participant. He would show the clips to his friend at work in order to wind the friend up about how badly his friend's team had done at the weekend. The issue here was not really one about quality of viewing experience. Indeed for both parties the content was not new as they had seen it before. The content was a pointer and the act of showing was sufficient to generate the humor.

Mobile Video Content

Content Choice

Comedy was the most popular genre of media content on our participants' mobile video devices. The great majority of the study's participants, across age and gender, downloaded short comedy-oriented, often animated, video clips. The positive experience of watching comedy on a mobile device is also supported by Repo et al. (2003), where animated films, karaoke recordings, and music videos were considered the most interesting content. Cartoons like "Family Guy," "South Park," and "The Simpsons" were popular with a range of ages, whereas several younger interviewees mentioned downloading "Saturday Night Live" comedy shorts. Another participant liked watching classic cartoons like "Felix the Cat," and downloaded contemporary cartoons such as "Sponge Bob" for her 5-year-old nephew. One interviewee, James H. (age 17) highlighted a few sensible reasons as to why comedy was an appealing source of content. He explained that since mobile video viewing is often done in short segments, usually 20 min or less, he prefers content that is not very long in duration and does not have a complicated plot to follow. He shared that it was easier to start watching comedy from the point where he last paused as it does not require as much immersion in the video. We were also told by another participant that comedy is good content for the mobile device because it continues to be funny when watched multiple times, whereas dramas and reality-based shows are only interesting the first time.

> "I like comedy … Futurama, Family Guy, The Simpsons. You can pick up on things when you watch it the 2nd time." James S., age 14

Content Ownership

Buying content was actually a relatively rare practice among our participants. Some participants downloaded just the free video clips from iTunes while others browsed on-line and through file-sharing networks. One participant always purchased her favorite TV drama to watch on her Video iPod because she does not have enough time at home to watch television. Some of the younger participants occasionally bought music videos. Other purchased content included UMD disks for the PSP but these had typically been purchased as gifts for the participants by other people. Part of this was attributed to limited content available for purchase at the time of the study with some participants hinting that they may have bought some content if something interesting had been available. Another participant owned all the DVDs to his favorite TV sitcom "Will and Grace." Although he felt ethically justified in doing so because he owns the content, he still expressed sincere concern about the fact that he was technically crossing a legal boundary by converting his DVDs to watch on his Video iPod. Several other participants expressed similar opinions about content ownership. They believed that if they purchased the content, then they should be able to watch the content on a variety of playback devices including their home television and mobile devices. Participants expressed interest in transferring their recorded television shows to their mobile devices, but some participants said it depended on the show and if they were willing to sacrifice the viewing experience of watching it on their HD TV.

> "I want the same experience across my devices." Michael, age 35

> "I would never watch 24 on my iPod." (due to preference for watching in HD) Chris, age 31

However, a large part of the reasoning here concerns the relationship of purchased content to the viewing opportunities within the broader ecology of viewing devices and situations such as watching TV at home with the family. That is, there was some reluctance to pay for content such as films or episodes from a TV series that would only be suitable or capable of being viewed on these portable devices. In paying for content they will keep, participants wanted the flexibility to use it on other devices:

> Its not just about buying content for the mobile device – when you buy content at full price you want to be able to use it on TV, projectors, etc. – you want the flexibility to use it in different formats … I think I would feel a bit cheated just to have a small version of it and you've paid probably the same price… watching it at home sometimes on the PSP isn't very good and if the whole family want to watch it its not very good – which means you will end up buying it twice – its silly.

Content Management

With this is mind, participants adopted strategies for getting free content onto their mobile devices. One such strategy was to look for free content on the Internet. Particularly popular sites were those where the free content was already formatted for iPod or PSP, e.g., Google Video. This search behavior was both a source of frustration and fun. Some of the younger participants really enjoyed the search for and discovery of new content, spending significant amounts of time doing so. For them it was an integral part of the mobile video consumption experience.

> I do a lot of browsing. I could do that for like 3 hours at a time. I like checking out the new videos. Lately iTunes has been really good adding a lot of new things that I can check out.

For others it was a source of frustration because of the time involved; especially if searching for particular content as opposed to more nonspecific browsing. Converting video was another strategy to get free content onto devices. Some of this was published content that had been downloaded from web sites and peer-to-peer sites and some was personally created content. Primarily, though, it involved the conversion of DVDs which the participants already owned. While there are subtle legalities at stake which actually prohibit such behavior with DVDs, participants who adopted this behavior generally felt it was morally acceptable to do so because they had already paid for the DVD. The conversion process though proved to be a significant area of frustration for participants and one of the key barriers to more frequent usage of mobile video. Not only was it too time-consuming, it was also somewhat of a black art in terms of knowing how to decrypt DVDs and the relevant parameters for formatting the files. The technical terms of industry standards such as bit-rate, frame-rate, and special resolution were a foreign language to many of our participants.

> I know there's this software you can use, like if you have season one of Friends, you can convert it onto your iPod. But I still haven't found out how to do that. Katie, age 16.

Preparing and putting content on the devices followed a number of different strategies. In one strategy people would prepare content on demand, putting it on their device in preparation for a specific purpose – a known upcoming opportunity for use, such as a specific trip. Others though would search for and load content onto the devices on a regular schedule in order to have content on there for nonspecific opportunities. So while this required advanced planning, it was planning for opportunistic use (Perry et al. 2001).

Social Currency

Within the context of these social motivations, certain content was seen to acquire high status. The video content was considered both social and physical currency that could be burned onto CDs and DVDs and traded with friends like baseball cards. In addition to the physical media serving as currency, the skills acquired in order to find and convert the content served as bragging rights. This helps explain the quite considerable lengths that certain individuals would go to in order to get exclusive content on the device because of the *kudos* associated with having it.

> This was in school. I watched the rest of Shaun of the Dead. Everybody loves this film – It's one of the best films ever – so they were all like 'do you reckon you can get Shaun of the Dead on there - so I was like ah 'I'll see what I can do'. So I transferred it over from the site I got it from and then put it in there. It takes ages about 3 hours but then once you've done it – and then you have to convert it which is another couple of hours so the next day I took it in and they were all like 'ahh no way.'

The value associated with the mobile video content and skills required to acquire it is part of an emerging market for the exchange of video material among peers. Peer-to-peer transfer of short video clips on mobile phones was common practice among school children:

> Pretty much they go 'ah I got this funny video the other day' – 'ah lets see then' and you'll laugh and go 'ah send it to me' and then the next day you go out and send it to about 10 other people - so it takes one person and then 2 days on the whole school has it. It spreads around so easily.

As with other forms of exchange, particular social motivations, rules, and consequences underpinned these behaviors such as reciprocity, exclusivity, and trust (Taylor & Harper 2002).

> It's sort of like exchanging them. If they see any they want you send it to them. If you see something you like they send it to you.

As one of our participants describes, some people in his school were happy to give content so long as they received credit for it. There was enough value in being the initial source of the video content. The participant also said how some people would not exchange particular content to retain exclusive rights over and make them feel important.

> Some people are like well I had that first and they send it and you just tell people they had it first…Most people aren't like I want to be the only person with it – they go just take it. But there are some people who are like I want to be the only one with it and you have to gather around their phone to make them look good – but that's a bit silly really.

Interestingly, the concerns here were never really with the legalities or illegalities of such behavior but rather with the particular social consequences. The social importance of ownership and exchange, then, was an important driver for people to obtain new content – having something to give has value over and above just having something to watch.

User-Generated Content

While the majority of our users watched published content on their mobile devices, several users did store user-generated content on their devices. As discussed previously, the users kept this content on their personal device in order to show to others when the situation was appropriate, such as to have visual aids during a conversation. Several of the users who had personal content on their video players, digital cameras, and mobile phones expressed interest in being able to share this content more easily. This aligns well with the growing support for sharing user-generated content on the web, such as via Google's YouTube which supports the sharing of personal content to the world (Grossman 2007). Similarly, many mobile phones now support MMS messages which allow users to send content from their phone to another person's phone or e-mail. A majority of our user's had watched personal other's video (such as from YouTube), but none of them had ever posted a video.

We wanted to understand why this was, since many of them had personal content. One user summed it up well when she said:

> I wouldn't mind sharing videos with my friends and family, but only with some of them. I don't want to receive spam video from some of my crazy friends...

In order to better understand the model of sharing wanted by our users, we asked them about how they would like to share their videos. In general, the users desired a way to share – both send and receive – videos privately with only specific people that they could choose. They wanted it to be easy, as some of them had many questions about how to get their videos off of their digital cameras and video-enabled cell phones in order to share with their friends. Some of them had succeeded by copying the personal content to their laptop, only to then fail when they tried to e-mail it to their parents because the file size was too large. Others had been able to copy the files to their friend's computers, only to fail because the computer did not have the correct video codec to support the playback of the specific file type.

In seeking to understand the consumption of user-generated video content on mobile devices, we can gain some important insights from the work of Kirk et al. (2007). In their study of video work, part of their analysis focused on the capture and consumption of video on mobile phones. In their characterization, the form factor and carry-everywhere characteristics of such devices changes how video content is both captured and consumed. Typically, they argue, video content on such devices is lightweight, spontaneous, and ephemeral, being used to "create visual traces of an engaged-in event, mostly used within the moment itself, to laugh, to rue, and to reflect on the activities by those participating"(Kirk et al. 2007). Sharing in the moment is crucial here, with content being used to augment the experience rather than capturing things that "really matter."

In our own study, there are certainly elements of Kirk et al.'s characterization that ring true. However, we observed other elements of people's creation and consumption behavior with respect to user-generated mobile video content that do not fall neatly within this model. While Kirk's arguments about the spontaneous, ephemeral nature of user-generated mobile video content are useful, the argument that such content does not "really matter" is at times overstated and underplays some aspects of mobile consumption of user-generated video. In our own studies, there were numerous examples where user's content is actually very important and of great personal significance in terms of capturing particular episodes. So, we would prefer to re-characterize Kirk et al.'s arguments to encompass this observation. That is, while recording video on mobile phones has enabled new spontaneous and ephemeral practices around user-generated mobile video content, these are not necessarily at the expense of other more significant episodic video capture. A good example in our study involved a teenage boy in a band. His band had performed their first gig at a friend's party. This was of great significance to the boy and his band – a special moment that they wanted to have captured. The teenage boy had given his phone to someone in the audience to get some video of the concert. He also saw that other people in the audience were recording video on their phones. In the days following the concert, he went to great lengths to get hold of the footage from the other people that he had seen in the audience. He wanted to collect as much content as possible. It was not simply about seeing the other footage, he also wanted to have it sent via Bluetooth across to his own phone in order to be able to own and keep it as a memory of the event. Of course, the lightweight nature of the capture was still important here, but the content was very much beyond what might be considered ephemeral use.

We also saw much more deliberate and creative uses of mobile video capture and consumption. A particular driver here was the notion of *emulation*, that is, the desire to copy, mimic, or spoof existing cultural video-based artifacts. An example of this came from another teenage male participant. This participant, along with his group of friends, used his mobile phone to recreate the Nike soccer commercial in which a sequence of high-profile soccer stars pass the ball to each other in intricate and skillful ways. In the commercial, continuity in the movie is created by the football leaving one part of the screen and then entering from another part of the screen as the next player in the sequence takes his turn to control the ball and then pass it on. The boys in the study recorded themselves and emulated these moves by pausing the recording on their phones, setting up the next shot, then continuing the video recording. The aim was to have a continuous sequence that was their unique version of the Nike video ad. The point here is that such mobile video use and consumption is more carefully, crafted, planned, and executed than some of the more spontaneous and ephemeral creations seen in the Kirk study. This kind of emulation was also seen in other participants, such as the skateboard enthusiast. In this particular case, the use of the mobile phone and its particular quality characteristics were an important feature in the emulation activities giving them an urban feel that was typical of the actual skateboard videos that they were trying to emulate. This emulation behavior is consistent with some of the viral video postings seen on YouTube where people copy other people's activities and content formats. What is important here though is that these aspects of user-generated mobile video content are more deliberate and creative as opposed to spontaneous and ephemeral.

An interesting example from our fieldwork, which goes beyond the ephemeral augmentation of the here-and-now experience,[1] concerns the use of mobile phone video in a mother–daughter relationship. In this particular episode, the mother was exasperated with the behavior of her young daughter of 8 years. The daughter had been throwing a tantrum and talking back to her mother repeatedly. Having exhausted the normal means for controlling the young girl's behavior, the mother resorted to using her mobile phone to video the bad behavior of the young girl in an attempt to get her to behave. What was particularly important here was the mother's threat to show the video to the young girl's teacher. The mother had recently received a report from the girl's teacher as to how well-behaved her daughter was at school and what an asset to the class she was. The mother knew that the daughter was pleased about these reports and was proud of her school "persona." Therefore, the mother threatened to show the teacher the video in order to reveal

---

[1] This particular example is an anecdote from a friend as opposed to that from a particular participant in this study, but is nevertheless of relevance to the arguments being made here.

the bad behavior of the daughter. While the threat was not real, the daughter did not know this, and the potential context of consumption of this video by her teacher was sufficient to get her to calm down and behave. In this instance, there are indeed some of the lightweight and ephemeral characteristics that Kirk et al. discuss, but the way the mobile video content was used is somewhat different from the augmentation of the in-the-moment experience. It was not about sharing in the moment; rather, the presence of the video and the ownership by the mother was most important. Longevity was also potentially important as an ever-present possibility that it could be consumed in ways that the daughter would not like.

In a further episode, a father used his mobile phone to video his daughter's hamster on a running wheel. The circumstances of the activity are important in understanding the father's motivations. His 4-year-old daughter had been asking whether her pet hamster liked the running wheel they had put in his cage because she had never seen him run on it. The father had said to her that the hamster did use it, but the little girl was not convinced and thought that perhaps the hamster was upset. With this conversation in mind, one evening after the father had just gotten into his bed, he heard the hamster get onto the wheel and start running. He immediately grabbed his phone and quietly went to where the hamster cage was located and recorded a short video of the hamster on the wheel. The next morning, the father was able to show the daughter the footage while they were getting ready for school. This made the young girl happy because she was able to see that her hamster was happy. The consumption of this user-generated content was done with a particular social purpose. It was an act of affection, in order to reassure a daughter in the context of her worries.

Finally, it is worth reflecting on how the carrying of such user-generated mobile video content comes to acquire significance as a consequence of being accessible all the time. At the time of capture, the importance of a video might not be immediately apparent. However, being stored on the mobile phone means the media is carried with a person at all times. This provides an opportunity for the carrier to revisit this content through occasional browsing. As with photos in a wallet, these particular videos can acquire significance over time as they are intermittently revisited and consumed.

Social Video Technologies

The goal of a social video technology is to replicate, as much as possible, the experience of interacting with another person as if you were in the same place together. In this section, we will describe two different technologies which were designed to offer mobile users the ability to have social interactions through their mobile media. The digital storytelling application provides users with the ability to add narration to their mobile video content, while the Conversa system allows users to share video easily within trusted groups. In describing early users of Conversa, we address some of the factors which may influence the adoption of video into social communities.

Mobile Storytelling

Building upon the significance described in the last section of carrying photos and videos on your mobile device for intermittent revisiting, social sharing of media often includes the act of user's telling stories about the circumstances and details of the media. A common scenario is when two people are sitting on a couch, shoulder-to-shoulder, flipping through a book of photographs. In this scenario, the storyteller points at photos and narrates the story while the listener interjects with questions.

In order to replicate this social experience digitally using a mobile phone, we created a mobile system which we called StoryCast. The software begins by displaying a collection of photo thumbnails on the device's screen. When the user is ready to tell her story, she presses the record button and begins talking. Throughout the narration, the user taps on photos just as she would point at photos in a physical photo book. When she is finished, the photos, audio narration, and timing sequence information are uploaded to the StoryCast web site and converted into a video. After the story is created and uploaded from the mobile device, others can download the story to their own mobile devices for playback. The story can also be viewed on a TV using the Windows Media Center interface, a feature which was added for convenience and was an important option for less technical users (see Fig. 3).

One advantage to the photo-centric approach of digital storytelling is that it reduces the element of stage fright that besets users when a video camera is pointed at them. The activity of pointing at photos and telling a story is fairly familiar and more natural than speaking into the lens of a video camera. The storyteller's focus is fixed on the content of the photograph while she speaks, reducing self-consciousness and distractions. On the other hand, the listener misses out on seeing the face of the storyteller and all the associated nonverbal communication while she is tell-

Fig. 3 Digital storytelling capture and playback via StoryCast

ing her story. Also, the solution does not account for feedback from the listener while the story is told or afterwards. The feedback factor in storytelling is significant and can change the direction and voice of the story.

Video in Social Communities

In order to alleviate some of the difficulty that exists in sharing personal video, we designed a system for sharing personal video messages in trusted communities. We call this system Conversa because its aim is to allow users to have asynchronous video conversations with their friends, families, and colleagues. The system is designed to offer the core experience (joining a group, browsing video conversation threads, posting/responding with video, etc.) on the user's mobile device as well as through a web service and via a desktop application.

While social communities are embraced currently on the web (MySpace, Facebook, Yahoo Groups), communicating through video is a vastly unexplored region of this space. As we begin to investigate the usage of our video community there are several factors which may influence adoption of video in social communities.

Generational Influences

Members of Generation Y have grown up with video on their mobile phones, SMS, and on-line networking. Many of them are comfortable sharing personal content on the web such as uploading and tagging pictures of themselves and friends on their Facebook pages and blogging about their daily activities. What about the parents of those in Generation Y – how will they feel sharing personal video content? What about their grandparents?

One generational difference that has emerged in early usage of Conversa is the filming of landscape scenes versus head shots (i.e., scenes where the user talks directly to the camera). Are younger people more comfortable talking to the camera? Will adults of today feel comfortable enough to record video responses that include their personal images?

Authorship and Environment

In many on-line social video sharing sites, the number of content *consumers* versus content *generators* is largely lacking with consumers vastly outnumbering generators in some cases at 100–1 (Arthur 2006). Through the support of private groups and the focus on sharing video through conversation threads, we hope to better encourage active participation by all Conversa users.

People who are likely to use social communication systems most likely fit into the following nonexclusive categories:

- People who already know each other
- People who are separated by distance and/or time zones
- People who share a common interests

These categories exist in multiple types of environments such as home, work, play, etc. The environments in which people operate on a day-to-day basis will influence how they interact through social video communities. For example, a group of teenagers will likely use the system vastly differently than a group of coworkers. Environment will likely have a large influence on mobile video creation and sharing.

Video Content

Video is a much richer medium than other forms of communication such as SMS, e-mail, or instant messaging. Not all communication opportunities require the richness of video content. For instance, if you are running late for an appointment, then an SMS message or short e-mail will suffice to let those who are waiting on you know that you are late. In other situations, such as when showing something is a crucial part of the conversation or when there is longing for face-to-face interaction, then the nonverbal communication possible only through video becomes important. It is in these scenarios that users may choose to interact through video-sharing communities.

With the richness of video also comes the need to support search and browsing features to enable community navigation. For example, it is quite simple to enable text-based search on a discussion board or to skim through text looking for words or links that are of interest. This skimming and search are not as easy for video. While there is work on video search through speech to text translation and object identification (Shibata et al. 2007; Volkmer & Natsev 2006), it is also possible with video to support *visual skimming*. Showing select scenes from several videos can help users browse discussion groups and draw attention to certain conversations through person and object recognition (Wang et al. 2005). This is an advantage that video offers over static text and pictures.

Discussion

What we can see in the findings presented here is that mobile video consumption is more than just watching TV anytime and anywhere in order to pass the time. It is also more than content "snacking" with a range of different viewing behaviors according to circumstances, some of which are quite substantial. By looking at people's everyday practices with different mobile video technologies, we have been able to highlight a range of motivations and values underlying usage of mobile video in a variety of different settings and circumstances. In addition, we have pointed to some of the factors that shape its use. For example, as an immersive solitary activity, mobile video was used as a privatizing technology – a way of claiming back their own time and space in shared spaces such as in urban environments, on public transport, in cars, the workplace, and even in the home when people actively wanted to be alone. Much of this solitary activity, though, had additional social underpinnings, thus allowing people to more effectively manage video-content consumption in the context of other social activities such as spending time with family. People shifted certain viewing activities to times and places where it did not compete with other activities in the home, and they coordinated content watched on the mobile with shared TV/DVD experiences at home. Further, by not confounding the sharing of space with sharing content (as with traditional TV viewing), mobile video facilitated togetherness in the home by allowing people to watch their own content while being in proximity to family.

Shared viewing experiences were also an important feature of mobile video consumption practices. People could bring content into social situations and places to create meaning and value in ways not possible with the traditional fixed TV. As well as viewing together, actively showing content to others in support of conversation was a key motivator for having and keeping content on the device over and above being viewed by the owner. We also saw the social importance of content ownership and exchange with others.

Device Design Implications

- Better integration with devices in the home (TV/DVD/etc.)
- Integrated speaker technology
- Mono feature to improve ear bud sharing
- Docking solutions with speakers/large-displays
- Integrated WiFi/Bluetooth or other technologies to enable content exchange between devices
- More storage capacity options

Content Distribution Design Implications

- Need for increased distribution of mobile content over the Internet
- Better licensing arrangements for mobile-content ownership
- Broadcast/Streaming supports on demand consumption
- Download/Save supports ownership/exchange

These experiences all have significant implications for the technology involved both at the device level and in terms of content distribution methods. For example, in terms of relationship with TV/DVD viewing experiences at the home, it is important to think about facilitating better integration with these technologies. One might think of these devices as mobile PVRs (as in the Archos) that can link to broadcast content available on normal TV. Broadcasters should also increase the distribution of content over the Internet that is formatted for mobile devices. Licensing arrangements that better fit with people's everyday understanding of content ownership should also be explored. Separate arrangements for mobile vs. DVD content, for example, only make sense to the industry and not to the consumer.

Different licensing varrangements might then allow DVDs to be shipped including mobile-ready content, avoiding need for any conversion processes.

With regards to shared viewing experiences, the findings suggest additional consideration be given to including integrated speaker technology into such devices. One might also consider features such as a mono feature to improve on earbud sharing practices, as well as docking solutions with speakers and larger displays to support a wider range of sharing experiences. In terms of exchanging content between devices, there are arguments for integrating WiFi or Bluetooth technology into these mobile devices, and we are indeed beginning to see this in emerging media player solutions such as those from Microsoft and Apple. Such technology will also facilitate other social aspects of content ownership and collecting. For example, it could allow people to browse and even consume video content collections of co-proximate others in the same ways that we have seen with music (e.g., Bassoli et al. 2006). Content ownership and collecting also relate directly to content distribution methods. Broadcast and streaming models may support some of the "killing time" aspects of mobile video consumption but only the download and store model support the value associated with ownership and exchange. Related to this model are design considerations regarding storage methods and capacity. Storage capacity on a device must depend on the range of social reasons why people want to keep content on the device which is more than just having content available to watch during any particular piece of downtime.

In addition, there are many design and usage implications in regards to user-generated content. This content was held in high regard by users. Previous studies have noted the spontaneous and ephemeral usage of this content, but we found the creation of this content to also be deliberate and creative. As opposed to sharing just in the moment, we saw that longevity was potentially important in regards to mobile consumption and that the sharing of user-generated content was done with a particular social purpose. In light of these findings, we described two mobile video technologies and analyzed potential factors that may influence video adoption in social communities.

In summary, we have started to characterize the ways mobile video is being integrated into people's everyday lives and social interactions. We have illustrated some of the ways in which these findings might inform the design space of these technologies and surrounding services. Such findings can also inform judgments about emerging adoption patterns and behavioral practices surrounding mobile video consumption and its relationship to a broader ecology of video and TV consumption technology.

Acknowledgments This work is based on earlier work:

Consuming Video on Mobile Devices, in Proceedings of the SIGCHI conference on Human factors in computing systems, {2, 1, (April 28-May 3, 2007)} © ACM, 2007. http://doi.acm.org/10.1145/1240624.1240754

"My iPod is my Pacifier:" An Investigation on the Everyday Practices of Mobile Video Consumption, in Proceedings of the Eighth IEEE Workshop on Mobile Computing Systems and Applications, {1, 1, (March 8–9, 2007)} © IEEE, 2007. http://doi.ieeecomputersociety.org/10.1109/HotMobile.2007.10

References

Arthur, C. (2006). What is the 1% rule? *The Guardian Newspaper*, Technology Section (p. 2), July 20 (Thursday), 2006.

Bassoli, A., Moore, J., & Agamanolis, S. (2006). tunA: Socialising music sharing on the move. In K. O'Hara & B. Brown (Eds.), *Consuming music together: Social and collaborative aspects of new music technologies*. New York: Springer-Verlag.

Black, A., Bayley, O., Burns, C., Kuuluvaineng, I., & Stoddard, J. (1994). Keeping-viewers in the picture: Real-world usability procedures in the development of a television control Interface. In *Proceedings of ACM CHI '94*.

Brown, B., & Barkhuus, L. (2006). The television will be revolutionised: Effects of PVRs and filesharing on television watching. In *Proceedings of ACM CHI '06*.

Brown, B., & Sellen, A. (2006). Sharing and listening to music. In K. O'Hara & B. Brown (Eds.), *Consuming music together: Social and collaborative aspects of new music technologies*. New York: Springer-Verlag.

Bull, M. (2000). *Sounding out the city: Personal stereos and the management of everyday life*. Oxford: Berg.

Bull, M. (2007). *Sound moves: IPod culture and urban experience*. London: Routledge.

du Gay, P., & Hall, S. (1997). *Doing cultural studies, the story of the Sony Walkman*. London: Sage.

Grossman, L. (2007). Time's person of the year: You. *Time Magazine*. Retrieved December 13, 2006, from http://www.time.com/time/magazine/article/0,9171,1569514,00.html

Kirk, D., Sellen, A., Harper, R., & Wood, K. (2007). Understanding Videowork. In *Proceedings of CHI '07, San Jose, CA, USA*.

Knoche, H., McCarthy, J. & Sasse, M. A. (2005). Can small be beautiful?: Assessing image resolution requirements for mobile TV. In *Proceedings ACM Multimedia 2005*.

Logan, R. L., Augaitis, S., Miller, R. H. & Wehmer, K. (1995). Living room culture – An anthropological study of television usage behaviors. In *Proceedings of Human Factors and Ergonomics Society*, pp. 326–330

Mateas, M., Salvador, T., Scholtz, J., & Sorensen, D. (1996). Engineering ethnography in the home. In Companion. In *Proceedings of ACM CHI '96*.

O'Brien, J., Rodden, T., Rouncefield, M., & Hughes, J. (1999). At home with the technology: An ethnographic study of a set-top-box trial. *ACM Transactions on Computer–Human Interaction, 6*(3), 282–308.

O'Hara, K., & Brown, B. (2006). *Consuming music together: Social and collaborative aspects of new music technologies*. New York: Springer-Verlag.

Palen, L., Salzman, M., & Youngs, E. (2000). Going wireless: Behavior & practice of new mobile phone users. In *Proceedings of CSCW '00, Philadelphia, PA, USA*.

Perry, M., O'Hara, K., Sellen, A., Brown, B., & Harper, R. (2001). Dealing with mobility: Understanding access anytime, anywhere. *ACM Transactions on Human–Computer Interaction, 8*(4), 323–347.

Repo, P., Hyvonen, K., Pantzar, M., & Timonen, P. (2003). Mobile Video. *National Consumer Research Centre Report, 2003*, 5.

Repo, P., Hyvonen, K., Pantzar, M and Timonen P.(2004) Users Inventing Ways To Enjoy New Mobile Services – The Case of Watching Mobile Videos. *In Proceedings of the 37th Hawaii International Conference on System Sciences*.

Rode, J., Toye, E. and Blackwell, A. (2005) The domestic economy: a broader unit of analysis for end user programming. *In Proceedings of ACM CHI'05*.

Shibata, T., Kato, N., & Kurohashi, S. (2007) Automatic Obect Model Acquisition and Object Recognition by Integrating Linguistic and Visual Information. *In Proceedings of ACM Multimedia '07*.

Silverstone, R. (1994) *Television and everyday life*. London: Routledge.

Södergård, C. (2003). *Mobile television – technology and user experiences* [Report on the Mobile TV project, VTT Publications].

Stockbridge, L. (2006). Mobile TV: Experience of the UK Vodafone and Sky service. In *Proceedings of EuroITV '06.*

Taylor, A., & Harper, R. (2002). Age-old practices in the new world: A study of gift giving between teenage mobile phone users. In *Proceedings of ACM CHI '02.*

Taylor, A., & Harper, R. (2003). Switching on to switch off. In R. Harper (Ed.), *Inside the smart home.* London: Springer-Verlag.

Volkmer, T., & Natsev, A. (2006). Exploring automatic query refinement for text-based video retrieval. In *Proceedings of the IEEE International Conference on Multimedia & Expo (ICME) 2006.*

Vorbau, A., Slayden Mitchell, A., & O'Hara, K. (2007). My iPod is my pacifier: An investigation on the everyday practices of mobile video consumption. In *Proceedings of IEEE Hot Mobile '07.*

Wang, Y., Zhang, T., & Tretter, D. (2005) Real time motion analysis toward semantic understanding of video content. In *Proceedings of Conference on Visual Communications and Image Processing 2005 (SPIE).*

m-YouTube Mobile UI: Video Selection Based on Social Influence

Aaron Marcus and Angel Perez

Abstract The ease-of-use of Web-based video-publishing services provided by applications like YouTube has encouraged a new means of asynchronous communication, in which users can post videos not only to make them public for review and criticism, but also as a way to express moods, feelings, or intentions to an ever-growing network of friends. Following the current trend of porting Web applications onto mobile platforms, the authors sought to explore user-interface design issues of a mobile-device-based YouTube, which they call m-YouTube. They first analyzed the elements of success of the current YouTube Web site and observed its functionality. Then, they looked for unsolved issues that could give benefit through information-visualization design for small screens on mobile phones to explore a mobile version of such a product/service. The biggest challenge was to reduce the number of functions and amount information to fit into a mobile phone screen, but still be usable, useful, and appealing within the YouTube context of use and user experience. Borrowing ideas from social research in the area of social influence processes, they made design decisions aiming to help YouTube users to make the decision of what video content to watch and to increase the chances of YouTube authors being evaluated and observed by peers. The paper proposes a means to visualize large amounts of video relevant to YouTube users by using their friendship network as a relevance indicator to help in the decision-making process.

Introduction

The popularization of the World-Wide Web among early technology adopters and younger generations, in addition to the new technologies giving faster and more reliable Internet connections, paved the way for new products and services that addressed, among others, one of the most basic human needs: social networking.

A. Marcus (✉) and A. Perez
Aaron Marcus and Associates, Inc, 1196 Euclid Avenue, Suite 1F, Berkeley, CA, 94708, USA
e-mail: Aaron.Marcus@AMandA.comm

A. Marcus et al. (eds.), *Mobile TV: Customizing Content and Experience*,
Human-Computer Interaction Series, DOI 10.1007/978-1-84882-701-1_17,
© Springer-Verlag London Limited 2010

In this way, a product/service that seems to make it easier to meet people, to keep in touch with friends and loved ones, and to share interests and opinions becomes the most successful one. The product/service success is not only given by its acceptance, but also by how effectively it opens new business opportunities. In fact, YouTube is arguably the most successful of the aforementioned "social network" products/services. The ease-of-use of the Web video publishing service provided by YouTube, encouraged a new way of asynchronous communication in which users can post videos not only to make them public for critique, but also as a way to express moods, feelings or intentions to an always growing network of friends. According to *Wired* magazine, YouTube went from 10,000 daily video uploads in December 2005, to about 65,000 in September 2006. Furthermore, Google, which acquired YouTube for \$1.6 billion, is betting on the reallocation of the money being currently invested in TV advertising (about \$67 billion) (Garfield 2006).

Nowadays, the Web is becoming mobile, meaning that mobile devices such as PDAs, mobile phones, and smart phones have ever-improving Web-browsing capabilities. However, the current trend of porting Web applications onto mobile platforms has focused primarily on mirroring desktop applications in mobile devices. Moreover, the nature of the mobile platform elements, such as screen size and interaction styles, has led to design efforts that purely reduce the functionality of the Web-desktop application to fit the constraints of the mobile platform (Jones & Marsden 2006; Lindholm et al. 2003; Miller 2007). Although necessary, functionality reduction is not sufficient to render a usable, useful, and appealing mobile user-experience version of a Web-desktop application. The lack of usability is due (1) to the basic unsolved problems and limitations initially inherited by the new platform from the desktop user interface and its WIMP paradigm and (2) to the further challenging and inherent constraints of the mobile platform. Within this context, the authors explored porting a Web-desktop application such as YouTube to a mobile platform, specifically, improving and extending the functionality reduction by using clues provided by human-to-human social interaction. In this way, the authors propose a mobile UI to visualize large amounts of video relevant to the YouTube users, and support quick video selection by using their friendship networks as a relevance indicator to help in the decision-making process (Kilduff 1992).

After observation of the practices of the YouTube community the authors borrowed ideas from social psychology research in the area of "social influence processes" and proposed a user-interface design solution that accomplishes the following:

- First, it reduces the amount of functions and the load of information to fit in a mobile phone, but seems to remain usable, useful, and appealing within an application context like that of YouTube.
- Second, it helps the YouTube users to make a fast decision about what video content to watch.
- Third, it increases the chances of YouTube authors to be evaluated and observed by peers.

Design Approach

Introduction to Design Approach

YouTube Anatomy: Key Success Aspects

A one-and-a-half-week observation of YouTube use by typical users and personal use revealed key concepts that contribute to the success of YouTube as a Web-desktop application.

First, the Web-based ubiquitous access to video, allows easy sharing of viral video hits (video that gains widespread popularity through Internet sharing) not only by simply sending the link to the video by e-mail, but also by allowing groups of friends to conglomerate around a screen in the same way they would do around a TV set. Furthermore, the interactivity given by the Web application (search, selection, rate, *etc*), supports social dynamics by involving in the process groups of friends who are either next to each other or connected through a remote communication service such as a messenger or a chat room (e.g., iChat, MSM, ICQ, AIM, *etc.*).

Second, YouTube shows a very easy-to-use publication environment. After registration, uploading a video takes only two steps. The simplicity of the uploading process allows users to focus on their final goal (the social interaction, e.g., making a friend laugh) rather than on a potentially cumbersome frustrating process (uploading the video).

Third, because the YouTube service is free, no exchange of money is involved at any part of the process (e.g., AOL video charges for some videos). Finally, there is little control of the video content to be posted, which is done by the YouTube self-organized community: if some video content is believed to be inappropriate, it will be flagged by the YouTube community and soon removed from the Web site by the service provider. This flexible means of control directly affects the user experience (UX) by giving immediate gratification to the YouTube user, because there are no major delays associated with posting a video.

YouTube Anatomy: YouTube Community Practices

First, YouTube users watch posted videos from either random sources, friends, contacts, or special interests lists. In turn, the URL of the videos can be copied and pasted by the users to be shared with others.

Second, any YouTube user can upload a video for Web publishing: virtually any kind of video can be uploaded, and for improved quality the YouTube Websites gives recommendations on the format of the video. In this way, the video repository is always growing and has a very large range of topics.

Third, YouTube users can add videos and authors to favored lists; among others, quick lists, groups' lists, play lists, and favorites lists. Furthermore, YouTube users vcan subscribe to channels, groups, and other users, and have videos delivered to them.

Fourth, YouTube users can post video responses, personal and copyrighted videos, text comments on videos watched. Also, they can rate and/or flag other YouTube members' videos.

YouTube Anatomy: New Design Opportunities

The variety in the user population, taking into account elements such as age, nationality, genre, occupation, etc., opens new design opportunities in many different directions, among others:

Corporate partners: establish new business relationships for content creation and distribution as currently explored with Warner to avoid copyright infringement.

Functionality: identify possible new applications on top of the current ones. As an example, some on-line providers give tools that allow easy, quick editing of video.

Incorporate Web 2.0: creation of products and services that make extensive use of APIs provided by YouTube to development communities.

Information design: taking into account the complexity of the information displayed to improve the UX.

Make it mobile: port YouTube to phones and PDAs freeing YouTube from the desktop usage and address the YouTube population on the go.

Markets: address both wide user population and different interests of each population sector.

New strategies: new strategies for traditional businesses such as advertisement, which are currently being explored by Google.

Personalization of functionality: direct functions to particular users' communities, as currently done by My Space with music artists.

Reinforce functionality: to improve self-expression with personal video by giving some extra functionality that reinforces the concept of easy Web publishing for regular users who see YouTube as a new space for art and media.

v-Mail: Although there is a wide variety of "kind of users," each one with different motivations to post videos, the YouTube functionality represents a *de facto* tool for asynchronous communication for which video is the media of preference.

Design Concept: m-YouTube

Considering the design opportunities previously described, the authors focused on the YouTube community always-on-the-go for a conceptual design. For users, the authors identified the most relevant functions in the YouTube application that potentially complement the YouTube easy video publishing, viewing, and sharing service when ported to mobile platform. Furthermore, in the proposal for m-YouTube, the authors generated added value in the form of information visualization that simplifies the video selection. In this way, they attempt to propose a design that takes full advantage of the mobile platform while supporting and extending some of the key elements of the YouTube UX.

In practice, with m-YouTube one wants to save "on the go" users from selecting irrelevant content by helping them choose videos that match their preferences. Additionally, one also aims to increase the chances for video authors to be reviewed by peers making it easier to be spotted and selected from large amount of videos.

The concept design is based on social psychology theories that suggest decision making is influenced by friendship networks. According to author Martin Kilduff (Kilduff 1992), social network as a decision-making resource, may be as much an expression of personality as it is a constraint on individual choice. In this way, Kilduff proposes that two personality variables, self-monitoring and social uniqueness moderate social influence on choices and the values of these variables differentiate between people on the basis of susceptibility to social comparisons. Furthermore, Kilduff suggests that self-monitoring and social uniqueness personality types differ in their preferences in relation to how much their decision patterns resembled those of their friends and with respect to the criteria they used in the decision-making process. Kilduff continues by stating that high self-monitoring actions relative to lows are more likely to shape people's behavior in accordance with cues supplied by the social circles to which they belong. Finally, Kilduff also states that social comparison theories imply that one's susceptibility to social influence depends on the availability of others who are perceived to be especially similar to oneself.

Context Approach to Video Recording

In m-YouTube, the results are grouped per page. In Fig. 1, assuming either a hypothetical outcome of a search (e.g., after searching YouTube for a video) or after

Fig. 1 m-YouTube user interface (UI) shows three pages, nine results per page, social affiliations, and number of hits. (**a**) Video thumbnail showing author's face. (**b**) Video thumbnail showing possible interesting content image. (**c**) Changed cursor position

having a default-state for the application (e.g., the very large list of featured videos on the YouTube main page), each page will show nine results in a 3 × 3 matrix. This arrangement not only allows five-way jog-pad navigation through the page, but also nine results can be quickly accessed (with just one click) via the numeric keys (Lindholm et al. 2003). Additionally, the design proposes a visual reinforcement given by a highlighted column. The column width varies per page hinting at the total amount of pages: a dramatic change in the page width when jumping from two consecutive pages suggests little content.

The presence of a thumbnail of the video content has a twofold intention: first, as shown in Fig. 1a, the thumbnail image could contain a face that can be recognized, hence selected (e.g., my best friend), or, as shown in Fig. 1a and b, the thumbnail has something that might interest the users (e.g., funny couples video or funny animals). Furthermore, within the YouTube community the posting user is as important as the video posted (e.g., the "famous" lonelygirl15). Consequently, the author's name is coupled with the video thumbnail.

In m-YouTube, the results are pre-filtered and sorted based on the number of times the video was seen, discussed, or linked by the rest of the YouTube community. Only the most watched, linked, and discussed are shown with the corresponding amount of hits. The intention of this design concept is to use the evidence that high self-monitors choose on the base of socially defined realities (e.g., image projected: the most discussed, must be good) whereas low self-monitors choose on the basis of intrinsic quality (e.g., most linked, must be good) (Kilduff 1992).

As previously mentioned, the susceptibility of a user to be socially influenced depends on the availability of other users who are perceived as similar. In this way in Fig. 2, visual cues are shown intended to link some of the video results with the

Fig. 2 The video in green has been rated three stars out of five by the friends of the user

users' affiliations. Assuming users subscribe to certain groups because they have similar interests, taste, humor, etc., the visual cues in the base design should not only speed the decision making, but also the chances of picking an enjoyable video to watch. Additionally, when the affiliations are present, the opinion of similar users is the best way to estimate the quality of a given video. The design, in consequence, includes a rating given by the members of the users' affiliations and reduces the hue of the numbers of hits emphasize the users peers' (similar users) opinion.

Conclusion

This conceptual design successfully explores information-visualization and social psychology in a UI to make decision making faster and more effective in a mobile platform. The proposed base design should simplify and speed the decision making with the several visual cues that address two types of users: high self-reflective and low self-reflective users. Additionally, the designs are sufficiently complete to take them to users for testing to fine-tune the UI elements that will render the best user experience. Finally, the design analysis was successful in that it showed a very diverse set of possibilities that can be further explored from the UX-design point of view and may illustrate how social psychology theory can be used as a catalyst for UX design. Design of a mobile user-interface for YouTube is taking place world-wide (see, e.g., Studio 7.5. 2005). The authors hope this work done in November 2006 contributes to the exploration of practical and effective possibilities.

Acknowledgments This chapter is based on the paper by Marcus and Perez (Marcus & Perez 2007) that appeared in the *Proceedings* of the 2007 Human–Computer Interface International conference in Beijing.

References

Garfield, B. (December 2006). The YouTube effect. *Wired*, p. 222.
Jones, M., & Marsden, G. (2006). *Mobile interaction design*. Chichester: Wiley.
Kilduff, M. (1992). The friendship network as a decision-making resource: Dispositional modera-
    tors of social influences on organizational choice. *Journal of Personality and Social
    Psychology, 61*, 168–180.
Lindholm, C., et al. (2003). *Mobile usability*. New York: McGraw-Hill.
Marcus, A., & Perez, A. (2007). m-YouTube Mobile UI: Video selection based on social influ-
    ence. *Proceedings 2009 HCI International Conference, Beijing, China, CD-ROM unpaged.*
Miller, P. (2007). Nokia's YouTube features in action. *Engadget.com,* from http://www.engadget.
    com/2007/02/13/nokias-youtube-features-in-action/ (last visited: February 15, 2007)
Studio 7.5. (2005). *Designing for small screens*. Lausanne: AVA Publishing.

Scenarios of Use for Sociable Mobile TV

Konstantinos Chorianopoulos

Abstract Mobile TVs have been available for many years, without ever becoming very popular. Moreover, the first wave of research has been mostly concerned with technology and standards, which are necessary to ensure interoperability and market acceptance. Although, there has been a significant body of computer-supported co-operative work (CSCW) and mobile human–computer interaction (HCI) research findings, there is limited investigation in the context of leisure activities, such as TV. In this article, we propose three concepts that drive the main paths for research and practice in mobile and social TV: (1) Mobile TV as a content format, (2) Mobile TV as user behavior, and (3) Mobile TV as interaction terminal. Finally, we provide particular directions to be considered in further research in social and mobile TV.

Introduction

One explanation for the slow diffusion of interactive TV (ITV) in the information society is that the difference between the broadcast and the telecommunications mentality has imposed an artificial distinction between content distribution and interpersonal communication. As a result, content has to be distributed and consumed through broadband, unidirectional, and inflexible TV channels, and interpersonal communication takes place over low-bandwidth bidirectional channels. However, the convergence of the telecommunication and content distribution platforms could be beneficial for viewers, as well as the commercial TV stakeholders. In addition, new devices and new types of content facilitate the emergence of novel consumer behaviors. In this article, we explore the interplay of these three concepts (device, content, and behavior) in the context of mobile and social TV.

TV content gradually finds its way through Internet and mobile platforms. Besides triple-play services, which offer integrated access to voice, content, and

K. Chorianopoulos (✉)
Ionian University, Greece
e-mail: choko@ionio.gr

A. Marcus et al. (eds.), *Mobile TV: Customizing Content and Experience*,
Human-Computer Interaction Series, DOI 10.1007/978-1-84882-701-1_18,
© Springer-Verlag London Limited 2010

data services, there are opportunities for new services enabled by the mobile infrastructure. Indeed, the convergence of broadcast, mobile, and data platforms has offered many opportunities for integrated content and communication services, which we refer to as "social TV." We define social TV as a socio-technical system that involves more than one user and networked audiovisual devices.

Previous definitions have been focused only on the technological aspects and ignored the fact that even traditional TV is inherently social. Nevertheless, the origin of traditional TV viewing is a social gathering event in the living room and not the isolated viewing typical of recent decades. For example, viewers compete mentally with quiz show participants, or between co-located groups. Moreover, viewers react emotionally to TV content, they record and share TV content with friends and discuss about shows either in real time, or afterwards. In this context, it is necessary not only to pay attention to usability issues, but also to the social practices that surround TV viewing. Indeed, ethnographic and survey studies have documented the social uses of TV (Ducheneaut et al. 2008; Lee & Lee 1995), but they have not described the user requirements of applications that facilitate the social uses of TV. For this purpose, we explore the related academic literature. We identify the user interface requirements of those computer-mediated communication applications that enhance the social dimension of TV.

The rest of the article is structured as follows. We begin with an analysis of the social uses of mobile TV. In Section "Social Value of TV," we outline the multiple roles of mobility in social TV. Finally, we describe the implication of such systems for practice and future research.

Social and Technological Aspects of Mobile TV

This section explores the social and technological dimensions of TV and other related audiovisual media. In addition, we present a brief overview of technological support for TV sociability.

Social Value of TV

Although TV has been blamed for the reduction of social interaction within the family and the local community, there is a significant body of previous research that considers TV as a social medium, because it provides opportunities for shared experiences and group viewing. In particular, mobile phone applications that support sociability within families or distant groups might enhance the attractiveness of ITV as a leisure activity. This section draws on interdisciplinary literature and empirical research in order to raise the main research issues of the multiple roles of mobility within social TV.

Despite the many criticisms on the quality of TV content and on the passive nature of the watching activity, the social uses of TV have been documented in acclaimed research (Gauntlett & Hill 1999; Kubey & Csikszentmihalyi 1990). It has also been established that viewers have adapted TV in many ways to meet their everyday life needs (Lee & Lee 1995; Rubin 1983). The findings of these works frame a set of opportunities for the design of social communication services in mobile TV.

The majority of previous research on ITV has overemphasized the benefit of increased choice of content and of the interactivity with content. Instead, a worthwhile effort would be the fulfillment of seamless communication over, or about televised content. Such services could support human connectedness (Agamanolis 2006) over a distance (e.g., synchronous communication over a TV program between diasporic households), or enhancement of the shared experience that comes with TV co-viewing. For this reason, we explore an integrated view of the interpersonal communication together with the shared experience of mass communication.

There is a growing academic interest on social TV systems, which consist of technological solutions for integrated interpersonal communication and content distribution. Although, there has been a significant body of computer-supported co-operative work (CSCW) research on supporting interaction among geographically distributed co-workers, there is limited investigation in the context of leisure activities, such as TV. Similarly, research on interpersonal communication in the human–computer interaction (HCI) field has regarded video-mediated communication at work (Veinott et al. 1999). As a matter of fact, there is not much knowledge on designing applications for leisure or informal content-enriched communication.

Cross-media Infrastructure

In the past, TV content in the living room has been provided either by broadcast, or optical disks, such as DVDs. A basic ITV system includes a set-top box (STB) that decodes the signal and provides processing and storage capabilities that enable interactive applications. Nevertheless, the disagreement on a common open middleware platform has been an obstacle for the development of sophisticated interactive applications that are independent from the STB hardware. On the other hand, there is agreement over the specifications for the digital video broadcasting (DVB-S/C/T/H specifications satellite, cable, terrestrial, mobile). Furthermore, TV content can be efficiently distributed over peer-to-peer (P2P) networks. In this way, the variety of video content has been increasing with the support of new Internet technologies, which allow new ways of distributing video (e.g., broadband-connected TV set-top-boxes). Thus, ITV applications are neither limited to the traditional TV device and broadcast delivery, nor to the typical channels of satellite, cable, and digital terrestrial networks. Alternative and complementary devices and distribution methods should be considered, such as mobile phones (mobile DTV).

Social TV builds upon the convergence between different technological infrastructure, such as broadcasting, telecommunication, and Internet. The convergence has been realized in different forms. On the one hand, Internet content may be accessed through television Web browsers, or linked to ITV programs (e.g., interactive advertisements). Communication applications such as messaging, chatting, or voting during certain programs (quizzes, contests, etc.) strengthen viewer's loyalty to the specific program. However, Internet access via television may disrupt current viewing patterns. Besides user interaction, at the network-level, Internet connection facilitates video transfer over P2P networks. Moreover, the distribution of TV content over IP-based platforms, known as IPTV (Internet protocol TV), provides additional opportunities for the delivery of a wide variety of TV programming. In addition, 3G mobile networks could be used to distribute and control TV content.

Related Research in the HCI and CSCW Fields

One of the first approaches for a closer integration between TV content and social communication was the "Inhabited TV" research effort (Craven et al. 2000), which developed a collaborative virtual environment, where viewers could interact with other viewers or virtual objects. In this case, viewers were watching TV within the virtual environment and not within the physical space. Thus, the TV experience was extended by enabling social interaction among participants and increased interaction with content. In an Inhabited TV application, the television becomes an actor and a part of a group interaction within a virtual online world.

There are various approaches to integrate social communication features into TV, such as chat, IM, and e-mail. There has been particular commercial interest on integrating the SMS into TV. Indeed, SMS TV is very popular, which is based on the familiarity with SMS and the availability of the technical infrastructure. Besides SMS services, there is a growing body of research and development, which is presented next.

Coppens et al. (2005) have reported the development of a "social TV" system, but their description focuses on the technical details, the features, and the potential of the system for end users. The "Amigo TV" system provides a technological platform for integrating content delivery, communities, and interpersonal communication (Coppens et al. 2005). In addition, the content of the broadcasts can be personalized by sharing personal photos and home videos. Amigo TV supports online user meetings and buddy lists. Interpersonal communication is based on voice, text, and video formats, as well as animated avatars.

Regan and Todd (2004) describe a system for messaging over TV content. The Media Centre Buddies system integrated TV technology into an instant messaging application. The main aim was to allow multiple users to log into an instant messaging client that was running next to a TV channel.

User-Generated and Distributed Content

TV content production has been regarded as a one-way activity that begins with the professional TV producers and editors and ends with post-production at the broadcast station.

As a matter of fact, television viewers have long been considered passive receivers of content, but a new generation of computer-literate TV viewers has been accustomed to make and share edits of video content online. Furthermore, the wide availability of video capture (e.g., in mobile phones, photo cameras, etc.) and easy-to-use video editing software (standard in many desktop computers), opens up additional opportunities for wider distribution of homemade content (e.g., through peer-to-peer, portable video players, etc.). User-generated content and social communication about media content have also been proposed by Resnick (2001), who suggested that interactions could create productive resources, which he refers to as socio-technical capital. This capital may consist of artifacts created from the interactions or relationships and practices developed through repeated social interactions. Such capital can enable future social interactions.

Although most mobile media players are inherently personal devices, they offer several technological features that can transform the traditionally solitary media consumption into a social experience. Mobile and wireless technology open up opportunities for new, interesting social practices, where media consumption and sharing can take place in a variety of social, physical, and temporal contexts. Advanced mobile phones are equipped with digital cameras, multimedia processing, and multiple mobile communication technologies (such as short- or long-range, low- or high-bandwidth). Since a mobile phone remains constantly with the user, it could potentially store a large amount of details about social interactions. Then, search and sharing of media content could benefit from this social dimension of smart phones: the user could share audiovisual content with those related (in terms of place or terms of social proximity) without investing effort to select these people. TunA (Agamanolis 2006) is one example of a mobile application where users can tune in to eavesdrop on the playlists of nearby users and listen to the same music in a synchronized way.

Content-Enriched Interpersonal Communication

Social TV systems offer one or more computer-mediated communication features, which are closely integrated with the TV watching experience. Computer-mediated interpersonal communication over distance or time could employ various communication modalities such as audio, text, video, photos, and nonverbal cues (e.g., emoticons, avatars). We refer to integrated content and communication services as "content-enriched communication." This over a distance refers to two types of sociability: (1) synchronous, when viewers get together and watch the same show at the same time, and (2) asynchronous, when viewers interact after the show has already been seen by each one, independently and at different times. Communication between spectators is realized at two levels: (1) direct communication, such as chat or instant messaging, and (2) indirect communication, such as cooperating in a team to win a quiz.

In brief, there are four basic scenarios of social TV (Chorianopoulos & Lekakos 2008):

- *Synchronous viewing over a distance:* This is probably the most interesting scenario, because the requirement it poses is to recreate the experience of co-located group viewing, when the viewers are located in two or more distant places. For example, distant viewers should be able to watch together popular social TV content, such as sports, quiz shows, series, and reality shows. A good starting point is to consider ways to disclose presence and status of viewers, to continue with support for multiple interpersonal communication modalities (nonverbal most notably), and to summarize the social experience with auto- mated highlight production, which could motivate further discussion and social bonding between the distant viewers.

- *Asynchronous viewing over a distance:* This is a feasible scenario if we consider that distance viewers might have very different time schedules, patterns of daily life activities, or even live in distant time zones. Then, the probability of syn- chronous co-viewing is rather limited. In this case, a social TV system could record and share shows and viewing habits with the members of the social circle. In addition, a social TV system should allow annotation of content and recording of interactions, such as pausing, skipping, replaying, and content browsing. In this way, each time a particular TV program is accessed, it keeps a trace, which is exploited at the next access, in order to personalize the content and most notably to provide a placeholder for interpersonal communication. This could be rather subtle, such as visual annotation of the content highlights, or could be more explicit such as audio and text comments.

- *Asynchronous viewing at the same place:* The main motivation for the develop- ment of social TV systems is based on the need to bridge the distance between social circles of people, but there is also the case that co-located groups of people do not manage to meet as often as they wish for a social TV night. A subset of the functionality that was described in the previous case might be the most appropriate here.

- In addition to the above, social TV designers should consider the *traditional TV watching scenario*, where a group of viewers gathers in the same place to enjoy a favorite TV program. Although this is a case that content-enriched communi- cation is least needed, there might be worthwhile benefits in employing a social TV system. In all cases, designers should consider extended functionality for user-generated content. For example, the ability to upload personal music, photos, and videos might be used to achieve communication through content. In particular, the automated production of personal TV channels that keep track of individual life streams captured with a mobile device (e.g., music, photos, and personal videos) could be multiplexed with broadcast TV watching behavior. Indeed, Kubey and Csikszentmihalyi (1990) have found that everyday life experience is correlated with TV watching behavior. Thus, interpersonal communication could start with a screen displaying media use of each party during the past few days or hours. In practice, this scenario is rather feasible to implement, because the respective services have been very popular (e.g., YouTube, MySpace, Flickr, etc.)

Although mobile and social TV is thought to be suitable for the distant and synchronous communication scenario, there are several other opportunities. For example, multiple mobile terminals could be employed at the same place to control content on a shared big screen. Moreover, user-generated mobile TV content could be posted online and latter-on be annotated by other mobile TV users, when triggered by a particular location or other condition. This could create a kind of public "wall" mosaic of individual image sources being combined in a large-scale matrix that would be viewed by many people at once.

Scenarios for Sociable Mobile TV

In this section, we propose three main directions of mobile TV research, and we offer suggestions for future research and market developments. Besides TV watching on-the-move, mobile TV has significant potential, both as a personal TV set and as a tool to establish a closer interaction with the television programs (e.g., TV voting).

Mobile TV as a Content Format

Digital mobile TV systems have been designed to complement mobile networks with broadcast and multicast capabilities for spectrum-efficient delivery of multimedia services on mobile devices in both outdoor and indoor environments. In particular, the DVB-H standard is based on the widely deployed series of DVB standards (DVB-S/C/T) and includes enhancements for mobile terminals, such as reduced power consumption and reception while on the move. Although the technical standards are suitable for mobile TV reception, it is clear that mobile TV prospects should be examined not as an alternative, but as a complementary service to traditional living-room TV. This is because the perceived quality of TV on a mobile phone and the solitary experience are not the favored mode of watching TV, at least with regard to popular living-room content formats (e.g., TV series, sports).

For some time television has been the only major media format that has been missing from mobile phones. Technological advancements in wireless broadband (e.g., WiFi, 3G, 4G, DVB-H) and multimedia mobile terminals (e.g., multimedia mobile phones) have made a reality the reception of digital TV on the move.

The distribution of TV content to mobile devices over broadband wireless raises the issue of video quality. Video quality depends on many aspects of the video-encoding systems, such as bit rate and algorithms that model human perception of video on small screens. Most of the research on the effect of screen sizes in the field of consumer electronics has examined the impact of increasing the image size in the viewer's visual field by means of large physical displays or projection areas. The results show that larger image sizes are more arousing, better remembered, and generally preferred to smaller ones (Reeves et al. 1999).

There are many services that aim to provide users with audiovisual content while on the move. Although many of these services sound appealing, the end users' subjectively perceived quality is an important factor for their success. The properties of video quality have many similarities between the different application domains (e.g., Internet, broadcast, etc.), but the characteristics of mobile devices define a special set of constraints. The biggest differences to other application domains are the limited bandwidth, which leads to high-level requirements of compression and the limitations of the mobile devices such as display size, power resources, processing capabilities, and memory. In addition, the wireless transmission of the content is prone to errors. Accordingly, the production of video under these special requirements should regard the possible distortions in the subjectively perceived quality (Knoche et al. 2008). For this reason, subjective quality evaluation tests during product development are necessary, in order to ensure acceptable quality of service. In particular, the subjective quality of service for mobile TV depends on the perceived audiovisual quality of the consumed content and the interaction through which the user has to go to access it (e.g., the delay between selecting content and start of play).

Further research in mobile TV should investigate authoring tools that enable automatic post-production of video that is targeted for viewing on the move. Currently, mobile service providers encode and deliver existing broadcast material and interactive applications without additional editing, because it is more cost-effective than re-editing. Future research should improve on intelligent cropping mechanisms that present only a part of the original shot. On the application side, cross-media multimedia authoring tools should consider the diversity of screen formats and sizes in mobile devices. Besides content adaptation, further research should investigate the uses of user-generated content and provide templates that facilitate creation and distribution (sharing) of end-user content.

Mobile TV as User Behavior

Early studies on user behavior and mobile TV systems have indicated short watching sessions (Södergård 2003), which are suitable for particular TV genres, such as news and sports highlights, and music videos. More recent research by the same group (VTT, Finland), has tracked the evolution of mobile TV usage (Oksman et al. 2007).

They have identified that in mobile TV there is no prime time, but only "prime place," such as while commuting.

In contrast to living-room TV sets, which are shared displays for audiovisual content, mobile phones are natively social devices. Since their introduction, users have learned to use them as social connectivity tools, with voice-calls and text messages as basic functions. Therefore, the mobile TV user behavior might be shaped by established practices of interpersonal communications over a distance. Indeed, researchers have identified that for some users mobile TV might be a rather personal activity (Cui et al. 2007). In particular, they have identified that mobile TV is employed to privately watch content, at places and situations that are not socially appropriate for TV watching (e.g., business meeting, school lectures). They have also reported that mobile TV is also employed at home, when other TV sets are employed for different programs than the ones preferred by the mobile TV users.

Mobility means that content consumption takes place in various dynamic mobile contexts, for example, on the go, in the bus or at work, a direct contrast to the static embeddedness of living-room TV. Mobility thus means limited attention spans, but with increased user readiness for interruptions and interactions. Furthermore, mobile displays are considerably smaller than living-room screens. The consequence of these contextual factors is that the living-room TV is superior in creating immersive, passive media experiences. Mobile TV might never be able to lull people in the same way as high-definition television, but on the other hand it allows for more interactive and intimate experiences. Although there is a significant body of research on sharing content such as photos and music through desktop and mobile media, there is not much research on video sharing through mobile devices. Therefore, further research should consider the practices of sharing user-generated video content.

Mobile TV as Interaction Terminal

Mobile phones include some kind of standard and familiar input and output facility. The most common input device on a mobile phone is a simple numeric keypad, a few function keys, and navigation keys. In short, in terms of input capabilities, a mobile phone is very similar to a common TV remote control. Some contemporary phones have removed the numeric keypad in favor of a larger touch screen, which might dynamically render a numeric keypad or many any other input arrangements depending on the application. Moreover, mobile phones feature media-rich output capabilities, such as full-color high-resolution (in comparison to size) screens and audio support. As a matter of fact, the output capabilities of contemporary mobile phones are equal or better to early TV sets. In addition to user input and output devices, mobile phones have several data networking capacities. Text messages are a common standard in mobile phones and they have been successfully exploited by TV channel operators as voting and chatting input devices.

The use of the input and output facilities of mobile phones as alternative communication channels for TV programs (e.g., voting, chatting, TV on the move) has been a straightforward and expected development. Cesar et al. (2007) has explored the use of mobile multimedia touch screens to augment the living room TV experience. They have demonstrated that besides remote control, personal mobile terminals could provide additional content, as well as annotation of content. Mobile TV broadcasts transmit content to all mobile terminals within the footprint of a base station, which is relatively narrow when compared with terrestrial broadcasts. The presence of multiple base stations is the main advantage of mobile broadcasting, because the content could be personalized to fit both the terminal and the context of use (e.g., time of the day, geographic location).

Conclusions

Mobile and social TV applications could be feasibly offered through triple-play infrastructures, which combine content delivery, voice, and data services. In this way, the network operator can provide interaction between the TV viewers on TV channels using an interactive broadband link. Triple-play services have been introduced on the assumption that telecommunication, content, and data services could be delivered over the same technological infrastructure thanks to the convergence of the respective technological platforms. Although the convergence of previously distinct technological platforms is a significant benefit for both consumers and service providers, there are also additional benefits from a closer integration of platforms at the user level. Content providers could be benefited by metered communication services, while telecom providers could be benefited by content distribution. In both cases, the users could gain access to intuitive content-enriched communication.

In addition, mobile DTV infrastructure offers many opportunities for converged personal communication and content services. In particular, the availability of broadband wireless technology is rather suitable for the delivery of content-enriched communication services (e.g., active content sharing, synchronous co-viewing, asynchronous notifications over a distance, or discussion and annotations about shared content). Wireless network operators have invested in broadband licenses and infrastructures, but most of the services offered are only video communication, or only video on demand. The introduction of content-enriched communication services is a worthwhile direction, because it offers an excellent balance between the basic need of users to communicate with a mobile device and the need of network providers for increased revenue by added value broadband services, such as mass media content distribution.

In further research, social TV should not only regard verbal and synchronous telecommunications. It seems likely in the future that being able to annotate video with one's comments will become as common as marking up a paper static text document and handing it off to someone else to appreciate or use. Until recently, it has been rare to experience a movie with someone's verbal and audio comments all over it. In upcoming social TV systems, comments could appear as speech or thought balloons over the imagery being viewed, or appear as sub-captions or in a panel below, like the crawling news headlines of standard broadcast video now. It seems likely that mobile multimedia terminal are a necessary user interface to perform content-enriched communication tasks, because they offer both a relatively rich input system, as well as a screen sufficient for personal views on the content.

In summary, multimedia mobile terminals are essential elements of the next generation of social TV services. They are established social connectivity providers, personal media interfaces, content capture and sharing tools, and thus complement stationary interactive TV setups very well. The proposition of mobile TV has a major difference with the analog predecessor. Most notably, it has the potential to offer localized and interactive programs and not just the same broadcasts as seen in living-room TV. In conclusion, while counterintuitive to many, the activities that happen during television watching can be very sociable. Therefore, the ultimate objective is to develop technological support and content for the social practices that surround mobile TV viewing, while retaining the centrality of TV as a leisure pursuit.

References

Agamanolis, S. (2006). At the intersection of broadband and broadcasting: How ITV technologies can support Human Connectedness. *Proceedings of the 4th European Interactive TV Conference*.

Cesar, P., Bulterman, D. C. A., Obrenovic, Z., Ducret, J., & Cruz-Lara, S. (2007). An architecture for non-intrusive user interfaces for interactive digital television. *EuroITV 2007*, 11–20. Springer LNCS.

Chorianopoulos, K., & Lekakos, G. (2008). Social TV: Enhancing the shared experience with interactive TV. *International Journal of Human-Computer Interaction, 24*(2), 113–120.

Coppens, T., Vanparijs, F., & Handekyn, K. (2005). *AmigoTV: A social TV experience through triple-play convergence*. White paper: Alcatel.

Craven, M., Benford, S., Greenhalgh, C., Wyver, J., Brazier, C., Oldroyd, A., & Regan, T. (2000). Ages of avatar: Community building for inhabited television. In *Proceedings of the Third international Conference on Collaborative Virtual Environments (CVE '00), ACM Press*, pp. 189–194.

Cui, Y., Chipchase, J., & Jung, Y. (2007). Personal TV: A qualitative study of mobile TV users. *EuroITV 2007*, 195–204. Springer LNCS.

Ducheneaut, N., Moore, R. J., Oehlberg, L., Thornton, J. D., & Nickell, E. (2008). Social TV: Designing for distributed, sociable television viewing. *International Journal of Human-Computer Interaction, 24*(2), 136–154.

Gauntlett, D., & Hill, A. (1999). TV living: Television, culture and everyday life. London: Routledge.

Knoche, H., McCarthy, J. D., & Sasse, M. A. (2008).How low can you go? The effect of low resolutions on shot types in mobile TV. *Multimedia Tools and Applications, 36*(1–2), 145–166.

Kubey, R., & Csikszentmihalyi, M. (1990). Television and the quality of life: How viewing shapes everyday experiences. Hillsdale, NJ: Lawrence Erlbaum.

Lee, B., & Lee, R. S. (1995). How and why people watch TV: Implications for the future of interactive television. *Journal of Advertising Research, 35*(6), 9–18.

Oksman, V. Noppari, E., Tammela, A., Mäkinen, M., & Ollikainen, V. (2007). Mobile TV in everyday life contexts – individual entertainment or shared experiences? *EuroITV 2007*, 215–225. Springer LNCS.

Reeves, B., Lang, A., Kim, E., & Tartar, D. (1999). The effects of screen size and message content on attention and arousal. *Media Psychology, 1*, 49–68.

Regan, T., & Todd, I. (2004). Media center buddies: Instant messaging around a media center. In *Proceedings of the Fourth Nordic Conference on Human-Computer Interaction, ACM press*, pp. 141–144.

Resnick, P. (2001). Beyond bowling together: Sociotechnical capital. In J. M. Carroll (Ed.), *Human–computer interaction in the new millennium* (pp. 647–672). New York: Addison-Wesley.

Rubin, A. (1983). Television uses and gratifications: The interaction of viewing patterns and motivations. *Journal of Broadcasting & Electronic Media, 27*(1), 37–51.

Södergård, C. (2003). Mobile television – technology and user experiences (Report on the Mobile-TV project (Rep. No. P506), VTT Information Technology).

Veinott, E. S., Olson, J., Olson, G. M., & Fu, X. (1999). Video helps remote work: Speakers who need to negotiate common ground benefit from seeing each other. In *Proceedings of the SIGCHI Conference on Human Factors in Computing Systems (CHI '99), ACM Press*, pp. 302–309.

"What Are You Viewing?" Exploring the Pervasive Social TV Experience

Raimund Schatz, Lynne Baillie, Peter Fröhlich, Sebastian Egger, and Thomas Grechenig

Abstract The vision of pervasive TV foresees users engaging with interactive video services across a variety of contexts and user interfaces. Following this idea, this chapter extends traditional Social TV toward the notion of pervasive Social TV (PSTV) by including mobile viewing scenarios. We discuss social interaction enablers that integrate TV content consumption and communication in the context of two case studies that evaluate Social TV on mobile smartphones as well as the traditional set-top-box-based setup. We report on the impact of social features such as text-chat, audio-chat, and synchronized channel-choice on the end-user's media experience. By analyzing the commonalities and the differences between mobile and living-room Social TV that we found, we provide guidance on the design of pervasive Social TV systems as well as on future research issues.

Introduction

In the traditional living-room context, TV viewing is a lean back, highly immersive, and often a collocated group activity. As can be seen from our own lives and key scenes from the 1990s and early 2000s in the most popular sitcoms ("Friends") and cartoons ("The Simpsons"), social gratification is an important aspect of watching TV together. However, there is a new move to "Participation TV," with new program concepts moving to higher levels of interaction, program input, personalization, and social sharing. This agenda setting gives rise to the concept of Social TV, as a form

R. Schatz, L. Baillie, P. Fröhlich and S. Egger
Telecommunications Research Center Vienna – ftw, A-1220, Vienna, Austria
e-mail: schatz@ftw.at baillie@ftw.at froehlich@ftw.at egger@ftw.at

T. Grechenig (✉)
Institute for Industrial Software (INSO), Vienna University of Technology, Wiedner Hauptstrasse, 76/2/2, A-1040, Vienna, Austria
e-mail: thomas.grechenig@inso.tuwien.ac.at

A. Marcus et al. (eds.), *Mobile TV: Customizing Content and Experience*,
Human-Computer Interaction Series, DOI 10.1007/978-1-84882-701-1_19,
© Springer-Verlag London Limited 2010

of computer-mediated communication (CMC) that aims to provide remote viewers with a joint watching experience at a distance using features such as voice-chat, text messaging, and mediated presence (Coppens et al. 2004).

Early user studies of Social TV systems in living-room settings have shown the huge potential as well as critical issues of connecting remote TV viewers via social enablers (Baillie 2002; Roibás et al. 2006; Weisz et al. 2007). Furthermore, the rapid diffusion of mobile TV has given rise to recent investigations of sociability and social features for mobile broadband media applications (Roibás et al. 2006; Schatz et al, 2007a). Given the complementary nature of mobile and home systems and the rise of the notion of *pervasive TV* (Roibás et al. 2006), it is surprising that so far no study has directly investigated and compared the two environments. In addition, there has only been very limited research into how Social TV might encourage social discourse or enhance the TV experience.

This chapter fills this gap by introducing the notion of pervasive Social TV (PSTV). The following section systematically elaborates the design dimensions of Social TV and extends traditional living-room social TV with pervasive use cases. We present two user studies about the acceptance of the Social TV concept. Case Study 1 is a lab-based evaluation of the set-top-box-based Social TV system, AmigoTV, (Coppens et al. 2004) that is geared toward traditional living-room settings. Case Study 2 addresses the design of our mobile Social TV prototype (see Fig. 1) for Symbian smartphones (Schatz et al. 2007a). In both studies, we investigated the user expectations and reactions to the Social TV concepts presented by the respective prototypes.

The studies have similar designs, enabling the direct comparison of Social TV issues and results across mobile and static home contexts: in both cases, we used controlled experiments involving 15 pairs of users each. Our studies present interesting results in terms of user and interaction-design aspects, yielding insights into varying user requirements and behaviors across the different contexts and platforms. In our conclusion section, we provide design guidance for realizing pervasive Social TV systems.

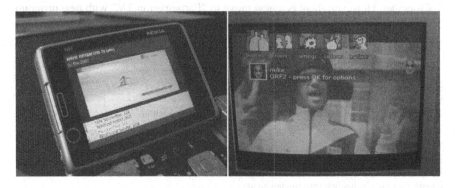

Fig. 1 Screenshots of Mobile TV (*left*) and AmigoTV (*right*) prototype systems used

Pervasive Social TV: Background and Motivation

From its very beginning, broadcast TV had elements of audience involvement. Prime examples are quiz shows, during which viewers mentally compete with each other or live sports coverage, where people congregate in front of the TV to jointly watch a game. Consequently, television has become an established provider of common ground necessary for socialization and bonding among viewers (Lull 1990). In recent times, the proliferation of networked set-top boxes and triple-play[1] concepts has enabled the widespread diffusion of convergent interactive TV services that blur the boundaries between content consumption and communication. For these reasons, the idea of "Social TV" has received increasing attention from industry and research in recent years.

Social TV as Integration of Content and Communication

The major aim of Social TV is to strengthen personal ties and perceived connectedness among remote viewers located in geographically disparate households. To this end, a key strategy is the usage of CMC technologies, such as audio-chat, instant messaging, and buddy lists, as illustrated in Fig. 2 below. These technologies enable shared experiences as well as mediated *social presence*, a "sense of being together" (Nardi 2005). We can define Social TV as *technology that enables sharing the TV experience in order to foster social interaction and the social uses of television among viewers*.

In this context, mediated sociability serves as a catalyst for interaction among viewers in two ways:

- *Direct* sociability: This refers to TV as *context* provider, exemplified by viewers using an audio-chat link parallel to watching the current program.
- *Indirect* sociability: This refers to social interaction that takes place before/after the related event (Oehlberg et al. 2006) and can be supported by features such as online discussion forums enabling discourse *about* a specific show and its episodes.

Key Drivers of Social TV

Two trends support the idea of Social TV: the decline of collocated watching and advances in networked communications. First, the most cited driver of Social TV is the need to counter the increasing isolation of people brought forth by the *decline*

---

[1] Triple-play is a term for the provisioning of content delivery, voice, and data services over a single broadband connection

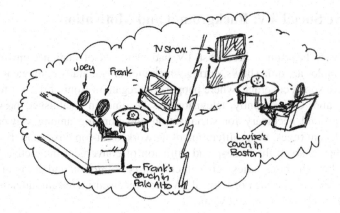

Fig. 2 Generic Social TV system sketch (Oehlberg et al. 2006)

of collocated TV watching (Becker-Beck et al. 2005; Harboe et al. 2007). This decline is caused by the following societal and media trends: the increasing number of single households, number of TV-sets per household, and the increasing mobility of people. In addition, individualization is fostered by the surge of TV channels with on-demand content and time-shifted media consumption (as enabled by PVRs[2]), and the increasing share of Internet usage for media access (Goldenberg 2007). These developments keep decreasing the probability of synchronous shared media experiences. The need to bridge the resulting sociability gaps has brought forward the Social TV paradigm of *"Connecting the Couches"* that refers to bringing remote living rooms closer together. Accordingly, a core functionality of Social TV systems is to emulate the collocated group watching setting by means of mediated presence and live communication links (Coppens et al. 2004; Regan & Todd 2004; Harboe et al. 2007).

The second key driver of Social TV is the *advanced diffusion of networked communication technologies* such as mobile voice telephony, SMS, Instant-messaging, and voice-over-Internet protocol (VoIP)[3]. This trend not only has led to an increased usage of networked communication but also to the frequent utilization simultaneous with TV consumption (Pilotta et al. 2004). For example, over 50% of US youngsters regularly chat on the phone or browse the Internet, effectively multitasking while watching TV (USC Center for the Digital Future 2007). Furthermore, the emergence of the Web 2.0 zeitgeist has caused growth of activity in online communities and networks, which people use to connect with each other by sharing content and experiences. Consequently, television itself is no longer marketed as a

---

[2] Personal Video Recorders, e.g., TiVO™

[3] An example is Skype (www.skype.com)

distinct, isolated channel, but as one center of gravity in an interconnected ecosystem that provides access to a large variety of forms of content and interaction.

The compound impact of these trends is the adoption of a widening portfolio of content and communication channels by their audiences, which turns Social TV from a merely theoretical concept into a viable hybrid medium.

The Design Dimensions of Social TV

Social TV is characterized by the convergence of mass media delivery and networked communication. Following the "connecting the couches" paradigm, the majority of the early Social TV initiatives have focused on recreating the direct sociability of collocated joint viewing experience in the classic living-room setting with live TV content (see the top-left quadrant of Fig. 3 below):

Systems such as PARC's SocialTV (Oehlberg et al. 2006) and Alcatel's AmigoTV (Coppens et al. 2004) enable communication via real-time, high-bandwidth audio links in order to *"facilitate television viewing"* (Oehlberg et al. 2006). In contrast, Media Center Buddies (Regan & Todd 2004) and Reality Instant Messenger (Chuah 2003) represent text-based approaches, including on-screen presence displays, a buddy lists, and invitations.

A number of Social TV projects have also started to conquer the hitherto neglected parts of the Social TV design space: motivated by the increasing prevalence of digital video recorders (DVRs), virtual couch (Goldenberg 2007) focuses on joint viewing of asynchronous media instead of live TV content. By extending a prototype TiVo™ DVR interface with social functions such as invitations, scheduling, Skype-calling and synchronized playback, the system stimulates remote users to engage in joint sessions for viewing asynchronous content such as time-shifted TV recordings and DVDs. CollaboraTV (Harrison & Amento 2007) addresses similar DVR usage scenarios, but focuses on asynchronous content consumption with

		Media Consumption	
		Synchronous	Asynchronous
Social Interaction	Synchronous	*Connecting the Couches:* **Media Center Buddies** **AmigoTV** **PARC Social TV**	Virtual Couch
	Asynchronous	-	CollaboraTV

Fig. 3 Social TV quadrants categorized by temporal variables of interaction and media consumption

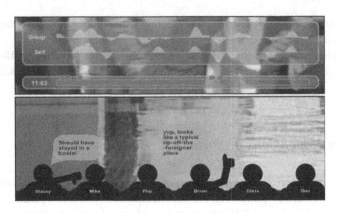

Fig. 4 Asynchronous annotations and avatar buddies in CollaboraTV (Harrison & Amento 2007)

functions for asynchronously annotating TV-shows with avatar gestures and text comments (see Fig. 4).

Table 1 depicts the main dimensions of the Social TV design space. It shows that the projects described above have in common that they all focus on the traditional, stationary set-top-box (STB)-based Social TV scenario. However, O'Brien et al.'s (1999) ethnographic study of set-top boxes in networked homes has shown that, even when being indoors, inhabitants can be very mobile and pursue various activities in parallel. Their findings suggest that home users require more flexible interfaces in order to naturally distribute activities across different people and spaces. Accordingly, two recent research projects address the opportunities of mixed device setups at home: Cesar et al. (2008) have developed a prototype system featuring handheld devices as a secondary screen for iTV in order to control, enrich, and share content. In similar ways, the "PresenceRemote" proposed by Sokoler & Svensson (2008) features a PDA serving as an enhanced remote control for senior citizens which also has a Social TV presence awareness display for communicating TV-activity related information to peers.

As this overview of related work and the depiction of its main design dimensions show, Social TV sill has been mainly confined to stationary settings. Due to the emergence of Mobile TV, however, an open issue is the inclusion of mobile video devices and contexts in Social TV.

From Mobile to Pervasive Social TV

The introduction of mobile 3G streaming and broadcast technologies (such as DVB-H and DMB) has led to the emergence of a new mass delivery channel which reaches beyond the living room: mobile TV. Mobile TV enables users to watch TV and video content on the go, on small-screen devices such as multimedia smartphones and handhelds.

Table 1 Main Social TV design dimensions

Category	Dimension	Example features	Example systems
Communication	Real-time vs. asynchronous	Voice conferencing vs. persistent user annotations	AmigoTV (Coppens et al. 2004) CollaboraTV (Harrison & Amento 2007)
	Direct vs. indirect sociability	Audio-chat vs. on-line discussion forum	AmigoTV "The Simpsons" online community portal
	Verbal vs. nonverbal/emotional	Text-chat vs. emoticons or thumbs up/down	Virtual Couch (Goldenberg 2007) offers both
	Single users vs. groups at endpoints	Headset vs. open microphone and speakers	AmigoTV SocialTV (Oehlberg et al. 2006)
	Private vs. public/strangers	Chat among buddies vs. public channel-chat	Media Center Buddies (Regan & Todd 2004) TV Cabo (Quico 2003)
	High-Bandwidth vs. low-bandwidth	Video-conferencing vs. text-chat	AmigoTV Reality IM (Chuah 2003)
Content	Real-time vs. asynchronous media	Live TV vs. DVD playback	AmigoTV DVD player
	Synchronous vs. asynchronous consumption	Playback synchronization vs. Asynchronous playback	Virtual Couch CollaboraTV
	Socially enabling vs. self-contained content	News/Society TV vs. dense/high-paced action movies and dramas	See Case Studies 1 and 2 in this book chapter
Context	Stationary vs. mobile	Living-room TV vs. mobile TV on the go	Amigo TV Mobile Social TV (Schatz et al. 2007a)
	Devices involved in experience	TV + Intell. Remote vs. TV + Handheld vs. cell-phone	Sokoler & Svensson (2008) Cesar et al. (2008) Mobile social TV

Mobile TV as a multimedia service should not be considered as TV simply scaled down for small devices. It seems destined to develop into a unique medium with its own distinct characteristics. According to Roibás & Sala (2004) traditional TV and small-screen Mobile TV differ in at least four fundamental dimensions: the physical diversity of user interfaces and devices, usage contexts, the history of mobiles being used as auxiliary devices, and the fact that interactive mobile devices in the user's hand constitute a "lean-forward" condition. Together with the phenomenon of interactive TV (or iTV) these findings have led to the notion of *everywhere TV* or *pervasive iTV* (Roibás & Johnson 2006). Pervasive iTV is characterized by user interfaces that operate in a cross-media system, effectively expanding iTV consumption beyond the domestic context.

But how does the sociability of mobile or pervasive iTV match the concept of Social TV? In their studies on mobile TV, Harper et al. (2006) and O'Hara et al. (2007) have found that mobile viewing is not an isolated activity. Similar to living-room TV, mobile TV has implicit social effects as it is experienced in public contexts, affecting persons nearby. Therefore, mobile TV creates social opportunities by watching something that involves bystanders or peers. Driven by a "watching to show" motive, mobile users engage in shared viewing despite practical difficulties such as small speakers or single-user earplugs (O'Hara et al. 2007). Similarly, Repo et al. (2004) report from their field study that among their participants mobile video was very popular particularly when they wanted to have fun together and when they wanted to share an experience. They state that this leads to new forms of watching, particularly on the mobile phone. Furthermore, the majority of mobile phone usage focuses on enhancing and maintaining personal relationships between friends and families (Fox 2001). This is confirmed by the fact that the most successful services (voice, SMS) on mobile phones so far relate to communications among peers (Vincent & Harper 2003).

These findings indicate that similarly to stationary Social TV, social interaction features bear high potential to equally enrich the mobile TV experience. Consequently, the idea of combining mobile content consumption with mediated presence and communication has given rise to the concept of Mobile Social TV services (Schatz et al. 2007a).

Furthermore, the seamless integration of stationary and mobile devices enables pervasive TV services that accompany users throughout their day. This is an attractive proposition, not only for people with a nomadic lifestyle. Just as mobility has created shifts in behaviors and perception of voice telephony, we foresee similar shifts in TV and Social TV watching patterns and attitudes. For example, the availability of a personal communication device might lower the spontaneity and privacy concerns which tend to hinder mediated social interaction, compared to a purely STB-based interactive TV scenario.

Achieving these mobility benefits in terms of a pervasive Social TV (PSTV) service demands the inclusion of mobile platforms and devices. The key dimensions of PSTV are: dynamically changing contexts, varying levels of user engagement, utilization of mobile and stationary devices, as well as dynamic transitions between social interaction modes. However, this integration of Social TV across different contexts and device types raises a number of issues. We have distilled the main issues into the following four research questions:

1. Can Social TV systems provide to remote users an experience similar to collocated TV watching?
2. Which types of social interaction and mediated communication are suitable enablers of pervasive Social TV?
3. In which ways do mediated communication and simultaneous content consumption influence each other?
4. How pervasive is Social TV? In which ways can it be extended beyond traditional living-room big-screen TV settings?

We focused our investigations on the most elementary and common Social TV situation: synchronous communication in the context of live viewing. We conducted two user studies on mobile and stationary Social TV prototypes, which are discussed in the following two sections. Since we used a coherent set of design principles and user experience measures, we are able to juxtapose and compare study results and gain profound insights on how users perceive and interact with pervasive Social TV services.

Study 1: Social TV Investigation in a Semi-Realistic Home Lab Environment

In order to gain more insight into the general expectations and acceptance of the Social TV concept and to investigate both the audio-chat and graphic symbol features of a Social TV system, we conducted a user study in our labs at our research institute to investigate the first three of the questions outlined at the end of the previous section.

Research Questions

Our first research question calls for investigation *whether or not Social TV lives up to its promise of providing remote users an experience similar to collocated TV.* However, there is the frequently observed and reported reluctance toward interactive television services, caused by the TV consumer's passive lean-back attitude (Baillie 2002; Chorianopoulos & Spinellis 2004). There are other concerns within the limits of our study such as privacy and a lack of usage contexts in which remote joint watching is more useful than collocated watching.

The second question was: which modes of social interaction and mediated communication are suitable for pervasive Social TV (e.g., audio-chat, text-chat, or graphical communication)? Social TV is a form of computer-mediated communication.

In this aspect it is comparable to conferencing and collaborative tools in the work or e-learning context (Sallnäs 2004). One fundamental concept and quality criterion for all these CMC application areas is social presence, which equally needs to be provided by Social TV systems.

Our third question refers to *how mediated communication and simultaneous content consumption influence each other.* As in other CMC application areas, it is generally important to minimize attention distraction from the primary content (in this case: TV). However, unlike in the more efficiency-oriented areas of CMC and e-learning, in the user's TV watching experience, enjoyment and satisfaction is also very important. TV consumers decide themselves which channel they want to watch and which service they use, mostly based on intrinsic and hedonistic motivation (Chorianopoulos & Spinellis 2004).

Social TV Application

The Social TV used was AmigoTV, a fusion of television programming with instant messaging (Coppens et al. 2004). It allows the users to form buddy groups with whom they can communicate while watching television, using audio-chat and predefined graphic symbols (e.g., avatar expressions and emoticons). Its main interaction feature – voice-chat – enables users to jointly comment on TV content, just as they are used to in collocated TV sessions. The second feature comprises graphic visual symbols overlaid over the TV content. Viewers can either express themselves by adjusting the appearance of their persistently displayed avatar or by sending symbols (such as emoticons) to their co-viewers. The idea behind this is to convey a sense of peripheral awareness of others' activities and to provide a means of non-verbal, nonbinding, means of communication. The application includes the following elements: group voice-chat, text-chat, list of channels that friends are watching, personalized avatars and emoticons for expressing viewer emotions (see Fig. 5).

Fig. 5 Example screenshots of Social TV system tested

Demographics and Study Setup

Fifteen pairs of friends (i.e., 30 subjects) were invited for the user study and received a small monetary incentive. The test sample corresponded to the young target user population identified for the Social TV system in several marketing-oriented focus groups. The users ranged in age from 20–35 (average age 27); gender, professional status, and technical expertise were balanced. On average, the users reported watching TV for approximately 18 h per week. Five had used the interactive services available on their televisions; all but one had prior experience with some form of chat service.

The evaluation of the Social TV system took place in the premises of our research institute. Two rooms where laid out like living rooms (e.g., there was a normal layout of a TV, sofa, and coffee table). We provided refreshments and snacks during the evaluation to make the situation even more like a living-room situation at home. Our focus was to let participants view the television programs but to also interact with the Social TV service in order to chat with their friend whenever they wanted. The test equipment consisted of two video cameras, video tapes, two television sets, two video player/recorders, one digital camera, and two laptops. The application infrastructure consisted of one video-streaming server, three Amino[4] set-top boxes, and four remote controls (one for the TV and one for the Social TV application in each room as depicted in Fig. 6).

Social TV User Experience Measurements

In order to reliably assess the key phenomena addressed by our research questions, our studies used the following three primary user-experience measurements[5]: social presence, affective connection, and joint TV experience.

A key aim of Social TV is to provide a joint viewing experience. Therefore, the degree of *social presence* felt is one of our main user experience measurements for gauging different Social TV mediated communication setups. Short et al. (1976) define social presence as *"degree of salience of other persons in the interaction and the consequent salience of the interpersonal relationships."* Since they propose social presence as a characteristic of the communication medium itself, their definition emphasizes that different media support different levels of social presence. Consequently, these variations exert strong influence on the ways individuals interact (Short et al. 1976: 65). Following Short's approach, we used the semantic differential technique (Osgood et al.

---

[4] http://www.aminocom.com/
[5] Our studies are not limited to these three measures, but include further independent variables such as distraction from TV, perceived privacy, and overall user satisfaction

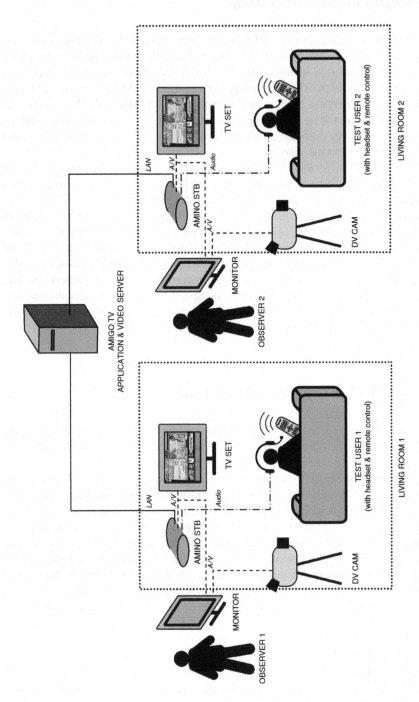

Fig. 6 Two-room setup of the Amigo TV user study

1957) in our studies to let subjects rate different communication conditions on a series of 7-point bipolar pairs such as "impersonal/personal," "insensitive/sensitive," "cold/warm." Using the unmediated face-to-face condition as the gold standard, subjects typically rate media with a high degree of social presence as sensitive, personal, and warm. This differential approach is still one of the most common ways of measuring social presence and has been confirmed to discriminate even between variations of the same communication medium (Hauber et al. 2005; Christie 1973).

Affective connection is a main contributor to a sociable atmosphere in interpersonal communication. Kelly (2004) summarizes mood, emotion, and dispositional affect as the main constituents of an affective experience in groups. Hence, an affective connection between remote peers can be established if the media used enables interaction, exchange, or evocation of these constituents. Such affective experiences can be short comments from several connected people or phatic responses and utterances which occur frequently during joint TV watching sessions (Oehlberg et al. 2006). We asked our study participants to rate the degree of affective connection they perceived, complemented by our coded observations of their actual behavior during the test tasks.

As discussed in the previous section, the additional benefits and TV experience enrichments that viewers gain from social interaction are a key motivator for introducing Social TV. We subsume these benefits under the umbrella term *joint TV experience*. We define the Joint TV experience as "the value added[6] to an individual's TV viewing experience generated by the mutual exchanges with co-viewers taking place on emotional, social, and informational levels as compared to solitary watching." For example, information exchange with peers takes place during watching a soccer match when a friend provides further information about players or specific team tactics. This way, co-viewers add information which might increase others' ability to interpret and better enjoy the current TV program. Our studies measured the Joint TV experience by letting participants rate to what extent the social interaction enriched (or harmed) their viewing experience as well as by asking them in which ways the added value was provided.

Study Design and Methodology

The experience prototype evaluation portion of the study had a one-factor, within-subjects design. In three situations throughout each of the 15 test sessions, the two subjects were asked to watch a set of five TV channels together. The channel consisted of prerecorded content from typical TV genres (Sports, Lifestyle TV, Soaps, Music

---

[6]This added value is reported in conjunction with group experiences frequently. Emile Durkheim (1965) associated this value with the feelings that a religious group relates to its deity, as a result of the group experience undergone during religious festivities. Another example are the public viewing areas in Berlin at the soccer world cup in 2006, which added so much value to the group experience that people decided that it was worth paying for

TV). The three communication situations of jointly watching TV were specified as follows (the order of these situations was varied between subjects; each situation had a duration of approximately 10 min):

1. *Face-to-face*: This situation had the function of a control condition. The users were jointly watching TV in the same room on a couch.
2. *Audio-chat*: The users were jointly watching TV in two separate rooms, using the audio-chat feature.
3. *Graphic symbolic communication*: While jointly watching TV, the users used the graphical symbolic communication feature. They were given a list with explanations about the meaning of each of the provided symbols.

After each of these conditions, the users were asked to fill in a questionnaire containing items for measuring perceived social presence, and further self-developed items to elicit attention focus toward the TV and the other person, privacy concerns, and six adjective pairs to characterize the enjoyment experienced in the situation. Furthermore, the subjects were asked to provide a ranking of the three media types. For four randomly chosen pairs of subjects (i.e., N=8), we conducted a behavioral analysis of the video material captured during the three previously mentioned different comparison conditions.

We then undertook a semi-structured final interview, which was designed to gather the users' reactions and opinions regarding the system concept, the different interaction modes, and design ideas for the audio-chat and graphical communications feature. We asked this range of questions because we wanted to gain insight into the users' expectations and acceptance of the Social TV concept.

To conclude, in this user study we investigated user expectations, reactions to the Social TV system, as well as other questions related to stationary Social TV. Section 5 will compare results of this study with the results of our mobile Social TV study, which is discussed in the next section.

Case Study 2: Mobile Social TV

With the proliferation of mobile multimedia streaming and broadcast technologies, TV for handhelds and related interactive services has become a subject of strong academic and commercial interest. Encouraged by the results of Case Study 1 and other studies (Harboe et al. 2007; Geerts 2006; Oehlberg et al. 2006), we were interested in investigating Social TV on multimedia phones (Schatz et al. 2007a). Although the idea of transferring Social TV to mobiles seems intriguing, mobility presents a number of potential barriers to the success of mobile Social TV, for example, device constraints (e.g., small screen size), the users' physical and social context, as well as cognitive load. Therefore, social enhancements for mobile TV raise questions of attention management, overall quality of the media experience, and social etiquette. In order to address these open issues, we set up a combined indoor/outdoor field study to answer the following research questions:

- Question 1: *How do users react to Social TV features offered on mobile devices?* The question addresses user reactions to mobile TV extended by parallel communication. Will users be overwhelmed or will they be able to divide their attention in a controlled manner?
- Question 2: *How is the Social TV user experience affected by TV content and other contextual factors?* The study needs to identify how user experience and the use of social interaction functions is related to the content shown and how contextual factors, like environment, ambient noise, other people, etc., influence the user experience.
- Question 3: *How do social interaction modes differ in sense of presence and which ones do users actually prefer?* The study should identify the relation between various interaction modes and the overall TV experience, as well as the variables determining the preferred interaction mode.
- Question 4: *Is it possible to create a sociable atmosphere in the context of Mobile TV at all?* Various studies have demonstrated that stationary Social TV successfully increases the sociability of TV (see Case Study 1 as well as Geerts (2006) and Harboe et al. (2007)). This effect needs to be proven for mobile contexts by assessing variables such as social presence, affective connection, and enjoyment.

Study Prototype

In order to obtain reliable answers to our mobile Social TV research questions, we avoided using low-fidelity mockups or early-stage prototypes for our user studies. Instead, we designed a mobile Social TV prototype system that features a custom interactive TV client[7] for current Symbian smartphones,[8] which provides a user experience equal to commercial solutions (Schatz et al. 2007b). The client features mobile TV enhanced by synchronous communication features, such as text-chat, messaging, audio-chat, and emoticons, within a split-screen user interface. The default top frame displays noninteractive data (such as information about the presence of other users or the current program), the middle frame presents the video content, while the bottom frame displays interactive elements such as chat (see Fig. 7 below).

Interaction Design

As Fig. 7 indicates, a major challenge for the interaction design was the simultaneous provision of TV and communication features on mobiles with a 320 × 240 pixel screen resolution. In order to obtain results that focused on Social TV we carefully

---

[7] For our MiViBES interactive video client, see the AMUSE project homepage http://amuse.ftw.at
[8] Smartphones such as the Nokia E61, N92, E70

Fig. 7 Screenshot of the Mobile TV client in text-chat mode during a newscast

limited the range of client features in order to avoid basic navigation flaws and usability issues. We decided to implement speech- and text-based user interfaces in order to offer both fundamental social interaction modes to the user:

- *Audio-chat*: Similar to mobile telephony, our users could engage with each other in an audio-chat session to directly communicate with each other. Voice audio was delivered via a headset (earplug) while the video sound was emitted from the built in speakers of the device.
- *Text-chat*: For the text-based interaction we offered the participants two different input methods, a QWERTY keypad and a 3 × 3 keypad. The messages sent were unrestricted in length, and users could type in emoticons that the system converted to small graphics.

Similar to AmigoTV, a *JointZapping* feature synchronizes two or more TV clients in a master/slave fashion. If the "master" user switches to another channel the others' (slaves) clients also switches to the channel specified by the master. This design has the advantage of avoiding confusion as it reflects the common collocated TV setup where only the person with the remote is in control. Furthermore, in order to facilitate session initiation, *ShareMarks* give the user the possibility to point friends to currently broadcasted programs of interest and invite them to join. We implemented ShareMarks as multimedia messages (MMS) that are automatically generated by the system and sent to their receivers via the mobile network. They consist of a current screenshot of the recommended program, relevant electronic program guide (EPG) information, and a short text message (see Fig. 8). The content should encourage the receiving users to join the recommended program and engage in joint watching.

Fig. 8 A ShareMark that encourages the receiver to join a TV-Channel

Methodology

We conducted a combined indoor/outdoor study to observe spatially separated pairs of friends or couples whilst using our mobile Social TV prototypes running on Nokia E61 and E70 smartphones (see Fig. 9). We performed a paired user test due to the following advantages for evaluating social applications: increased realism, less need for facilitator intervention, and higher quality of results (Shrimpton-Smith et al. 2006). We only tested with pairs of users and not with groups in order to assure comparability with the results of Case Study 1. Furthermore, this method also enables the reliable assessment of the basic Social TV setting (single users in each location), because any social experience measurements can be related to the mediated communication and not interference of collocated buddies.

Test Setting and Demographics

The user tests took place in our lab and in the surroundings of Tech Gate Vienna. The lab itself offers a living-room-like environment where the users can feel nearly as comfortable as being in front of their own TV sets at home. We recruited 15 pairs of friends via public announcements and the test-person database of our institution. By this means, we had 30 participants in total, 16 male and 14 female, aged between

Fig. 9 Nokia E61 (QWERTY keypad) and E70 (3 × 3 text input)

14 and 72 years (mean = 29.8 years, median = 27.0 years). Other variables such as profession, educational background, TV/Internet usage, and messaging usage habits were varied to account for the broad target group of future mobile TV users.

Study Design

We conceived the study as series of controlled user experiments in order to be able to vary chosen variables (such as interaction mode and TV content) and observe the impact on user feedback and behaviors in comparison to the reference condition. The duration of a full test was about 2 h with a break after the first hour. The duration of the tasks was roughly 10 min. The course of the user tests included two reference conditions (joint watching of a standard TV and a shared mobile), followed by sessions in four different contexts: at home (living room), café, bus-stop, and walking within the surroundings of our research centre. In each context, participants were able to remotely interact with each other via the mobile TV client (see Fig. 10). Eight TV channels were broadcast via our hybrid DVB-H/UMTS test platform (Schatz et al. 2007b) during the tests. The channels covered a variety of genres, including classic mobile TV genres, such as live sports, music TV, and news. Furthermore, we included content that is potentially suitable for facilitating social interaction, e.g., lifestyle TV (coverage of celebrities and events) and user-generated content clips (from YouTube.com). We included these genres because the overall purpose of lifestyle TV is to function as social currency, whereas user-generated video clips are widely considered to work very well for mobile viewing (cf. Orgad 2006) because of their being short and self-contained.

Fig. 10 Study participant in the café filmed by cameras mounted on a hat

Similar to Study 1, participants filled out a questionnaire after each condition in order to rate the tested feature and provide feedback concerning the Social TV experience, in particular concerning our key user-experience measurements. Finally, we conducted debriefing interviews to assess participants' overall satisfaction with the Social TV features experienced. The fact that both studies were based on the same principles and methods enabled us to analyze results aggregated as one pervasive setup. This analysis is presented in the following section.

Comparative Analysis of Study Results

This section presents our findings on pervasive Social TV based on consolidation and comparison of the results of the two previously described Social TV studies. The benefit of this comparative approach is the coverage of a wide spectrum of settings, reflecting the important everyday situations where users engage in TV and in communication activities. Since both studies share a consistent set of experimental design principles, the combination of the user samples allows for a consolidated analysis of the phenomena involved. In addition, different situations, such as stationary *vs.* mobile, can be compared with regard to behavior and subjective experience.

Table 2 Factors of pervasive Social TV considered in the two case studies

Case study – condition	Collocation	Interaction mode	Device	Mobility
1–1	Collocated	–	TV	Stationary
1–2	Mediated	Audio	TV	Stationary
1–3	Mediated	Graphic	TV	Stationary
2–1	Collocated	–	Phone	Stationary
2–2	Mediated	Audio	Phone	Stationary
2–3	Mediated	Text (qwerty)	Phone	Stationary
2–4	Mediated	Text (3×3^9)	Phone	Stationary
2–5	Mediated	Audio	Phone	Mobile (café)
2–6	Mediated	Text (qwerty)	Phone	Mobile (café)
2–7	Mediated	Text (qwerty)	Phone	Mobile (walk)

Table 2 shows that, taken together, the studies cover a fairly wide design space. The combined results provide guidance about how PSTV systems should be designed in order to truly blend with their users' everyday life.

The factors that we used in the comparative analysis are: collocation, mobility, device, and interaction mode. Both studies juxtaposed the traditional form of collocated joint TV watching with various mediated communication modes (audio chat, text chat, and graphic). While case study 1 focused on big-screen Social TV in a living-room context, case study 2 investigated small-screen Social TV on smartphones in different contexts ranging from stationary domestic to mobile (living-room, café, and walking, respectively). The main dependent variables were joint TV experience, social presence, affective connection between users, as well as distraction from the media experience. These variables constitute our main quantitative user-experience measures in the context of Social TV.

In the following discussion, we present the key results of both studies to gain a better understanding of the major factors involved. The key findings were derived both from inferential statistics and qualitative data from observations and interviews. Each finding is interpreted and contrasted with related research results. Our key findings are these:

1. Social TV creates levels of joint TV experience, social presence, and affective connections that are sufficiently high to emulate collocated watching.
2. Audio is the most effortless, universal, and therefore most essential communication channel for Social TV.
3. Audio- and text-chat are complementary.

---

[9] 3×3 refers to text entry via a standard phone's keypad which demands for multiple keypresses for certain letters

4. The user's readiness to engage in text-chat primarily depends on personal background and actual input method available.
5. Graphical communication is not sufficient to provide a joint TV experience.
6. Mediated communication distracts significantly more from TV watching than collocated face-to-face communication.
7. TV content has a significant influence on users' readiness for social exchange.
8. Social TV is indeed pervasive. User ratings vary only little across different contexts and device setups.

Finding 1: Social TV creates levels of joint TV experience, social presence, and affective connections that are sufficiently high to emulate collocated watching.

Social TV systems only meet end-user expectations if they create levels of perceived "togetherness" which come close to the traditional collocated situation. To this end, we have begun to contextualize the phenomenon of social presence and to operationalize the notion of a "joint TV experience" as discussed in the context of Case Study 1. In both case studies, we used the traditional living-room situation of collocated joint TV watching as a baseline and contrasted it to its mediated counterparts.

Our data suggest that particularly mediated audio and text communications succeed in providing similar experience levels (see Fig. 11). The joint TV experience of audio- and text-chat was clearly higher than medium (mean = 5.0 and 4.8 on a 1–7 scale) and did not differ significantly from the collocated reference situation[10] (p > 0.05). The reason for these results, we believe, is the fact that viewers normally remain focused on the TV during social interactions. We observed that our participants rarely turned their heads to see their conversation partners during communication, indicating that visual gesture and facial turn-taking has only a minor impact on communication quality. Therefore, low-bandwidth communication links via audio and text are sufficient to emulate collocated watching, while the visual channel is of relatively low importance for creating social presence in this setting. Therefore, communication in front of the TV set happens as a "shoulder-to-shoulder" rather than "face-to-face" experience. Similar studies on Social TV such as Oehlberg et al. (2006) and collocated TV watching experiences (Lull 1990; Jerslev 2001) support these results in that they identify social interactions between viewers as "visually peripheral," with little reliance on visual cues, particularly when it comes to watching in groups. Therefore, we can safely conclude that the requirements of Social TV users on the mediated social interaction channel are significantly lower compared with face-to-face applications such as video-conferencing.

Concerning features that complement communication, TV channel-switching synchronization (i.e., *JointZapping*) was rated as highly realistic and essential feature, also in mobile setups (average 4.43 out of 7). According to user comments,

---

[10] For identification of statistical differences, Wilcoxon signed ranks tests were calculated in case of paired samples, and Mann-Whitney-U tests in case of independent samples, respectively

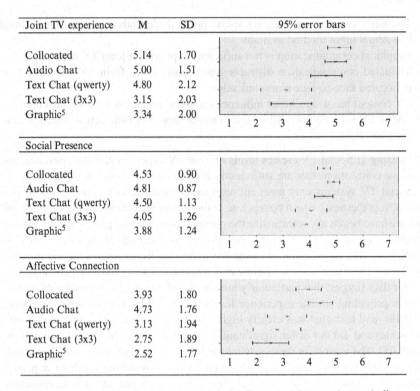

Joint TV experience	M	SD	95% error bars
Collocated	5.14	1.70	
Audio Chat	5.00	1.51	
Text Chat (qwerty)	4.80	2.12	
Text Chat (3x3)	3.15	2.03	
Graphic[5]	3.34	2.00	
Social Presence			
Collocated	4.53	0.90	
Audio Chat	4.81	0.87	
Text Chat (qwerty)	4.50	1.13	
Text Chat (3x3)	4.05	1.26	
Graphic[5]	3.88	1.24	
Affective Connection			
Collocated	3.93	1.80	
Audio Chat	4.73	1.76	
Text Chat (qwerty)	3.13	1.94	
Text Chat (3x3)	2.75	1.89	
Graphic[5]	2.52	1.77	

Fig. 11 Comparison of collocated TV watching and different social interaction modes[11]

this synchronized zapping simplified the logistics and degree of realism of remote joint watching. Interestingly, text-chat on average was rated as sufficient interaction mode for negotiating TV-program choice (average 4.86 out of 7). Furthermore, the following user feedback excerpts also provide further, insights on overall perceived usefulness of the systems tested:

Viewing becomes more fun, particularly during ad breaks (male, age 30).

Particularly interesting when you are away from the person you normally watch with. This regularly happens in our case (male part of a young couple, night worker, age 29, about the mobile system).

I was even more chatting as I usually do if I jointly watch TV at home (female commenting on the audio chat, age 22)

Finding 2: Audio is the most effortless, universal, and therefore most essential interaction mode for Social TV.

---

[11] The overall sample size of both studies was originally 60. However, the data of one person in case study 1 could not be analyzed. Different sample sizes are due to differences in experimental design between the two case studies and by nested design in Case Study 2

The central role of the auditory channel for Social TV was confirmed by the participants of both studies. Audio-chat conveyed a significantly higher extent of social presence and joint TV experience compared to text-chat (the 3×3 and QWERTY input methods combined, $Z = -2.01$, $p = 0.44$; $Z = -2.18$, $p = 0.29$). Audio-chat was even more strongly preferred to graphical communication in matters of social presence and joint TV experience ($Z = -3.08$, $p = 0.02$; $Z = -2.83$, $p = 0.05$). A graphical representation of this finding is depicted in Fig. 11. User comments while using the audio-chat also affirm that: *"While speaking I can more concentrate on the video again"*, *"now you don't have to wait minutes until I reply"* or *"Ah, nice to hear your voice."* This yields from the ease of use and the fact that people are accustomed to using audio-chat. Geerts (2006) has also shown that people are less distracted when using audio-chat and therefore can concentrate more on the video and the other user. It was obvious in the observations that the emotional component of speech (cf. Froehlich 2007) was of immense importance also in this TV-related communication context. When asked about their communication channel preferences in the final interviews, the majority of our subjects commented on audio-chat being *"more natural,"* *"easy to learn,"* and *"effortless to use."*

Another interesting finding related to audio-chat was that social presence and affective connection ratings were significantly higher than in the tested collocated settings ($Z = -2.19$, $p = 0.028$; $Z = -1.97$, $p = 0.49$). Our observations have shown that participants talked significantly more when using remote audio communications compared to when they were collocated. This increased communication activity correlates with increased perceived social presence. This is to some extent contrary to the findings of Geerts and Harboe as they did not conclude that audio-chat was more sociable than face-to-face. We believe that our finding was different because we included single users in separated locations in our study while the other studies used groups in each location. In such a group setting a sociable atmosphere might exist even without communication through a Social TV system.

Finding 3: Audio- and text-chat are complementary.

Aside from a general preference of voice-chat, our results also show that both text and audio communication have compensatory strengths and, consequently, different roles in Social TV. The general strengths of audio as being a very natural, low-effort, low-delay and high-bandwidth communication modality were evident in both user studies. This was also confirmed by participants' comments such as *"audio is more personal and feels more natural than writing,"* *"I am faster when I can talk"* or *"it is more easy than typing on the keypad."*

Both studies have revealed a particular advantage of audio over text: emotional expression capabilities and subjective ratings of emotional connection were much higher for audio than for text communication ($Z = -4.55$, $p < 0.001$). A general observation of participant behavior was the intense and spontaneous use of affective cues, such as emotional prosody, emphatic responses, and affect bursts (e.g., laughter). Furthermore, audio enables communication nonverbal cues such as prosody, phatic response, and utterances, which make audio a richer and more universal channel compared to textual and graphical communications (see for example Froehlich 2007).

However, the need to manage two different audio sources (TV, chat) along with the sound of one's own voice was identified as a major drawback of audio-chat in both setups, mobile and STB-based. Participants complained about TV interfering with audio-chat or vice versa, resulting in frequent attempts to adjust audio levels, particularly when someone was talking on TV, too. Although we ended up using separate headsets and speakers, the problem remained. Particularly in public mobile settings, where environmental noise became an issue, many participants commented that they would rather switch to text-chat in order to avoid audio-interference. Geerts (2006), who conducted a user study that compared between text- and audio-chat for stationary Social TV, confirm these findings. The majority of their participants stated a clear preference for audio-chat because of ease-of-use and no requirements to divide attention between different actions (e.g., reading, typing, and watching). However, participants also complained about stress from the need to attune to different audio sources which they identified as an issue that should be gracefully handled by the system.

Finding 4: The user's readiness to engage in text-chat primarily depends on personal background and actual input method available.

Several contextual factors affect users' preference of text-chat over audio-chat. Firstly, the input method had strong influence on users' ratings. In case study 2, users reported to have a significantly higher joint TV experience with the Blackberry style QWERTY method than with the 3×3 text-entry method (4.8 vs. 3.5 rating points; $Z = -2.34$; $p = 0.19$). In general, the 3×3 method was rated significantly lower than audio-chat in all four dimensions of interest in Fig. 11 ($p < 0.053$). Also when QWERTY input was used, less mediated social presence and affective connection than in the audio-chat condition was perceived by our subjects. However, in contrast to the 3×3 condition, the joint TV experience and distraction were comparable to audio-chat situations.

Secondly, the user's background, especially age and communication habits, exerts a significant influence on willingness to engage with text-chat. User age significantly correlated with the preference of chat modality (audio-chat vs. text-chat, $r = 0.32$, $p = 0.49$). This finding is substantiated by our observations during the tests. Younger users tended to be much more proficient and creative in using mobile text input than older participants. Furthermore, the heavy SMS or Instant-messaging user among our subjects stated a preference of text-chat over audio-chat in the final interviews. The main reasons given state by participants was that: using text matched existing communication habits (such as texting others during TV watching) and high skill levels in mobile text-entry. Notably, the influence of existing skill levels was so strong that heavy SMS users explicitly preferred the 3×3 keypad (to which they were accustomed to) over the QWERTY layout.

Finding 5: Graphical communication is not sufficient to provide a satisfying joint TV experience on its own.

Both case studies investigated features for communication on a graphical/symbolic basis. Case Study 1 featured animations that viewers could send to each other. In one dedicated test condition, participants were asked to use *only* graphic communications, whereas, in the other task settings, they could use graphic communications as an optional enrichment. According to user feedback, the richness and usefulness of this interaction mode was perceived as very limited. This was also reflected in the significantly lower subjective ratings of joint TV experience, social presence, and affective connection ($p > 0.05$), as shown in Fig. 11. Concerning the pure graphical communication condition, participants commented that they could not establish a meaningful dialogue with their peers. In Case Study 2, viewers could use standard symbols (such as emoticons and thumbs up/down) via text-chat. However, these symbols were rarely used in practice. In the debriefings, the majority of our subjects mentioned they actually would have used the symbols more often if they were easier to access.[12] However, all participants rejected the idea of pure symbolic communications and preferred textual or audio communications "spiced up" by graphical communication.

Finding 6: Mediated communication distracts more from TV watching than collocated face-to-face communication.

The more intensely one communicates with another person, the more the communication activities tend to distract from the TV content. Distraction of attention should therefore be even stronger when the interlocutor is located somewhere else and mediated communication is required. We confirmed both hypotheses in our studies. In the collocated situation, distraction from TV content was at close to medium (mean = 3.8 on a 1–7 scale). Compared to that, audio-chat and text-chat were significantly more distracting. Due to the high levels of attention and skill required for 3 × 3 input, the distraction ratings were highest here (see Fig. 12). Nevertheless, although mediated communication distracts from watching to a certain amount, it does not affect the sociable atmosphere created, as Finding 1 has shown.

From our observations, ratings, and user comments we arrived at the following ranking of communication modes (from least to highest distraction):

1. Text (receiving)
2. Audio (speaking)
3. Audio (listening)
4. Text (writing)

Distraction of TV watching attention by personal communication (1=high; 7=low)		
Collocated	3.20	1.57
Audio Chat	2.49	1.39
Text Chat (qwerty)	2.07	1.29
Text Chat (3x3)	1.85	1.39
Graphic	3.00	1.97

Fig. 12 Distraction from TV content by collocated and different mediated communication types

---

[12] Participants stated that the main barrier were the key combinations required for accessing the emoticons and that a pop-dialogue for direct access would be the preferred design

We propose the following explanations for this ranking:

1. Reading text can be done asynchronously and enables the user to decide when he or she wants to read the message. Thus, it puts least pressure on user.
2. Speaking is in line with one's desire for keeping control of the media consumption and communication process and does not require special skills. Our participants automatically started to speak when content needed less attention from their side or when it was appropriate for them.
3. Listening to voice-chat interferes with TV audio and environmental sound and thus tends to be perceived as uncontrolled disturbance in contrast to speaking or reading.
4. Text entry on mobile devices is a generic problem and detracts high levels of attention particularly if users do not text regularly.

These explanations are in line with the findings of Weisz et al. (2007) who also investigated the ability of attention management connected with text communication. Although text-chat lacks some of the features offered by audio-chat, their users also stated that it allows for better attention management. One reason is that text-chat also functions as persistent history log which allows for more flexible communication timing (Weisz et al. 2007). In contrast to Geerts (2006), we think that users are capable of multitasking since nowadays TV consumers are used to doing household chores, surfing the web, etc., while watching. Similar to Oehlberg et al. (2006), we observed that if the system allows for multitasking users time, their interactions are such that distractions are minimized.

Finding 7: TV Content has a significant influence on users' readiness for social exchange.

In order to verify Oehlberg et al.'s (2006) observation that TV content *serves as resource as well as a constraint* for social interaction, we tested whether the content of the TV program impacted on the user willingness to engage in conversation. After having been exposed to different content genres, our subjects rated the chat-suitability of lifestyle TV (i.e., light shows about celebrities, events, etc.) and news-casts as highest (average 3.81 and 4.4, out of 5). On the other hand, documentaries and user-generated content were rated toward the low end (2.79 and 2.42 respectively). These user ratings matched our observations of participants' actual chat behavior during the studies.

The explanation for these results is that Lifestyle and News are deliberately designed to function as social currency. Both genres rely on bite-sized stories that users can easily connect with and relate to in conversations *"have you seen the crazy wig of …,"* *"I have read this already today on the Web."* In the same way, our users identified sports as one of the most suitable Social TV genres, since it is most commonly watched in group settings. Harboe et al. (2007) confirm this result, with sports being identified as optimal type of Social TV content because sports coverage is easy to follow and provides common ground necessary for social interaction. On the other hand, the documentaries and more art-oriented user-generated content samples[13] we showed were perceived as more lengthy, self-contained, and intel-

---

[13] We used user-generated content clips taken from www.youtube.com such as "Tony vs. Paul" http://www.youtube.com/watch?v=AJzU3NjDikY

lectually challenging *"wait a moment I want to see first what he does next."* Therefore, these formats kept our participants concentrating on figuring out the content rather than on engaging in conversation. However, since our set of user-generated videos was a very small subset of a very heterogeneous genre, our results on user-generated content cannot be generalized. For example, viewer ratings might be very different if they were chatting while watching videos of their last holiday.

Finding 8: Social TV is indeed pervasive. User ratings and perceptions vary only little across different contexts and device setups.

One of the main aims behind juxtaposing both studies was to assess whether Social TV is a truly pervasive phenomenon and what differences exist between *stationary* living-room and *mobile* settings. The mean rating scores of our main quantitative experience measures (joint TV experience, social presence, and affective connection) were highly consistent and clearly above average, ranging between 4.82 and 5.13 (see Table 3 below). On first sight, most mean scores seem slightly higher for mobile settings. However, the difference was not significant in most cases.

Audio-chat was neither perceived differently in terms of Joint TV Experience (U = 300.0; p = 0.59), nor Social Presence (U = 264.5, p = 0.25). As the only signifi-

Table 3 Comparison between stationary and mobile settings for audio-chat and text-chat in terms of our main quantitative user-experience measures

		Stationary	Mobile
Audio-chat[14]			
Joint-TV experience	Mean	4.95	5.13
	SD	1.54	1.51
Social presence	Mean	4.83	5.10
	SD	0.87	0.87
Affective connection	Mean	4.14	5.01
	SD	1.76	1.63
Text-chat[15]			
Joint-TV experience	Mean	4.93	4.13
	SD	1.96	2.25
Social presence	Mean	4.66	5.10
	SD	1.04	0.87
Affective connection	Mean	2.94	3.33
	SD	1.75	2.16

[14] The data for stationary audio-chat has been computed from both studies (conditions 1–2 and 2–2 in Table 2), and the data for mobile audio-chat is from Study 2 (condition 2–5). The samples for the mobile and stationary conditions were independent. Consequently, in order to investigate statistical significance, Mann-Whitney-U tests were calculated instead of Wilcoxon tests

[15] Stationary text-chat is equivalent to condition 2–3 of Table 2, and mobile text-chat is equivalent to condition 2–7. As also here the samples were independent, Mann-Whitney-U tests were calculated

cant difference, the affective connection was perceived higher for the mobile than for the stationary setting (mean rating scores: 5.07 and 4.14; U = 209.5, p = 0.032). A plausible interpretation of this may be that audio is a very familiar way of communicating in mobile settings, much more than when sitting in front of the TV.

The experience of Social TV by using text-chat appeared even less influenced by the type of setting. No statistical differences between mobile and stationary conditions were found for the main measures Joint TV Experience, Social Presence, and Affective Connection (U = 339.0, p = 0.14, U = 395.0, p = 0.54, U = 99.5, p = 0.60).

This overall consistency in our data is a surprising outcome, because one might expect strong influences by dynamic mobile contexts such as interruptions of attention (Oulasvirta et al. 2005; Blom et al. 2005). To a certain extent, these influences were also present in our study. For example, users felt significantly more distracted using text-chat in mobile than in stationary situations (Z = −1.99; p < 0.046). Some of them also expressed their worries about being too absorbed by the TV content and chat in highly mobile situations and the resulting risk of accidents. Nonetheless, the stability of the main experience measures shows that Social TV worked almost as effectively in pervasive as in purely stationary setups.

The design space covered by our user studies is characterized by interaction with two different device types, namely *TV-based and cellphone-based interaction*. The major related question is whether the differences entailed by the device type, such as display size, video quality, and input device, have an influence on our experience measures. The focus here was on audio-chat in home settings, which serves as the common denominator of both studies. Table 4 shows that the mean experience scores did not differ strongly between TV-based and cellphone-based interaction. As could be expected, taking into account the relatively high standard deviations, we did not find any statistical significance regarding joint TV experience, social presence, and affective connection. Also, the distraction ratings did not differ significantly between our TV-based and cellphone-based conditions.

Table 4 Comparison of TV-based and cellphone-based interaction for audio-chat in terms of our main experience measures[16]

		TV	Cellphone
Joint-TV experience	Mean	4.76	5.33
	SD	1.57	1.45
Social presence	Mean	4.73	5.10
	SD	0.83	0.87
Affective connection	Mean	4.03	4.33
	SD	1.68	1.95

[16] TV = 19 "TV set (case study 1); phone = Nokia e61 2.8" (case study 2). We could only compare the audio conditions, as these were the 'common denominator' of both studies: Conditions 1–2 of Table 5.1 (case study 1, audio-chat) vs. 2–2 (case study 2, audio-chat) were compared

While the final results particularly call for further empirical examination, they nevertheless show that TV-related shared communication is a pervasive phenomenon worth of further study. The following final section will reflect on these findings in order to provide answers to our initial research questions on pervasive Social TV.

Conclusions and Outlook

This section answers the four key questions concerning pervasive Social TV stated at the outset of this chapter. To this end we synthesize the findings of our comparative analysis with those from related mobile and Social TV literature. Furthermore, we will derive implications for the design of Pervasive Interactive TV applications as well as an agenda for future research in this field.

Question 1: Can Social TV systems provide to remote users an experience similar to collocated TV watching?

On the most fundamental level, our study results show that Social TV systems (as represented by our mobile and stationary prototypes) can successfully emulate a collocated joint TV experience by providing CMC in parallel to media consumption. The main reason is that whilst in front of the TV, peripheral awareness among co-viewers is sufficient, designating a "shoulder-to-shoulder" rather than a "face-to-face" condition (see Finding 1 in the previous section). Therefore, Social TV only requires low-effort, low-bandwidth communication links between viewers rather than rich, sophisticated channels such as video-conferencing. This fact facilitates design and practical implementation of Social TV systems, particularly when involving mobile devices with their constrained interfaces. Furthermore, in the context of TV viewing, social exchange by default is a background activity secondary to the actual media consumption. Therefore, designers of Social TV systems should focus on providing mutual awareness and communication interfaces that require minimal user effort, tolerate swift user attention and cope with sporadic bursts of interaction. For example, an ambient chat-activity indicator combined with instant access to the recent communication history allows the user to focus on the TV content without the fear of missing important parts of the ongoing dialogue. Furthermore, designing for connectedness requires synchronization features (such as *JointZapping*) that help maintain a shared media context among peers.

Question 2: Which types of social interaction and mediated communication are suitable enablers of pervasive Social TV?

Concerning the design of social interaction mechanisms, we found that audio-chat is pivotal to Social TV adoption since it provides the ease of use and richness necessary to naturally interact with each other during TV watching. This holds particularly true for target audiences that are not experienced in other forms of mediated communication such as text-chat. Nonetheless, audio-chat also creates a number of practical and social difficulties, particularly in mobile setups: annoyance, privacy, noise, and having to handle multiple audio sources. Headsets significantly mitigate these difficulties, since users can talk or whisper while holding the device in their hands. However, most people regard their handling as too cumbersome for practical everyday usage (cf. O'Hara et al. 2007). As a practical alternative, loud-speakers are suitable for more private indoor settings. However, interference of chat with the TV sound demands for sophisticated audio mixing and echo-canceling features (cf. Oehlberg et al. 2006). For both setups we therefore propose to separate the different audio sources (TV, chat) in the stereo panorama as well as to provide a simple switch for assigning each source into the foreground or background.

In addition, the results of our own and similar studies (cf. Rettie 2003; Geerts 2006) demonstrate that low-bandwidth communication such as text-chat provide levels of connectedness sufficiently high to enable strong social bonding among viewers. Particularly younger users rated text-chat as less intrusive, more fun, and as a more intimate medium for social exchange. However, text-chat also suffers from delays, visual distraction, and the need for multitasking. In this context, the key issue is text-entry: the QWERTY keypad is the optimal tool; however, the majority of today's phones use the 3×3 Keypad. This keypad was deemed to be too onerous and distracting for simultaneous TV viewing by our users. The text-entry interface therefore is currently one of the main bottlenecks for pervasive Social TV[17]. A partial remedy could be to offer users a choice of preconfigured text phrases similar to SMS templates. In addition, impulsive expressions such as emotional utterances and phatic responses are essential affective Social TV elements that pure textual communication is lacking. Therefore, providing graphical symbols (such as smileys or thumbs up/down) is vital, but features of this kind only have practical value if users can also spontaneously access them with ease (e.g., via shortcuts or a dedicated pop-up menu).

However, despite the influence of user background such as age and messaging skills, actual preference of interaction type often is a rather dynamic decision depending on viewers' current context, chat-content, and communication needs. For example, audio was preferred for more lengthy, side-conversations. In contrast, our participants switched to textual communication for shorter comments on the TV content or when they felt uncomfortable due to the presence of bystanders. Therefore, providing only a single type of social interaction channel is not suffi-cient, since the different modalities tend to complement each other very well. To this end, Social TV systems should offer viewers flexible choice of communication channels and enable seamless transitions between them.

Question 3: In which ways do mediated communication and simultaneous video content consumption influence each other?

One of the key questions concerning Social TV is whether its mediated interac-tion features actually enhance or distract from the viewing experience. We found that content and communication affect each other in both, positive and negative ways. On the positive side, our study participants appreciated the possibility to turn

---

[17] We regard touch-screen text-input (e.g. Nokia N800, Apple iPhone) not as an adequate replace-ment for a QWERTY keypad, since the interface visually distracts and consumes considerable amounts of screen real estate

mere TV watching into a social event that gives the TV content a shared meaning. This holds especially true for content that builds on already established social practices. Particularly, sports coverage tends to be viewed in groups, which transfers well to Social TV (cf. Harboe et al. 2007). Furthermore, we found that News and Lifestyle TV, formats that are deliberately designed to function as social currency, are Social TV enabler genres. Corroborating the results of Oehlberg et al. (2006), social interaction also proved to enhance the TV experience as complementary activity that bridges periods of low-interest content (e.g., advertising breaks) or lapses in plot density. Summarizing these results, we found that suitable TV content actually fulfilled its purpose as "common ground" that viewers actively refer to in their (mediated) conversations. Particularly at the beginning of communication sessions or when zapping, participants tend to ask orientating questions such as "What are you viewing?" or "What is going on in this show?" This behavior underlines the importance of common-ground functions such as a smart EPG[18] and chat history that informs newcomers about the current show and enables them to catch up instantly. In this context, providing richer presence information to co-viewers (such as current channel/show viewed) serves as complementary means to increase the sociability of TV. This enriched presence can go as far as extending the chat with a micro-blogging option (similar to Twitter[19] or Jaiku[20]) that allows viewers to leave a commented trail of their viewing experience (accompanied with contextual data such as a TV-screenshot).

On the other hand, the primary position of TV has always been one of a leisure pursuit that requires little or no effort. Therefore, division of attention between media consumption and social interaction and resulting distraction phenomena constitute recurring themes (cf. Oehlberg et al. 2006; Geerts 2006; Harboe et al. 2007) which challenge the design of Social TV systems. First, social interaction is not always welcome and can even be considered intrusive, particularly when viewers want to relax or concentrate on the media content. Therefore, presence and availability management constitute essential Social TV features that enable users to signal whether and how they want to interact. Furthermore, mechanisms for session initiation and exiting (such as our mobile *ShareMarks* and similar invitation mechanisms) are further key elements for maintaining social etiquette. Second, mediated communication significantly distracts viewers' attention from TV content as well as from their immediate physical and social environment. The need to divide attention and multitask between the front channel (i.e., TV) and social interaction interfaces is a frequently reported source of stress for end-users and probably one of the biggest practical obstacles to Social TV adoption[21]. While following a stream of chat messages or uttering into a microphone is not perceived as problematic by users, attuning to two audio

---

[18] EPG = Electronic Program Guide

[19] www.twitter.com

[20] www.jaiku.com

[21] Distraction is even more critical on mobile media terminals due to their tiny keypads and small screens, where TV is less immersive and easily cluttered

sources or even having to type and watch simultaneously tends to significantly detract attention.[22] The ideal solution for addressing this asymmetry would consist of a recognition module that transcribes voice-chat into text on the screen that users can easily follow. Unfortunately, the current state of the art in speaker-independent, large-vocabulary recognition of continuous unstructured speech is not advanced enough to provide practical solutions to this problem in the near future (Stolcke et al. 2005). Alternatively, a visual indicator that signals when a program requires attention – as suggested by Geerts (2006) – or a shared pause-button that pauses the TV in case the conversation becomes too important.

Question 4: How pervasive is Social TV? In which ways can it be extended beyond traditional living-room settings?

Social TV has been confined to stationary contexts such as the living room, building on television watching behaviors and practices established over decades. In contrast, mobile TV is a fairly novel phenomenon involving new usage patterns, contexts, and a diversity of devices which are still evolving. Therefore, it is reasonable to expect that stationary and pervasive Social TV exhibit substantial differences in terms of both perception by the user and overall success in providing remote viewers with a shared media experience. However, to our surprise, we found strong similarities regarding key Social TV user-experience measurements across the different conditions that we evaluated. Our test participants perceived similar degrees of social presence and felt the same quality of joint TV experience on big and small-screen TV devices as well as in mobile and stationary contexts alike. Across all conditions, it was rather the mode of social interaction (e.g., text, audio, graphical) and related interfaces (e.g., QWERTY 3 × 3, headsets) that had the biggest influence on user experience and approbation of Social TV. This result is also substantiated by the fact that observed user behaviors, reported benefits, and positive acceptance ratings for both Social TV system types were consistent. Further reasons for differences were users' experience and willingness to interact with mobiles (due to the lean-forward condition) as well as the immediate physical and social context as sources of distractions, particularly when users were on the move. The implications of these results are that, from a communications perspective, *Social TV also functions on mobile devices and in mobile contexts.* Therefore, Social TV should be considered as a service that forms part of the user's pervasive media environment.

This outcome leads to more user-related acceptance questions: Does Social TV as a pervasive service make sense to users at all? Do they actually need it and will they actively use it as "sticky" service that forms part of their everyday lives? Will they enact sociability *through* the TV in the same way as in front of the TV? These questions are significantly harder to answer, since our studies were conducted as time-constrained lab/field user tests. Controlled experiments are suitable for comparing

---

[22] According to our case study results as well as the findings of Geerts (2006) and Weisz et al. (2007)

different setups and contexts. However, they tend to create artificial situations and therefore are methodologically less apt for reliably assessing long-term user acceptance. In addition, mobile or pervasive Social TV applications have not been deployed on a larger scale and related longitudinal research studies are yet to be undertaken. However, in addition to positive user study results, we see several reasons to be optimistic about the adoption of pervasive Social TV in the long run: the success of mobile peer-to-peer communications and communities (Vincent & Harper 2003), the inherent sociability of mobile content and Mobile TV (O'Hara et al. 2007; Harper et al. 2006), and the ongoing convergence of media consumption and communication services (Fox 2001; Schatz et al. 2007a).

Summary and Future Research Agenda

In this chapter we have proposed the extension of Social TV toward an understanding as a pervasive service concept that integrates Mobile TV and mobile communications. By comparing two case studies on mediated co-viewing for living-room IPTV and mobile broadcast television, we showed that Social TV systems are capable of providing a social experience in stationary and mobile setups alike. Therefore, we argue that Social TV should be conceived as a pervasive media service that reaches beyond the Triple-play home sphere by leveraging the connectivity provided by multimedia phones. Such a service effectively addresses users' needs for mobility and socializing in the context of TV. However, designing for Social TV on mobiles does not only face classical Social TV challenges that come from enabling simultaneous communication and content consumption. It also has to deal with limited device capabilities, increased distraction potential in mobile contexts, and the need to integrate heterogeneous platforms and standards. Nonetheless, pervasive Social TV is an attractive proposition for mobile and Triple-play service providers as it generates new revenues from added-value broadband and integrated communication services.

We need to emphasize that the two case studies presented can only serve as a starting point and motivation for further research. First, long-term field studies are required to observe user acceptance and behaviors under realistic conditions. While field studies on stationary Social TV are already on their way (cf. Harboe et al. 2007), we see the need for long-term studies that equally address pervasive TV setups. Second, our studies so far were limited to one-to-one communications, since this is the most fundamental use case that enables reliable assessment and comparison of conditions. Therefore, the next step is the support of group viewing (cf. Oehlberg et al. 2006; Harboe et al. 2007) across different contexts and device setups. To this end, we are currently evaluating mixed scenarios where coviewing involves ensembles of different stationary and mobile devices. Third, our research so far has focused on synchronous communications in the context of live TV. However, asynchronous use cases such as offline content playback are highly practical in the context of pervasive Social TV. A large share of mobile video consumption actually happens "on demand," complementary to live Mobile TV (O'Hara et al. 2007), which requires support in the form of text and multimedia annotations as well as shared browsing of playlists.

Although TV (and Mobile TV particular) remains a heavily disputed medium, it also is an established social enabler. To this end, development of future media technology should have the goal to leverage the existing sociability of TV not only in order to provide better entertainment, but also to engage users beyond mere "watching."

Acknowledgments This research has been performed within the projects M2 AMUSE 2.0 and U0 SUPRA++ at the Telecommunications Research Center Vienna (ftw.) and has been funded by the Austrian Government and by the City of Vienna within the competence center program COMET. We would like to thank our colleagues Peter Reichl and Andreas Berger for their fruitful contributions to this work.

References

Baillie, L. (2002) The home workshop: A method for investigating the home. Ph.D. thesis, Napier University, Edinburgh.

Becker-Beck, U., Wintermantel, M., & Borg, A. (2005). Principles of regulating interaction in teams practicing face-to-face communication versus teams practicing computer-mediated communication. *Small Group Research, 36*(4), 499–536, SAGE.

Blom, J., Chipchase, J., & Lehikoinen, J. (2005). Contextual and cultural challenges for user mobility research. *Commun ACM, 48*(7), 37–41.

Cesar, P., Bulterman, D., & Jansen, A. (2008). Usages of the secondary screen in an interactive television environment: Control, enrich, share, and transfer television content. In *Proceedings of 6th European Conference EuroITV 2008, Salzburg, Austria, Springer-Verlag, Berlin, Heidelberg*, July 3–4, 168–177.

Chorianopoulos, K., & Spinellis, D. (2004). Affective usability evaluation for an interactive music televisionchannel. *Computers in Entertainment, 2*(3), 14.

Christie, B. (1973). Appendix M. In P. C. Goldmark et al. (Eds.), *The 1972/73 new rural society project* [Research report available from Fairfield University, Conneticut].

Chuah, M. (2003). Reality instant messaging: Injecting a dose of reality into online chat. *CHI'03 Extended Abstracts, ACM Press, New York*, 926–927.

Coppens, T., Trappeniers, L., & Godon, M. (2004). Amigo TV: Towards a Social TV experience. In *Proceedings of the 2nd European conference on Interactive Television: Enhancing the experience, Brighton, U.K.*

Durkheim, E. (1965). The elementary forms of the religious life (J. W. Swain, Trans.). New York: The Free Press.

Fox, K. (2001). Evolution, alienation and gossip: The role of mobile telecommunications in the 21st century. London: Social Issues Research Centre: London.

Froehlich, P. (2007). Auditory human-computer interaction: An integrated approach. Ph.D. thesis at the University of Vienna, Austria.

Geerts, D. (2006). Comparing voice chat and text chat in a communication tool for interactive television. *NordiCHI 2006*, 461–464.

Goldenberg, S. (2007). *Digital video recorders and micro-social networking: Recreating the shared watching experience of television*. Paper presented at the 5th European Conference, EuroITV 2007, Amsterdam, The Netherlands, Springer Berlin/Heidelberg, May 24–25.

Harboe, G., Massey, N., Metcalf, C., Wheatley, D., & Romano, G. (2007). Perceptions of value: The uses of social television. In *Proceedings of the 5th European Conference, EuroITV 2007, Amsterdam, The Netherlands, Springer Berlin/Heidelberg*, May 24–25.

Harper, R., Regan, T., & Rouncefield, M. (2006). Taking hold of TV: Learning from the literature. In *Proceedings of the 20th Conference of the Computer-Human Interaction Special interest Group (CHISIG) of Australia on Computer-Human interaction: Design, activities, artefacts and environments OZCHI '06, Sydney, Australia, ACM, New York,* (Vol. 206; pp. 79–86), November 20–24.

Harrison, C., & Amento, B. (2007). CollaboraTV – Making TV social again. In *EuroITV 2007 Workshop on Social Interactive Television, Amsterdam, The Netherlands,* May 24–25.

Hauber, J., Regenbrecht, H., Hills, A., Cockburn, A., & Billinghurst, M. (2005). Social presence in two- and three-dimensional videoconferencing. In *Proceedings of 8th Annual International Workshop on Presence, London, UK,* September 21–23, 189–198.

Jerslev, A. (2001). Video nights: Young people watching videos together – A youth cultural phenomenon. *Young, 9*(2), 2–18.

Kelly, J. R. (2004). Mood and emotion in groups. In M. B. Brewer & M. Hewstone (Eds.), *Motivation and Emotion.* Oxford: Blackwell Publishing.

Lull, J. (1990). The social uses of television. *Human Communication Research, 6,* 197–209.

Nardi, B. A. (2005). Beyond bandwidth: Dimensions of connection in interpersonal communication. *Computer Supported Cooperative Work, 14*(2), 91–130.

O'Brien, J., Rodden, T., Rouncefield, M., & Hughes, J. (1999). At home with the technology: An ethnographic study of a set-top-box trial. *ACM Transactions on Computer-Human Interaction (TOCHI), 6,* 282–308.

O'Hara, K., Mitchell, A. S., & Vorbau, A. (2007). Consuming video on mobile devices. In *Proceedings of the CHI 2007 Conference, San Jose, California, USA,* April 28–May 03.

Oehlberg, L., Ducheneaut, N., Thornton, J. D., Moore, R. J., & Nickell, E. (2006). Social TV: Designing for distributed, sociable television viewing. In *Proceedings of EuroITV 2006, Athens, Greece,* 251–259.

Orgad, S. (2006). This Box was Made for Walking. Mobile TV Study Report, London School of Economics, UK, from http://www.lse.ac.uk/collections/media@lse/pdf/Mobile_TV_Report_Orgad.pdf

Osgood, C. E., Suci, G. J., & Tannenbaum, P. R. (1957). *The measurement of meaning.* Chicago: University of Illinois Press.

Oulasvirta, A., Tamminen, S., Rotol, V., & Kuorelahti, J. (2005). Interaction in 4-second bursts: The fragmented nature of attentional resources in mobile HCI. In *Proceedings of the SIGCHI Conference on Human Factors in Computing Systems (CHI'05), Portland, Oregon, USA, ACM, New York,* 919–928, April 02–07.

Pilotta, J. J., Schultz, D. E., Drenik, G., & Philip, R. (March 2004). Simultaneous media usage: A critical consumer orientation to media planning. *Journal of Consumer Behaviour, 3*(3).

Quico, C. (2003). *Are communication services the killer application for interactive TV? Or: 'I left my wife because I am in love with the TV set.'* Paper presented at the 1st EuroITV: From Viewers to Actors, Brighton, U.K.

Regan, T., & Todd, I. (2004). Media center buddies: Instant messaging around a media center. In *Proceedings of the Third Nordic Conference on Human-computer interaction (NordiCHI '04), Tampere, Finland, ACM, New York,* October 23–27.

Repo, P., Hyvonen, K., Pantzar, M., & Timonen, P. (2004). Users inventing ways to enjoy new mobile services – the case of watching Mobile videos. In *Proceedings of the 37th Hawaii International Conference on System Sciences.*

Rettie, R. (2003). A Comparison of Four New Communication Technologies. *Human-computer interaction: Theory and practice,* Part I, 686–690. Mahwah, NJ: Lawrence Erlbaum Associates.

Roibás, A. R., Geerts, D., Furtado, E., & Calvi, L. (2006). Investigating new user experience challenges in iTV: Mobility & sociability. In *CHI Extended Abstracts 2006,* 1659–1662.

Roibás, A. R., & Johnson, S. (2006). Unfolding the user experience in new scenarios of pervasive interactive TV. *CHI 2006 Extended Abstracts, Montreal, Quebec, Canada,* 1259–1264.

Roibás, A. R., & Sala, R. (2004). Main HCI issues for the design of interfaces for ubiquitous interactive multimedia broadcast. *Interactions, 11*(2), 51–53.

Sallnäs, E. (2004). The effect of modality on social presence, presence and performance in collaborative virtual Environments. Doctoral thesis, KTH Stockholm, Sweden.

Schatz, R., Wagner, S., & Berger, A. (2007b). AMUSE – A platform for prototyping live Mobile TV services. *16th IST Mobile and Wireless Communications Summit, Budapest, Hungary,* 1–5.

Schatz, R., Wagner, S., Egger, S., & Jordan, N. (2007a). Mobile TV becomes social – integrating content with communications. In *Proceedings of the International Conference on Information Technology Interfaces (ITI'07), Dubrovnik, Croatia.*

Short, J., Williams, E., & Christie, B. (1976). *The social psychology of telecommunications.* London: Wiley.

Shrimpton-Smith, T., Zaman, B., & Geerts, D. (2006). Coupling the users: The benefits of paired user testing for iDTV. In *Proceedings of the 4th Euro iTV Conference, Athens, Greece,* 214–221.

Sokoler, T., & Svensson, M. S. (2008). PresenceRemote: Embracing ambiguity in the design of Social TV for senior citizens. In *Proceedings of 6th European Conference EuroITV 2008, Salzburg, Austria, Springer-Verlag, Berlin, Heidelberg,* 158–162, July 3–4.

Stolcke, A., Anguera, X., Boakye, K., Cetin, O., Grezl, F., Janin, A., Mandal, A., Peskin, B., Wooters, C., & Zheng, J. (2005). Further progress in meeting recognition: The ICSI-SRI Spring 2005 Speech-to-Text Evaluation System. NIST RT-05 Meeting Recognition Workshop, UK.

USC Center for the Digital Future. (2007). *Sixth Study of the Internet by the Digital Future Project,* from http://www.digitalcenter.org

Vincent, J., & Harper, R. (2003). The social shaping of UMTS-preparing the 3G customer [UMTS Forum Report 26].

Weisz, J. D., Kiesler, S., Zhang, H., Ren, Y., Kraut, R. E., & Konstan, J. A. (2007). Watching together: Integrating text chat with video. In *Proceedings of SIGCHI 2007, ACM, New York,* 877–886.

Part VI
Advanced Interaction Modalities with Mobile Digital Content

m-LoCoS UI: A Universal Visible Language for Global Mobile Communication

Aaron Marcus

Abstract The LoCoS universal visible language developed by the graphic/sign designer Yukio Ota in Japan in 1964 may serve as a usable, useful, and appealing basis for a mobile phone application that can provide capabilities for communication and storytelling among people who do not share a spoken language. User-interface design issues including display and input are discussed in conjunction with prototype screens showing the use of LoCoS for a mobile phone.

Introduction

Universal Visible Languages

Over the centuries, many different theorists and designers have been interested in and proposed artificial, universal sign or visible languages intended for easy learning and use by people all over the world, a kind of visual Esperanto. For example, in the last century, C.K. Bliss in Australia invented Blissymbolics (Bliss 1965), a language of signs, and attempted to convince the United Nations to declare Blissymbolics a world auxiliary visible language. Likewise, in 1964, the graphic designer and sign designer Yukio Ota introduced his own version of a universal sign language called LoCoS (Marcus 2007; Ota 1973a; Ota 1973b; Ota 1987), which stands for Lovers Communication System. The LoCoS language, invented in 1964, was published in a Japanese LoCoS reference book in 1973 (Ota 1973a). Ota has presented lectures about LoCoS around the world since he designed the signs, and published several articles in English explaining his design, for example, Ota (1973b). The author has written about Ota's work (Marcus 2003a), and the author's firm maintains an extranet about LoCoS at this URL: http://clients.amanda.com/

A. Marcus(✉)
Aaron Marcus and Associates, Inc., 1196, Euclid Avenue, Suite 1F, Berkeley, CA 94708, USA
e-mail: aaron.marcus@amanda.com

A. Marcus et al. (eds.), *Mobile TV: Customizing Content and Experience*,
Human-Computer Interaction Series, DOI 10.1007/978-1-84882-701-1_20,
© Springer-Verlag London Limited 2010

locos/. One of the significant features of LoCoS is that it can be learned in one day. Participants at Ota's lectures have been able to write him messages after hearing about the system and learning the basics of its vocabulary and grammar.

Based on this background, the author's firm worked with Mr. Ota over a period of several months in 2005, and in the ensuing months since then, to design prototypes of how LoCoS could be used on a mobile device. This paper presents an introduction to LoCoS, the design issues presented by trying to adapt LoCoS to a mobile phone use, an initial set of prototype screens, and future design challenges. The author and associates of the author's firm worked with the inventor of LoCoS in early 2005 and subsequently to adapt the language to the context of mobile device use.

Basics of LoCoS

LoCoS is an artificial, nonverbal, generally nonspoken, visible language system designed for use by any human being to communicate with others who may not share spoken or written natural languages. Individual signs may be combined to form expressions and sentences in somewhat linear arrangements, as shown in Fig. 1.

The signs may be combined into complete LoCoS expressions or sentences, formed by three horizontal rows of square area typically reading from left to right. Note this culture/localization issue: Many, but not all symbols could be flipped left to right for readers/writers who are used to right-to-left verbal languages. The main contents of a sentence are placed in the center row. Signs in the top and bottom rows act as adverbs and adjectives, respectively. Looking ahead to the possible use of

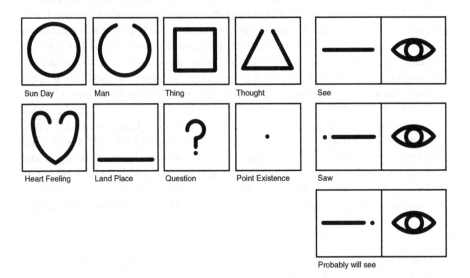

Fig. 1 Individual and combined signs

LoCoS in mobile devices with limited space for sign display, a mobile-oriented version of LoCoS can use only one line. The grammar of the signs is similar to English (subject–verb–object). This aspect of the language, also, is an issue for those users who are used to other paradigms from natural verbal languages.

LoCoS differs from alphabetic natural languages in that the semantic reference (sometimes called "meaning") and the visual form are closely related. LoCoS differs from some other visible languages; for example, Bliss symbols use more abstract symbols, while LoCoS signs are more iconic. LoCoS is similar to, but different from Chinese ideograms, like those incorporated into Japanese Kanji signs. It is less abstract in that symbols of concrete objects like a road sign shows pictures of those objects. Like Chinese signs or Kanji, one sign refers to one concept, although there are compound concepts. According to Ota, LoCoS reuses signs more efficiently than traditional Chinese signs. Note that the rules of LoCoS did not result from careful analysis across major world languages for phonetic efficiency. LoCoS does have rules for pronunciation (rarely used), but audio input/out was not explored in the project to be described for a mobile-LoCoS.

LoCoS has several benefits that would make it potentially usable, useful, and appealing as a sign language displayable on mobile devices. First, it is easy to learn in a progressive manner, starting with just a few basics. The learning curve is not steep, and users can guess correctly at new signs. Second, it is easy to display; the signs are relatively simple. Third, it is robust. People can understand the sense of the language without knowing all signs. Fourth, the language is suitable for mass media and the general public. People may find it challenging, appealing, mysterious, and fun.

Design Approaches for m-LoCoS

Universal Visible Messaging

m-LoCoS could be used in a universal visual messaging application, as opposed to text messaging. People who do not speak the same language can communicate with each other. People who need to interact via a user interface (UI) that has *not* been localized to their own language normally would find the experience daunting. People who speak the same language but want to communicate in a fresh new medium may find LoCoS especially appealing, for example, teenagers and children. People who may have some speech or accessibility issues may find m-LoCoS especially useful.

Currently, the author's firm has developed initial prototype screens showing how LoCoS could be used in mobile devices. The HTML prototype screens have been developed showing a Motorola V505 and a Nokia 7610 phone. A LoCoS-English dictionary was begun and is in progress. Future needs include expanding LoCoS, exploring new, different visual attributes for the signs of LoCoS, including color, animation, and nonlinear arrangements (called LoCoS 2.0), and developing the prototype more completely so that it is more complete and interactive.

The assumptions and objectives for m-LoCoS include the following:

For the developing world, there is remarkable growth in the use of mobile phones. China has over 300 million phones, larger than the US population, and India is growing rapidly. People seem to be willing to spend up to 10% of their income for phones and services, which is often their only link to the world at large. For many users, the mobile phone is the first one that they have ever used. In addition, literacy levels are low, especially familiarity with computer user-interfaces. Thus, if mobile voice communication is expensive and unreliable, mobile messaging may be slower but cheaper, and more reliable texting may be preferred to voice communication in some social settings. m-LoCoS may make it easier for people in developing countries to communicate with each other and with those abroad. The fact that LoCoS can be learned in one day makes it an appealing choice.

In the industrialized world, young people (e.g., ages 2–25) have a high aptitude for learning new languages and user-interface paradigms. It is a much-published phenomenon that young people like to text-message, in addition to, and sometimes in preference to talking on their mobile phones. In Japan, additional signs, called emoticons have been popular for years. In fact, newspaper accounts chronicle the rise of *gyaru-moji* ("girl-signs"), a "secret" texting language of symbols improvised by Japanese teenage girls. They are a mixture of Japanese syllables, numbers, mathematical symbols, and Greek characters. Even though using gyaru-moji takes twice as long for input as standard Japanese, they are still popular. This phenomenon suggests that young people might enjoy sign-messaging using LoCoS. The signs might be unlike anything they have used before, they would be easy to learn, would be expressive, and would be aesthetically pleasing. A mobile-device-enabled LoCoS might offer a fresh new way of sending messages.

User Profiles and Use Scenarios

Regarding users and their use-context, although one billion people use mobile phones now, there are a next one billion people, many in developing countries, who have never used any phone before. A mobile phone's entire user interface (UI) could be displayed in LoCoS, not only for messaging, but also for all applications, including voice. For younger users interested in a "cool" or "secret" form of communication in the industrialized world, they would be veteran mobile phone users. LoCoS would be an add-on application, and the success of *gyaru-moji* in Japan, as well as emoticon-use, suggests that an m-LoCoS could be successful. Finally, one could consider the case of travelers in countries that do not speak the traveler's language. Bearing in mind these circumstances, the author's firm developed three representative user profiles and use scenarios for exploring m-LoCoS applications and its UI. Use Scenario 1 concerns the micro-office in a less-developed country: Srini is a man in a small town in India. User Scenario 2 concerns young lovers in a developed country: Jack and Jill, boyfriend and girlfriend, in the USA. Use Scenario 3 concerns a traveler in a foreign country: Jaako is a Finnish tourist in a restaurant in France. Each of these is described briefly below.

Use Scenario 1: Micro-office in a less-developed country. Srini in India lives in a remote village that does not have running water, but just started having access to a new wireless network. The network is not reliable or affordable enough for long voice conversations, but is adequate for text-messaging. Srini's mobile phone is the only means for non-face-to-face communication with his business partners. His typical communication topic is this: should he go to a next village to sell his products, or wait for the prices to rise?

Use Scenario 2: Young lovers in the USA. Jack and Jill, boyfriend and girl friend, text-message each other frequently, using five to ten words per message, and two to three messages per conversation thread. They think that text-messaging is "cool," that is, highly desirable. They think that it would be even "cooler" to send text messages in a private, personal, or secret language not familiar to most people looking over their shoulders or somehow intercepting their messages.

Use Scenario 3: Tourist in a foreign country. Jaako, a Finnish tourist in a restaurant in Paris, France, is trying to communicate with the waiter; however, he and the waiter do not speak a common language. A typical restaurant dialogue would be: "May I sit here?" "Would you like to start with an appetizer?" "I'm sorry; we ran out of that." "Do you have lamb?" All communications take place via a single LoCoS-enabled device. Jaako and the waiter take turns reading and replying, using LoCoS.

Design Implications and Design Challenges

The design implications for developing m-LoCoS are that the language must be simple and unambiguous, input must occur quickly and reliably, and several dozen m-LoCoS signs must fit onto one mobile-device screen. Another challenge is that LoCoS as a system of signs must be extended for everyday use. Currently, there are about 1,000 signs, as noted in the guidebook published in Japanese (Ota 1973a). However, these signs are not sufficient for many common use scenarios. The author, working with his firm's associates, estimates that about 3,000 signs are required, which is similar to basic Chinese. The new signs to be added cannot be arbitrary, but should follow the current patterns of LoCoS and should be appropriate for modern contexts a half-century after its invention. Even supposedly universal, timeless sign systems like those of Otto Neurath's group's invention called Isotypes (Marcus 2003a; Ota 1987) featured some signs that almost a century later are hard to interpret, like a small triangular shape representing sugar, based on a familiar commercial pyramidal paper packaging of individual sugar portions in Europe in the early part of the twentieth century.

Another design challenge for m-LoCoS is that the mobile phone UI itself should utilize LoCoS (optionally, like language switching). For the user in developing countries, it might be the case that telecom manufacturers and service providers might not have localized, or localized well, the UI to the specific users' preferred language. M-LoCoS would enable the user to comfortably rely on a language for the controls and for help. For users in more developed countries, the "cool" factor or the interest in LoCoS would make an m-LoCoS UI desirable. Figure 2 shows an initial sketch by the author's firm for some signs.

Not only must the repertoire of the current LoCoS signs be extended, but the existing signs must be revised to update them, as mentioned earlier in relation to Isotype. Despite Ota's best efforts, some of the signs are culturally or religiously biased. Of course, it is difficult to make signs that are clear to everyone in the world and are pleasing to everyone. What is needed is a practical compromise that achieves tested success with the cultures of the target users. Examples of current challenges are shown in Fig. 3. The current LoCoS sign for "restaurant" might often be mistaken for a "bar" because of the wine glass sign inside the building sign. The cross as a sign for "religion" might not be understood correctly, considered inappropriate, or even be welcomed in Moslem countries such as Indonesia.

Another challenge would be to enable and encourage users to try LoCoS. Target users must be convinced to try to learn the visible language in one day. Non-English speakers might need to accommodate themselves to the English subject–verb–object structure. In contrast, in Japanese, the verb comes last, as it does in German-dependent phrases. Despite Ota's best efforts, some expressions can be ambiguous. Therefore, there seems to be a need for dictionary support, preferably on the mobile device itself. Users should be able to ask, "what is the LoCoS sign for the X, if any?, or "what does this LoCoS sign mean?"

⌐	⊃	✕	◇	‑‑	⤴
add	back	Cancel	close	continue	edit
≣	⊢⊣	○	◇	▯	⌂
menu	next	Ok	open	PHONE	remove

Fig. 2 Sketch of user-interface control signs based on LoCoS

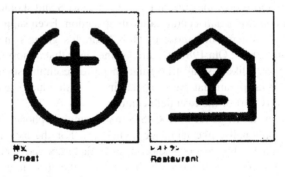

Fig. 3 LoCoS signs for priest and restaurant

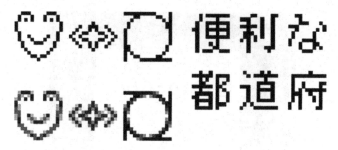

Fig. 4 Examples of signs drawn with and without anti-aliasing

In general, displaying m-LoCoS on small screens is a fundamental challenge. There are design trade-offs among the dimensions of legibility, readability, and density of signs. Immediately, one must ask, what should be the dimensions in pixels of a sign? Figure 4 shows some comparative sketches of small signs.

Japanese phones and web sites often seem to use 13 × 13 pixels. In discussions between the author's firm and Yukio Ota, it was decided to use 15 × 15 pixels for the signs. This density is the same as smaller, more numerous English signs. There were some discussions about whether signs should be anti-aliased; unfortunately, not enough was known about support of mobile devices with grayscale pixels to know what to recommend. Are signs easier to recognize and understand if anti-aliased? This issue is a topic for future user research.

Classifying, Selecting, and Entering Signs

There are several issues related to how users can enter m-LoCoS signs quickly and reliably. Users may not know for sure what the signs look like. What the user has in mind might not be in the vocabulary yet, or might not ever become a convention. One solution t is to select a sign from a list (menu), the technique used in millions of Japanese mobile phones. Here, an issue is how to locate 1 of 3,000 signs by means of a matrix of 36 signs that may be displayed in a typical 128 × 128 pixel screen (or a larger number of signs in the larger displays of many current high-end phones).

The current prototype developed by the author's firm uses a two-level hierarchy to organize the signs. Each sign is in of 18 domains of subject matter. Each domain's list of signs is accessible with two to three key strokes. Three thousand signs divided into 18 domains would yield approximately 170 signs per domain, which could be shown in five screens of 36 signs each. A three-level hierarchy might also be considered. As with many issues, these would have to be user-tested carefully to determine optimum design trade-offs. Figure 5 shows a sample display.

To navigate among a screen-full of signs to a desired one, numerical keys can be used for eight-direction movement from a central position at the 5-key, which also acts as a Select key. For cases in which signs do not fit onto one screen (i.e., more than 36 signs),

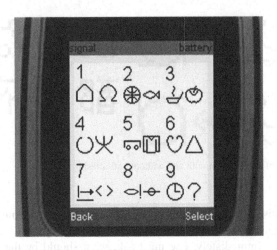

Fig. 5 Sample prototype display of a symbol menu for a dictionary

the 0-key might be used to scroll upward or downward with one or two taps. There are challenges with strict hierarchical navigation. It seems very difficult to make intuitive the taxonomy of all concepts in a language. Users may have to learn which concept is in which category. Shortcuts may help for frequently used signs.

In addition, there are different (complementary) taxonomies. Form taxonomies could group signs that look similar (e.g., those containing a circle). Properties taxonomies could group signs that are concrete vs. abstract, artificial vs. natural, micro-scaled vs. macro-scaled, etc. Schemas (domains in the current prototype) would group "apple" and "frying pan" in the same domain because both are in the "food/eating" schema.

Most objects/concepts belong to several independent (orthogonal) hierarchies. Might it not be better to be able to select from several? This challenge is similar to multifaceted navigation in mobile phones. It is also similar to the "20 Questions" game, but would require fewer questions because users can choose from up to one dozen answers each, not just two choices. Software should sort hierarchies presented to users by most granular to more general "chunking." It is also possible to navigate two hierarchies with just one key press.

A realistic, practical solution would incorporate context-sensitive guessing of what sign the user is likely to use next. The algorithm could be based on the context of a sentence or phrase the user is assembling, or on what signs/patterns the user frequently selects. Figure 6 illustrates multiple categories selection scheme.

If the phone has a camera, like most recent phones, the user could always write signs on paper and send that image-capture to a distant person or show the paper to a person nearby. However, the user might still require and benefit from a dictionary (in both directions of translation) to assist in assembling the correct signs for a message.

There are other alternatives to navigate-and-select paradigms. For example, the user could actually draw the signs, much like Palm® Graffiti ™, but this would

	Concrete	Abstract	Don't know
Man-Made	1	2	3
Naturally -Occurring	4	5	6
Both	7	8	9
Don't Know	*	0	#

Fig. 6 Possible combinations of schema choices for signs

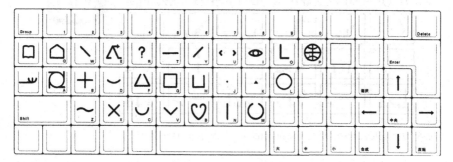

Fig. 7 LoCoS keyboard designed by Yukio Ota

require a mobile device with a touch screen (as earlier PDAs and the Apple iPhone and its competitors provide). One could construct each sign by combining, rotating, and resizing approximately 16 basic shapes. Ota has also suggested another, more traditional approach, the LoCoS keyboard, but this direction was not pursued. The keyboard is illustrated in Figure 7.

Still another alternative is the Motorola iTAP® technique, which uses stroke-order sequential selection. In recent years, there have been approximately 320 m Chinese phones, with 90 m using text messaging in 2003, using sign input via either Pinyin or iTAP. m-LoCoS might be able to use sequential selection, or a mixed stroke/semantic method. Figure 8 shows examples of stroke-order sign usage for Chinese input.

Future Challenges

Beyond the matters described above, there are other challenges to secure a successful design and implementation of m-LoCoS on mobile devices that would enable visible language communication among disparate, geographically distant users.

For example, the infrastructure challenges are daunting, but seem surmountable. One would need to establish protocols for encoding and transmitting LoCoS over wireless networks. In conjunction, one would need to secure interest and support from telecom hardware manufacturers and mobile communication services.

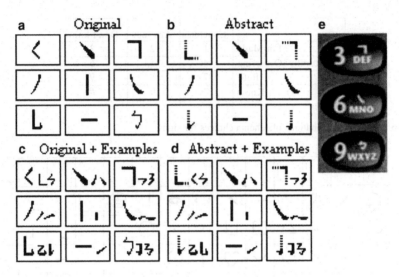

Fig. 8 Examples of stroke-order sequential selection from (Lin 2005)

Conclusion: Current and Future Prototypes

The author's firm, with the assistance and cooperation of Yukio Ota, investigated the design issues and designed prototype screens for m-LoCoS in early 2005, with subsequent adjustments since that time. About 1,000 signs were assumed for LoCoS, which is not quite sufficient to converse for modern, urban, and technical situations. There is a need for a larger community of users and contributors of new signs. The current prototype is a set of designed screens that have been transmitted as images and show the commercial viability of LoCoS. Figure 9 shows a sample screen.

Among next steps contemplated for the development of m-LoCoS are to develop an online community for interested students, teachers, and users of LoCoS. For this reason, the author's firm designed and implemented an extranet about LoCoS at the URL cited earlier. In addition, new sign designs to extend the sign set and to update the existing one, ideal taxonomies of the language, working interactive implementations on mobile devices from multiple manufactures, and the resolution of technical and business issues mentioned previously lie ahead.

Of special interest to the design community is research into LoCoS 2.0, which is currently underway through Yukio Ota and colleagues in Japan. The author's firm has also consulted with Mr. Ota on these design issues: alternative two-dimensional layouts; enhanced graphics; color of strokes, including solid colors and gradients; font-like characteristics, for example, thick-thins, serifs, cursives, italics, etc.; backgrounds of signs: solid colors, patterns, photos, etc.; animation of signs; and additional signs from other international sets, for example, vehicle transportation, operating systems, etc.

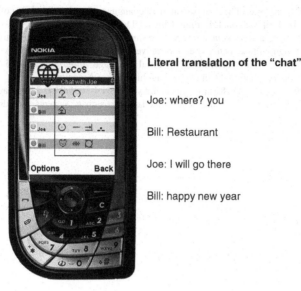

Literal translation of the "chat"

Joe: where? you

Bill: Restaurant

Joe: I will go there

Bill: happy new year

Fig. 9 Example of a prototype chat screen with m-LoCoS on a mobile phone

m-LoCoS, when implemented in an interactive prototype on a commercial mobile device would be ready for a large deployment experiment, which would provide a context to study its use and suitability for work and leisure environments. The deployment would provide, also, a situation for trying out LoCoS 2.0 enhancements. A wealth of opportunities for planning, analysis, design, and evaluation lies ahead.

Acknowledgments The author acknowledges the assistance of Yukio Ota, President, Sign Center, and Professor, Tama Art University, Tokyo, Japan, in preparing this text. In addition, the author thanks Designer/Analyst Dmitry Kantorovich of the author's firm for his extensive assistance in preparing the outline for this chapter and for preparing the figures used in it. This chapter is based on a paper (Marcus 2007) that appeared in the *Proceedings of the 2009 Human-Computer Interface International*, Beijing, China.

References

Bliss, C. K. (1965). *Semantography (Blissymbolocs)* (The book presents a system for universal writing, or pasigraphy) (2nd ed., pp. 882). Sidney, Australia: Semantography Publications.
Lin, S. (2005). Graphics matters: A case study of mobile phone keypad design for Chinese input. *Proceedings of the Conference on Human Factors in Computing Systems (CHI 2005), Extended Abstracts for Late-Breaking Results, Short Papers, Portland, OR, USA*, 1593–1596.
Marcus, A. (2003a). "Icons, symbols, and more," Fast forward column. *Interactions*, 10(3, May–June), 28–34.
Marcus, A. (2003b). "Universal, ubiquitous, user-interface design for the disabled and elderly," Fast forward column. *Interactions*, 10(2, March–April), 23–27.

Marcus, A. (2007). m-LoCoS UI: A universal visible language for global mobile communication. *Proceedings*. HCI International, Beijing, China, CD-ROM, unpaged.

Ota, Y. (1973). *LoCoS: Lovers communications system* (in Japanese). Tokyo: Pictorial Institute. (The author/designer presents the system of universal writing that he invented.)

Ota, Y. (1973). LoCoS: An experimental pictorial language. *Icographic, 6*, 15–19. London: ICOGRADA, the International Council of Graphic Design Associations.

Ota, Y. (1987). *Pictogram design*. Kashiwashobo, Tokyo, ISBN 4-7601-0300-7. (The author presents a world-wide collection of case studies in visible language signage systems, including LoCoS.)

The Future of Mobile TV: When Mobile TV Meets the Internet and Social Networking

Marie-José Montpetit, Natalie Klym, and Emmanuel Blain

Abstract First-generation mobile TV has involved delivering content to cell phones. But as mobile TV evolves, it will find greater significance as part of a multifaceted video offering that combines multiple screens, devices, networks, and content types. Content, or a particular viewing session, moves with the user, across devices and across networks. Furthermore, in addition to providing an alternate screen, a mobile device may provide complementary functions like programming TiVo remotely, streaming video from the cell phone to the TV set, or creating video content for distribution on the Web and uploading it directly over wireless networks. In the new TV ecosystem, all end-user devices collaborate across the whole video value chain, from content creation to distribution to consumption. Finally, as mobile devices become integral components of the new video ecosystem, their personal nature will drive the development of social TV, defined as a new way of delivering TV based on users sharing all aspects of the experience within the context of social networks. This chapter presents our view of mobile social TV: a shared TV experience that uses the power of the Internet and social networks to "move" from screen to screen and network to network to unite family and friends.

Introduction

Over the past few years, on-line video services and telco IPTV have rocked the traditional model of television. As content delivery moves to an all-IP platform, connecting old and new providers to a growing array of increasingly personal and multipurpose devices over fixed and mobile networks, the TV experience has become extremely versatile. Mobile TV is not immune to these upheavals, and is itself a disruptive force. In fact, it will soon make little sense to think of mobile TV as distinct from TV in general. Rather, it will be an integral part of an increasingly rich TV experience.

M.-J. Montpetit (✉), N. Klym, and E. Blair
Massachusetts Institute of Technology, Communications Futures Program,
32 Vassar Street, 32-G820, Cambridge, MA 02139, USA
e-mail: mariejo@media.mit.edu

A. Marcus et al. (eds.), *Mobile TV: Customizing Content and Experience*,   305
Human-Computer Interaction Series, DOI 10.1007/978-1-84882-701-1_21,
© Springer-Verlag London Limited 2010

This chapter provides a vision for the future of mobile TV as it evolves from stand-alone to integrated service. This shift will be examined in context of the more general transformation of television, with a focus on the recent integration of social networking. Our vision will thus build toward community-based approaches that harness the power of individuals, from their technologies to their behaviors.

We begin by redefining mobile TV, and then give a brief overview of the key trends related to the television infrastructure and industry landscape. From there, we outline the mobile TV ecosystem of content, connections, and devices in more detail, and then demonstrate the growing importance of service features in this new environment, particularly in terms of integrating mobile and social TV.

We would like to point out up front that many of the scenarios described in the paper are fraught with issues related to usability, technical difficulties, business models, and/or legalities. We do not intend to provide solutions for resolving these challenges here; rather, we provide a conceptual framework for understanding the evolution of a multi-platform TV experience. (Also note that in this chapter we use the terms "TV" and "video" interchangeably when referring to content, as any distinction between the two has sufficiently blurred.)

Redefining Mobile TV

The term mobile TV typically refers to the delivery of video content to cell phones, including the carriers' packaged subscription services like VCast and premium mobile Web services like MobiTV, or more recently, mobile versions of on-line video services like YouTube. Mobile video adoption in the USA and in Europe is still low. According to Nielsen Mobile,[1] the percent of mobile subscribers who access mobile video each month in North America and Europe does not exceed 5%. In comparison, 50% of cell phone owners in Japan and South Korea watch video content on their phones. The number of mobile phone users who watch video on their cell phones, along with the number of mobile video applications, is, however, increasing. Overall, subscriptions to carrier mobile video services in the USA have risen by 24% from September 2007 to September 2008, to reach 16.4 million subscribers.

Despite the growing interest in mobile TV, both its definition and use value are still not clearly understood. The first generation of mobile TV has emerged mainly as a stand-alone service – separate from home delivery models – and valued strictly in terms of the ability to consume video on the go. As such, the first-generation mobile TV experience is often considered secondary (and inferior) to that of the increasingly rich home theater, but market expectations are high, in line with the billions of mobile phone users around the world.

However, in this chapter we demonstrate that as mobile TV evolves, it will find additional, if not greater significance as part of a multifaceted video offering that

---

[1] Nielsen Media, "Turned into the Phone: Mobile video use in the U.S. and abroad," January 2009, available at http://www.nielsen.com/solutions/Nielsen_MobileVideo_January2009.pdf

combines multiple screens, devices, networks, and content types. Cell phones and other mobile devices are being integrated into a cross-platform offering so that content, or more importantly, a particular viewing session, moves with the user, across devices and across networks. Video service providers must integrate solutions into their offerings that enable consumers to purchase content once and enjoy it anytime, anywhere, on any device. In this sense, when we think about mobile TV, it is not just the devices that are mobile; content too, is mobile.

Furthermore, the other functions of a mobile device besides viewing, or "rendering" must be considered. In other words, rather than serving as an alternate screen, a mobile device may provide a variety of complementary functions (some of which may have nothing to do with mobility per se) like voting on American Idol via SMS, purchasing a product seen in a show or advertisement, programming TiVo remotely, streaming video from the cell phone to the TV set (or even projecting it onto a wall, eventually), or using a cell phone's video camera to create content for distribution on the Web and uploading it directly from the phone over wireless networks. In the new TV ecosystem, all end-user devices collaborate across the whole video value chain, from content creation to distribution to consumption.

Finally, as they become integral components of the new video ecosystem, the personal nature of mobile devices will drive the development of social TV.

The Evolving TV Landscape

This next section looks at the evolving TV landscape into which the elements of mobile TV are being integrated. The television industry has become complex enough to warrant a high-level mapping of its evolution, highlighting some of its more salient technical, business, regulatory, and behavioral aspects. A historical perspective is especially relevant since, at the time of writing, all delivery platforms from the original analog broadcast model to IPTV, are currently in operation (to one degree or another) presenting numerous challenges related to user expectations, legacy infrastructure, regulatory regimes, and business models.

Disrupting the Original Broadcast Model

We begin with a brief history of television in order to establish what we mean by "traditional TV," and point out that the TV systems that are being disrupted today – over-the-air, cable, and satellite – are themselves disruptors of the original broadcast model. In this sense, traditional TV constitutes the first reinvention of television, while the more recent trends mark the beginnings of its second reinvention.

Television began as an over-the-air (OTA) analog radio transmission service in the 1930s. The industry was dominated by three large networks (ABC, CBC, and NBC

– and later joined by Fox in the late 1980s) and their affiliates, all delivering content over licensed spectrum to a device designed specifically to receive their signals – the TV set. For several decades, the TV set was the exclusive domain of the big networks along with the smaller individual stations, and the sole receiving and viewing (end-user) device. By the mid-1970s the industry had undergone a couple of important technological transformations that precede today's disruptive trends.

The first transformation involved the rise of alternate transmission systems, starting with cable. In the late 1940s, cable operators began retransmitting local broadcast programming to rural areas that were outside the reach of broadcast signals. By the early 1950s, the cable providers had started retransmitting signals from TV stations in other regional markets across the country, which they could now receive via satellite. In this way, cable companies began competing with local broadcasters by offering additional programming, which in turn initiated the regulation of the cable industry. By the mid-1970s, cable *programming* networks had emerged, producing original content for the cable operators. Initially considered inferior to the broadcast networks, cable TV networks have evolved tremendously, particularly during the 1980s, to produce award-winning shows.[2] Thus, what began as an *access* service evolved into a highly competitive *content* service.

Satellite delivery followed suit in the early 1980s, transmitting both traditional broadcast and cable programming to TV sets via consumer satellite dishes, and providing competition for the cable operators (and leading to more regulation).

Although these new transmission systems gave birth to a new content industry (the cable networks) and introduced multichannel, subscription-based business models, they did not fundamentally change the user experience; TV viewing remained a passive, push-based activity, meaning users basically turned on the TV and watched whatever was being broadcast at the time – a model compared to spam by today's technologically savvy youth.

Furthermore, while the increase in the number of channels and content providers expanded programming choices, the distribution model essentially remained a closed system in the sense that the cable and satellite operators delivered a "walled garden" of acquired content over their pipes, keeping content and conduit ownership tightly linked, and maintaining their role as content aggregators.

The second important technological transformation during this period was the introduction of the video cassette recorder (VCR) in the late 1970s. The VCR was the first TV add-on and was intended for recording TV content onto tape cassettes for time-shifted viewing and archiving. The entertainment industry attempted to stop its distribution in a case that made it to the Supreme Court, where it was declared that copying programs was a legitimate use, as long as the copied material was not used for profit. Ironically, few people could figure out how to set the clock or program the VCR, so its primary recording function went largely unused.

---

[2] Broadband directions LLC, "The Top 75 Basic Cable TV Networks: An Analysis of Their Broadband-Delivered Video Opportunities and Current Initiatives" July 25, 2005, available at http://www.broadbanddirections.com/pdf/BroadbandDirectionsTop75reportnew.pdf

Instead, the playback function reigned, and the VCR became more important as a new distribution channel to the TV, spawning the retail video tape industry and becoming a crucial source of revenue for the entertainment industry.

Although a rather primitive playback technology by today's standards, the VCR is significant because it introduced the concept of time-shifting, even though the practice was not widely adopted. It can even be considered an early form of video on demand, especially given that the video rental business is now threatened by the operators' VOD offerings (as well as on-line streaming and downloading services like Amazon, Netflix, and iTunes). Additionally, the recordings of TV programs comprised the first instances of user-generated content, where viewers strung together episodes of their favorite shows (with the ads roughly chopped out) or random clips that resembled many of the playlists compiled on YouTube today. Furthermore, these were shared with friends, often by bringing tapes over to one another's homes – a rather rudimentary form of mobile social TV. And as a channel for both user-generated content tapes and those rented or purchased from the video store, the VCR gave the first important non-broadcast function to the TV. The other non-broadcast function available at the time was video gaming (e.g., Pong), introduced in the early 1970s. (While gaming has not figured prominently in the TV ecosystem until recently, the gaming console is now positioned to compete with both the PC and the STB to become the media hub in the home.) In this sense, the seeds of today's disruptions were already planted three decades ago.

In summary, by the end of the 1970s, a new ecosystem of competing delivery platforms (OTA, cable, and satellite) and the first non-TV end-user device (the VCR) had completely engulfed the original OTA landscape. This became the new standard – the new "traditional" TV – and experienced more incremental than disruptive innovation for about 20 years.

Starting in the mid-late 1990s, several technological developments have been fundamentally reshaping the TV industry once again, comprising what is actually television's second reinvention. These include a new set of transmission technologies (digital, IP, and mobile networks) and new end-user devices.

The Era of Digital Television

The next part of our discussion will look at the digitization of television, including transmission and recording, and the subsequent integration of TV with the PC, PDAs, and broadband value chains.

Digital Transmission

All traditional delivery platforms started off transmitting analog signals but are now switching, or have already switched to digital. Most satellite services in the USA went digital by the mid-1990s, while cable and OTA are in the final phases of the transition.

Transmitting digital signals enables the delivery of more data, which means the ability to deliver HDTV (and now 3D) and, for the cable and satellite operators, a greater number of channels. But more significantly, digital TV introduced interactive services like the electronic program guide and video on demand.

Most cable companies in the USA have started to deploy *switched* digital video (SDV), an advanced digital transmission architecture that delivers signals more efficiently in order to free up further bandwidth for more programming, HD and 3D content in particular. SDV is viewed as a transition strategy toward the eventual migration to IPTV because it provides some of the advantages of IPTV but leverages the installed base of digital cable STBs.

Digital Recording

The digital video recorder (DVR) enables the recording and storing of TV programs on a hard disk. The original models were designed to digitize and compress analog video signals, while subsequent models were made for digital delivery platforms. The concept of recording live TV had already been introduced with the VCR, but as noted above, it was not a widely adopted practice, even among VCR owners. The DVR provided a more friendly user interface that was integrated with the electronic program guide, so that selecting a program to record was as easy as selecting a program to watch. The instances of recording and time-shifted viewing among DVR owners has doubled compared to VCR owners, disrupting programming and content development strategies for networks and advertisers.

Same as the VCR, the DVR was introduced to the market as a third-party, standalone device, but the digital cable and satellite network operators began adding DVR functions to their digital STBs shortly thereafter, taking away market share from third-party DVR providers, currently dominated by TiVo. TiVo's strategic response has been to work with operators to provide the UI on their proprietary boxes, since TiVo's UI has thus far provided a superior user experience than most of the operators, who have been impaired by legacy agreements with traditional UI providers.

Software has also been developed to enable PCs (equipped with TV tuners) to function as a DVR, including Linux-based SageTV and MythTV, and Windows Media Center (and more recently MediaRoom for IPTV).

Following several years of legal battles, the network DVR (nDVR) reemerged in 2008 as a centralized solution to digital recording by storing recorded content remotely, i.e., on a DVR that is owned by the MSO and part of the network core, rather than locally, on a home DVR (think of voice mail versus an answering machine). For MSOs, the nDVR eliminates the cost of supplying and installing STBs for each customer (cable operators reportedly spend around 10% of capital investment on DVR boxes[3]).

---

[3] Reuters, "Court rules in favor of Cablevision network DVR" August 4, 2008, available at http://www.reuters.com/article/marketsNews/idINN0448712120080804?rpc=44&sp=true

In effect, the recording function has become less tied to a single-purpose device (which has become commoditized) and integrated in other points in the value chain including the PC and operators' STB at the edge of the network, and the operators' servers (the nDVR) at the core.

As more content is consumed on demand, the function of recording becomes less relevant, but it will nonetheless remain valuable to viewers, programmers, and advertisers for scheduled TV.

Transferring and Redistribution

Like its analog tape predecessor, the DVR serves other purposes besides recording, and some of these have likewise proven to be more significant than the ability to record and archive content.

The first of these involves the transfer and redistribution of operator content to devices and networks that are outside the control of the operator. From a value-chain perspective, the DVR is perhaps most disruptive in that it has led to a second-ary, edge-based redistribution network for recorded content.

When connected to home networks (or as PC software), the DVR functions as an "outbound" channel to other devices by enabling the transfer of recorded pro-grams (as well as other personal data like family photos or home videos) to new viewing devices including the PC and portable media players via USB or other connection standards. Transferring recorded TV content by cracking DRM systems is illegal, but services like TiVoToGo offer a legitimate way to transfer content to the PC and certain PDAs. Again, the cable or satellite operator does not provide this functionality, i.e., it is not part of the cable or satellite offering.[4]

Once on the PC however, recorded content can also be redistributed over other networks. In this way, the DVR provides an integration point between traditional TV content and the Internet. The merging of these two value chains has been one of the major sources of disruption of traditional TV. Recorded and subsequently edited (sliced and diced) TV programs are an important – albeit often unauthorized – source of user-generated content (UGC) for on-line video services like YouTube, representing both a threat (piracy) and opportunity (promotion) for traditional con-tent providers. Although the majority of content found on UGC sites today are amateur-produced, YouTube in particular initially gained popularity after clips of recorded content showed up on its site. It could be argued that the networked TiVo was instrumental in making on-line video analogous, and therefore a potential competitor, to traditional operator-based services. While video was certainly avail-able on the Internet prior to YouTube and Hulu, it was not quite perceived by viewers as "TV," until traditional TV started showing up on PC screens.

---

[4]The TiVoToGo service was offered on the TiVo Series2; however, the TiVo Series 3 HD does not include this feature. Cnet reviews, "TiVo Series3 HD DVR (32-HD hours)", September 11, 2006, avail-able at http://reviews.cnet.com/digital-video-recorders-dvrs/tivo-series3-hd-dvr/4505-6474_7-32065631.html

Placeshifting technology is another form of redistribution, although in this case the operator's video feed is literally rebroadcast over the Internet, making a subscriber's content package accessible from any broadband connected device. Today's placeshifting market is largely based on hardware, the most popular device being the Slingbox STB. In addition to the original PC client software, versions now exist for cell phones and the Blackberry. Software solutions are becoming more popular, where a PC equipped with TV tuner functions as the STB, redirecting content over the Internet.

Placeshifting technology, the Slingbox in particular, has (not surprisingly) led to some interesting unauthorized business models. While it is legal for a Slingbox user to tune in to their cable subscription remotely over the Internet, it is not legal to use the technology as a broadcast platform to third parties. In December 2008, *Newsweek* reported on the growing practice of "Slingbox hosting," where certain Slingbox owners share their video feeds with third parties, often for a fee.[5] As the article explains, these Slingbox owners effectively function as mini-cable companies, using the Internet as an unauthorized distribution channel.

Third-party placeshifting, like transferring recorded content, is outside the control of the operators; however, satellite operator DishTV has integrated placeshifting into its service through a "Slingloaded" STB. But for most cable and satellite providers, the Slingbox is a user-managed solution for remote access.

Inbound Channels

Just as the VCR created a new content channel to the TV, the DVR and other set-top-boxes, when connected to the Internet, have also come to serve as an "inbound channel" for on-line video services. The inbound channel tends to support more authorized services than the outbound channel. The more recent TiVo models for example, can download or stream select Web content like YouTube and Netflix, for easy viewing on a TV set. In this way, the DVR competes with the Internet-to-TV devices that have appeared on the market, most of them single-purpose, proprietary boxes that deliver a Web-based video service providers' content to the TV. These will be discussed in the section on on-line video services below.

The Internet Changes Everything

While digital delivery and recording set the stage for interactivity and have expanded the boundaries of the TV industry, IP delivery platforms will truly reinvent television.

---

[5] Newsweek, "The Slingbox was built to stream your favorite TV shows to your laptop via the Internet. But users are finding other new and controversial uses," December 17, 2008, available at http://www.newsweek.com/id/175602

IP provides a standard way to enable interactive services that seamlessly integrate video, voice, and data communication, as well as fixed and mobile networks and devices, to facilitate the multi-platform vision of TV.

We distinguish between two basic types of IP-based video delivery systems – IPTV and Internet TV or on-line video. These are typically described as closed or open delivery platforms respectively and as we will discuss below, the introduction of an open delivery platform has been another major driver of disruption in the TV industry.

IPTV

Although the term IPTV (Internet Protocol Television) is often used to include on-line video, we use it specifically to refer to video services delivered end-to-end (from the head-end to the STB) over the carriers' closed IP networks, as opposed to the public Internet. Like cable and satellite services, connectivity and content services are tied (i.e., the connectivity and video service provider are one and the same), and the connection offers a guaranteed quality of service as opposed to the public Internet's best-effort delivery. Content is delivered directly to the TV via an IP-enabled STB.

Telcos are currently leading the IPTV trend, primarily as a strategic response to cable companies' provision of bundled voice, data, and interactive video services (the triple play). Their goal is to reduce customer churn and generate revenue from proprietary video services and advertising. The cable companies are currently upgrading their existing networks to switched digital video as a transition to IPTV. As the mobile carriers' upgrade from 3G to all-IP 4G networks over the next few years, they will enter the IPTV game, but in its early incarnations, IPTV is focused on the home-delivery model. Mobile IPTV will be discussed in greater detail below.

There is currently relatively little IPTV activity in North America. Most deployments are in Western Europe and Asia, with Europe accounting for about 61% of IPTV subscribers worldwide – 8.2 million subscribers total. North America, with less than 5% of IPTV subscribers is behind other markets primarily because of the well-established cable and satellite offerings, which, as premium services, compete with IPTV, whereas in Europe in particular, the market is dominated by free antenna TV.[6]

On-line Video

On-line video, or Internet TV as it is sometimes called, refers to services that deliver content over the public Internet. These include P2P services and the more commonly known Web services like YouTube and Hulu, the traditional programming

---

[6] Communications Technology, "The Yanks Are Coming – Eventually," March 8, 2007, available at http://www.cable360.net/ct/news/ctreports/22406.html

networks' sites like NBC.com and History.com, and the latest breed of Web-original content producers like Tiki Bar TV.

On-line video is largely consumed on the PC in "lean forward" mode; however, there are more and more solutions for watching on-line content on the TV in "lean back" mode including proprietary STBs like the Apple TV that streams iTunes to the TV, as well as YouTube and potentially other Web content. Other boxes of this type include the Roku for streaming Netflix's "Watch Instantly" service from the PC to the TV, and the Vudu, which connects the TV set to a proprietary on-line catalog of movies and TV shows. In addition, the recently available Boxee service moves the lean-back experience to the PC platform and combines it with the lean-forward activities related to social TV.

In addition to stand-alone boxes like the DVR and AppleTV, etc., the PC-based media hub is another model for bringing on-line video to the TV, streaming video content acquired from Web video services from the PC to the TV, and increasingly via mobile devices.

Internet-enabled TVs began appearing on the market in 2009. For the time being, these TVs do not offer general Web browsing capabilities, rather, the TV manufacturers have partnered with software providers to enable widget-based access to limited sets of content. For example, Toshiba has partnered with Intel, Microsoft, and Yahoo to create its Combo TV. As the end user has access to the Web uniquely through the Yahoo widget, it is the software provider that controls (for now) what content will be available from the device.

On-line video is becoming increasingly accessible over the mobile Web – and has proven thus far to be more popular than the mobile carriers' services – with some services providing special on-line versions designed specifically for the mobile experience, like YouTube Mobile. Mobile on-line video will be discussed in the next section.

With on-line video services, the content provider is usually a third-party to the ISP. This model thereby challenges the closed "content-conduit"[7] model of traditional, as well as the emerging telco IPTV and cell phone TV services. This fundamental difference in the business model for video content provision – where content is decoupled from connectivity—is at the heart of the net neutrality debate, and the basis of what has become known as the "over-the-top threat." For operators who function as both ISPs and TV service providers, the risk is that TV subscribers will cancel or downgrade their subscriptions in favor of "free" or *a la carte* online content that runs "over-the-top" of the broadband service provided by the same company. Anecdotal evidence is increasing, especially during the economic crisis, that people are cutting their cable or satellite service and only watching video on-line. Nonetheless, statistics show that while on-line video consumption is increasing, it is not necessarily at the expense of traditional TV. Rather that substituting for traditional TV, on-line video often complements it. Some studies have shown that it may even lead to more viewing on traditional platforms.

---

[7]David Clark, "Network Neutrality: Words of Power and 800-Pound Gorillas," International Journal of Communication 1 (2007)

This second reinvention of television triggered by digital and IP-based platforms has initiated the upheaval of a traditionally operator-controlled industry. Not only has the Internet provided new opportunities for content distribution – by content owners themselves and new third-party aggregators – but also a whole world of end-user devices has emerged. The "edge" occupied by these end-user devices comprises a very dynamic part of the value chain for all new TV systems. Devices integrate multiple content and value-added services – both authorized and unauthorized – and their respective value chains into the TV ecosystem, expanding its boundaries and creating new opportunities for both network operators and non-network players to create and capture value while dramatically changing the TV experience for consumers. The next section will look more closely at the role of mobile networks and devices in the new TV ecosystem and its impact on edge innovation.

The Mobile TV Ecosystem

As we pointed out at the beginning of this chapter, the first generation of mobile TV has emerged primarily as a stand-alone service created specifically for viewing on cell phones. We use the term stand-alone to imply a single platform solution. For example, while the popular show CSI can be watched on Verizon's VCast mobile service, on-line at cbs.com (over both the fixed or mobile Web), or as part of a cable TV subscription, these represent three separate services from the user's perspective. In other words, it is not an integrated, cross-platform solution provided by a single entity.

The most typical model is the subscription packages offered by the cell phone carriers. These come in two basic flavors: unicast services delivered over 3G networks, and broadcast services delivered over a separate, dedicated network that uses different frequencies than those for voice and data but still controlled by the carriers.

3G networks are used to deliver both "clipcasting" services – short, on-demand video clips that are downloaded to the phone – and direct streaming of content to the phone. The service may be the carrier's branded service, like Verizon's VCast, or a premium Web video service provided by a third-party aggregator like MobiTV. Because the network used to deliver video content is the same as that used to transport voice and data, bandwidth is a limiting factor in this model, especially when considering delivering video to a mass audience.

The separate, dedicated networks are a proposed solution to the problem of video's high bandwidth consumption. However, there are still few dual-tuner handsets available on the market. A variety of standards have been adopted around the world for these networks. MediaFlo is leading in the USA, while DVB-H is used in Europe and Asia. Some carriers, like Verizon, offer services over the two different types of networks (VCast over its 3G network and VCast Mobile TV over MediaFlo).

While some users have valued the ability to watch TV on the go enabled by these early mobile TV offerings, for a lot of them it has been a frustrating and expensive proposition, and we believe that mobile TV will eventually find greater value as part of a multifaceted, cross-platform offering. In this section, the focus will go beyond the mobility of the *device* to include the mobility of the *content,* and perhaps even more intriguing, we will explore some of the roles played by mobile devices other than receiving and viewing content, some of which have little or nothing to do with mobility per se. The emphasis in this next stage of mobile TV is on the personal and social nature of mobile devices and the influence they will have in taking social TV to the next level.

Multi-Screen TV

As mobile TV becomes integrated into a multi-screen, cross-platform experience – typically called "3-screen TV" in reference to the PC and cell phone as the second and third screens – there are several strategies for designing and delivering these types of experiences. As a preamble, it is interesting to note that while the TV is still considered the first screen, there is increasing anecdotal evidence that the lean-forward PC experience, once considered inferior to the lean-back mode of traditional TV viewing, is gaining importance as behaviors change. Similarly, some mobile phone users have blogged that the only way they have been able to watch TV is on their phones, in transit, because they are perpetually too busy to lie on the couch to watch a show on a regular basis. The traditional TV set, while valued for its own qualities, including size and the ability to connect to fatter residential pipes for delivering high-definition services, may not always be held as the standard. Rather, each screen will be equally valued on its own terms as behaviors evolve, and screen ranking will be different for different users.

Conceptually speaking, the most basic model for 3-screen TV involves treating the mobile device as an alternate screen; one that is smaller but mobile. This view is accurately reflected in the promotional images used for multi-screen TV, which typically show the same image on each screen, in different sizes and proportions. In this way, 3-screen TV essentially means a service provider's content is available on all device types, a trend that is often referred to as "device-shifting."

For on-line video providers, the key challenge thus far – in the absence of truly Internet-enabled TVs – has been to bridge the technical gap between PC and TV. Some of the solutions have been discussed above, for example, using TiVo as a distribution channel to the TV, or via proprietary boxes like Apple TV or the Roku for Netflix.

With regards to the third screen, many cell phone subscribers use the carriers' 3G network as well as WiFi hotspots and home networks for Internet access to connect to on-line video content, some of which is formatted specifically for the mobile experience, like YouTube Mobile or Joost's iPhone application. In this scenario, users bypass the carriers' content offerings (the mobile version of the "over-the-top" threat). A survey conducted by ABI in 2007 found that of the relatively small number (14%) of subscribers who did watch video on their cell phones, 35% had watched content from Internet sites like YouTube, compared to 31% who watched the carrier services, and 5% who watched from a third-party service like MobiTV. Although these mobile services are in their very early stages

– and complaints regarding the experience abound – they indicate a general trend toward 3-screen TV among Web video content providers. Side-loading models that copy downloaded content from one device to another, like iTunes + video iPod have been around for several years.

For operator-based services (i.e., cable, satellite, and telco offerings), delivering to multiple screens is more challenging for a variety of reasons including that the rights for the content they have acquired apply to their delivery platform only. Several operators are developing Web video services positioned as "device-shifting" strategies. In these models, the operators are essentially on-line video providers, distributing a limited selection of their acquired content over any broadband service, in other words, separate from connectivity provision.

Most of these models have started as a PC-only service with mobile versions to be added for access via the mobile Web. Comcast's Fancast is perhaps the most advanced of these. For its latest version Comcast partnered with Hulu to offer content from various broadcast and cable networks like NBC, CBS, Fox, MTV, and BET. Comcast announced last September that a mobile version of its Fancast service would be available for cell phones. The mobile application should include the same features as the original service: allow users to watch TV shows on their phones and share them, as well as interact remotely with their DVR to schedule recordings. This model is in contrast to the placeshifting model described above, where the operators' actual video package is accessible by the subscriber via the Internet.

AT&T U-Verse's 3-screen model called OnTheGo lies somewhere in between Fancast and Slingbox in the sense that it rebroadcasts (as opposed to redistributes via on-line channels) a limited selection of its live and on demand programming to U-Verse subscribers via the Internet to a PC or cell phone (although there are only a few cell phones with this capability at this time). The video is rebroadcast from the U-Verse head end rather than the subscriber's STB.

It is difficult to say at this time which of the operator-based models for content mobility will be more successful. As more traditional content is available on-line, cable and satellite subscribers may increasingly log onto Hulu, or their favorite network's Web site to watch content on their PC rather than logging onto their traditional service provider's Web site. On the one hand, services like Fancast may drive the reported trend that on-line viewing stimulates demand for traditional TV by enhancing Comcast's traditional offering, e.g., providing an enriched PC-based electronic program guide as a complement to their traditional TV service. On the other hand, Fancast may end up cannibalizing its traditional TV business. But if cable subscribers are going to give up their cable TV service for Web TV, the cableco would prefer it be their own Web TV service. A Web TV offering is one strategy for retaining control over the customer and maintaining its role as a content aggregator.

A more primitive (and less common) mobile TV model involves broadcasting traditional over-the-air (OTA) television to cell phones or other mobile devices that are equipped with an analog or digital TV tuner – basically a miniaturized version of old-fashioned broadcast TV. Mobile analog OTA cell phones became available in the early 2000s but these were not successful because of the poor quality of reception and battery drain. More recently, the ATSC (Advanced Television Standards Committee) approved a mobile version of its digital TV standard for cell phones, laptops, portable media players, and other mobile devices called ATSC-M/H. Mobile digital OTA – often referred to as mobile DTV – is viewed by the ATSC as an alternative to building out separate broadcast networks as discussed below, since the spectrum and transmitting equipment are already available, and most content will be free. In 2007, several major local and national TV stations in the USA formed the Open Mobile Video Coalition Mobile[8] to develop mobile DTV products and services that would complement existing free, ad-supported content, including interactive services and paid content (broadcast and download). Although Japan and Korea have enjoyed some success with mobile DTV, critics point to the inferiority of the ATSC standard and the greater rate of adoption of other standards for both digital OTA TV and dedicated mobile TV networks (e.g., DVB-H and MediaFLo) around the world. Overall, mobile OTA has not been very popular.

The 2- and 3-screen services that we have looked at so far provide the means for the user of a particular service to access the provider's content over various devices and networks, however, another differentiator involves the mobility of a *viewing session* across devices for a persistent experience. As video services become multi-platform, providers – whether cable and satellite operators, or aggregators like iTunes, or content owners like NBC – have recognized that mobility of a TV session is an important application. The typical scenario involves starting a program at home on TV, pausing, and then picking up where you left off from your mobile device. In this scenario, all end-user devices are connected to a media server or DVR, either in the home (at the edge of the network) or at the network core.

This vision requires several conditions to be successful, including all IP delivery to the edge; ubiquity of broadband access; transcoding services to adapt content for each of the screens in the rendering ecosystem, and – perhaps the most challenging – a multi-platform business model. The latter enables the vision of personal broadband, defined by the MIT Communications Future Program (CFP) as "a set of capabilities and interfaces that allow users (or their agents) to select the connections that best meet their needs within a particular context." [9] Personal broadband is essentially about connecting a service to a person, rather than to a specific device.

While we are close technologically to such a vision, the biggest obstacle is business-related. Operators are reluctant to open their STBs to other network operators; however, as we will discuss in the section below, they may be encouraged to do so to remain competitive. Personal broadband will be the new "triple-play."

---

[8] http://www.omvc.org/about%2Domvc/

[9] A Vision of Personal Broadband, MIT Communications Futures Program, January 2006, http://cfp.mit.edu/publications/index.shtml

Complementary Devices

So far we have looked at the role of mobile devices as small, portable screens in a multi-platform TV experience. But mobile devices can play complementary roles that use the mobile device's other capabilities besides image rendering.

Typically, the mobile phone (as well as the PC and even the traditional landline phone) is used to complement the living room TV experience. This may involve loosely coupled processes like voting on American Idol, or more technically integrated processes such as programming a TiVo remotely, or streaming from a cell phone to the TV. A more advanced level of technical integration occurs when all end-user devices become part of a community of collaborating devices. This is especially useful when the peering device contains more storage and complements the mobile's own capabilities. This vision of a peer network of collaborating devices will be discussed in more detail in the section on community TV at the end of this chapter.

Mobile phones are also increasingly being used as cameras for user-generated videos, and like Web cams, are directly integrated into the distribution infrastructure. They effectively function as mobile TV studios, broadcasting to sites like Kyte, Qik, and Flixwagon, and providing interesting insider perspectives on public events.

It Is All About the Applications

The TV landscape is becoming more exciting, more diverse and, as a consequence, complicated. Leveraging the opportunities of the new offerings will mean the difference between success and failure for many services. Recent work by Chintan Vaishnav at MIT provides interesting insights regarding competitive dynamics in this complicated industry landscape.

Vaishnav's research applied systems dynamics theory to model innovation in the TV industry. The results show that for video service providers to keep market share in a highly competitive environment, they must offer ancillary services; those services that are secondary, or supplemental to the "me too TV" of linear and VOD offerings. Such ancillary services eventually become integrated into the normal or primary offering as users start expecting these services as part of the mainstream offering.

This perspective reflects a shift in the competitive dynamics of the TV industry, which, with the introduction of each new delivery platform, started off as platform vs. platform (e.g., cable vs. satellite, cable and satellite vs. telcos, etc.). But competition is now more accurately described as service versus service (on-demand vs. live, mobile vs. fixed) and even feature vs. feature (interactive vs. noninteractive).

At this stage in the evolution of TV, both mobile and social TV are considered ancillary. Both services emerged independently, but not surprisingly, their trajectories have now begun to intersect, particularly as social networking applications in general and social TV applications in particular are being developed for mobile devices. In this next section, we explore the relationship between mobile and social TV.

Social TV

The meaning of mobile TV was discussed at the beginning of this chapter; this section addresses its relationship to social TV, and how social TV will win its place in the multi-screen TV world.

While the social aspect of TV is not new, the term "social TV" has emerged fairly recently to describe a new breed of video services that integrate other communication services like voice, chat, context awareness, recommendations, and peer ratings. Its goal is to support a shared TV experience with one's peer groups, defined more and more by social networking sites like Facebook and YouTube. Social TV applications are currently geared primarily at real-time interactivity with friends such as shared viewing and peer recommendations, e.g., What are my friends watching right now? What are their "favorite" shows? How can I watch what they watch?

The adoption of social TV services is driven, on the one hand, by the rise of social networking, and on the other by the availability of Web applications across the TV ecosystem. It is also fueled by the seemingly paradoxical trend of individualized viewing on personal devices like PCs, smart phones, other PDAs and cell phones, or simply one's own TV.

Social TV involves the rediscovery of TV as a shared activity. Back in the 1950s, when television came of age, watching TV was typically a communal activity, with family and friends gathered in the living room around the TV, choosing what to watch and reacting to the same program and exchanging comments. In the 2000s, TVs are no more a luxury item and it has become common for the typical home to have more than one, where individuals or smaller family groups watch their preferred programs separately. In 2006, Nielsen Media Research reported that only 19% of American homes have no more than one TV, and the typical home now has more TVs than people – 2.73 TVs for 2.55 people.

In effect, we have seen the growth of "anti-social TV" watching, where the social aspect of exchanging comments and making program recommendations is delayed – or asynchronous – occurring the next day around the water cooler and in other social contexts. A lot of the social aspects of the living room TV have moved to sports bars and other more public spaces.

But the shared TV experience is now returning, in a new form. A person's social networks are replacing the typical family room of the 1950s. These virtual communities can extend far beyond the home to span entire neighborhoods, cities, countries, and hemispheres. And like the traditional living room, they are increasingly organized around video, connecting families, friends, and some strangers alike in a shared video space defined by interactions, common interest, or location.

In the world of cable and IPTV services, efforts to integrate social networking features began in the early 2000s, with STB-to-STB communications provided by a few operators. Today, social TV offerings are on many operators' roadmaps. IPTV middleware like MediaRoom as well as next generation versions of OCAP (recently branded as Tru2way) middleware for digital cable, are offering shared viewing applications and converged telecommunication services. These systems use Instant Messaging-like capabilities with buddy lists, etc. that overlay the watched content, text bubbles, or even avatars to convey the friend's messages, enabling friends watching the same program in separate homes to exchange comments about the show they were watching. Other early incarnations of social TV have involved traditional TVs with added interaction and widgets.

Nonetheless, most of today's social TV experiences originated online with services like YouTube, Joost, Hulu, and now Boxee integrating social networking features like sharing content among peer groups, program ratings, "favorites" lists, discussion forums, and multi-user chat sessions directly into their offerings.

At the same time, Web-based social networks like Facebook and MySpace have been embedding video applications into their sites, both user-generated and professional content from commercial sites, thereby becoming both video viewing sites and video distribution platforms in their own right. Viewing on those sites is, by definition, a social experience. In addition to getting movie and TV recommendations from their peers, subscribers to these social networks can now stream selected content on a personal page for a shared viewing experience with visitors and "friends."

Video-oriented social networks essentially become "virtual operators," servicing the user and their group of friends. This changes the traditional role of the user in the video consumption value chain. The members of a peer group influence and alter each other's behavior. Like a traditional operator, the virtual operator (the social network) effectively programs the service (chooses and rates content) but based on peer recommendation lists and ratings, not generic population statistics.

While enhancing the user experience by making it more relevant, peer-based programming also creates tremendous opportunity for targeted advertisement, and the ad industry is taking note. Already one can see a huge difference in the advertisements for a given show when viewed on prime time TV versus video on demand versus on-line. Social networks take ad targeting to a new level: identify the main programmer – or "power influencer" – and use their social graph to influence the group. It is useful to note here that there has also been a rise in social features in gaming, where users can connect to friends or meet new people using various applications. These developments in gaming will influence user expectations vis-à-vis the TV experience, especially as gaming becomes more integrated with TV viewing.

Operators are also starting to incorporate aspects of Web-based social networking directly into their offerings via the STB. Sites like Facebook and MySpace have been complementing operator services with features like movie recommendations for the past few years, but in a loosely coupled way. Consumers discover content through their on-line communities, and then turn on the TV and interface with the EPG (electronic program guide). Although the process can be more synchronous than the water cooler scenario, it is a technically separate process.

Recent work with social networking extensions to the TV user interface, like TiVo for example, show that various social features can now be technically integrated with the actual TV viewing experience, similar to on-line video services described above. The social network look and feel is incorporated into the TV user interface with some minor changes, e.g., a menu item (e.g., my friends' favorites) and/or a real-time chat application for shared viewing. For example, the "favorites" list can be influenced by what a subscriber's friends in their social network are watching.

The list of one friend's favorites can also be used to determine what to record on another friend's DVR.[3] As in the on-line examples above, this creates the opportunity for more targeted advertising. While some critics are skeptical, claiming that too much of the information about users is fake or out-of-date, or that connections to social groups can be meaningless because they are so remote (many degrees of separation) or no longer relevant, the social network for a typical user is still considered valuable by advertisers.

The Facebook TV prototype, developed at MIT's Media Lab, has shown that commercial operators see value in the opportunity to build a new type of user interface – the social network user interface – over and above the services they already offer. This raises more general questions regarding the value of social networks beyond target audiences for advertisers. As David Reed of the MIT Media Lab notes, "From a business point of view, almost all of the value (economic utility) of our communications arises out of the shared context that we have created, so as part of understanding what the communications business is about, we should be studying the value that is created through the elements of context, rather than the speeds and technologies of the particular pipe."

Social TV Goes Mobile

Mobile social TV is a natural evolution of the current trends. YouTube and Facebook, for example, have launched mobile versions of their applications (YouTube Mobile and Facebook Mobile Video). Twitter offers a platform to comment on mobile (and traditional) TV. And according to Opera Software Mobile Web report, 63% mobile traffic in the USA is to mobile-social sites, most of those now having a video component. YouTube Mobile is the leading mobile social TV service because of its availability on a variety of mobile platforms. Developers working on the mobile version of YouTube ensured that the interface and the features are the same on a smart phone as on a PC and use a variety of wireless media from 3G to WiFi, and soon to 4G, it is offering an Internet service that is network agnostic.

However, YouTube mobile offers only basic social features. One can only rate, share, flag, and add a video to a list of favorites. Only user-generated content is offered, and advanced social features like multi-user chat sessions are not supported yet. This service is used mostly because it allows users to easily upload videos taken from their phones. Overall, the ability to upload and share videos shot directly from the cell phone seems to be the most salient feature of mobile social TV. And those tend to be short clips not full featured videos.

Itsmy.com offers a more complete mobile social TV experience. Itsmy.com is a portal that offers several services: chat with friends, video and picture uploading and viewing, forums, flirting, etc.; however, not all of these features are integrated. These types of services are developing extremely rapidly, especially among the younger demographic. According to the recent Opera Software Mobile Web report, itsmy.com ranks amongst the top ten most-visited mobile sites.

At this point, the most advanced mobile social TV initiative is Mogulus. This Internet and mobile platform allows users to watch and shoot videos from their PCs and cell phones. Chat rooms are associated with the shows, and videos can also be shared, flagged, and rated. Mogulus' creators boast more than 5.8 million unique viewers each month, and more than 400 million unique viewer minutes watched each month, and the 2,972th Alexa rank. A number of other services resemble Mogulus. These services are however also still emerging, and are currently much less significant in terms of traffic. Kyte, mogulus' most threatening competitor has only the 65,325th Alexa rank. Other emerging services include Qik, Flixwagon, Phanfare.

So what does it mean for wireless networks and operators? According to Alexa. com, the YouTube.com domain accounts for 15% of the total Web traffic. Even thinking that 1/1,000 of YouTube's traffic is mobile, this is still a hugely successful Mobile TV service, one that is both social (YouTube connect feature) and viral (top video recommendations) and risks to drain all capacity from current networks. But can it be stopped? And can mobile social TV become even more social? As was shown by the recent CNN/Facebook event for the American presidential inauguration the use of peer-to-peer technologies could alleviate some of the network congestion associated with mass social events.

True Community TV

Most social TV applications offered by cable operators, IPTV, and IP video services, and mobile portals alike still follow traditional head-end/STB mechanisms or client/server models of TV delivery. However, once TV becomes truly social – a shared experience among peers – the next logical step is to consider user-controlled, peer-to-peer (P2P) *delivery networks* for rights-protected and user-generated content.

Mobile devices are perfect for peering and exchanging information at close range. Can that include video? Peering is the basis of a community-focused approach that harnesses the combination of the now almost ubiquitous WiFi hotspot at home and on the road; Bluetooth file exchanges; related protocol stacks including Digital Life Network Alliance (DLNA); end-user technologies (like the whole-home DVR) for content distribution to local communities, and the collective knowledge of these communities for programming and content discovery via social interaction. It also enables the ever-growing number of power users – those who tend to use the more advanced features of technology – to shape the social consumption of content.

Unfortunately, *peer-to-peer* is still often associated with stolen bandwidth and illegal file sharing. But it can also enable the legitimate exchange of TV content. Bringing peer-to-peer to the TV experience means both P2P in the network sense, using short-range or local connectivity, and in the more literal sense of sharing content among a social group. It is social mobile TV based on physical proximity and shared interests.

The peering model may be more advantageous than the client/server model (mostly unicast) in terms of bandwidth and supports the sharing of nearby resources. As early business card exchanges via infrared on cell phones have shown, if the required information is available nearby, you do not have to go fetch it from the other end of the network. The availability of Bluetooth and the development of interface specifications from the DLNA, for example, have demonstrated the value of storing and exchanging content among devices in a home ecosystem. With WiFi or other wireless access, the ecosystem can be extended to a city block or neighborhood or even a small town, and profit from shared resources like DVRs or other storage. The social networks, as mentioned in the previous section add a wider distribution area and an element of content management.

If we want to take peer-to-peer "out of prison," then the shared content should not be commercial, unless it is DRM-free. But as a starting point, the availability of both camera phones and Internet-enabled digital cameras makes it easier to exchange user-generated content within a local community. While this practice is still in its infancy, and the issue of content storage and cell bandwidth remain unresolved, the concept of streaming UCG in a peering network that could also include PCs and other video-ready devices is carving a very compelling path for social media.

This vision of mobile TV is not just social; it is "neighborly." It creates a "social mobile TV" experience at the local level, whether the peer groups are based on Facebook friends, or real-world connections (e.g., parents of the children of the neighborhood school), etc. In this context mobile TV is also "social" in the sense that the content itself relates to a community.

Several trends are overlapping to support this vision of community TV. First of all, the combination of social networking and personalization is driving a shift in the distribution of the TV experience away from the living-room TV in a single household to multiple homes as well as to a multi-device ecosystem. More specifically, social networks are driving the transition from the whole-home DVR – a centralized hub serving a single household (an approach supporting the traditional living room scenario) – to the community DVR. The community DVR is essentially a social version of the core-based network DVR, where one household's DVR serves a community of users who are defined by their membership to a social network. This trend will eventually progress toward true "community TV," as described above, where members of a social network will connect to each other's mobile devices via peer-to-peer networking technologies.

Secondly, although consumers are concerned with the security of locally stored – un-backedup—data, concerns about the reliability of the operator-controlled network devices are equally important. As one analyst puts it, "[w]e're ... looking at a living-room analog to cloud computing. What if the cloud goes offline? What service expectations should consumers have? Should there be TV service-level agreements that somehow translate into community requirements?"[10]

A tremendous opportunity therefore exists for a shift from distribution based on a core network infrastructure and a single content source to community-based distribution. This change can happen, and is happening, at many levels including the physical layer, where autonomous systems manage the organization of the network;

---

[10] http://www.techlare.com/blog/entry/23528/A-Cablevision-Win-for-Network-DVR-AKA-Cloud-TV/

the architecture level, where users are both content sources and/or consumers; and the management level, where power users are responsible for guaranteeing connectivity and the legality of the experience. It is even more impacted by the mobile Internet requirements and affecting the distribution and consumption of TV content at the edge. Users will have different expectations for live popular events like the Olympics than for user-generated content dedicated to local consumption.

In order for this P2P network to be functional, intelligence must be added to otherwise dumb devices; adding "self" capabilities like self-configuration, self-detection, and self-management. As the MIT Media Lab's work on the P2P platform is demonstrating, P2P-based community TV will encourage the move away from the monster media hubs of the early 2000s – where a single device is overloaded with features – toward a peer network of collaborating devices that share functions based on service and user profiles. For example, the DVR with large enough disk space could become the designated community storage device while an attached PC can provide the transcoding to allow image rendering (viewing) on a handset. The community can also extend beyond a geographical area with one member in the USA, for example, watching content subscribed to by a friend in France via a super peer in New York – the global-based "Slingbox" adding community to the mobile (content) experience.

Community TV closes the circle in defining the future of Mobile TV as it is affected by and in turn affects viewing behavior and the sharing of the TV experience inside and outside the home. The community is essentially where TV started and it is appropriate that it is where TV returns.

Conclusion

Mobile TV is still in its infancy. We still think of it as a distinct service. We still think that its main purpose is to offer the ability to watch timely, "snacky" content like sports and news when we are away from home. But as a more general TV experience in itself, we find it frustrating and not worth the high cost; it is simply an overpriced, lesser version of the real thing. These sentiments were eloquently expressed in the following statement:

"Why put long-form video on a linear service? Mobile viewing by definition isn't appointment viewing. Who wants to miss both the start and end of something, watch what's in between and then try to figure out what it was all about? Why ask us to pay $5 or $10 on top of the $50 or so we already pay for phone service so that we can watch ancient television episodes in low resolution on a tiny screen? Sorry, this is not a compelling proposition."

Our understanding of mobile TV has to change. As this chapter has demonstrated, the role of mobile networks and devices must be reconceptualized and their development must be examined in context of the more general transformation of TV itself. Furthermore, the definition of mobility per se, and the means to provide it must be expanded. This perspective takes us away from the *mobile TV = mobile network + mobile device* view to a much richer world in which our original notions of mobile TV all but disappear.

To turn this vision into reality, mobile TV initiatives must move from the lab to the street. Focus must shift from technology features like screen size and bandwidth to real benefits like content choice, social networking, community TV, location based services, etc. User behaviors are key (even the unauthorized ones – *especially* the unauthorized ones) and must be carefully studied. This is a world where doing things with content once you get it, as well as creating your own content, has become more important than just watching a live broadcast video feed. It all started with recording shows off the TV onto tape about 30 years ago, and has evolved to wonderfully creative endeavors like YouTube and personal mobile TV broadcasting networks as end-users are increasingly empowered.

The mobile dimension of TV will remain largely in control of the operators as long as handsets (and content) are locked in. But this model is changing. At the same time, on-line video, with its expansive range of choice, is increasingly moving to the mobile Web as wireless broadband improves. The 4G era will undoubtedly open more capacity and more channels, further encouraging the growth of open, rather than walled-garden services. Combined with social networking, where peer groups become de facto operators recommending and rating content, operators face some tough competition. We believe, however, that the benefits of mobile TV will arise through competition as well as cooperation. One of the key conditions of our vision – a multi-platform business model for personal broadband – requires a new approach to partnerships.

We believe that the future of mobile TV is embedded in the future of TV in general. This chapter has provided a vision for the future of mobile TV as it evolves from stand-alone to integrated service.

From One to Many Boxes: Mobile Devices as Primary and Secondary Screens

Pablo Cesar, Hendrik Knoche, and Dick C.A. Bulterman

Abstract This chapter looks at the current changing habits on audiovisual content consumption at home, with special focus on potential uses of mobile devices. Standard television plus a remote control impose a use that is too coarse to support the various personal needs of people, while mobile devices open new possibilities from engagement and immersion into content and deliberately controlled disengagement with others to providing a screen that can be offered to include others in sharing experiences in a huddled setting.

Introduction

Mobile devices provide users finer levels of control over where and how to consume multimedia content. Due to inherent properties of these devices, portability and privacy among others, media consumption has undergone fundamental changes in the last years. The intention of this chapter is to shed light on the current viewing and interaction behaviors in our complex multidevice, multiuser world. Two major functionalities include selecting and viewing multimedia content. Mobile devices can be used as primary screens for watching content (Södergård 2003). Moreover, due to portability, they can be used for bringing movies and photos into places and situations where such content was not available before (O'Hara et al. 2007). On the other hand, mobile devices can be used in conjunction with other platforms, extending their functionality (Cesar et al. 2009).

In order to scope the contribution of this chapter we will focus on media consumption at home, where fixed television sets used to be the default media player.

P. Cesar (✉)
Centrum voor Wiskunde en Informatica, Amsterdam, The Netherlands
e-mail: P.S.Cesar@cwi.nl

H. Knoche
University College London, London, UK

D.C. Bulterman
Centrum voor Wiskunde en Informatica, Amsterdam, The Netherlands

A. Marcus et al. (eds.), *Mobile TV: Customizing Content and Experience*,
Human-Computer Interaction Series, DOI 10.1007/978-1-84882-701-1_22,
© Springer-Verlag London Limited 2010

At home, people's watching of standard TV is driven by ritualistic (Taylor and Harper 2002) and instrumental motives (Rubin 1981) as in "electronic wallpaper" (Gauntlett and Hill 1999), mood management (Zillman 1988), escapism, information, entertainment, social grease, social activity, and social learning (Lee and Lee 1995). For many of these drivers watching TV constitutes a group activity. Whereas the drivers behind standard TV consumption are fairly well understood, we lack comparable knowledge in media consumption at home, where individuals can make use of mobile devices, television sets, or can use both of them at the same time. The current shift can be classified as "from one box to many boxes."

The rest of this section will describe our multidevice world, our multiuser world, an overview of existing interaction paradigms and services, and a further elaboration of the motivation of our work.

A Multidevice World

Traditionally, research on multimedia consumption mostly focused on the effective delivery and rendering of content in a given screen. Such a line of research resulted in the proposal of several transmission protocols and in the development of efficient multimedia players tailored to specific platforms: television set-top boxes, mobile phones, and web browser plug-ins. Today, because of the number of devices a user is surrounded by at a specific moment, context-aware consumption has gained increasing importance. We can define the user's digital sphere as the digital devices that a user can employ for rendering multimedia content and/or for interacting with the content. Depending on the contextual situation of the viewer and on the nature of the content, parts of the content can be rendered in a specific device, while other devices can be used for controlling content playback. In this chapter, we will only consider the home sphere of a given user. That is, the sphere composed of a mobile device and a television set connected with a personal video recorder. We are aware that outside the home there are a number of other interactive/passive devices, such as public screens, but such situations are out of the scope of this particular contribution.

We can classify the devices surrounding the user based on the resolution, or viewing experience, based on their private nature, interaction role, and rendering role:

- **TV**: it represents a shared device, with none or little privacy, obtrusive in the sense that it draws the attention of people located in the living room, with a large screen, normally used as a primary screen, and that it provides a lean-back attitude to the users.
- **Mobile Device**: mobile devices are normally portable and personal devices with smaller screens that can be used as primary or secondary screens, and people often employ it with a more active attitude.

We can identify a major issue that arises in our multidevice world: necessity of interoperability among devices and networks. It has been reported that people use different devices at the same time in the same room. For example, research into people's use of audiovisual entertainment at home has suggested a need for spatially distributed access and concurrent service use within the same room (Seager et al. 2007). Unfortunately, in the majority of the cases other devices surrounding the user at a specific moment are underused due to the lack of interoperability among them (Dearman and Pierce 2008).

A Multiuser World

In our fast-paced society, it is becoming increasingly complicated for families and friends to find time to gather in the same location for social events, such as television watching. Nevertheless, people continue to share interest and want to socialize around content (Coppens et al. 2005) even though they are not located at the same place. There is a need for the community to actualize the definition of togetherness under the new living habits and norms.

Television watching on mobile devices, due to their nature and limitations, might be more individualistic and private. The smaller viewing angle afforded by the screens, the ensuing of the required proximity with other viewers – possibly uncomfortable for some (Hall 1966) – while sharing, and the fact that the mobile phone is a rather personal device with intimate information might curb group usage. Despite this, mobile devices are becoming an increasingly popular means to consume and interact with audiovisual TV content. Moreover, mobile devices have been shown to be used to enjoy content with other people, when people let others to look into their private content over their shoulders (O'Hara et al. 2007).

Even though the natural tendency is to conclude that mobile devices at home will tend to fragment the socializing capabilities provided by television watching, we are inclined to follow O'Hara et al.'s (2007) view that redefined the traditional view on togetherness from a task-oriented concept into a more spatially-oriented one. Although mobile devices constitute a privatizing technology, it might facilitate togetherness at home as people can watch *"their own content while being in proximity to family,"* Based on a literature review on mobile TV, Harper et al. identified that people include others in their mobile phone TV use and dubbed this salient property *watching-to-show.*

Interaction Paradigms

There are multiple views and opinions on what interactivity actually means in the new media landscape (Jensen 2005, 2008). Nevertheless, we can distinguish two different levels at which it happens: user-to-user and user-to-media interaction. The first level refers to a social activity, or parasocial interaction (Horton and Wohl 1956), and includes actions such as initiating a (text, audio, or video) chat with others, while watching television. The latter one refers to the potential impact the viewer has on the multimedia content he is watching. Examples of user-to-media interactivity include switching on/off a media player, selecting a program to be watched, or creating a slide show from the family photo album.

The level of user-to-media interaction can be seen, at the same time, on a continuum ranging from zero to one (Cesar 2006), as shown in Fig. 1. Zero interaction stands for passive situations, in which the multimedia presentation is presented to the user, but he does not have any control over it. At the other end of the spectrum stand highly interactive situations such as the user authoring of content. Between levels 1 and 0, one can align activities such as selecting a piece of content to be watched, switching on/off extra features (e.g., subtitles), and changing the state of a running presentation (e.g., playing a game or time-shifting).

The interest of this article in terms of interactivity lies in the user-to-media interaction, defined as the potential impact of the user on the content being watched. Thus, we can distinguish three major levels of interaction:

- Content viewing: passive viewing activity
- Content selection: active selection of media content to be watched
- Extra features selection: active control over enhanced content
- Content Enrichment: active authoring on the media content being watched

Overview of Existing Services

As indicated above we can identify a number of dimensions in which mobile devices at home can influence the way people consume and interact with media. We can highlight a number of usages: watching videos at home and enhancing the capabilities of other devices.

Historically, portable TV sets were the only way to watch TV anywhere but they were large and consumed a lot of energy. Nowadays, people can choose from a range of devices such as portable DVD players, laptops, mobile music players, PDAs, mobile phones, and mobile digital TVs that vary in size and energy consumption and follow different paradigms in terms of consumption. The content can be either played back from storage (e.g., DVDs) or device memory (e.g., iPod), delivered on demand by mobile operators, received live by broadcasters, or downloaded or streamed from computers (e.g., Slingbox) or set-top box solutions (e.g., AppleTV).

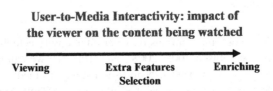

Fig. 1 Levels of user-to-media interactivity (as a continuum ranging from zero to one)

The existing number of solutions implies that mobile devices are popular ways for watching videos and television. In terms of home consumption, Mäki (2005) identified home, work, and transit as the three top places for mobile TV. Between 30% and 50% of the participants used mobile TV at home in different mobile TV field trials (Mason 2006; Lloyd et al. 2006; Nokia 2006). In Södergård's (2003) study people used PDAs and tablet PCs in the home context suggesting that screen size does not affect this choice much. Cui et al. (2007) observed that mobile TV constitutes rather a personal TV which is therefore used in the home context, too.

In terms of enhancing other devices' capabilities, it has been shown that people tend to multitask and, for example, browse the web on their laptops while watching television (Kap 2008). People have already started integrating the use of laptops, mobile music, and video players (e.g., iPods) to allow for more flexible media use at home (Seager et al. 2007). We can highlight a number of services such as content selection and T-Learning enhanced by the use of handheld devices. Cesar et al. (2009) use an architecture that integrates the personal video recorder at home with the different mobile devices from the users for provision, selection, and previewing functionality over media content and extra information about a current program, among other things.

Motivation

The motivation of this chapter is the current shift on multimedia consumption that occurs because of latest advances in mobile media, ubiquitous computing, and interactive digital television. A number of trends have been observed:

- Mobile devices are a private, personal, and portable means to consume audiovisual content, even at home.
- Viewers tend to perform other tasks, such as web browsing or e-mailing with their laptops whilst watching television. Unfortunately, devices do not seamlessly integrate at home (Edwards and Grinter 2001).
- Such multitasking behavior does not necessarily translate into an antisocial attitude since we can reconsider togetherness basing it more on spatial location rather than on activities.
- Mobile devices provide ways to enhance social behavior in the form of sending images that reflect an experience and by bringing content to places where it was not available previously.

Figure 2 shows two different contextual situations of a media user. In the first case (left), we can see a user within her digital sphere that can be used for rendering audiovisual content. The second one (right) shows that the viewer might not be alone. Thus, some of the audiovisual resources might be shared among collocated viewers, while other resources might be used as personal devices. For example, the television set has traditionally been considered as a shared display because of its size and historical reasons (in the olden days, there was one television set per block,

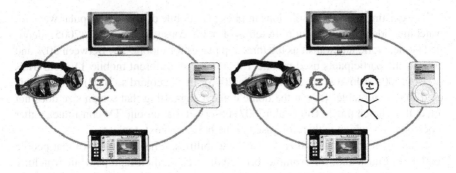

Fig. 2 Digital environment of the user(s). (*Left*) private consumption of media; (*Right*) shared consumption of media

if any) (cf. Mobile Devices as Primary Screens). As an analogy, the shared landline telephone at home has evolved first to multiple telephones in different locations and is now facing replacement by personal mobile devices.

The assumption of this chapter is that a shift on multimedia viewing habits is underway. First, mobile devices are becoming popular audiovisual content front-ends. Moreover, the traditional monolithic media rendering, in which one box is in charge of managing the audiovisual stream served from one source, is becoming outdated. Media consumption is thus shifting from one box to multiple boxes.

Summary and Overview of the Chapter

People live with, and adapt, technologies to their needs (McCarthy and Wright 2004). But new technologies need to support relationships and activities that enrich people's experience in order to be successful (Shneiderman 2003). The intention of this chapter is to provide an understanding on how mobile devices in the home context provide increase flexibility for users to consume and interact with multimedia content. This section has presented an overview of related work in terms of interaction paradigms, existing services, and potential user behavior. The remainder of the chapter provides a more detailed discussion on the two most significant use cases: mobile devices as primary screens for watching media content and mobile devices as secondary screens that provide more personal viewing and interaction capabilities.

Mobile Devices as Primary Screens

We have described above that people are making increasing use of mobile devices for content consumption. Mobile devices come with a large range of screen sizes smaller than standard TV sets. Insufficient screen size is a common but hasty criticism of mobile TV that ignores a much shorter viewing distance. That is not to say that many compact mobile phones have screens that result in a smaller image in the eye of the beholder compared to their TV sets.

Another driver for small depictions of video on mobile devices might be people's desire to access interactive and communication services in parallel with the media. We will discuss these services in detail in the section on Mobile Devices as Secondary Screens. Furthermore, most content of mobile TV services is much lower than that for standard or high-definition TV.

We will describe in this section that the preferred viewing ratio of mobile TV is similar to that of standard TV or an even bigger picture and that the major difference is the resolution of the content that is delivered to mobile devices, compared to standard television (SDTV).

Viewing Constraints

Viewing distance is often expressed in terms of the ratio between the distance of the observer and the height of the visible screen. A viewing ratio of 5 H describes a viewing distance five times the picture height (H). The visual angle (VA) or angular size (AS) θ expresses the viewing ratio in degrees regardless of D as illustrated in Fig. 3.

Viewing distance has an effect on the possible social uses of a screen. In general, short viewing distances cannot support as many viewers to share a screen as in comparison to longer viewing distances even if the viewing ratio is kept constant. This is further exacerbated by the fact that the angle from which a screen can be viewed is limited and portable devices tend to have smaller *viewing angles* than the more powerful TV sets. On the positive side, smaller viewing distances allow for more private content consumption.

The human visual system uses two mechanisms to focus on objects: convergence and accommodation. Convergence denotes the eyes moving inward when focusing on nearby objects, and accommodation describes the focusing on objects of different distance by means of physically deforming the lens of the eye. The resting point of accommodation (RPA), i.e., the default distance at which objects appear sharp, for example, when opening the eyes, is around 75 cm for younger people and increases in distance with age (Owens and Wolfe-Kelly 1987). The resting point of vergence (RPV) is 114 cm when looking straight ahead, and drops to 89 cm when looking 30° down.

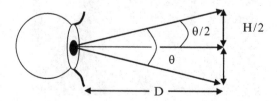

Fig. 3 Viewing ratio and the visual angle

This is a posture often seen in mobile TV consumption (cf. Fig. 4). People use their legs or bags on their laps as support for the hand holding of the device (Cui et al. 2007). The stress of convergence contributes more to visual discomfort than the stress of accommodation. Continued viewing at distances closer than the RPV can contribute to eyestrain (Owens and Wolfe-Kelly 1987). When viewing distances come close to 15 cm, people experience discomfort (Ankrum 1996). Boff and Lincoln (1988) showed that visual acuity decreases as viewing distance increases, and so for close viewing distances people's acuity is at its maximum.

Screen Sizes and Viewing Ratios

People unfamiliar with watching content on mobile devices usually mention the screen size as an obstacle to a satisfying experience (Knoche and McCarthy 2004; Cui et al. 2007). Talking about the size or the resolution of videos and screens only

Fig. 4 Mobile viewing ratios (from l.t.r) varying from 15 H to 1.5 H

makes sense when we consider the distance (D) at which it is used. For that reason research often reports viewing distances in relation to screen heights. A viewing ratio of 5 describes a viewing distance D five times the picture height H.

From research on traditional TV viewing in the living room, we know that a range of factors such as spatial layout of the living room, screen size, and ambient lighting can influence people's decision on their chosen viewing distance. Early research by Thompson on preferred TV viewing distance suggested that people chose their viewing distance so that the TV lines were not visible anymore (Thompson 1957). More recent research, however, has refuted this assumption (see Lund below). Due to the layout of the average living room, people typically watch TV at the so-called Lechner (USA, 9 ft) or Jackson (Europe, 3 m) distance (Diamant 1989). Unfortunately, both of these values are often cited but poorly documented and their original sources are not readily accessible. As recently as 2004, the median viewing distance for standard definition TV of BBC employees was reported as 2.7 m (8.5 H) (Tanton 2004a). Nathan et al. (1985) showed that the viewing distance of regular TV at home varied with the age of the viewers. The average viewing distance for 17-year olds and younger was 2.25 m (7.8 H), whereas adults watched from 3.37 m (11.7 H). The study did not explain this difference, but it did report that children were more mobile than adults, and much less likely to sit or lie on furniture while watching TV.

For mobile devices the viewing distance can be considered fixed at about arm's length (20–50 cm). Kato et al. (2005) found an average viewing distance of 35 cm for standing or sitting participants and Knoche and Sasse (2008) found no differences in response to two low resolutions (120 × 90 and 168 × 126) and sizes between 11 mm and 45 mm in height. Mobile TV viewing distances might depend partly on the posture of people within a given environment and whether they are sharing it with other viewers.

Hatada et al. (1980) discovered that it required a picture with a 20° horizontal visual angle to induce a *sense of reality* of a landscape depicting picture (cf. extreme long shot in Fig. 5) and that with 30° this effect became conspicuous. When given the choice people prefer widescreen (16:9) over standard 4:3 aspect ratio for TV content. This holds true when both formats are presented at equal height, equal diagonal, equal area, and equal width (albeit to a lesser degree) irrespective of viewing distance and screen size (Pitts and Hurst 1989). With a 16:9 display a visual angle of 30° can be achieved at a viewing distance of 3 H. On a mobile device held at 35 cm an immersive visual angle of 30° can be achieved with a screen height of just 12 cm possibly on most laptops and portable DVD players.

In a series of five studies Lund showed that participants' preferred viewing ratio was not a constant 7 H. With increasing image size, independent of resolution, the preferred viewing ratio approached 3 H or 4 H (Lund 1993) in a dark room with a projected picture with a 74 in. diagonal. Based on Yuyama's (2008) and his own results, Lund hypothesized that viewers might select their viewing distance not to maximize perceived visual quality but "to optimize a sense of presence or reality."

Ardito found that when brightness was reduced, there was a trend of participants sitting closer to the screen (Ardito 1994). When watching HDTV content on a 38 in. screen (in a completely dark room), the average preferred viewing ratio was 3.8

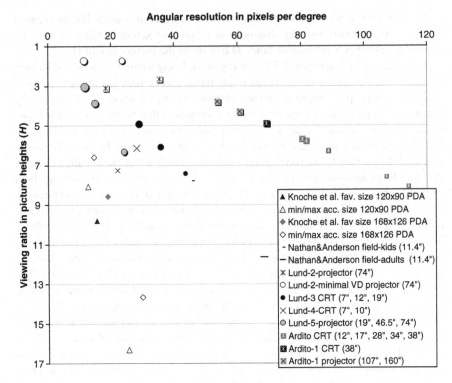

Angular resolution in pixels per degree

Legend:
▲ Knoche et al. fav. size 120x90 PDA
△ min/max acc. size 120x90 PDA
◆ Knoche et al. fav size 168x126 PDA
◇ min/max acc. size 168x126 PDA
- Nathan&Anderson field-kids (11.4")
— Nathan&Anderson field-adults (11.4")
✳ Lund-2-projector (74")
○ Lund-2-minimal VD projector (74")
● Lund-3 CRT (7", 12", 19")
✕ Lund-4-CRT (7", 10")
◎ Lund-5-projector (19", 46.5", 74")
▨ Ardito CRT (12", 17", 28", 34", 38")
▣ Ardito-1 CRT (38")
✖ Ardito-1 projector (107", 160")

Fig. 5 From left to right top to bottom: XLS, VLS, LS, MS, MCU, and CU

H, compared to 6.3 H when viewing the same footage in brighter surroundings. For HDTV content, Ardito predicted a viewing distance (in cm) of $D = (3.55 H + 90)/H$. Although he did not test small mobile screens, he interpolated from a range of HDTV screen heights from 198 cm to 15 cm that for screens with a screen height close to zero the viewing distance would be 90 cm (Ardito 1994).

When content is presented "full screen" on a mobile device with screen height H, e.g., 3.5 cm, the viewing ratio (*VR*) – the quotient of *D* and H – is (10 H) not radically different from the average home TV settings (8.5 H) reported by Tanton (2004b). A large range of viewing ratios is possible not only due to different screen sizes (cf. Fig. 4), but also due to the fact that content could be displayed at nonnative sizes, i.e., stretched or squeezed especially if other content or controls are depicted on the same screen (see Section "On Mobile Devices as Secondary").

Resolution

The amount of detail resolvable by the human eye is primarily limited by the density of the light-sensitive rods and cones on the eye's retina. Normal 20/20 vision is classified as the ability to resolve 1 min of arc (1/60°) (Luther 1996) and is translated to an angular resolution of 60 pixels per degree (ppd). The maximum amount of pixels p_{max} that can be resolved by a human at a given viewing distance D and a picture height H can be computed by the following equation:

$$p_{max} = \frac{H}{D} \times 2\tan\left(\frac{1}{120}\right)$$

Boff and Lincoln showed that visual acuity decreases as viewing distance increases – for close viewing distances people's acuity is at its maximum (Boff and Lincoln 1988). The highest acuity as detailed above is in the *discriminatory visual field* an area of roughly 3° from the center of the fovea.

Thresholds are possible concerns but in terms of watching TV people might not require that much detail. According to Birkmaier (2000) moving images of approximately 22 cycles per degree (44 ppd) are perceived as *sharp*. This value is achieved when a typical standard resolution TV display is viewed from 7 H.

In practice the resolution of digital video content depends to a large degree on the encoding bitrate that is available to compress the spatiotemporal information present in the video frames. The degree of quantization during compression of video frames reduces the resolution as well as the depth at which colors are encoded. The nominal dimensions in pixels in the x and y dimension can be misleading if the encoding bitrate is not sufficiently high. For video encoders, there are numerous trade-offs between parameters involved.

Trade-Off Between Size and Resolution

Both size and the available resolution of the content have to be taken into account for the best presentation of mobile TV material (Knoche and Sasse 2008), but size is more important. Results showed that participants' preferences for watching low-resolution content depended first on size – they required at the very minimum sizes of 19.6 mm (16.3 H) for 120 × 90 resolution content but preferred sizes of 32.6 mm (VR 9.8) for 120 × 90 and 37 mm (VR 8.6) for 168 × 126 resolution content. This matches with findings from the industry. According to Strategy Analytics (Strategy Analytics 2006), Samsung stated that screens of their first mobile TV phones (27 mm in height; a VR of 10.4 at 35 cm) were probably too small and Nokia and Telia Sonera found that usage rates almost doubled with a screen diagonal larger than 7.6 cm (9.5 H). A general limit for upscaling video clips regardless of content and shot types was a resulting angular resolution of about 14 ppd close to the 11 ppd observed by Lund, derived from minimum viewing distances of large projections of TV content in a dark room (Lund 1993) (Fig. 6).

Shot Types

We use Thompson's classification (Thompson 1998) for medium close-ups (MCU), medium shots (MS), long shots (LS), very long shots (VLS), and extreme long shots (XLS). Faced with the more constrained visual real estate, content producers are considering a different mix of shot types for mobile TV.

Fig. 6 Combinations of viewing ratios and angular resolution

Based on the findings on the *sense of reality* of Hatada et al., Tanton and Stone (1989) carried out a study to evaluate the preferred viewing ratios of HDTV at home. He remarked that some participants objected to watching "a *'talking-heads' interview scene on such a large screen from such a close distance*" as talking heads shot types might not and this would need to be addressed through zooming out of the picture.

With mobile content the opposite end of the shot type spectrum represents the main concern. In Asia, content creators produce soap operas especially for mobile devices, which are short and rely heavily on close-up shots with little dialogue. Most emotions have to be conveyed by means of facial expressions and "*there is very little dialogue and a lot of close-ups of characters striking exaggerated poses*" (Guardian 2005). ESPN minimizes the use of extreme long shots in sports coverage for mobile devices (Gwinn and Hughlett 2005); instead it uses more high-lights with close-up shots. These decisions are not backed by research. Little research has been done on how small screen sizes and resolutions might affect the presentation of shot types. In the first study this depended on the content type (Knoche et al. 2006a), but subsequent research has shown that a lot depends on the presence and absence of actors in extreme long shots (XLS).

Apart from XLS, *shot types* are only a concern at the lower limits of acceptable size. MCU and MS could still be presented at slightly smaller sizes than other shot types, but their *favorite sizes* do not differ from other shot types (Knoche and Sasse 2008). To rely on them in production would only make sense for content that would be shown on screens smaller than 22 mm in height. Results from field studies, however, indicate that these will not be met by much user approval (Knoche and Sasse 2008). The acceptability gains for XLS through zooming are substantial. Content adaptation employing zooming approaches should consider a resulting angular size of actors in XLS of at least 0.5° as a lower limit but ideally between 0.7° and 1.3° (Knoche et al. 2007).

Text

For people with 20/20 visual acuity, the minimum readable text size is 5 min of arc (Bailey and Lovie 1976). Broadcasting companies have come up with guidelines on the use of text in TV content. In BBCi's standard (Hansen 2005), the display of text within their interactive television application's body text should generally not be smaller than 24 point (where 1 point equals 0.353 mm) and no text should be smaller than 18 point under any circumstances. The BBCi guidelines mention 12 min of arc close to the limit of 16 min of arc specified by ANSI (American National Standards Institute (ANSI) 1988). The US military standard is 15 min of arc for the principal viewer and 10 min at the maximum viewing distance (Musgrave 2001). In terms of resolution, fonts need to be at least 5 pixels in height to be legible for standard ASCII fonts. The letter "E," for example, needs three rows for the strokes and two for the spaces in between. The television channel MTV is using larger, shorter, and sharper fonts for their made-for-mobile content.

If people are aiming at achieving viewing ratios on mobile devices that are close to those of standard TV, size may not be as much a concern as the lower resolution. Research has shown that both the legibility and the visual quality of text in video have a strong impact on the overall acceptability of video quality (Knoche et al. 2006b). Poor contrast due to low video encoding bitrates can render text illegible.

Frame Rate

For standard TV, frame rates of 25 frames (50 fields) per second are used to display video and induce apparent motion for the viewer. In analog TV, frame rates were fixed but for digital content the frame rates used at recording, encoding, and display can differ. When lower frame rates are used for encoding less data need to be transmitted to the displays – see (Curran and Annesley 2005) for example values.

In a study by Apteker et al. (1994), subject assessments of video clips dropped significantly with each 5 fps decrease in frame rate (15, 10, 5 fps). Song et al. (2004) found no significant difference in users' ratings of 15 and 25 fps displays of content. McCarthy et al. (2004) showed that the video quality of football content became less acceptable when the frame rate dropped below 12 fps. They found that when trading-off smoothness of motion for resolution in terms of encoding quantization, video quality was more based on blocking effects (i.e., resolution) and information value than on the smoothness of movement.

User Experience of Television on Mobile Devices

The quality of audiovisual material depends on the bitrates at which the audio and video is encoded. A number of studies have addressed the values necessary to provide an acceptable or higher-quality experience for mobile TV (Jumisko-Pyykkö et al. 2006; Hauske et al. 2003; Winkler and Dufaux 2003; Jumisko-Pyykkö and Hannuksela 2008; Knoche and McCarthy 2005; Knoche et al. 2005). The required encoding bitrate depends on the content, e.g., the amount of motion, the encoder, and the loss profile of the channel that is transmitting the information. For broadcast services, the typical parameter for a television channel is QVGA resolution (320×240) at 25 fps at a bitrate of around 250 kbit/s (Mason 2006). But the resulting perceived quality when transcoding content from TV (see e.g., Curran and Annesley 2005) and trading-off different parameters for each other, e.g., color depth, quantization, resolution, and frame rates, is currently not sufficiently understood. When taking into account specific encoders and the combined effects of video quality, text in the video, and audio quality together with the effects due to imperfect transmission such as bit errors and packet loss (Jumisko-Pyykkö et al. 2006) the situation becomes even more complex. This optimization problem is tackled from various angles with subjective, objective, and combined approaches.

While most of the research around mobile television studies technical factors or the perceived quality, there are studies that focus on people's current usage of mobile devices for the consumption of video (see Harper et al. 2008 for an overview). Koskinen and Repo (2006) found that people moderated their use of mobile TV devices in shared spaces to save face. They used it either politely to avoid disturbing others and adjusted this further in case of disapproval or aggressively used the devices to draw attention. Södergård (2003) and Repo et al. (2004) reported both individual and collective viewing on mobile devices. O'Hara et al. (2007) and Cui et al. (2007) provided studies on how and why people consume video material on mobile devices. O'Hara argued that even though consuming video in mobile devices is a privatizing technology, it might facilitate togetherness at home as people can watch "*their own content while being in proximity to family.*" Harper et al. (2008) pointed out the active and social component of TV watching on mobile phones and used the term *watching to show* as a maxim to describe this salient property.

Summary – Mobile TV Bigger Than You Think and You Might Not be Alone

People are content with consuming video at various viewing ratios and ensuing resolutions. With mobile devices they can easily adjust and tremendously vary size and resolution if they wish by changing the viewing distance or if supported by changing the size of the video on the mobile device. With larger viewing distances they can share the screen with more people. People prefer to watch even low-resolution content (e.g., QCIF) that is encoded sufficiently high at viewing ratios which yield a picture size in the order of typical (8.5 H) living room setups. The large range of sizes and angular resolution that people find acceptable show that many other factors such as ambient lighting, furniture arrangement, screen size, age, and desire for immersion need to be considered to find the optimal trade-off between size and resolution.

A large range of possible viewing ratios is especially promising when other information should be presented in connection with the video footage, e.g., for control, navigation, or annotation purposes. These kinds of interactions on mobile devices as a secondary screen in conjunction with a primary TV screen will be further explained in the following section.

Mobile Devices as Secondary Screens

The previous section discussed how mobile devices can be used as primary devices for audiovisual content consumption. Nevertheless, as shown in Fig. 7, mobile devices can be used in conjunction with television sets (Cesar et al. 2009). In the figure, the television experience is enriched by the digital capabilities of mobile devices. In this case, an iPod Touch and/or a Nokia 770 tablet PC. For example, the mobile devices can be used for displaying extra information or for providing an easier content selection process.

There have been a number of studies on the usage of secondary screens in the home environment. This section is an attempt to structure them into the different levels of user-to-media interactivity identified previously.

Back in 1996, the seminal work from Roberston et al. (1996) introduced a system in which mobile phones were used for house hunting. The phone provided a floor map of different houses; the user could select a room and activate an internal view of the room as a movie in the television screen. This usage can be classified as provision of extra information in a secondary screen, in this case the television set.

More recently, researchers have focused on high-end remote controls in the form of mobile devices. Research on how to design, evaluate, and implement a mobile Electronic Program Guide (EPG) has become very popular in the last couple of years. The mobile device can be used for selecting television programs, finding more information about a specific program, and for typical remote control functionality (e.g., change channel or volume). For example, Cruickshank et al. (2007)

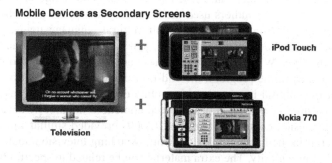

Fig. 7 Usages of mobile devices together with shared screens such as television sets

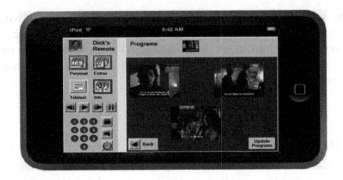

Fig. 8 Scene navigation using a handheld device

presented a detailed study on how a PDA can be used as an extended remote control. They reported on a working system in which the PDA displays a personalized EPG and provides functionality such as channel selection. While Karanastasi et al. (2005) provided a solution for a ubiquitous personal video recording interface in handheld devices, their system was capable of recording, deleting, and summarizing recorded television content. The two clear benefits from such solutions are personalization and mobility. In terms of personalization we can highlight that the mobile device is the most personal device a user carries around. For example, when traveling to a new environment such as a hotel room in another country, the mobile device can provide specific information about the user in terms of profile and preferences that the hotel room environment could not easily infer. In terms of content selection, Cesar et al. (2009) extended the typical EPG model by providing fine-grained selection capabilities. The viewer was capable not only of selecting multimedia programs, but fragments within the content. Figure 8 shows how an iPod Touch can be used in conjunction with the television content for activating specific fragments of a movie.

Apart from content selection, another active field of research for combining the shared nature of television screens and the private nature of mobile devices is T-Learning. Fallahkhair et al. (2005) argued that nondesktop technologies fit learning activities. The authors used the secondary screen for a number of scenarios such as providing help for difficult cultural language items, providing extra information about specific concepts, and managing the personal learning sphere of the user. When difficult cultural concepts or words unknown by the learner appeared in the program, the end-user could translate them or get more info about the cultural items using his mobile device. This line of research can be classified into the provision of enhanced content to the mobile device, while watching television content. Cesar et al. (2009) provided similar functionality, extra material in the handheld device, while watching television content with a finer-level of granularity. The extra material can be related to specific fragments of the content, as shown in Fig. 9.

Fig. 9 Extra content visualization of a media presentation viewed in the television display

Discussion

In the previous sections we have explained the limitations and interdependencies of various factors for consumption of audiovisual content on standard TV and mobile devices. We looked at what kind of activities and scenarios are possible with mobile devices as secondary screens. We believe that a number of drivers exist for the adoption of mobile devices as both primary and secondary devices at home.

One big driver is the current lack of screens at home which will result in further mobile TV usage at home as apparent by the current appropriation of other mobile devices e.g., laptops equipped with TV-tuners or wifi and the starting integration of set-top boxes with both mobile devices and computers.

Mobile TV screens provide a more granular control of space. This might change the relation between technology use and ownership of space that Hughes et al. (1998) pointed out. The use of television or stereo systems indicate a control of space that might not be intended in every case but might be a by-product of convenience and the limitation of the existing technologies. Mobile devices especially when equipped with earphones or headphones do not impose this ownership of space. In that case a mobile TV makes for a *quiet technology* such as text messaging (Grinter and Eldridge 2001) which does neither create nor require sound that might disturb others in a shared space. This could be a driver especially for younger users who do not have a large say in the use of shared space at home. Mobile devices allow for a straddle of media use and shared space, as well as a choice of whether or not to conform to social norms while watching.

The medium and how it is used in which space serves as a message to others. Mobile TV screens offer a greater range of indicators which people can use to signal their availability and inclination to engage in a shared activity or experience.

Mobile device screens are easily shared within small groups, and from screen heights of 4 cm they can result in a satisfactory viewing experience as shown in the previous sections. Watching content on a mobile device in a group requires initiation by the device owner and involves a gesture that carries more social meaning than if a living room TV was turned on and watched by multiple people. The required act of offering to jointly watch or letting someone watch content on one's personal device and thereby share content will further reciprocity. Watching-to-show might support a different kind of social TV viewing that focuses on "being together" as described by Taylor and Harper (2002) but includes intimate spatial proximity. This has been proven popular for parents when watching content with children (Södergård 2003) which on mobile devices is marked by intimate proximity of the involved viewers.

Conclusion

The adoption of mobile technologies at home for multimedia consumption brings along a number of research challenges. In terms of togetherness, we still need to better understand and further research the impact mobile devices will have in traditional television consumption patterns and behaviors. People will be able to moderate their participation from being completely committed to what a group is watching, shadowing or screening different content on a mobile device and deciding to just share a common space and be immersed mostly in the content on the mobile device. Headphones enable a high degree of immersion into the content and disengagement from others especially in conjunction with a personal screen (O'Hara et al. 2007). They can moderate their presence as they can gradually retreat from shared into a more private space and still follow content on their device.

Use of the device as a secondary screen allows for various activities that might only be of personal interest while still being able to monitor a primary screen. A range of possible interactions with the content, additional information, and communication needs can be supported. Any of this can be shared with other people who are close by. On the one hand this might contribute to a fragmented experience of what is being followed on the primary screen but at the same time more involved with the people who are present. A more socially engaged use of TV will be furthered by allowing people to share with – or to personalize and annotate content for – other people. At the same time people can engage with people who are not present through the communication services provided by the mobile device. Due to the viewing restrictions provided by small screens people will be able to switch between these different modes – private or shared – with little effort.

Figure 10 provides a visualization of the different level of togetherness as a result of the adoption of mobile technologies in the home environment. In the figure we identify two dimensions – spatial and activity – in order to categorize the different current habits of end users. By spatial togetherness we refer to the spatial collocation of people, who might not be performing the same activity. The value $(0, 0)$ corresponds to a single person watching media content alone (photo a). While several people watching (and laughing) together represents the highest level of togetherness (represented in photo d). Finally, we can discover a number of situations, in which there is a lower level of spatial togetherness (photo c) or a lower level of activity togetherness (photo b), since there is one person doing something on his own with a tablet PC. Such taxonomy is helpful to further design, deploy, and

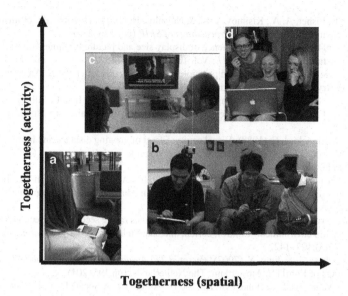

Fig. 10 Taxonomy of current habits in our multidevice, multiviewer world

evaluate user experiences at home, where there is a common space and several media-related activities can take place at the same time. It is easy to extend such taxonomy, such that mediated communication is taken into account. In our connected world, people can be together across distances (e.g., video conferencing, instant messaging, social television), thus leveraging the togetherness level. For example, in the photo marked as b, the person on the left is actually communicating with a friend located in a different house.

This chapter looked at the current changing habits on audiovisual content consumption with special focus on current and potential uses of mobile devices. Standard TV imposes a use at home that is too coarse to support the various personal needs of people from engagement and immersion into content and deliberately controlled disengagement with others to providing a screen that can be offered to include others in sharing experiences in a huddled setting. Future research should be targeted to build on top of our findings and better categorize and quantify the different aspects that will influence togetherness – collocated and through mediated interaction – in the coming years.

References

American National Standards Institute (ANSI). (1988). *American national standard for human factors engineering of visual display terminal workstations* (Report No. ANSI/HFS Standard No.100–1988). Santa Monica, CA: The Human Factors Society Inc.

Ankrum, D. R. (1996). Viewing distance at computer workstations. *Work Place Ergonomics,* 10–12.

Apteker, R. T., Fisher, A. A., Kisimov, V. S., & Neishlos, H. (1994). Distributed multimedia: User perception and dynamic QoS. In *Proceedings of SPIE* (pp. 226–234).

Ardito, M. (1994). Studies on the influence of display size and picture brightness on the preferred viewing distance for HDTV. *SMPTE,* Vol. 103(9), (pp. 517–522).

Bailey IL, Lovie JE (1976) New design principles for visual acuity letter charts. American Journal of Optometry & Physiological Optics 53:740–745

Birkmaier, C. (2000). Understanding digital: Advanced theory. In M. Silbergleid & M. Pescatore (Eds.), *The guide to digital television.* (United Entertainment Media) New York (NY), USA.

Boff, K. R., & Lincoln, J. E. (1988). Visual acuity: Effect of viewing distance and luminance level. In *Engineering Data Compendium, Human Perception and Performance.* Ohio: AAMRL/ Wright-Patterson AFB.

Cesar, P., Vuorimaa, P., & Vierinen, J. (2006). "A Graphics Architecture for High-End Interactive Television Terminals," ACM Transactions on Multimedia Computing, Communications, and Applications (TOMCCAP), 2(4):343–357.

Cesar, P., Bulterman, D. C. A., & Jansen, J. (2009). Usages of the secondary screen in an interactive television environment: Control, enrich, and share television content. *Multimedia Systems Journal* 15(3):127–142.

Cui, Y., Chipchase, J. & Jung, Y. (2007). *Personal TV: A qualitative study of mobile TV users, In* Proceedings of EuroITV, Amsterdam, The Netherlands, (pp.195–204).

Coppens, T., Vanparijs, F. & Handekyn, K. (2005). "AmigoTV: A Social TV Experience Through Triple-Play Convergence", Alcetel-Lucent white paper.

Cruickshank, L., Tsekleves, E., Whitham, R., Hill, A., & Kondo, K. (2007). Making interactive TV Easier to Use: Interface design for a second screen approach. *The Design Journal,* p. 10.

Curran K, Annesley S (2005) Transcoding media for bandwidth constrained mobile devices. International Journal of Network Management 15:75–88

Dearman, D., & Pierce, J. S. (2008). It's on my other computer!: Computing with multiple devices. In *Proceedings of the SIGCHI Conference on Human factors in Computing Systems* (pp. 767–776).

Diamant, L. (1989). *The broadcast communications dictionary.* (3rd ed.). Greenwood Press. Santa Barbara (CA), USA.

Edwards, W. K., & Grinter, R. E. (2001). At home with ubiquitous computing: Seven challenges. In *Proceedings of the 3rd international conference on ubiquitous computing* (pp. 256–272). London: Springer.

Fallahkhair, S., Pemberton, L., & Griffiths, R. (2005). Dual device user interface design for ubiquitous language learning: Mobile phone and interactive television (iTV). In *Proceedings of the IEEE International Workshop on Wireless and Mobile Technologies in Education* (pp. 85–92).

Gauntlett, D., & Hill, A. (1999). *TV living: Television, culture and everyday life.* London: Routledge.

Grinter, R. E., & Eldridge, M. (2001). y do tngrs luv 2 txt msg? In *Proceedings of the seventh conference on European Conference on Computer Supported Cooperative Work.* Dordrecht, Netherlands: Kluwer.

Guardian. (2005). Romantic drama in China soap opera only for mobile phones. *Guardian Newspapers Limited,* from http://www.buzzle.com/editorials/6-28-2005-72274.asp

Gwinn, E., & Hughlett, M. (2005). Mobile TV for your cell phone. *Chicago Tribune,* from http://home.hamptonroads.com/stories/story.cfm?story=93423&ran=38197

Hall ET (1966) The hidden dimension. Doubleday & Company Inc., New York

Hansen, V. (2005). *Designing for interactive television: version 1.0.* British Broadcasting Corporation (BBC).

Harper, R., Regan, T., & Rouncefield, M. (2008). Taking hold of TV: Learning from the literature. In *Proceedings of the 18th Australia conference on Computer-Human Interaction: Design, activities, artefacts and environments* (pp. 79–86).

Hatada T, Sakata H, Kusaka H (1980) Psychophysical analysis of the 'sensation of reality' induced by a visual wide-field display. SMPTE 89:560–569

Hauske, G., Stockhammer, T., & Hofmaier, R. (2003). Subjective image quality of low-rate and low-resolution video sequences. In *Proceedings of the 8th International Workshop on Mobile Multimedia Communications*.

Horton D, Wohl RR (1956) Mass communication and para-social interaction: Observations on intimacy at a distance. Psychiatry 19:215–229

Hughes, J., O'Brien, J., & Rodden, T. (1998). Understanding technology in domestic environments: Lessons for cooperative buildings. In *Proceedings of the First International Workshop on Cooperative Buildings (CoBuild'98)* (pp. 248–261). Heidelberg, Germany: Springer.

Jensen, J. F. (2005). Interactive television: New genres, new format, new content. In *Proceedings of the Second Australasian Conference on Interactive Entertainment* (pp. 89–96).

Jensen, J. F. (2008). The concept of interactivity – revisited: Four new typologies for a new media landscape. In *Proceedings of UXTV* (pp. 129–132).

Jumisko-Pyykkö, S., & Hannuksela, M. (2008). Does context matter in quality evaluation of mobile television. In *Proceedings of mobile HCI*.

Jumisko-Pyykkö, S., Kumar, V. M. V., Liinasuo, M., & Hannuksela, M. (2006). Acceptance of audiovisual quality in erroneous television sequences over a DVB-H channel. In *Proceedings of the Second International Workshop in Video Processing and Quality Metrics for Consumer Electronics*.

Kap, D. (2008, November 4). Americans surf internet while watching TV: Nielsen. *New York Post*.

Karanastasi A, Kazasis FG, Christodoulakis S (2005) A natural language model for managing TV-anytime information in mobile environments. Personal and Ubiquitous Computing 9:262–272

Kato, S., Boon, C. S., Fujibayashi, A., Hangai, S., & Hamamoto, T. (2005). Perceptual quality of motion of video sequences on mobile terminals. In *Proceedings of the IASTED International Conference* (pp. 442–447).

Knoche, H., & McCarthy, J. (2004). Mobile users' needs and expectations of future multimedia services. In *Proceedings of the WWRF12*.

Knoche, H., & McCarthy, J. (2005). Design requirements for mobile TV. In *Proceedings of Mobile HCI* (pp. 69–76).

Knoche, H., McCarthy, J., & Sasse, M. A. (2005). Can small be beautiful? Assessing image resolution requirements for mobile TV. In *Proceedings of ACM Multimedia 2005* (pp. 829–838). ACM.

Knoche, H., McCarthy, J., & Sasse, M. A. (2006a). A close-up on mobile TV: The effect of low resolutions on shot types. In *Proceedings of EuroITV '06 – beyond usability, broadcast and TV* (pp. 359–367).

Knoche, H., McCarthy, J., & Sasse, M. A. (2006b). Reading the fine print: The effect of text legibility on perceived video quality in mobile TV. In *Proceedings of ACM Multimedia* (pp. 727–730).

Knoche, H., Papaleo, M., Sasse, M. A., & Vanelli-Coralli, A. (2007). The kindest cut: Enhancing the user experience of mobile TV through adequate zooming. In *Proceedings of ACM Multimedia 2007* (pp. 87–96). ACM.

Knoche, H., & Sasse, M. A. (2008). The sweet spot: How people trade off size and definition on mobile devices. In *Proceedings of ACM Multimedia 2008*.

Koskinen, I., & Repo, P. (2006). *Personal technology in public places – face and mobile video* (Rep. No. 94). Helsinki, Finland: National Consumer Research Centre.

Lee B, Lee RS (1995) How and why people watch TV: Implications for the future of interactive television. Journal of Advertising Research 35:9–18

Lloyd, E., Maclean, R., & Stirling, A. (2006). *Mobile TV – results from the BT Movio DAB-IP pilot in London* (Rep. No. Technical Review). EBU.

Lund AM (1993) The influence of video image size and resolution on viewing-distance preference. SMPTE 102:406–415

Luther AC (1996) Principles of digital audio and video. Artech House Publishers, Boston, London

Mäki, J. (2005). *Finnish mobile TV pilot*. Research International Finland.

Mason, S. (2006). *Mobile TV – results from the BT Movio DAB-IP trial in Oxford* EBU (Technical Review).

McCarthy, J., Sasse, M. A., & Miras, D. (2004). Sharp or smooth? Comparing the effects of quantization vs. frame rate for streamed video. In *Proceedings of the CHI* (pp. 535–542).

McCarthy J, Wright P (2004) Technology as experience. MIT Press, Cambridge, MA

Musgrave, G. (2001). Legibility of projected information, from www.conceptron.com/articles/pdf/legibility_of_projected_information.pdf

Nathan JG, Anderson DR, Field DE, Collins P (1985) Television viewing at home: Distances and visual angles of children and adults. Human Factors 27:467–476

Nokia. (2006). *Abertis telecom, Nokia and Telefonica Moviles unveil results of first digital mobile TV pilot in Spain.*

O'Hara, K., Mitchell, A. S., & Vorbau, A. (2007). Consuming video on mobile devices. In *Proceedings of CHI'07* (pp. 857–866). ACM Press.

Owens DA, Wolfe-Kelly K (1987) Near work, visual fatigue, and variations of oculomotor tonus. Investigative Ophthalmology and Visual Science 28:743–749

Pitts K, Hurst N (1989) How much do people prefer widescreen (16 × 9) to standard NTSC (4 × 3)? IEEE Transactions on Consumer Electronics 35:160–169

Repo, P., Hyvönen, K., Pantzar, M., & Timonen, P. (2004). Users inventing ways to enjoy new mobile services – the case of watching mobile videos. In *Proceedings of the 37th Annual Hawaii International Conference on System Sciences.*

Robertson, S., Wharton, C., Ashworth, C., & Franzke, M. (1996). Dual device user interface design: PDAs and interactive television. In *Proceedings of the SIGCHI Conference on Human factors in Computing Systems* (pp. 79–86).

Rubin AM (1981) An examination of television viewing motivations. Communication Research 9:141–165

Seager, W., Knoche, H., & Sasse, M. A. (2007). TV-centricity – Requirements gathering for triple play services. In *Interactive TV: A shared experience TICSP adjunct proceedings of EuroITV 2007* (pp. 274–278).

Shneiderman, B. (2003). *Leonardo's laptop: Human needs and the new computing technologies.* Cambridge, MA: MIT Press.

Södergård, C. (2003). *Mobile television – technology and user experiences report on the mobile-TV project* (Rep. No. P506). VTT Information Technology.

Song, S., Won, Y., & Song, I. (2004). Empirical study of user perception behavior for mobile streaming. In *Proceedings of the tenth ACM international conference on Multimedia* (pp. 327–330). New York: ACM Press.

Strategy Analytics. (2006). *TV phones: Integration and power improvements needed to reach 100 million sales.*

Tanton, N. E. (2004b). *Results of a survey on television viewing distance* (Rep. No. WHP 090). British Broadcasting Corporation.

Tanton, N. E. (2004a). *Results of a survey on television viewing distance* (Rep. No. WHP 090.). British Broadcasting Corporation.

Tanton, N. E., & Stone, M. A. (1989). *HDTV displays* (Rep. No. BBC RD 1989/9 PH-295). BBC Research Department, Engineering Division.

Taylor, A., & Harper, R. (2002). Switching on to switch off: An analysis of routine TV watching habits and their implications for electronic programme guide design. *usableiTV, 1,* 7–13.

Thompson FT (1957) Television line structure suppression. SMPTE 66:603–606

Thompson, R. (1998). *Grammar of the shot.* Elsevier/Focal Press, Oxford, UK.

Winkler, S., & Dufaux, F. (2003). Video quality for mobile applications. In *Proceedings of SPIE* (Vol. 5150), Jun. 2003, San Jose, CA, USA (pp. 593–603).

Yuyama, I. (2008). Fundamental requirements for high-definition television. In *High-Definition Television NHK Technical Monograph* (NHK Advanced broadcasting systems research division).

Zillman, D. (1988). Mood management: Using entertainment to full advantage. In L. Donohew, H. E. Sypher, & E. T. Higgins (Eds.), *Communication, social cognition, and affect* (pp. 147–172). Hillsdale: Erlbaum.

Watch-and-Comment as an Approach to Collaboratively Annotate Points of Interest in Video and Interactive-TV Programs

Maria da Graça C. Pimentel, Renan G. Cattelan, Erick L. Melo, Giliard B. Freitas, and Cesar A. Teixeira

Abstract In earlier work we proposed the Watch-and-Comment (WaC) paradigm as the seamless capture of multimodal comments made by one or more users while watching a video, resulting in the automatic generation of multimedia documents specifying annotated interactive videos. The aim is to allow services to be offered by applying document engineering techniques to the multimedia document generated automatically. The WaC paradigm was demonstrated with a WaCTool prototype application which supports multimodal annotation over video frames and segments, producing a corresponding interactive video. In this chapter, we extend the WaC paradigm to consider contexts in which several viewers may use their own mobile devices while watching and commenting on an interactive-TV program. We first review our previous work. Next, we discuss scenarios in which mobile users can collaborate via the WaC paradigm. We then present a new prototype application which allows users to employ their mobile devices to collaboratively annotate points of interest in video and interactive-TV programs. We also detail the current software infrastructure which supports our new prototype; the infrastructure extends the Ginga middleware for the Brazilian Digital TV with an implementation of the UPnP protocol – the aim is to provide the seamless integration of the users' mobile devices into the TV environment. As a result, the work reported in this chapter defines the WaC paradigm for the mobile-user as an approach to allow the collaborative annotation of the points of interest in video and interactive-TV programs.

M.G.C. Pimentel (✉) and R.G. Cattelan
Universidade de São Paulo, 13560-970, São Carlos - SP, Brazil
e-mail: mgp@icmc.usp.br; renan@icmc.usp.br

E.L. Melo, G.B. Freitas and C.A. Teixeira
Universidade Federal de São Carlos, 13565-905, São Carlos - SP, Brazil
e-mail: erick melo@dc.ufscar.br; cesar@dc.ufscar.br

A. Marcus et al. (eds.), *Mobile TV: Customizing Content and Experience*,
Human-Computer Interaction Series, DOI 10.1007/978-1-84882-701-1_23,
© Springer-Verlag London Limited 2010

Introduction

In their literature survey, César and Chorianopoulos identify "content creation" and "content and experience sharing process" among the concepts that have been inherent in interactive-TV research. More specifically, they identify authoring tools, content metadata modeling, and user-generated content as important research themes associated with content creation (César and Chorianopoulos 2008).

The authoring of interactive multimedia contents to be presented in interactive-TV platforms has led to the research associated with tools to support the creation of declarative documents (e.g. César et al. 2006; Guimarães et al. 2008), as well as interactive screen media narratives for the TV (Ursu et al. 2008). Researchers have also investigated alternatives to support the authoring of interactive contents based on the user interaction with mobile devices in the context of live video production (Engström et al. 2008).

In the area of ubiquitous computing, which investigates the alternatives for providing services to users in a transparent way (Weiser 1991), the expression capture and access refers to the task of "preserving a record of some live experience that is then reviewed at some point in the future" (Abowd et al. 2002). In earlier work we proposed the Watch-and-Comment (WaC) paradigm as the seamless capture of multimodal comments made by one or more users while watching a video, resulting in the automatic generation of multimedia documents specifying annotated interactive videos. The aim is to allow services to be offered by applying document engineering techniques to the multimedia document generated automatically: for example, an interactive video described in NCL, as detailed in our original proposal (Pimentel et al. 2007). The paradigm takes advantage of the fact that watching and commenting a video with someone else is a practice many people enjoy and feel comfortable with. For example, participants talked most while watching the news, soap, quiz, and sport programs in a study reported by Geerts et al. (2008).

We have previously explored such ideas by defining (Pimentel et al. 2007b) and demonstrating (Pimentel et al. 2008) the WaC paradigm. The original prototype application WaCTool supports the capture of digital ink and voice comments over individual video frames and segments, producing interactive multimedia documents in SMIL[1] and Ginga-NCL that synchronize the different media streams. Ginga-NCL[2] is the Brazilian Digital TV Standard for declarative interactive multimedia programs.

We have extended our original proposal for the WaC paradigm in a number of ways, as summarized in the next section and detailed elsewhere (Cattelan et al. 2008). First, we associate user–video interactions with edit commands (loop, seek, skip, and slow motion) and digital ink operations. This aims to demonstrate the possibility that users have to seamlessly author interactive video considering those conventional editing options. Second, focusing on collaboration and distribution

---

[1]http://www.w3.org/TR/2008/REC-SMIL3-20081201, visited on March 13, 2009.
[2]http://www.ncl.org.br, visited on March 13, 2009.

issues, we employ annotations as simple containers for context information by using them as tags in order to organize, store, and distribute information in our P2P-based multimedia capture platform (Cattelan and Pimentel 2008).

People use mobile phones with ease to interact with the TV, as observed by Tuomi while investigating the usage of SMS messages by viewers who interact with human hosts in interactive-TV programs (Tuomi 2008). In order to leverage the ubiquitous property of the WaC paradigm, in this chapter we propose an infrastructure that allows viewers to use their own individual mobile phones to interact with TV programs – and seamlessly author corresponding interactive multimedia documents.

The remaining of this chapter is organized as follows. We review our previous work regarding the Watch-and-Comment paradigm in Section "The Watch-and-Comment Paradigm: Previous Work". We discuss several scenarios in which collaborative applications incorporating the WaC paradigm may be deployed by mobile users in Section "Beyond Mobile TV: Scene Discrimination Scenarios". We present the prototype application we built to demonstrate our proposal in Section "The 'Match the Master' WaC Tool Prototype". We detail the infrastructure we built to support that prototype as well as other similar applications in Section "The WaC Tool Underlying the Framework". In Section "Related Work", we discuss how our research can be compared to others reported in the literature. We present our final remarks and discuss future work in Section "Final Remarks".

The Watch-and-Comment Paradigm: Previous Work

Considering that watching and commenting a video with someone else is a practice many people enjoy and feel comfortable with, the main premise underlying the WaC paradigm is that, while a user watches a video, any natural user–video interaction (such as a voice comment) can be captured and reported in an interactive video specified by means of a declarative document (e.g., one described in SMIL or NCL). We call the period during which this interaction occurs a watch-and-comment session. The approach is a general one (Cattelan et al. 2008):

- There is no restriction with respect to the source of the video: the media can be obtained live from a camera, from TV broadcasting, or played back from a computer storage device, from the set-top box or from a media player.
- There is no restriction with respect to the type of the video: for instance, the video can be generated from a set of images.
- There is no restriction with respect to the language of the resulting document: Ginga-NCL, SMIL or any other declarative language can be used.
- The session can be collaborative, distributed, and synchronous: more than one user (remote or collocated) can collaborate in a watch-and-comment session of the same source video at the same time.
- The declarative document generated keeps annotations separate from the original media: this means that the annotations and edits can be distributed independently

from the video stream – which is an important feature as far as digital rights are concerned.

- There is no restriction with respect to the media used for commenting as long as the media can be captured. The capture can be transparent from the user's perspective (e.g., voice captured by a microphone, electronic ink from pen-based devices, gestures captured by sensors such as accelerometer and compass as those present in the Wii[3] remote control or the iTouch[4]).
- There is no restriction with respect to how the capture interaction is to be used. This means that applications can be innovative in terms of what to do with the captured interaction.
- There is no restriction with respect to how the resulting declarative document is distributed. This means that the interactive video could be stored and played back only on the device it has been captured (say, the user's own next generation remote control), or there may exist an integration of the user's environment with a Web repository (such as YouTube[5] or AsterPix[6], for instance);
- A watch-and-comment session can start with an interactive document: users can watch-and-comment an interactive video as well as a linear one, which requires that the annotation tool include parsers for the corresponding format, as is the case for the Ambulant Annotator (César et al. 2006) and the NCL Composer (Guimarães et al. 2008).

It is important to observe that, from the digital rights perspective, the fact that annotations are kept separate from the original media means that they can be distributed independently.

The principles outlined above stress how general the overall WaC paradigm is: the prototypes presented in this chapter illustrate a few of the many possibilities one may be able to envision by applying the WaC paradigm in the context of interactive TV in general, and of end-user authoring interactive documents using their own mobile devices in particular.

In the remaining of this section, we present a brief review of the TabletPC version of the WaCTool, which allows a user to add multimodal annotations to a video. Design issues relative to the use of a minimum remote control are discussed elsewhere (Pimentel et al. forthcoming).

The Tablet PC version of the WaCTool prototype includes, besides the multimodal annotation features demonstrated elsewhere (Pimentel et al. 2008), support to edit commands and a set of P2P capabilities that allow user collaboration and content and metadata sharing (Cattelan et al. 2008).

When the user executes the tool, he opens an existing video[7] file: the WaCTool presents four panels as illustrated in Fig. 1 (clockwise from the top left): (a) the

---

[3]http://www.nintendo.com/wii/what/accessories, visited on March 13, 2009.

[4]http://www.apple.com/ipodtouch, visited on March 13, 2009.

[5]http://www.youtube.com, visited on March 13, 2009.

[6]http://www.asterpix.com, visited on March 13, 2009.

[7]In this text we use video to refer to digital (non-interactive) video, and interactive video to refer to digital interactive video.

Fig. 1 TabletPC WaCTool (clockwise from the top left): video playback window; ink window for pen-based annotation on top of a video frame grabbed from the playback window; shared content window; and the chat window

playback window containing a panel for video playback with buttons for play/pause/stop, as well as buttons for recording text and audio notes; (b) the ink window containing a panel for pen-based annotation (among other resources); (c) the shared content window presenting content (video and annotations) related to the video being watched or the result of user search queries (based on the video ID and the text annotations/tags); and (d) the chat window for collaboration via text chat among users currently active in the system.

Figures 2, 3, 4 illustrate a watch-and-comment session being played back in the Ginga player, which allows interactive multimedia programs encoded in NCL to be presented in the Brazilian interactive-TV infrastructure. The figures assume that the user interacts with the program using a remote control containing four buttons dedicated to user interaction with the program (referenced as square, triangle, diamond, and circle due to their standardized shapes). When the playback starts:

- At each occurrence of an ink comment, a miniature icon of the corresponding annotated frame is presented on the bottom-right corner of the video window (Fig. 2 (left)): if the square button is pressed, the video is paused and the annotated frame is presented (Fig. 2 (right)) until the triangle button is pressed, causing the playback of the original program to be resumed;
- At each occurrence of an audio note, an audio icon is presented on the upper-right corner of the video (Fig. 3 (left)): if the diamond button is pressed, the original audio is muted and the audio comment is played back; the original audio is resumed automatically at the end;

Fig. 2 A miniature image of the annotated frame is presented (left) to indicate that an ink note is available and is presented (right) if the user selects the square button on remote control; the triangle button resumes the playback

Fig. 3 Left: an audio icon indicates that an audio comment is available and is played back when the user selects the diamond button on the remote control. Right: a text icon indicates that a text comment is available and is presented as subtitle when the user selects the diamond button

- At each occurrence of a text note, a text icon is presented on the upper-right corner of the video (Fig. 3 (right)): if the diamond button is pressed, the text commentary is presented as a subtitle for as long as it was necessary for the user to write it.
- At each occurrence of a video to be skipped, a skip icon is presented on the bottom-left corner of the video (Fig. 4 (top-left)): if the circle button is pressed, the portion of video indicated by the user is skipped.
- At each occurrence of a loop command, a loop icon is presented on the bottom-left corner of the video (Fig. 4 (top-right)): if the circle is pressed, the portion of the video specified by the user is replayed once.
- At each occurrence of a slow motion command, a slow motion icon is presented on the bottom-left corner of the video (Fig. 4 (bottom)): if the circle button is pressed, the video is presented in slow motion as specified by the user.

Fig. 4 Top-left: a skip icon indicates that a portion of the video can be skipped if the user selects the (circle) button on the remote control. Top-Right: a loop icon indicates that a portion of the video can be replayed if the user selects the circle button. Bottom: a slow motion icon indicates that a portion of the video can be played back in slow motion if the user selects the circle button

Compared to related work, we argue that the WaC approach brings the following contributions (Cattelan et al. 2008):

- The support for the user to personalize linear media in order to produce interactive video.
- The support for remote communication among users beyond colocated settings enables broad social aspects of video watching.
- The use of video identifiers and tagging as context containers, which organize information and enable collaboration among active participants via P2P groups.
- The support to complementary digital ink manipulation operation, including ink filters and ink expanders.
- The use of tags to index specific portions of the video timeline, allowing search in the shared annotations.
- The provision of personalized, tag-oriented, context-based content search and retrieval of related media.

Next, we discuss several scenarios in which collaborative applications incorporating the WaC paradigm may be deployed by mobile users.

Beyond Mobile TV: Scene Discrimination Scenarios

This section provides application scenarios of our concept of ubiquitous collaborative video watching and TV programs scene discrimination. It is worth highlighting that the meaning of the word discrimination, in the context of the work reported in this chapter, is the following: recognition of the difference between one thing and another.[8] More specifically, in the scenarios we present, the users discriminate one or more scenes when they recognize a particular value in them while watching the video, the value being associated with the users' context and their watching-TV experience. We also use, from now on, the word select with a meaning equivalent to discriminate.

It is relevant to observe that the scenarios we discuss in this chapter are neither exhaustive nor limiting. Our intention is to provide a framework to facilitate the understanding of our architecture.

In all scenarios, we assume that the video is previously recorded or, in the case of broadcast video from interactive TV, we assume that the video is recorded during its presentation. We also assume that viewers have their own mobile devices.

The scenarios illustrate situations in which a client application, running on the viewers' mobile devices, exploits wireless protocols to communicate with a server-side application running on the set-top box. In our implementation, detailed in Section "The 'Match the Master' WaC Tool Prototype", the following applies:

- To support the necessary communications, we experimented the UPnP protocol, which allows both the automatic detection of the presence of the mobile devices and the negotiation of services.
- To support the capture of viewers' interaction.
- Viewers are able to select scenes using the keyboard on their own mobile device.
- The scenes selected by the viewers are registered in a markup document which refers to the original video.

As suggested by the scenarios described next, specific applications can be built that make use of the scenes discriminated and registered in the document to offer a variety of services.

Educational Scenarios

The original motivation of the proposal came from the education domain, in which we identified the opportunity to provide mechanisms to support psychology classes that need to develop in the students the skill to classify different human behaviors.

---

[8]Compact Oxford English Dictionary of Current English http://www.askoxford.com/concise oed/ discrimination, visited on March 13, 2009.

A video, presented without interruptions to a group of students, contains scenes that should be classified by the student according to the instructions given by the Professor. Using their mobile devices, the students classify the scenes as the video is played back. At the end of the presentation of the video, an application offers the instructor the option to review the annotations of each student individually, or of the whole group. The review is presented by means of a new interactive video – a new structured document generated automatically defines the interactive video by organizing the data from the selections made by the students and referring to the original video. This new interactive video can be used by the instructor to investigate the selections made by the students individually or as a group.

The same model applies to several other educational scenarios. A karate instructor, for example, can ask his students to watch a competition presented on TV during the Olympic games and classify, using the numerical keyboard of their mobile phones, the name of each karate move used by the contenders. Later, in the training area, students can send their annotations to an application running on the instructor's interactive-TV set where he recorded the competition while it was broadcast. The instructor, along with the students, can review the annotations as a group or individually using an application that synchronizes all annotations with respect to the start of the original broadcast. The collective vision can provide rich feedback to the group's skills.

Selection of Scenes for Replay

The Talky family, congregated in the living room, watches together a family movie which is broadcast on TV for the first time. In several moments one of the family members – say, the Grandpa – recognizes the scenario and wants to talk about the visit he made to the same spot. In other moments, the twins start arguing about a dangerous action scene. A few minutes later, the teenage girl gets upset when she recognizes her favorite actor in a secondary role. To avoid so many interruptions by the family members while the movie is broadcast, Mr. and Mrs. Talky program their interactive-TV set to allow everyone to select the scenes they want to review by using their mobile phones. During the breaks, the family members can review the movie using the annotations.

Waiting Room Scenarios

John Flyer is frustrated because he has been waiting for his flight which is delayed by more than an hour. Seated in the boarding gate area, he watches the video presented in one of the many TV sets located in the area along with many other passengers waiting for the same flight. Giving that there are a number of vacant seats in the business class of that particular flight, the company, having made previous arrangements with business partners who advertise on TV sets in the departure lounge, decides to offer free upgrades to business class to a few passengers. To earn the prize, the passengers must use their mobile phones to interact with videos associated with one of the partners: for instance, a quiz-based contest related to the most recent model from a car company. John Flyer wins the contest and an upgrade to the business class.

Jane Doe is at the hospital waiting for her turn to see the doctor. While she waits, she watches a video program that offers those who wait the opportunity to provide information about their health condition using their mobile phones. While the application asks the same questions to everyone, Jane provides her answers in the privacy of her own mobile device. This type of service has several potential benefits, for instance the use of the waiting time to collect valuable information. Moreover, the fact that the users are given the opportunity to use the waiting time in a productive way may reduce the sensation of frustration while the time passes.

Product Selection in Sale Scenarios

Mary D'Ollar, tired of her day-long shopping, enters a department store where she can sit comfortably. In the resting area, she watches well-produced videos while drinking a complimentary ice drink offered by the store. While watching the interactive video, she is offered the opportunity to order the items advertised using her mobile phone – to buy or just to view them in more detail. Her selection is sent to the sales team which gets prepared to show her all the items she has selected while resting and sipping her ice drink.

Discussion

The scenarios above illustrate specific situations in which the WaC paradigm can be exploited: all scenarios assume the selection of scenes or programmed options, and all scenarios exploit the fact that the users can interact with the video they are watching using their own mobile device.

The value of the specialization of WaC paradigm, as proposed in this section, lies on its simplicity and generality. The adoption of personal portable devices, such as mobile smartphones, demands the use of a protocol that allows the discovery and the negotiation of services automatically – as is the case of the UPnP protocol. It also demands the provision of accessible and intuitive user interfaces and support from the underlying iTV middleware.

The simplicity and ubiquity of the model allow the applications to be collaborative. The distributed nature of the model is evidenced in applications where the users make the selection of scenes individually, but can later review the selections collaboratively.

These scenarios bring up the following question: How to make these scenarios possible using interactive-TV-related solutions?

We propose the integration of the facilities provided by interactive-TV middlewares to those offered by mobile devices to allow the implementation of the applications discussed in the previous section.

One point of particular relevance in our proposal is the possibility a group of viewers has to collaboratively annotate points of interest in video and interactive-TV programs in a simple and ubiquitous way. The use of a ubiquitous capture and access approach implies that, on the one hand, the viewers can use their own mobile devices to make scene selections and, on the other hand, the interaction can be captured and processed in many ways to provide useful services, such as the one proposed previously.

However, the construction of such applications without a proper support from the interactive-TV middleware infrastructure would demand that each application had its own communication software infrastructure in the mobile devices, which would have several drawbacks. Moreover, some of the scenarios could not be implemented in the general way, in particular those demanding collaborative annotation with respect to any program broadcast.

As a result, our proposal is that a basic resident application providing scene discrimination be available at the set-top box: this application could be deployed by viewers in several scenarios that demand the selection of scenes for reply. Moreover, its underlying infrastructure can be used to build even more complex applications that users, then, may wish to install in their mobiles and/or set-top boxes.

In the next section (Section "The 'Match the Master' WaC Tool Prototype"), we present an application we built to demonstrate our approach. In the section that follows (Section "The WaC Tool Underlying the Framework"), we detail the software infrastructure we built to support it.

The "Match the Master" WaCTool Prototype

To experiment with our proposal, we have designed a prototype application called Match the Master, which implements the WaC paradigm by (a) capturing the interaction of a group of users with a TV via their own mobile devices; (b) analyzing the interaction by comparing the interaction of one user identified as master with the interaction performed by all the other users; and (c) creating a new interactive-TV document which shows the scores of how close the interaction of each user is with the interaction of the master.

The Match the Master application, which has been made available in the TV set-top box, is executed as follows:

- A group of viewers who watch a program on the same TV set (e.g., the movie shown on Fig. 5(left)) decides to play Match the Master;
- The group chooses, in an informal face-to-face conversation, one of the members as the master. Using their own mobile devices, each member activates the

Fig. 5 While watching TV (left), users activate the WaC application in their mobile devices: the TVWaCMiflet application, previously installed, is listed on the mobile device and can be initialized/executed (Select one to launch menu at the right upper corner), starting the search for available UPnP services

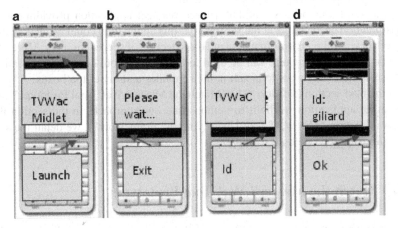

Fig. 6 WaC mobile in use: (**a**) the user selects the TVWaC application from the list of pre-loaded applications and presses Launch; (**b**) a message Please wait... is shown while the mobile client communicates with the server on the set-top-box; (**c**) A message TVWaC is shown when the WaC service has started: from now on, all keys pressed by the user will be sent to the server, or the user may select Exit or Id; (**d**) the user selects Id to enter a string for identification

generic WaC application which has been previously installed in their mobile devices. The client WaC application, then, searchs for services broadcasting their availability via the UPnP protocol and lists all the UPnP services found: Fig. 5(right) shows the list of application preloaded on the mobile, including WaC (TVWaCMidlet), which can then be initialized/executed.

- All users activate the TVWacMidlet application as shown in Fig. 6(a): selecting TVWacMidlet and pressing Launch.

- All users wait while the message Please wait ... is presented (Fig. 6(b)), indicating the mobile synchronizes with the server on the set-top box – the figure also shows that the user has the option to select Exit to end the application.
- The message TVWaC is presented (Fig. 6(c)) when the WaC service starts from now on, all keys pressed by the user will be sent to the server – the user may select Exit or Id. To play Match the Master, the users informally agree on which key has to be pressed: for instance, they can agree all users have to press 1 when one character in the movie is found in a dangerous situation.
- All users may select the Id option to enter the identification string: one of them is required to register as the master. (If a user does not register, the physical address of his mobile device will be used). Figure 6(d) illustrates the user called Giliard registering his name.
- Using the TV remote control, the user may, at any time, press the stop key on the remote: this causes the server portion of the application to compute the "matching score" of all users in comparison with the master, and generate a suitable interactive multimedia document to be presented on the TV, as illustrated in Fig. 7.

Next, in Section "The WaC Tool Underlying the Framework", we discuss the software infrastructure we have built to support applications such as the Match the Master.

Fig. 7 The stop button on the TV remote control can be pressed at any time, causing the generation and presentation, on the TV, of an interactive multimedia document showing the "matching score" of all users in comparison with the master

The WaCTool Underlying the Framework

Our prototype application contains two parts: a portion on the user's mobile device contains the client portion, and the portion on the set-top box contains the service provider's portion of the application.

In the user's device, the client portion of the application consists of a UPnP control point responsible for finding and using the service provided by TV. The main advantage of exploring UPnP in this scenario is the use of the plug-and-play alternative to the communication network: this means that viewers can use the services without having to perform complex configurations. An important feature of the architecture is the support to different mobile devices such as smartphones, handhelds, and tablet PCs. As a result, our prototype supports multiuser interaction with the interactive-TV platform because the UPnP communication is not limited to a specific device type, operating system, or programming language.

The service provider portion of our application demands the extension of the original Ginga-NCL middleware architecture (Soares et al. 2007), as shown in Fig. 8: the original modules are presented in white (e.g., the Formatter in the Ginga-NCL Presentation Environment Layer), our new modules are shown in black, and a module we extended from the original Ginga-NCL middleware is shown in gray. We present further details of both portions of the application next.

Components of the Service Provider

We have designed the extension to the original Ginga-NCL middleware architecture (Soares et al. 2007), and so it can be used by any application that may want to take advantage of (a) the UPnP protocol for communication, and (b) the WaC paradigm for the capture of the viewer interaction, and the presentation of associated interactive programs generated on the fly by the server-side portion of application.

Given that the Ginga-NCL middleware can be extended, as defined by its specification (Soares et al. 2007), our extension is composed of:

- The new UPnP module, added to Protocol Stack layer, which implements a code relative to the UPnP protocols so as to provide its functions to other devices throughout the network.
- The new implementation of the Input Manager module, which enables the original module in Ginga Common Core layer to allow user input to be directed not only to the middleware declarative and procedural environments, but also to other modules and native applications.
- The new Bookmark Annotator module which, added to the Resident Applications layer, treats the input provided by the user's mobile device.
- A new Matching Reporter module which, added to the Resident Applications layer, is activated when the stop button on the remote control is pressed, causing the interactive multimedia report to be produced and presented – the presentation is activated when the stop key on the remote control is pressed (Fig. 7).

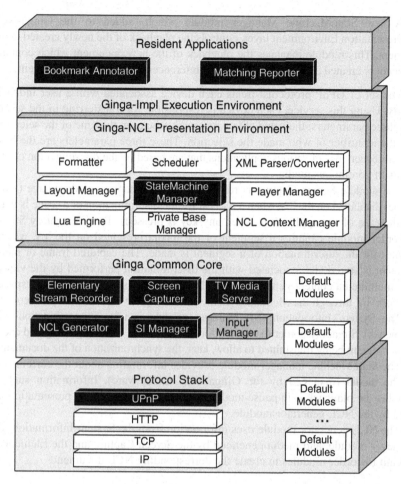

Fig. 8 Architecture used in WaCTV: Original Ginga modules are indicated in white boxes, modified Ginga modules are indicated in light gray boxes, new modules are indicated in dark gray

- Five new modules to the Ginga Common Core layer.
- Elementary Stream Recorder module: allows the recording of all elementary streams in a way that it can be later referenced for presentation.
- Screen Capture module: captures the selected video frame so that it can be presented later.
- TVMedia Server module: provides audiovisual content transparently in the network.
- Information System (SI) Manager: registers information relative to the synchronization of all elementary streams of the original program, and controls the later play back of that information in concordance with the additional user selections.
- NCL Generator module: produces an interactive multimedia document (in the NCL declarative language) aggregating the information captured by the other modules.

- A new StateMachine Manager module which, added to the Ginga-NCL Presentation Environment layer, controls the playback of the newly created document. This module manages the playback of the new document which contains anchors created according to the users' references to the original document.

The set of UPnP protocols[9] treats each device associated with a user independently. Using this service, each device is responsible for transferring to the set-top box three parameters: the value of key pressed by the user, the time of the selection, and the identifier of who made the selection. These three parameters are the basis for subsequent use in various applications that are based on the discrimination of segments of continuous media.

The module Screen Capture is responsible for the capture of the image (video frame) displayed on the TV when a request for the discrimination of a scene is made (in the case of our application, when any key is pressed). The Elementary Stream Recorder module captures a segment of the media presented on the TV when a request for the discrimination of a segment is made. The captured frame or media segment is stored and associated with the discrimination performed by the viewer. The multimedia content generated from these modules is available in a transparent network TV through the Media Server module, using the set of UPnP protocols.

The System Information (SI) Manager module is used in combination with Elementary Stream Recorder to obtain information relative to the beginning and end of a TV program being transmitted to allow, later, the synchronization of the documents.

The StateMachine manager module provides information about the current state of the media (managed by the Ginga-NCL middleware). Information such as whether the playback is in pause mode and the current time of the presentation are used by the NCL generator module.

The NCL generator module uses information from the System Information (SI) Manager module, and media generated by the Screen Capture and the Elementary Stream Recorder modules to create the corresponding NCL document.

Components of Client Application

Our prototype supports several types of devices that support Java.[10] In the user's mobile device, the main client component is the UPnP control point, which is responsible for finding a UPnP device on the network and allowing the viewer to use the services provided by the device.

When the application is started on the client, a search for UPnP devices is automatically performed. If a device with a service of the type TV scene discrimination

---

[9]Implemented using the Cyberlink UPnP API for C ++ http://clinkcc.sourceforge.net, visited on March 13, 2009.

[10]Java 2 Micro Edition for mobile devices and Java 2 Standard Edition to other devices such as a netbook computer or a tablet PC.

of segments of continuous media is found, the application automatically enables the viewer to use this service via a graphical interface on the device.

When any number key is pressed by the viewer, the device sends to the server portion of the application two parameters: an identifier of the device itself and the identification of the key which was pressed.

The device identifier is generated automatically with information gathered from the device's operating system. However, our sample application allows the user to change the device's identifier to other information, such as the user's name, and one of the viewers is required to set that name to master.

As designed, our framework provides both watch-and-comment and UPnP protocol services for any application.

Related Work

Typical video authoring tools may not be considered as worth learning by home users (Kirk et al. 2007). One factor is that such tools have not been designed for the average home user: the tools assume expert users with complex authoring tasks at hand. By specialized authoring tools we mean, for non-interactive video, simple tools such as Movie Maker[11] and iMovie,[12] as well as more sophisticated tools such as Premiere[13] Pro CS4.

Considering our own previous experience with a capture and access general platform (Pimentel et al. 2007a), we have previously exploited the ubiquitous computing paradigm to associate user annotations with video streams in the design of the Multimedia Multimodal Annotation tool (M4Note), which supports annotations in two complementary methods: context-based metadata association and content enrichment (Goularte et al. 2004).

While we exploit an ubiquitous capture and access approach, several authors report having used explicit authoring techniques (e.g., Girgensohn et al. 2000; Hua and Li 2006; Hua et al. 2004). Targeting at the home user, Hua and Li's LazyMedia aims at facilitating editing and sharing home videos using techniques such as content analysis in association with authoring composition and presentation templates (Hua and Li 2006).

While our proposal aims at achieving authoring via transparent interaction, other authors opt for the explicit manipulation of tangible objects representing video artifacts. In the multiuser Tangible Video Editor (Zigelbaum et al. 2007), users edit video clips by manipulating active handheld computers embedded in plastic cases; in the mediaBlocks system, children capture, edit, and display media by manipulating passive wooden blocks (Ullmer et al. 1998).

---

[11]http://www.microsoft.com/windowsxp/using/moviemaker, visited on March 13, 2009.
[12]http://www.apple.com/imovie, visited on March 13, 2009.
[13]http://www.adobe.com/products/premiere, visited on March 13, 2009.

Our work is mostly related to efforts targeted at nonexpert users, as in the architecture proposed by César et al. which provides an approach for end-user enrichment of video streams via many alternative end-user devices (César et al. 2007), and the use of a secondary screen to allow users to control, enrich, share, and transfer interactive television content (César et al. 2008). Also similar to our approach is the investigation of alternatives to support the authoring of interactive contents based on the user interaction with mobile devices in the context of live video production (Engström et al. 2008).

In work targeting interactive digital TV, Bulterman et al. address the viewer-side enrichment of multimedia content (Bulterman et al. 2006; César et al. 2006). We move toward this goal by giving the user increased control for customizing the review of annotations.

As far as the usage of UPnP as the underlying support for communication among the interactive-TV infrastructure and mobile devices is concerned, our work is most related to that reported by Holbling et al. (2008), who first supported multiuser access to interactive-TV platforms using the UPnP architecture. Compared to their work, our approach is already integrated in the Brazilian middleware. Moreover, our infrastructure is general enough to support building a variety of applications – including those which exploit the watch-and-comment paradigm.

Final Remarks

In this chapter, we have proposed an extension of the watch-and-comment paradigm by allowing interactive-TV viewers to make annotations using their own personal mobile devices. After presenting an overview of the original WaC proposal, we discussed scenarios in which the annotations may be useful for an individual as well as for a group of users, in public spaces or in the privacy of their home.

To demonstrate the feasibility of the WaC paradigm for the mobile user proposal, we presented an application allowing the use of a mobile device to provide information to data gathering applications, and detailed how we have extended the original Brazilian Interactive-TV Ginga Middleware to support that and similar applications.

The work presented in the chapter will continue in several research directions. In the short term, with respect to the Match the Master application, we plan to perform usability tests with typical users, and a discount usability evaluation with user-interface specialists.

We also plan to work in collaboration with domain specialists to detail and extend the scenarios we have presented.

In future, we plan to formalize an API corresponding to our current implementation to facilitate the building of novel applications. The experimentation with the scenarios introduced in this chapter is also planned, as it would allow, on the one hand, the evaluation of the API and, on the other, the leverage of the implementation of further applications based on the WaC paradigm for the mobile user.

Acknowledgements We thank the following organizations for their financial support: FINEP, FAPESP, CAPES, and CNPq. We thank Dick Bulterman for great discussions on this topic. We thank Luiz F. G. Soares for inspiring us with Ginga-NCL. We thank Felipe S. Santos, Bruno C. Furtado, and Rudinei Goularte for their collaboration in our previous work.

References

Abowd, G. D., Mynatt, E. D., & Rodden, T. (2002). The human experience. *IEEE Pervasive Computing, 1*(1), 48–57.

Bulterman, D. C. A., C´esar, P., & Jansen, A. J. (2006). An architecture for viewer-side enrichment of tv content. In *Proceedings of the ACM International Conference on Multimedia* (pp. 651–654). New York: ACM.

César, P., Bulterman, D. C. A., & Jansen, A. J. (2006). The Ambulant Annotator: Empowering viewer-side enrichment of multimedia content. In *Proceedings of the ACM Symposium on Document Engineering* (pp. 186–187). New York: ACM.

César, P., Bulterman, D. C. A., & Jansen, A. J. (2008). Usages of the secondary screen in an interactive television environment: Control, enrich, share, and transfer television content. In *European Interactive TV Conference, Lecture Notes in Computer Science* (Vol. 5066, pp. 168–177).

César, P., Bulterman, D. C. A., Obrenovic, Z., Ducret, J., & Cruz-Lara, S. (2007). An architecture for non-intrusive user interfaces for interactive digital television. In *European Interactive TV Conference, Lecture Notes in Computer Science* (Vol. 4471, pp. 11–20). Heidelberg, Germany: Springer.

César, P., & Chorianopoulos, K. (2008). Interactivity and user participation in the television life-cycle: Creating, sharing, and controlling content. In *Proceedings of the UXTV* (pp. 125–128).

Cattelan, R. G., & Pimentel, M. G. C. (2008). Supporting multimedia capture in mobile computing environments through a peer-to-peer platform. In *Proceedings of the ACM Symposium on Applied Computing* (pp. 1246–1251). New York: ACM.

Cattelan, R. G., Teixeira, C. A. C., Goularte, R., & Pimentel, M. G. C. (2008). Watch-and-comment as a paradigm toward ubiquitous interactive video editing. *ACM Transactions on Multimedia Computing, Communications and Applications, 4*(4), 1–24.

Engström, A., Esbj¨ornsson, M., & Juhlin, O. (2008). Mobile collaborative live video mixing. In *Mobile HCI* (pp. 157–166).

Geerts, D., C´esar, P., & Bultermand, D. A. (2008). The implications of program genres for the design of social television systems. In *Proceedings of the UXTV* (pp. 71–80).

Girgensohn, A., Boreczky, J., Chiu, P., Doherty, J., Foote, J., Golovchinsky, G., Uchihashi, S., & Wilcox, L. (2000). A semi-automatic approach to home video editing. In *Proceedings of ACM Symposium on User Interface Software and Technology* (pp. 81–89). New York: ACM.

Goularte, R., Cattelan, R. G., Camacho-Guerrero, J. A., Inácio, V. I., & Pimentel, M. G. C. (2004). Interactive multimedia annotations: enriching and extending content. In *Proceedings of the ACM Symposium on Document Engineering* (pp. 84–86). New York: ACM.

Guimarães, R. L., Costa, R. M. R., & Soares, L. F. G. (2008). Composer: Authoring tool for iTV programs. In *European Interactive TV Conference, Lecture Notes in Computer Science* (Vol. 5066, pp. 61–71). Berlin: Springer.

Holbling, G., Rabl, T., Coquil, D., & Kosch, H. (2008). Interactive tv services on mobile devices. *IEEE MultiMedia, 15*(2), 72–76.

Hua, X. S., & Li, S. (2006). Interactive video authoring and sharing based on two-layer templates. In *Proceedings of the ACM International Workshop on Human-centered Multimedia* (pp. 65–74). New York: ACM.

Hua, X. S., Lu, L., & Zhang, H. J. (2004). P-karaoke: Personalized karaoke system. In *Proceedings of the ACM International Conference on Multimedia* (pp. 172–173). New York: ACM.

Kirk, D., Sellen, A., Harper, R., & Wood. K. (2007). Understanding videowork. In *Proceedings of the ACM International Conference on Human Factors in Computing Systems* (pp. 61–70). New York: ACM.

Pimentel, M. G. C., Baldochi, L. A., & Cattelan, R. G. (2007). Prototyping applications to document human experiences. *IEEE Pervasive Computing, 6*(2), 93–100.

Pimentel, M. G. C., Cattelan, R. G., Melo, E. L., & Teixeira, C. A. (forthcoming). Ubiquitous end-user live editing of itv programs. *International Journal of Advanced Multimedia and Communications,* p. 25p.

Pimentel, M. G. C., Goularte, R., Cattelan, R. G., Santos, F. S., & Teixeira, C. A. (2007). Enhancing multimodal annotations with pen-based information. In *Workshop on New Techniques for Consuming, Managing, and Manipulating Interactive Digital Media at Home* (pp. 207–213).

Pimentel, M. G. C., Goularte, R., Cattelan, R. G., Santos, F. S., & Teixeira, C. A. (2008). Ubiquitous interactive video editing via multimodal annotations. In *European Interactive TV Conference, Lecture Notes in Computer Science* (Vol. 5066, pp. 72–81). Berlin: Springer

Soares, L. F. G., Ferreira, R. R., & Moreno, M. F. (2007). Ginga-NCL: The declarative environment of the Brazilian Digital TV System. *Journal of the Brazilian Computer Society, 13*(1), 37–46.

Tuomi, P. (2008). SMS-based human-hosted interactive tv in Finland. In *Proceedings of the UXTV* (pp. 67–70).

Ullmer, B., Ishii, H., & Glas, D. (1998). mediaBlocks: Physical containers, transports, and controls for online media. In *Proceedings of the Conference on Computer Graphics and Interactive Techniques* (pp. 379–386). New York: ACM.

Ursu, M. F., Kegel, I., Williams, D., Thomas, M., Mayer, H., Zsombori, V., et al. (2008). ShapeShifting TV: Interactive screen media narratives. *Multimedia Systems, 14*(2), 115–132.

Weiser, M. (1991). The computer for the 21st century. *Scientific American, 265*(3), 94–104.

Zigelbaum, J., Horn, M. S., Shaer, O., Jacob, R. J. K. (2007). The tangible video editor: collaborative video editing with active tokens. In *Proceedings of the International Conference on Tangible and Embedded Interaction* (pp. 43–46). New York: ACM.

Conclusion (The Mobile Future)

The Mobile Future

There are a couple of fundamental beliefs that I hold about the future of technology and media. First, I believe that, absolutely, most, if not all, media will be delivered, at least intermittently in its lifecycle, over an IP network. It is an efficient carrier, it is scalable, and it can be organically evolved. Whether this is IPV6 or some other technology is inconsequential, it will just work.

Secondly, I believe that, despite certain commercial business efforts and the occasional spell in the middle of the film where the villain appears to be winning, the audience ALWAYS gets what they want. History is littered with the corpses of those who attempted to thwart consumer desire through legislation, technology, or social manipulation. In the long-run, these never work. The Audience always get what they want at the end.

Thirdly, I believe that everything software related is in some interim stage of its inevitable migration to the cloud – the Internet of computers in the sky. More and more we are going to be less and less aware of where our content is, software and related services live physically, happy in the knowledge that we have a contract with someone to provide them and relieved that we do not have to keep track of them physically any more. Google is a great first step example of this – today I use Google for my email, I trust that they have backed it up, and I never make a copy for myself (where it might be less secure). This idea of the cloud being somehow more trustworthy than a physical copy is completely different than every computer revolution before. Security is about controlled, appropriate, and traceable access and about the ability to take punitive measures when these principles are breached or when inappropriate access occurs.

Thus, all of these digital devices evolve into simple, variable size/shape/connectivity-caching devices. They hold a local copy of some portion of your data for you, manage which data they think you will need (whether it is the London phone numbers when you are in the UK vs NYC when you land at JFK, or pre-caching the HD content for the newest episodes from Ceebeebies at Grandmother's house where the connection is slow for the children's weekend viewing delight).

A. Marcus et al. (eds.), *Mobile TV: Customizing Content and Experience*,
Human-Computer Interaction Series, DOI 10.1007/978-1-84882-701-1_24,
© Springer-Verlag London Limited 2010

Personalization – this data – that lives in the cloud, starts to have multiple nodes – connections, places (or is it "connection places") where aggregations and relationships between bits of data are noticed, tracked, and confirmed – Amazon is a great example of a node, as is my financial institution. Others are more complicated; Facebook is a node, as is yahoo.com or even pricegrabber. As our @social fabric and the complexity of our behavior evolve online (browsing, consuming, buying, chatting, sharing, etc.) we build profiles, which allow others to know things about us, whether these are benign (you have a mac, lets give you the QuickTime version of that file), benevolent (you hate Cricket, lets just delete it from your program guide), or malevolent (you are on a diet so I'm going to deliver Haagen Daaz ads at you every 30 s!).

Mobile devices are the perfect connectors to data space – they are the repositories and collectors today for some of the most sensitive and personal elements of our digital lives. They have keypads for security and can act as one half of a dual key encryption system. Lastly, your phone can become the collector and keeper of your preferences, such as things you like and things you hate, and it can communicate these preferences, overtly or subvertly to others, to commercial partners (with your permission), i.e., I am really in a mood for a coffee anywhere handy?, to your other devices (your telly will know you were watching six nations and let you finish the game when you arrive home) and to the cloud (google! Again).

One of my favorite stories refers to an audience research session we ran a while ago, where we asked some audience whether they had used their phone to access the Internet; to which they all resoundingly replied NO (much to our surprise). When probed, asking what did they do with their mobile devices, when they were not calling or SMS'ing, or taking pictures they replied: "Oh I use Facebook", "I check the scores on Sky Sport," or my favorite "Oh I like to watch programs on iPlayer(BBC)." The fact that all three of these activities were using the mobile Internet was completely lost on this young audience, much to my colleagues chagrin and my secret delight.

The fact is, why should they know it is the Internet? The icons came with their phone, or they downloaded them from the store. Why should they care about the transport technology? Over the past 10 years or so living through the Internet revolution (remember the "E-Commerce" businesses) we have evolved from a place where connectivity was a question mark, something you hoped for, to a status where it is like oxygen – required for life. This striving for a state of ubiquity of connectivity is a real-time journey; and while we have not arrived yet, we are further down the way than ever. Real questions about the future include: Is there a universal connectivity?, if so, how fast?, does it drop out?, or can I disconnect?

I think the answer, as things always are, is more complicated. The latest devices, mobiles netbooks, etc. leverage a veritable cornocopia of mobile network technologies, seamlessly. My N98 and blackberry are as comfortable on wifi as they are on 3g. What is missing is a seamless hand-off, and an intelligent bandwidth maximization, and the simple mechanisms for monetizing this connectivity for both carrier and intermediary (I can imagine a world where you "make" money for providing someone with secure "guest access" to your wifi, like winding your electric bill backward with your solar panels.) In the future, gone will be the days of consumer awareness of 3g or GRPS – it will just work; sometimes faster, and sometimes slower. The network becomes smart.

What else does the network do? Well, it can be linked to your bank account (or at least a billing relationship) it has got a keypad for your Pin code (though we will likely be using gestural security – paired with biometrics). It is going to be smart about managing your cache and help keep what you need handy, and the rest safely in the cloud somewhere, double-key encrypted. My personal mobile data device ("mobi" I suspect it will be called) in the future will have some attributes similar to a phone or netbook today. It will be a bit bigger than an iphone (folding out to twice that side with an invisible seam and an optional extending qwerty keyboard), and it will keep a copy of all of my personal details, secure with a bio-metric sensor on its touch screen interface. It will interface with vendors (taxis, restaurants, airports), confirming my identity, allowing me frictionless purchasing, and alerting me to the presence of friends (and enemies!) in my vicinity. It will be constantly updating content from the network, the latest rugby games, television from iplayer, new music from Zane Lowe, and the latest news from egos.alltop.com – so that I can consume it whenever I have a few free moments (on the tube, train, car, etc.). I will be able to flag this information to other devices, which may either grab a copy or in the case of my 100" television, download their own higher-resolution one from the net. Triggered by my mobi that I am halfway through the game where England scores on Wales as I arrive home.

My mobi will sync with my accounts with spotify, iPlayer, itunes, emusic, and hulu, all of which have varying kinds of specialty content as well as some crossover. It will also sync with any content owner-specific channels though many of those will have collapsed into larger collectives and aggregators. I will also have subscribed to video search keywords, which scour the net and collect audio and video on my favorite topics from UGC, as well as commercial and semicommercial providers and sites. Based on my previous consumption some of these will even be caught on my device in case I want to consume them when I enter a tunnel on the train or in a "dead zone" – which I fear, may be with us for some time to come. The device will also aggregate all available radio, both Internet only, DAB and FM, optimized based on my previous listening behavior, and "pivots" points will have been inserted in the music to let me know there is other content similar to this available, should I, at that moment have the urge to channel/content surf.

Back to the device, 20 gig of storage will be standard 100 gig premium, but I will hardly notice since this is mostly managed by software behind the scenes. So in terms of storage it will seem infinite to me – since only rarely will something not be at least partially available to me.

When I am tired of watching video and listening, the screen will be converted to a Kindle-like readability level for text and images, whether I am doing some heavy reading or just thumbing through (or in the future it will be sliding through – think iPhone gestural) the pages. Lastly, the device will intelligently manage its own trash. Content I have not used in a while will be politely deleted, with a permanent copy stored in the cloud in case I want to find it later. Old emails, old radio programs, last month's news clippings, etc. are safely moved out of my scarce device memory, but accessible in case I just had not gotten to them, but really wanted one.

My mobi will give me really useful information about where I am. It knows where I am, and what I am looking for. It should enhance every moment with useful info, weather, news, best place for a proper latte, scores of the recent sports news (for conversation with the locals), or that the tube is on strike and to take another route. Or better yet, it will know I am at the airport and help me rebook a flight, or a hotel if there is a snowstorm around. Always updated, always on, always aware, always discreet. It is like having a real Jeeves, 6 in. by 4 in. by ½ an inch when extended. With behavioral data and modeling my devices intuition will grow and develop until I really cannot remember a time when I had to do the work. In short, a perfect butler/personal assistant who is a mild mind-reader with a deep desire to fill every waking minute with data, entertainment, utility, and pleasure – all will be delivered digitally over the net.

Oh yes, and it should be able to lie to people when I do not want to be reached – i.e., maybe I am on vacation, but want you to think that I am in a critical meeting. It is also possible to set, via software out of office, to tell you that I am in someplace I am not, preserving my solitude but breaking it if something critical comes. The biggest issue for me in the future of mobile devices and ubiquitous connectivity is how vacations work. How do you get off the grid? The killer app for the future will be a brief, managed, anonymous disconnection that would be a luxury to me even today.

Index